RSF: The Russell Sage Foundation Journal of the Social Sciences

Immigration and Changing Identities

VOLUME 4, NUMBER 5, AUGUST 2018

RSF: The Russell Sage Foundation Journal of the Social Sciences ISSN 2377-8261

The Russell Sage Foundation

The Russell Sage Foundation, one of the oldest of America's general purpose foundations, was established in 1907 by Mrs. Margaret Olivia Sage for "the improvement of social and living conditions in the United States." The foundation seeks to fulfill this mandate by fostering the development and dissemination of knowledge about the country's political, social, and economic problems. While the foundation endeavors to assure the accuracy and objectivity of each book it publishes, the conclusions and interpretations in Russell Sage Foundation publications are those of the authors and not of the foundation, its trustees, or its staff. Publication by Russell Sage, therefore, does not imply foundation endorsement.

Board of Trustees

Claude M. Steele, *Chair*

Larry M. Bartels
Karen S. Cook
Sheldon H. Danziger
Kathryn Edin
Michael Jones-Correa
Lawrence F. Katz
David Laibson

Nicholas Lemann
Sara S. McLanahan
Martha Minow
Peter R. Orszag
Mario Luis Small
Shelley E. Taylor
Hirokazu Yoshikawa

Mission Statement

RSF: The Russell Sage Foundation Journal of the Social Sciences is a peer-reviewed, open-access journal of original empirical research articles by both established and emerging scholars. It is designed to promote cross-disciplinary collaborations on timely issues of interest to academics, policymakers, and the public at large. Each issue is thematic in nature and focuses on a specific research question or area of interest. The introduction to each issue will include an accessible, broad, and synthetic overview of the research question under consideration and the current thinking from the various social sciences.

RSF Journal Editorial Board

Elizabeth O. Ananat, Duke University
Sheldon H. Danziger, Russell Sage Foundation
Mesmin Destin, Northwestern University
Shigeo Hirano, Columbia University
Maria Krysan, University of Illinois, Chicago
Michal Kurlaender, University of California, Davis

Helen Levy, University of Michigan
Martha Minow, Harvard University
Mary E. Pattillo, Northwestern University
Becky Pettit, University of Texas at Austin
Miguel S. Urquiola, Columbia University

Copyright © 2018 by Russell Sage Foundation. All rights reserved. Printed in the United States of America. No part of this publication may be reproduced, stored in a retrieval system, or transmitted in any form or by any means, electronic, mechanical, photocopying, recording, or otherwise, without the prior written permission of the publisher. Reproduction by the United States Government in whole or in part is permitted for any purpose.

Opinions expressed in this journal are not necessarily those of the editors, editorial board, trustees, or the Russell Sage Foundation.

We invite scholars to submit proposals for potential issues through the *RSF* application portal: https://rsfjournal.onlineapplicationportal.com/. Submissions should be addressed to Suzanne Nichols, Director of Publications.

To view the complete text and additional features online please go to **www.rsfjournal.org**.

Open Access Policy

RSF: The Russell Sage Foundation Journal of the Social Sciences is an open access journal. It is published under a Creative Commons Attribution-NonCommercial-No Derivs 3.0 Unported License

Russell Sage Foundation
112 East 64th Street
New York, NY 10065

ISSN (print):	2377-8253
ISSN (electronic):	2377-8261
ISBN:	978-0-87154-017-1

Carnegie Corporation of New York

Carnegie Corporation of New York was established in 1911 by Andrew Carnegie to promote the advancement and diffusion of knowledge and understanding. In keeping with this mandate, the Corporation's work focuses on the issues that Andrew Carnegie considered of paramount importance: international peace, education and knowledge, and a strong democracy.
https://www.carnegie.org.

RSF: The Russell Sage Foundation Journal of the Social Sciences

VOLUME 4, NUMBER 5,
AUGUST 2018

Immigration and Changing Identities

ISSUE EDITORS
Kay Deaux, City University of New York
Katharine M. Donato, Georgetown University
Nancy Foner, City University of New York

CONTENTS

Introduction: Immigration and Changing Identities **1**
Nancy Foner, Kay Deaux, and Katharine M. Donato

Varieties of Ethnic Self-Identities: Children of Immigrants in Middle Adulthood **26**
Cynthia Feliciano and Rubén G. Rumbaut

Immigrant Perceptions of U.S.-Born Receptivity and the Shaping of American Identity **47**
Michael Jones-Correa, Helen B. Marrow, Dina G. Okamoto, and Linda R. Tropp

Shifting U.S. Racial and Ethnic Identities and Sikh American Activism **81**
Prema Kurien

Making Americans: Schooling, Diversity, and Assimilation in the Twenty-First Century **99**
Cristina L. Lash

The Racialization of Latino Immigrants in New Destinations: Criminality, Ascription, and Countermobilization **118**
Hana E. Brown, Jennifer A. Jones, and Andrea Becker

Majority No More? The Influence of Neighborhood Racial Diversity and Salient National Population Changes on Whites' Perceptions of Racial Discrimination **141**
Maureen A. Craig and Jennifer A. Richeson

Assessing the Political Distinctiveness of White Millennials: How Race and Generation Shape Racial and Political Attitudes in a Changing America **158**
Deborah J. Schildkraut and Satia A. Marotta

Hyper-selectivity, Racial Mobility, and the Remaking of Race **188**
Van C. Tran, Jennifer Lee, Oshin Khachikian, and Jess Lee

Introduction: Immigration and Changing Identities

NANCY FONER, KAY DEAUX, AND KATHARINE M. DONATO

In the last half century, the United States has undergone a profound demographic transformation in the wake of a massive inflow of immigrants. In 2016, immigrants represented approximately 14 percent of the U.S. population; together with their U.S.-born children the figure was more than 25 percent, a remarkable eighty-six million people. This growth in immigration, mainly from Latin America, Asia, and the Caribbean, has altered the racial and ethnic composition of the nation. The non-Hispanic white population in the United States declined from 83 to 62 percent between 1970 and 2015, and the Hispanic population grew from 4 to 18 percent in the same period. Asians, fewer than 1 percent of the U.S. population in 1970, are now 6 percent. The number of black immigrants (from Africa and the Caribbean) has also increased, and close to 10 percent of blacks in the United States are now foreign born. The result has been greater racial and ethnic diversity in a wide swath of both urban and rural neighborhoods across the country. While policymakers deliberate about controlling future immigration or dealing with those who are already here (particularly those who lack documentation), the reality of a changed ethnic-racial population plays out in the lives of millions of Americans, immigrants and nonimmigrants alike.

In distinction from earlier immigration issues in *RSF* that have highlighted questions of legal status (Gonzales and Rafael 2017) and political representation (McCann and Jones-Correa 2016), we examine fundamental issues of identity definition and group categorization with a focus on the U.S. context: how immigrants, the children of immigrants, and long-established Americans see themselves in terms of race and ethnicity, as well as how members of each group view and label the others. What has increased diversity meant for the way people define their ethnicity and that of others? How do these conceptions influence the ways in which members of different ethnic groups

---

Nancy Foner is Distinguished Professor of Sociology at Hunter College and the Graduate Center of the City University of New York. **Kay Deaux** is Distinguished Professor Emerita at the Graduate Center of the City University of New York and visiting research scholar in psychology at New York University. **Katharine M. Donato** is Donald G. Herzberg Professor of International Migration and director of the Institute for the Study of International Migration at Georgetown University's School of Foreign Service.

© 2018 Russell Sage Foundation. Foner, Nancy, Kay Deaux, and Katharine M. Donato. 2018. "Introduction: Immigration and Changing Identities." *RSF: The Russell Sage Foundation Journal of the Social Sciences* 4(5): 1–25. DOI: 10.7758/RSF.2018.4.5.01. Direct correspondence to: Nancy Foner at nfoner@hunter.cuny.edu, 785 Park Ave., 5E, New York, NY 10021; Kay Deaux at kdeaux@gc.cuny.edu, 20 East 9th St., Apt. 20E, New York, NY 10003; and Katharine M. Donato at kmd285@georgetown.edu, School of Foreign Service, Institute for Study of International Migration, Georgetown University, 3300 Whitehaven St., Washington, D.C. 20007.

Open Access Policy: *RSF: The Russell Sage Foundation Journal of the Social Sciences* is an open access journal. This article is published under a Creative Commons Attribution-NonCommercial-NoDerivs 3.0 Unported License.

interact with one another? To put it another way, how has the massive immigration inflow of the last half century altered the social and psychological reality that people experience in the United States today?

In exploring these questions, this introduction brings together insights and perspectives from a variety of social science disciplines, from social psychology to demography to social history. Questions about identity and identity change, intergroup relations, and indeed the field of immigration itself, cannot be relegated to any single discipline. We firmly believe that a multidisciplinary strategy is the most productive choice. Some topics and questions do of course fall more easily into one domain than another. But we have consistently tried to link the domains and broaden the perspective, in the hope that readers from each discipline will find both the familiar and the new.

We begin by addressing identity, a concept that can be defined in terms of basic cognitive and social psychological processes, but at the same time depends on social norms, accepted demographic classifications, and historical developments. Later, in discussing the historical context for identity development and change, we draw heavily on work from history and sociology, at the same time pointing to processes that may have implications for individual functioning. In examining changing identities and intergroup relations, we again bring in work from several disciplines, including demographic and sociological analyses of intermarriage, social psychological work on identity and intergroup contact, and the work of sociologists and political scientists on panethnicity. Finally, we take stock of where we are and we look ahead to possible future developments. How might immigration, ethnic and racial identity, and relations between diverse ethnic and racial groups continue to develop and change? What additional factors need to be taken into account and what new research is needed?

IDENTITY AS CONCEPT AND PROCESS

Fundamental to our analysis is the recognition that racial and ethnic identities are socially constructed and amenable to change. Although these categories are often assumed to be fixed and constant, the historical, sociological, and psychological evidence convincingly document their dynamic and flexible nature. Historically, both the categories of usage and the accepted conventions for assigning certain groups to certain categories have changed over time (and place) and continue to do so as large-scale post-1965 immigration influences the demographic profile of the United States. Given that flow and shifting demographic patterns, how do individuals see themselves and how do others see them? We know from psychological research that people have many identity options open to them (for example, age, gender, social class, and religion). Although these identity categories are surely not irrelevant to immigration, in this issue we focus primarily on ethnic, racial, and national identities. From the census to the media to the marches on the street, these identities are what are most debated and contested in the context of immigration. On the one hand, historical precedents and assumptions establish a framework for contemporary usage of identity as a subject for ethnic, racial, and national discussion. Yet, at the same time, social forces and current experiences create a process by which previous notions of identity may be challenged, redefined, and individually selected and used. These possibilities for change, both over time and circumstance, impel us to give greater attention to the processes of ethnic and racial identification and to the forces that promote one choice over another.

Constructing Identity Categories

Ethnic and racial identities are, like other social identities such as gender, religion, or occupation, categories that people use to place themselves and others in the social world (Gleason 1983; Deaux 2015). As such, they not only are forms of self-definition, articulating the aspects of self that one sees as most central to who they are, but also serve to organize a person's social world, viewing others as members of identifiable categories in which members share some common features (Vignoles, forthcoming). These categories are more than mere labels. They carry beliefs about content and meaning, have evaluative connotations, and are affirmed with varying degrees of importance. Moreover, they link individuals to social groups, shape interactions within and between groups, and provide viable links to past histories and future goals (Ashmore, Deaux, and McLaughlin-Volpe 2004).

How and why people choose particular identity categories for self-definition or for the description of others have been increasingly explored in recent years, opening up possibilities previously thought to be settled issues. A major shift in the conversation has been the recognition that identity is not an objectively determined category but instead a construction, reflecting and substantiating a particular set of assumptions about the world or a particular position for viewing the social structure in which one exists.

Across time and continents, racial categories have often been an accepted way of sorting people into groups. From the early eighteenth-century proposal by the Swedish botanist Carl Linnaeus of four basic races, defined in terms of physical features (such as color of skin, texture of hair) and elaborated by assumed traits and behaviors (such as haughty, indolent, inventive, or capricious) through contemporary census categories, race has continued to be a demarcation tool (Prewitt 2013). Extended to five categories by the German scientist Johann Blumenbach, racial classification soon became a simple color chart of white, yellow, brown, red, and black—the *ethnoracial pentagon*, a term offered by David Hollinger (2006). In various forms, these color-coded categories have long been used and continue to be used in this country, both in official and bureaucratic documents and in everyday usage, both descriptive and sometimes pejorative.

Although racial categorization has been ubiquitous in the United States, and in many other countries as well, the finer distinctions of ethnicity and culture have also been pervasive. The felt need to make these distinctions in the United States has often been prompted by the increasing inflow of new immigrant groups, exemplified by Robert Park and Herbert Miller's *Old World Traits Transplanted* (1921). As in the case of racial categories, ethnic distinctions have continued to be used, both by researchers and in common parlance, the latter documented in a series of studies of ethnic stereotypes begun by Daniel Katz and Kenneth Braly in the 1930s and continuing to the present day (Katz and Braly 1933; Fiske and Lee 2012).

Currently, the U.S. Census contains a mixture of racial and ethnic bases of classification (Prewitt 2013). A question on race asks people whether they are one of three races—white, black–African American–Negro, or American Indian–Alaska native—or some other race, which respondents are asked to specify. A fifth option, covering the broad Asian category, offers more specificity, listing ten possibilities (such as Chinese, Filipino, Samoan) and an additional Other category. The race question on the census is preceded by a question focusing specifically on Hispanic-origin respondents ("Is person of Hispanic, Latino, or Spanish origin?"), with a yes response allowing four choices (for example, "yes, Puerto Rican"), one of which is again an invitation to state a specific heritage not included in the answers provided.

As Kenneth Prewitt discusses in detail, the census exemplifies the statistical definition of race, "constructed and reconstructed by the government" (2013, 4). The categories are both cause and consequence: their inception is typically the result of political decisions and pressures, and their existence in turn influences the way that our understandings are shaped and political policies are enacted. Yet, as Richard Alba convincingly argues, the seeming impartiality of statistics does not preclude arbitrary coding and allocation practices that affect the interpretation and use of these statistics (2016a). Such biases are particularly likely to emerge in the classification of the growing multiracial population in the country.

To use a general *multiracial* category for the myriad of combinations that are possible in a diverse society has serious limitations, as the particular combinations are often distinctive and consequential. For example, those with an Asian-white background are likely to claim a multiracial identity whereas black-white mixed-race individuals tilt more often toward a black identity (Alba 2016b; Bratter 2016). Gender can further complicate the picture, in that women of mixed-race heritage—particularly younger women—are more likely to identity as multiracial than men are (Morning and Saperstein 2016; Pew Research Center 2015). These variations, when coupled with evidence that the multiracial population is growing (though still small in absolute terms) provide further reason to take notions of identity seriously.

Selecting an Identity: What and Why

Societal formulations make certain categories more available for regular usage, both by those who want to describe others and by individuals and groups who seek to define their own position in the society that they inhabit. In some cases, the labels commonly used in the United States are unfamiliar to immigrants or were not used (or less often used) in their countries of origin. Immigrants from Jamaica, for example, may shift from an identification with their specific country or ethnic origin to a more general West Indian or black label when they are assumed by others to be part of these larger groups in the United States (Waters 1999). Similar issues arise for many migrants from Latin America, who are categorized as Hispanic when they settle in the United States and less often distinguished by their country or culture of origin.

A variety of categories are available for a person to use in self-attribution, but clearly some are more suitable or more desirable than others. How the individual comes to define his or her identity within the set of possibilities is a multidetermined process. Certainly, the immediate environment in which a person lives—the family constellation and traditions and the neighborhood, for example—plays a role in making certain identity options both available and feasible. A person's physical features can also be influential: individuals who look more prototypical of their ethnic group in terms of physical features are more likely to be assigned to that ethnic category by others and to identify with that category themselves (Wilkins, Kaiser, and Rieck 2010). The choice of a particular racial-ethnic identity can also reflect personal motives and desired goals. Dominican immigrants, for example, often adopt the identity of Hispanic as a way of placing themselves in a category distinct from black and white (Itzigsohn 2009). Individuals from Vietnam, China, or the Philippines may opt for the more general label of Asian American because they see strategic value in adopting a panethnic identity (Okamoto 2014).

In discussions of race and ethnicity, the emphasis is often on the nonwhite sectors of the population, that is, those who are differentiated from the normative white category. Yet, in recent years, white identity has also been recognized as an important racial as well as ethnic identity category (McDermott and Samson 2005), and one that has become more prominent in the current U.S. political climate. Whereas only a decade ago some social scientists could confidently say that "Whites' whiteness is usually likely to be no more noteworthy to them than is breathing the air around them" (Sears and Savalei 2006, 901), more recent research has shown an array of behaviors that are moderated by white ethnic identification (Knowles and Peng 2005), including voting patterns in the 2016 U.S. presidential election (Major, Blodorn, and Blascovich 2016).

My Choice Versus Your Assumption: Discrepancies in Category Usage

Categories used for classification by others do not always match the identity categories that the person uses. Although both outsiders and insiders are likely to draw from the same available set of societally defined options, criteria for a particular endorsement can differ. As noted earlier, visibility of some physical features such as skin color can make agreement more likely (Wilkins, Kaiser, and Rieck 2010). Yet in other cases, physical features carry more weight for observers than for the targets of their view. For example, people of Asian descent born in the United States are often assumed by others to be immigrants rather than natural-born citizens, illustrating the outsider's preference for an ethnic-racial category, whereas the Asian insider might want to be seen in terms of the national identity of American (Tuan 1998). This difference in priorities might seem relatively harmless; however, research has shown that the target person is likely to be angered by what is seen as an offensive mistake in categorization (Cheryan and Monin 2005; Wang, Minerva, and Cheryan 2013).

Distinctions within a panethnic grouping can also be more important for self-identification than for categorization by others. Panethnic identities, such as those made available in census forms, can be accepted and used, particularly for political mobilization (Okamoto 2014; Schildkraut 2011). At the same time, interethnic distinctions remain important. The failure of others to correctly identify a person's national-origin identity—such as by assuming that a person speaking Vietnamese is Japanese, or that a Venezuelan would celebrate Mexican Independence Day—can elicit adverse reactions (Flores and Huo 2013).

Discrepancies such as these between identities preferred by an individual (or group) and categorical assignment by others have numerous implications for interactions between the two. At a minimum, one cannot assume equivalence of the label and the interpretations that follow from the use of that label when shifting between the two vantage points. More broadly, discrepancies in the preference for and use of identity categories can potentially disrupt, or at least make problematic, interactions between those representing one versus the other perspective.

Identity Change

The available options for identity categorization within a society can change, as the frequently modified U.S. Census illustrates. Yet even when categories remain stable, people's claims to those categories vary over time and circumstance. Evidence of this variability in the use of census categories is provided by Carolyn Liebler and her colleagues (2017), who used matched 2000 to 2010 census files to determine the extent to which self-selected ethnoracial categories remained stable or changed over the period. They find not only that 6 percent of respondents differed in self-labeling between the two periods, but also that individuals in particular groups were most likely to show flexibility in their responses. Respondents who reported a multiracial background at one point in time, for example, frequently chose only a single category at another. This pattern was particularly true of those who combined white and Asian or white and Hispanic labels in one of their self-descriptions.

Possible reasons for changes in an identity category during a ten-year period are numerous, from methodological (such as unreliability of categories that were not common-use terms for respondents) to experiential (such as a substantial change in a person's social network during the period that makes one ethnic identity category more salient or relevant than another). More longitudinal research on the self-labeling of identity would be helpful in sorting out possible causes.

At the same time, social psychological research provides ample evidence that people can easily shift from one identity to another in shorter, more situationally dependent circumstances. Evidence for these shifts is both cognitive and behavioral. In what is termed *cultural frame-switching*, the availability of cognitive cues relevant to one or another identity can affect the thoughts and expressions of multicultural persons, often in wholly nonconscious and automatic ways (Benet-Martínez 2012). At a more behavioral level, in a process that has been termed *bicultural* (or *multicultural*) identity performance, it has been shown that people will strategically make choices among possible identities when presenting themselves to others (Wiley and Deaux 2011; see also Klein, Spears, and Reicher 2007). Numerous factors influence these choices. For example, people are likely to emphasize a version of self that is consistent with the situation or with the characteristics of those around them, such as identifying as a student in a classroom or as a Muslim when in a mosque. Norms and social pressures influence many of these choices: for example, the American-born daughter of Chinese immigrant parents would be likely to express her Chinese identity more strongly when at home, but her American identity in a more diverse school setting. Individual differences in the importance of a particular identification or in allegiance to an ethnic group also moderate presentational choices. Not surprisingly, those who strongly identify with a category are more likely to show consistency across situations than are those whose subjective investment in the category is weaker (Wiley and Deaux 2011). Thus change, both short-term and long-term, must be considered an essential part of any account of ethnic and racial identity.

CHANGEABILITY OF ETHNORACIAL CATEGORIES AND IDENTITIES: PUTTING THE PRESENT IN HISTORICAL CONTEXT

If our theme is immigration's impact on changing identities in the contemporary United States, it is useful to view the present in light of the past. Looking back to earlier periods in U.S. history brings out in a powerful way how racial and ethnic identities are socially constructed in the context of large-scale immigration and points to underlying factors that have led to specific changes over time. Racial differences may seem permanent and immutable—this is the essence of race, which refers to the belief that visible physical characteristics or putative ancestry define groups or categories of people in ways seen to be innate and unchangeable. But "race has only the meaning that culture gives it," and in fact race is a changeable perception (Robinson 2017, 16). So, too, are ethnic categories and ethnic identities, which not only may shift in meaning in different everyday situations, but also have been viewed in different ways in earlier eras. Ethnicity is often defined by ancestry and descent as opposed to physical markers, but such distinctions are not as easy or unambiguous as is sometimes assumed. George Fredrickson argues that race refers to what happens when ethnicity is deemed essential or indelible and made hierarchical (2002, 155); Stephen Cornell and Douglas Hartmann emphasize that race is a construction imposed on a group against its will and that ethnic consciousness is a self-construction of the group (2004). Indeed, it has been argued that the very concept of ethnic group in American discourse to refer to groups with common cultural characteristics and ancestry did not emerge until the early twentieth century, when it was used by Jewish intellectuals to resist being assimilated into the melting pot while avoiding racialization (Foner and Fredrickson 2004, 4; Hattam 2004).

As these comments suggest, debates about the use of race versus ethnicity as conceptual categories have a lengthy and continuing history, and usage of the terms can vary both within and between disciplines. Such differences of opinion and usage attest to the fluid character of identity construction and definition.

The Meaning of Whiteness: Eastern and Southern Europeans in the Past

The commonly taken-for-granted meaning of white or whiteness has undergone significant shifts over time. It is often said that a major distinction between today's immigrants and those a hundred years ago is that then they were, in the main, white Europeans and today they are, in significant numbers, people of color, but this is to impose early twenty-first century understandings of racial categories on the past. Race today is basically a color word, but when it came to the millions of southern and eastern European immigrants a century ago, race and color were not "perfect synonyms"; in the first half of the twentieth century, "one could be considered both white (color) and racially inferior to other whites (race)" (Fox and Guglielmo 2012, 334).

Southern and eastern European immigrants at the time were widely viewed as racially inferior to those with origins in northern and western Europe. At the same time, although their whiteness was sometimes questioned, they were legally white—that is, not prevented from naturalizing as Asians were, for example, or subject to the antimiscegenation laws that existed in many states. They were also placed in the white category by federal agencies, including the U.S. Census (Fox and Guglielmo 2012, 364). Historians have sought terms to describe the ambiguous racial position of Jews and Italians a century ago: "inbetween peoples," in the words of the historians James Barrett and David Roediger (1997), "probationary" whites in those of the historian Matthew Frye Jacobson (1998), or, as Thomas Guglielmo suggests (2003), racial outsiders but color insiders—that is, racially inferior to other whites on the basis of notions of stock, heredity, blood, and selectively chosen physical characteristics (Fox and Guglielmo 2012, 343). As Jacobson aptly puts it, eastern and southern Europeans were both white and racially distinct from other whites (1998).

In the early twentieth century, Jewish and Italian immigrants, who then made up more than half of the southern, central, and eastern European immigrants in the United States, were seen as belonging to inferior "mongrel" races that would alter the essential character of the United States and pollute the nation's Anglo-Saxon or Nordic stock. They were thought to have distinct biological features, mental abilities, and innate character traits and many Americans believed that they were physically identifiable: facial features (including the "Jewish" nose) were often noted in the case of Jews, "swarthy" skin in the case of Italians. Even as late as the 1930s, an American history textbook asked whether it would be possible to absorb the "millions of olive-skinned Italians and swarthy black-haired Slavs and dark-eyed Hebrews into the body of the American people" (Barker, Dodd, and Commager 1934, cited in Fitzgerald 1979, 79–80).

What factors eventually led Jews and Italians to become part of an all-encompassing white community and no longer set apart in the popular mind as inferior, in racial terms, from those with northern and western European ancestry (Alba 2009; Foner 2000, 2005)? The economic and occupational successes of Jews and Italians were critical: economic prosperity and the enormous expansion of higher education in the post–World War II years and the benefits that came with postwar policies, such as the GI Bill of 1944, provided opportunities for educational and job mobility for both the Jewish and the Italian second generations. Climbing the social and economic ladder was accompanied by increased intermixing—in neighborhoods, at work, and eventually in marriage—with those whose roots were in different parts of Europe.

A combination of other factors was also involved. That those with origins in eastern and southern Europe shared a safe haven of legal whiteness with other European groups from the very beginning—and were not subject to the same kind of systematic legal and official discrimination facing black, Asian, and Mexican immigrants—was important in their eventual racial inclusion into the white mainstream. Also, because many Jews and Italians physically resembled members of the older European groups, it was often possible for them to blend into the majority population ("to pass") if they shed cultural features such as distinctive dialects or dress.

Nor can we dismiss the ending of the massive eastern and southern European immigrant influx following restrictive U.S. legislation in the 1920s, which reduced fears of old-stock Americans about the deluge of racial inferiors and contributed to cultural assimilation. Moreover, the massive migration of African Americans from the rural South to northern cities from World War I on likely facilitated the acceptance of Jews and Italians as full-fledged whites by changing the racial order in these cities from one marked by the multiplicity of white races to one focused on race as color (see, for example, Guterl 2001). As blacks became a significant proportion of the population in cities like New York and Chicago (where they were less than 2 percent of the population in 1900), Jews and Italians often sought to distinguish themselves from (and claim superiority to) African Americans—which they did by emphasizing their whiteness.

The Nazi genocide made anti-Semitism less respectable. World War II had another effect as well, occurring when the mass inflow of immigration had receded and the army was filled with U.S.-born generations with origins in all parts of Europe. Fighting in segregated white platoons "brought about a self-conscious wartime unity that transcended ethnic lines among whites" (Alba 2009, 80; see also Gerstle 2001). Especially after the war, struggles by the groups themselves—most notably Jewish organizations such as the Anti-Defamation League—to eliminate racial exclusionary barriers in housing, higher education, resorts, and social clubs were key in the passage of laws prohibiting racial and religious bias in employment and higher education. Whether any of these factors will play a role in changing the social construction of racial and ethnic categories in the future is one of the topics we take up in the conclusion.

Whiteness in Flux Today
Whatever the course of change in the future, we already see shifts as a result of the massive immigration of the last half century, and this includes the meaning of whiteness. The scholarship on white racial identity in the United States has highlighted how much it is taken for granted as well as rooted in social and eco-

nomic privileges, with these privileges often invisible to many whites who do not think of themselves as having a race at all. Although white racial identity continues to encompass European Americans' advantaged position in the ethnoracial hierarchy, it is also very much in flux (McDermott and Samson 2005).

One issue that has come into prominence, particularly in analyses of the last presidential election campaign and support for President Donald Trump, is the degree to which many whites feel that their "natural" privileges as whites are in jeopardy, indeed under siege, in the context of demographic change fueled by immigration and the economic and political gains of nonwhite groups in the post–civil rights era—something dramatically symbolized by the election of the nation's first black president. In the midst of growing ethnic and racial diversity across the country, whiteness has become more salient to many Americans who believe that nonwhites are undeservedly receiving advantages and "cutting in line" (Hochschild 2016). The historian Nell Irvin Painter argues that in the Trump era what it means to be white has fundamentally changed "from unmarked default to racially marked . . . from *of course* being beauty queen and *of course* being the cute young people selling things in ads to having to make space for other, nonwhite people to fill those roles" (2016).

In their article in this issue, Maureen Craig and Jennifer Richeson report empirical evidence of group-status threat—that is, the threat or fear that whites will lose their privileged and dominant position in America's racial hierarchy (2018). They note that many white Americans believe that antiwhite discrimination is on the rise, a view especially likely to be held by whites living in areas with relatively large racial minority populations. Deborah Schildkraut and Satia Marotta (also this issue) ask whether white millennials, born after 1980, might be less conservative in their political views than older whites, given their greater experience with a diverse society (2018). Although white millennials are more liberal on some issues, the stronger message from Schildkraut and Marotta is that differences between whites and nonwhites are much stronger than the generation difference among whites.

Another shift, although unusual, is worth attention. In some communities where Asian immigrants are numerically dominant, highly educated, and well off (and blacks and Latinos virtually absent), whiteness may well be downgraded. This has happened in Cupertino, California, an affluent white-Asian city in Silicon Valley where high academic achievement is no longer associated with whiteness: whiteness has come to stand for lower achievement, laziness, and academic mediocrity, and Asianness is linked with academic success, hard work, and achievement (Jiménez and Horowitz 2013).

There are also intriguing questions about white identities among groups classified as white on the census but who do not see themselves, and may not be seen by others, as white. Whereas for the descendants of earlier European immigrants, ethnic identity has become optional and white ethnic distinctions have gradually blurred into a more diffuse European American identity, especially by the third and fourth generations, this may not be the case for groups such as Arab and Middle Eastern Americans. Although they are officially considered white by the U.S. Census, they often have a stronger identification with their home country, region of origin, or religion than with whiteness, in good part owing to the widespread public suspicion and discrimination they face, especially among the many who are Muslim (Tehranian 2010). In fact, advocacy groups have pressured the census to adopt a separate Middle Eastern and North African (MENA) category because of the discomfort many have with checking off white, as well as a desire to increase opportunities for federal funding and gain more political clout; in early 2018, however, the Census Bureau announced that it would not add MENA to the next census.

Asians and the Elasticity of Race

Asians, especially those with origins in East Asia, have experienced a remarkable change in racial status, undergoing a metamorphosis in the last seven decades from "yellow peril" to model minority. Indeed, when whites stereotype Asian Americans today it is often for being economically successful (Abrajano and Hajnal 2015, 54).

It is hard to imagine that the Chinese and

Japanese in the United States used to be cast, as Yen Le Espiritu puts it, as "almost blacks but not black" given that now they are frequently seen as "almost whites but not whites" (1997, 109). In the past, racial prejudice against Asians was inscribed in restrictive immigration and naturalization laws. The Chinese Exclusion Act of 1882 singled out the Chinese as the first and only group to be excluded from the United States on the basis of race, ethnicity, or nationality; by 1917 Congress had also banned the immigration of most other Asians. For much of the nation's history, Asian immigrants were denied the right to become citizens; the 1882 Chinese Exclusion Act decreed that the Chinese were "aliens ineligible for citizenship," and over the next few decades the rule was extended, through a series of decisions in state and federal courts, to all other immigrants from east and south Asia (see Kurien 2018). It was not until 1943 that Chinese immigrants gained the right to become citizens and that the discriminatory immigration laws affecting Asians began to be relaxed. Only in 1952 was naturalization eligibility extended to all Asians.

Anti-Asian sentiments were particularly virulent on the West Coast, where several states adopted laws prohibiting Asian-white intermarriage. A 1913 law, targeting Japanese farmers, barred Asian immigrants from owning land. When a California court held in 1885 that the public schools had to admit Chinese children, the state legislature passed a bill allowing school districts to set up separate schools for "Mongolians" (Wollenberg 1995). Most devastating of all, during World War II more than one hundred thousand Japanese who lived on the Pacific Coast were forcibly evacuated and moved to internment camps.

Changes in U.S. immigration policy, foreign relations, and law set the stage for radically altered perceptions of Asians, including the abolition of the exclusion regime in the mid-twentieth century and revocation of Asian immigrants' ineligibility to citizenship. Also, Asian immigrants' home countries have changed over time. Americans once saw Asia as a backward region; now Japan, Taiwan, South Korea, and China are modern advanced nations and world economic powers. Of greater importance, however, in the higher racial status of Asians is that a large proportion of post-1965 Asian immigrants are highly educated and highly selected from their countries of origin. As Jennifer Lee and Min Zhou note, Chinese and Korean (as well as Asian Indian) immigrants are not only more highly educated than nonmigrants from their countries of origin, they are also more highly educated than the general U.S. population (Lee and Zhou 2015; on the Chinese, see Tran et al. 2018). Hyperselectivity goes a long way toward explaining another significant, and related, factor in East Asians' altered racial status: the extraordinary educational success of the second generation, including their significant overrepresentation in the nation's most competitive magnet schools and elite private universities. "Despite decades of institutional discrimination and racial prejudice," Lee and Zhou observe, "the status of Asian Americans has risen dramatically in less than a century. Today, Asian Americans are the most highly-educated [racial] group in the country, have the highest median household incomes, the highest rates of intermarriage, and the lowest rates of residential segregation" (2014, 8).

The substantial rates of intermarriage between Asian Americans and whites not only reflect the more positive views of Asians in the current period but also support and strengthen them. About one in three U.S.-born Asian Americans is married to a non-Hispanic white (Alba and Foner 2015); in 2010, among new marriages contracted in the past year, the figure was comparable, nearly four in ten U.S-born Asians marrying a non-Asian, by and large a non-Hispanic white (Wang 2012).

The frequent experience of marriage to whites among the second generation does not mean that negative stereotypes of Asians have disappeared; they have not. East Asians may seem *almost* white to many Americans, but as Mia Tuan puts it, yellow is not white (1998, 164). One persistent negative stereotype about Asian Americans is that they are newcomers, or thought of as "forever foreign" no matter how many generations their families have been in the United States, a perception that may be reinforced by continued large-scale inflows of Asian immigrants (Tran and Valdez, n.d.). Another is the model minority stereotype, which labels Asians as a racial group distinct from the white majority at the same time as they are lauded as culturally programmed for success, "well assimilated, upwardly mobile . . . and definitively not-black" (Wu 2015, 2). Hailing Asian Americans as a model minority, it has been argued, overlooks the heterogeneity among Asian immigrant ethnic groups, diverts attention away from the existence of continued racism against Asian Americans, and pits them against blacks and Latinos. Still, that Asian Americans are often now touted as a model minority reflects a positive change from the "yellow peril caricatures" of the past that described Asians as illiterate, undesirable, and unassimilable immigrants (Lee and Zhou 2014, 8).

Another change that should be mentioned is the increasing use of the Asian label as a marker of self-identity and identity attribution by others. In the pre-1960s era—when the Asian population was overwhelmingly of Chinese, Japanese, and Filipino origin—those with roots in Asia strongly identified with their national-origin identities, but not in terms of a shared Asian label. To what extent those seen as Asian Americans today identify that way themselves is an open question; their national-origin identities, associated with distinctive languages, religions, national histories, and cultures, seem to supersede the broader Asian identity much, perhaps most, of the time. Still, as Okamoto argues, the use of the category Asian "by mainstream institutions . . . [has become] institutionalized and . . . taken for granted in everyday interactions" (2014, 48). That the census and frequently the mainstream media as well use the term *Asian* has had an impact. Before 1970, the U.S. Census Bureau categorized Asian groups as different "races"—Chinese, Japanese, and Filipino in 1950. In 1990, the racial category Asian and Pacific Islander was used for the first time in the decennial census, partly in response to civil rights legislation and the need for a standard system to collect data to enforce equal opportunity and affirmative action policies. Researchers, businesses, public agencies, educational institutions, foundations, hospitals, and industry adopted the category *Asian* to collect data, award grants, and allocate resources (Okamoto 2014), which encouraged a panethnic Asian identity. By the mid-1980s, Asian panethnicity had become well established as an organizing principle for building a community among groups of different ethnic origins, replete with many panethnic organizations and institutions (Okamoto 2014, 45–46; see also Espiritu 1992).

Creating Hispanics

The case of Hispanics also represents a contemporary sea change, in large part because the very category *Hispanic* is a modern-day invention. Hispanics are now the largest minority group in the nation, attributable to high levels of immigrant inflows as well as relatively high fertility among Latino immigrants and U.S.-born Latinos in recent decades (Durand, Telles, and Flashman 2006). It is now normal to hear about the Hispanic vote and Hispanic organizations, but in the mid-twentieth century the press and pundits wrote about Mexicans or Puerto Ricans, not about Hispanics (Fischer 2014). A key development occurred in 1980, when the census adopted the term Hispanic as an enumeration category; this decision both reflected changes in American society and, at the same time, entrenched Hispanic as a legitimate official category, contributing to its importance as an identity label for Hispanics themselves as well as non-Hispanics.

The emergence of Hispanic (and Latino) as categories of identity is to a large degree the result of the politics of ethnic and racial classification (Itzigsohn 2009; see also Rumbaut 2006). As Cristina Mora tells it in *Making Hispanics*, the creation of this new identity label in the 1970s and 1980s involved a combination of activists seeking political clout, government funds, and philanthropic support by uniting under the Hispanic banner; Spanish-language television broadcasters seeking a larger national market; and activists and politicians successfully campaigning to have the census adopt the Hispanic category (2014). To this day, Mora argues, the web of media, state, and activist networks has upheld the notion of Hispanic panethnicity (2014, 16).

A key question, of course, is the extent to which those with origins in Latin America actually identify as Hispanic or Latino. It is not an either-or situation. Although many, perhaps most, Latin American immigrants prefer to be known by and primarily identify in terms of their national origins, they also often identify as Hispanic or Latino; the two identities, in other words, are not mutually exclusive but instead complementary. What seems clear is that what started out as a statistical term of convenience or tool to bring those of Latin American origin together has been transformed into a real social entity.

Whether Hispanics should be considered a race or an ethnic group is an issue characterized by confusion and debate. On the ethnic group side is the fact that the Census Bureau classifies Hispanics in terms of ethnicity, not race, and, as a group, they have varying skin tones, many being phenotypically white and more than half checking white on the 2010 Census. Hispanics who have light skin color and European features, are well educated, or are well to do may gain acceptance as whites, at least in some contexts and places; by the same token, dark-skinned Hispanics may suffer many of the same disadvantages as African Americans (see Kibria, Bowman, and O'Leary 2013, 129; Fox and Guglielmo 2012).

Yet a scheme that treats Latinos as a race between whites and blacks, as Wendy Roth puts it, is winning out in the United States today (2012, 64). In the media, public discourse, some government reporting standards, and everyday language used by Latinos and non-Latinos alike, the view of Latinos as a separate racial group has increasingly come to dominate. The term tends to conjure up images of people who are brown or tan-skinned and foreign in speech and manner. Or as Nazli Kibria and her colleagues observe, notions of intrinsic difference from and inferiority to whites are long-standing features of the stigmatization of Latino/a populations in the United States (2014, 126; see also Brown, Jones, and Becker 2018).

The case of Mexicans, by far the largest national-origin group of Latinos, illustrates some of the complexities of their position on the white-nonwhite boundary in the past and their racial status today. Looking to the past, the census classified Mexicans as white before 1930 and official instructions in World War II called on local draft boards to classify Mexicans as white; no state miscegenation law specifically barred unions between whites and Mexicans and the federal government accepted Mexicans as white for purposes of naturalization. Yet, at the same time, the boundary between whites and Mexicans appeared bright "in the sense that a wide range of individuals and non-state institutions recognized Mexicans as nonwhite. Many race scientists [in the early twentieth century] categorized the vast majority of Mexicans as nonwhite. Numerous Anglos did as well, a point that became most obvious when Mexicans [in many parts of the Midwest and Southwest] found themselves excluded from white-only public accommodations, when realtors refused to sell them homes in white neighborhoods, or when school officials excluded them from white schools" (Fox and Guglielmo 2012, 367).

Fast forward to the present and Mexicans have come to be seen, as some scholars argue, as a racialized ethnic group, often stigmatized as inferior, illegal, and foreign and regarded as nonwhite (see Alba and Foner 2015, 107). Another view stresses that Mexican Americans are targets of prejudice and discrimination because of nativism, or intense opposition based on their foreign connections, rather than because of beliefs about their racial inferiority. According to one argument, Mexican Americans experience a racialized form of nativism in which their presumed foreignness is central and their right to be in the country is questioned; third- and later-generation Mexican Americans, in this perspective, may encounter discrimination because they are associated with and often mistaken for new Mexican immigrants (Jiménez 2010). Pigmentation and other physical features also appear to be involved. Skin color among Mexicans and other Latinos has been shown to matter for socioeconomic standing and residential integration, the lighter, not surprisingly, the better—light skin color (along with social class standing) enabling some, at least some of the time, to be seen as white. A recent ethnographic study shows that Mexican Americans and Mexican immigrants, including those attaining middle-class status, often experience discrimination in their daily lives because of their skin color and surnames (Dowling 2014). Indigenous ancestry, manifested in physical features such as facial appearance and height as well as skin color, also poses racial challenges. As David Lopez and Ricardo Stanton-Salazar put it, speaking of Mexicans, "those who fit the mestizo/Indian phenotype, who 'look Mexican,' cannot escape racial stereotyping any more than African Americans, though the stigma is usually not so severe" (2001, 75).

Black Immigrants: Persistence in the Context of Change

This brings us to blacks, who are currently nearly one in ten immigrants in the nation. Blacks are the quintessentially racialized Americans with a history of special disadvantage—slavery, Jim Crow, ghettoization, and, most recently, massive incarceration (Foner and Fredrickson 2004, 8). The particular history of blacks in America has led to a highly rigid boundary surrounding them and a pattern of what might be called black exceptionalism. The historical legacy of deeply entrenched antiblack racism, combined with continued racial inequalities, has meant that the way contemporary black immigrants and their children identify, and are identified by others, is in many ways eerily like it was a hundred years ago. Overall, critical aspects of the dynamics of race, ethnicity, and identity for blacks of immigrant origin appear to be at least as much a matter of persistence as change across historical time.

Of course, not all is the same: many changes for the better have occurred since the early and mid-twentieth century. When tens of thousands of Afro Caribbean immigrants arrived in the United States a hundred years ago, a harsh regime of institutionalized racial oppression and legal segregation prevailed in the South, confining blacks there to separate (and inferior) schools, hospitals, and public places, putting them under threat of violence and lynching, and depriving most of the right to vote. Indeed, these conditions were a major reason why black immigrants at the time avoided the South and headed for northern cities, most notably New York. Although New York did not have a Jim Crow regime like the one in the South, it was no racial paradise. The housing market was rigidly segregated. Relatively few Afro Caribbean immigrant women had jobs in the manufacturing sector where so many eastern and southern European immigrant women clustered; black immigrant women overwhelmingly worked as household servants (Model 2001; Watkins-Owens 2001). During World War II, blacks in the armed forces were relegated to segregated units and after the war, as Ira Katznelson details, black veterans generally were unable to reap the benefits of the GI bill that enabled so many in the eastern and southern European second generation to attend college and buy homes (2005). In an environment of intense antiblack racism, the children and grandchildren of early twentieth-century Afro Caribbean immigrants had little choice as they incorporated into American society: they became African American (Vickerman 2016, 74–75).

Post-1965 black immigrants, who include a growing number of Africans as well as Afro Caribbeans, have entered a post–civil rights America that has seen declines in the grip of racial inequality on the life chances of blacks; the growing presence of blacks in the upper middle class and visibility in elite positions, from the heads of large companies, well-known newscasters and other personalities in the media, to the first black president; a rise in the number and proportion of mixed-race (black-white) individuals; and evidence of a greater willingness among whites to see differences among African Americans and more acceptance of middle- and upper-class African Americans (Waters and Kasinitz 2015; Edsall 2017; on the integration of African American history into school curricula, see Lash 2018).

Yet despite these improvements, stark social cleavages involving people of African ancestry remain. Rates of black-white intermarriage are much lower than those of Asian- and Hispanic-white intermarriage. Whether native or foreign-born, blacks in the United States are still highly residentially segregated from whites—more so than Hispanics and Asians—and the New York City metropolitan area, still home to the largest black immigrant population in the country, is one of the most segregated (Alba and Foner 2015; Foner 2001, 2015, 2016). In a large-scale study of young adult members of the second generation in the New York metropolitan area, West Indians reported the most discrimination (compared to Dominicans, South Americans, Chinese, and Russian Jews), especially in public places on the streets, in stores, and from the police (Kasinitz et al. 2008). Anonymous encounters with shopkeepers, security guards, and particularly the police in public spaces "are powerful because they are so purely 'racial.' In such confrontations class differences do not count . . . Nor do ethnic differences. . . . A police officer rarely has a basis for knowing if a young man on a public street is African American or West Indian, middle class or poor. If the police officer discriminates, it is on the basis of race alone" (Waters 2014, 159).

How blacks of immigrant origin are identified also shows considerable continuity over time. Much like the early and mid-twentieth century pattern, the descendants of black immigrants continue to face great difficulties today in being recognized by others in terms of their ethnicity rather than their race. Moreover, black immigrants, at least so far, have not had a significant impact on how blackness is widely seen in the United States.

To be sure, some changes are apparent. It might even be said that contemporary black immigration is contributing to "tweaking" notions of a monolithic blackness in cities like New York where black immigrants have become a considerable presence (Vickerman 2001). In early twentieth-century New York, for example, Afro Caribbean politicians played down their ethnic identity in the quest for office, putting themselves forward as representatives of the broader black community (Kasinitz 1992). Today, when the number of black immigrants is so much larger in New York City—more than ten times the 1920 figure—several sizable West Indian neighborhoods have provided the base for politicians to use the "ethnic card" to gain support in campaigns for local office. In general, the larger populations of Africans and West Indians provide more scope for ethnic identities to thrive within their communities in private interactions as well as public spaces. It has been suggested, as well, that in some instances second- and third-generation West Indians have actively tried to create a hybrid identity with younger African Americans, based in part on melding aspects of Caribbean and African American popular culture (Vickerman 2016, 77).

To tweak notions of a monolithic blackness, however, is not to create substantial change.

Even when their ethnicity is recognized in certain places and contexts, blacks of immigrant origin are seen as an ethnic group within the larger black population, with all the negative stereotypes that this so often involves. Their racial status as blacks, in other words, is always salient.

Identity issues take on special significance for the second generation, born and raised in the United States, as research on Afro Caribbeans reveals. Without an accent or other cues to immediately telegraph their ethnic status to others, second-generation Afro Caribbeans, in the words of Philip Kasinitz and his colleagues, are likely to fade to black (Kasinitz, Battle, and Miyeres 2001). Second-generation Afro Caribbeans who continue to identify with their ethnic backgrounds are aware that unless they are active in conveying their ethnic identities, they are seen as African Americans and that the status of their black race is what matters in encounters with whites. Or, as Milton Vickerman puts it, "the general public has yet to discard the reflexive habit of identifying 'black' with 'African American'" (2016, 78). The crux of the problem is that being seen as black American, they are subject to the same kind of racial prejudice and exclusion that black Americans are (see Waters 1999). The children of African immigrants face the same problem, although it is unclear whether they will have an easier time establishing an ethnic identity given, among other things, their distinctive surnames and whether they will be more or less likely than the Afro Caribbean second generation to want to do so (see, for example, D'Alisera 2009; Imoagene 2017; Ludwig 2013).

If, so far, contemporary black immigration has brought no significant change in the meaning of the racial categories black or African American, there still may be shifts ahead to incorporate the large and growing populations of recent West Indian and African origin. On the one hand, the children and grandchildren of today's black immigrants are likely to assimilate as African Americans, but, on the other, the meaning of African American may expand, if only in the African American community itself. It is not inconceivable that in the years ahead African American will be seen as a product not just of centuries on American soil but also of intermixing with black foreigners (Vickerman 2016, 2001).

CHANGING IDENTITIES AND INTERGROUP RELATIONS

As the array of ethnic groups increases in number and presence, interactions between people almost inevitably are influenced by ethnic and racial group membership—and by the members' identification with those groups and their perceived membership by others. These interactions can be positive or negative, can result in cooperation or competition, and can create occasions for unifying groups under a superordinate umbrella or for sharpening group boundaries and increasing distinctiveness. Further, these encounters occur for individuals as well as groups. At the individual level, contacts between members of different ethnic groups take place in casual encounters, friendships formed at work or in the neighborhood, or, perhaps with the greatest consequences for future identity issues, in the context of the family and kinship circles as a result of intermarriage. At the group level, ethnicity can structure interactions at work, in neighborhoods, and in political organizations, sometimes pitting groups against each other in conflict over resources, either imagined or real, and at other times, laying the groundwork for the development of panethnic (superordinate) identity groups that can unite for common goals.

Intermarriage

Intermarriage is perhaps the most intimate of all intergroup relations. It is, of course, an outcome of interpersonal relations between individuals in different ethnic and racial groups. But it also both affects relations between those of different race and ethnicity within families, kinship networks, and other contexts and has an impact on the identities of the partners and their multiethnic or multiracial children. Ethnoracial intermarriage is on the rise in the United States: about one out of every six marriages in 2015 was an interracial or interethnic marriage, more than twice the rate in 1980 (Livingston and Brown 2017). According to a Pew Research Center's analysis of census data, intermarriages of Asians, Hispanics, and blacks mainly involve a white spouse (some seven in ten new intermarriages in 2010), and this is the type of mixed union we focus on here; in most cases, both partners are native born, many of the nonwhite spouses being the children or grandchildren of immigrants (Wang 2012). Immigrants are much less likely to intermarry than the second and third generations, partly because many are already married when they arrive and because they may lack English fluency and other skills that facilitate easy interaction with the native born. The children and grandchildren of immigrants, born and raised in the United States, not only speak English but also often have many opportunities to mingle with those in the white majority in such places as schools, colleges, and work (Alba and Foner 2015, 208).

Whether considering rates of intermarriage or their consequences, the boundary separating blacks and whites stands out. Although marriage between blacks and whites in the United States has increased appreciably in recent decades (antimiscegenation laws were still on the books in sixteen states when the Supreme Court declared them illegal in 1967), it falls well short of the levels between whites and Hispanics and between whites and Asians. The frequency of intermarriage among the second generation is revealing. According to a recent summary, for second-generation Hispanics and for the largest group Mexicans, the rates of marriage to non-Hispanic whites are 35 to 40 percent; for second-generation Asians in general and most Asian national-origin groups (except Indians and Vietnamese) the rates vary roughly between 30 and 45 percent, depending on gender, women being more likely to intermarry. By comparison, only about 10 percent of the Afro Caribbean second generation have white partners (Alba and Foner 2015, 209–10). These low figures for Afro Caribbeans reflect a continued deep social cleavage involving groups with visible African ancestry, including the persistent stigma attached to blacks and the high levels of residential segregation they experience, which reduce opportunities for close social contacts and intimate relations with whites to develop.

The identity options of children of mixed unions also reflect continued black exceptionalism. Admittedly, mixed-race individuals' identities are fluid and change over time, no doubt more so than among individuals with ethnoracially unmixed backgrounds (Alba, Beck, and Sahin 2018), and what we know about these identities is sparse, if only because the mixed-race population, though now rapidly growing, historically has been a small share of the U.S. population as a whole. Still, a study based on in-depth interviews with interracial couples and their children suggests greater constraints facing the children of black-white unions in how they identify (Lee and Bean 2010). The study found that Asians and Hispanics married to whites felt that their U.S.-born children had the option to identify as whites, without having their decisions questioned by outsiders or institutions. The experiences of the children of black-white unions were different. Blacks who intermarried with whites said that their children were often seen as black only, underscoring that the "one drop rule" is not altogether a relic of the past. In fact, black-white couples emphasized that nobody would take them seriously if they tried to identify their children as white, and their children chose to identify as black rather than as multiracial or nonblack (Lee and Bean 2010, 108–9). Although a recent Pew Research Center survey (2015) found that a similar percentage of adults with a white-Asian (70 percent) and white-black (61 percent) background identified as multiracial, it was a different story in terms of how they thought others saw them: six in ten with a black-white background said a person passing them on the street would see them as black (only 7 percent said strangers would see them as white); around four in ten of those with an Asian-white background said that they would be seen as white, and one in four as Asian. Experimental work in social psychology supports these findings: although both biracial Asian whites and black-whites are more likely to be perceived as minorities than as whites by white observers (a pattern that has been determined by hypodescent), the threshold for being perceived as white was higher for biracial black-whites (Ho et al. 2011). Perhaps the best-known example of the identity issues facing black-white multiracials is Barack Obama, the son of a Kenyan father and white mother, who is seen, without question, as the nation's first black president, and as an adult defined himself as a black American.

The former president aside, similar patterns emerge with regard to friendship and family relations that can be viewed as a manifestation of how multiracial adults are identified by others and see themselves. The social worlds of biracial adults with Asian and white backgrounds in the Pew Research Center survey were more likely to lean to the white side of their ancestry than were those of biracial adults with black-white backgrounds (2015). Biracial white and Asian adults had more close friends who were white than Asian and more contact with white than Asian family members; most said they felt accepted by white relatives and by whites in general. Indeed, the Asian-white biracials were more likely to feel very well accepted by whites than by Asians. In contrast, black-white biracial adults tended to tilt more to the black side: they had more close friends who were black than white, had much more contact with black than white family members, and felt a much greater sense of acceptance from black people than whites (see also Chito Childs 2005).

Not unexpectedly, multiracial adults with a black background were far more likely than those with Asian-white ancestry to say they had experienced discrimination because of their racial background. A large proportion of those who said that casual observers would describe them as black also said that they had been unfairly stopped by the police—the same proportion, it turns out, as single-race blacks who reported receiving unfair treatment from the police. One young black-white biracial man summed up the feelings of many others in the survey: "No matter how I see myself, at the end of the day I'm still black" (Pew Research Center 2015, 58). Even so, by virtue of having parents in two ethnoracial groups, biracial children, whether the nonwhite parent is black, Asian, or Hispanic, inevitably have intimate contact with members of two groups. Just how this contact, as well as relations within wider kinship and friendship circles, affects the children's identities and interactions is one of the many topics about which we have much to learn.

Intergroup Contact

Whereas intermarriage can foster contacts with an ethnic or racial community other than one's own, in some ways a by-product of original interpersonal goals and attachments, direct contacts between ethnic groups are shaped by a variety of other factors. Some of these are idiosyncratic, the product of specific individual histories and encounters with particular people; others are structured by larger social and economic forces such as patterns of residence, labor market incorporation, and political mobilization and alliances. At the same time, the form of intergroup contact is shaped by widely shared and indeed normative views based on prevailing categorization practices and the narratives associated with those categories. These "normative ideas in circulation" influence individuals' views of those in different groups and how they should be treated (Appiah 2016, 164). Fundamentally, intergroup interactions are energized by issues of identity: how strongly does a black, white, Latino, or Asian person, for example, identify with his or her ethnic and racial group, and how readily does the other party view them as representatives of that group?

The tradition of research on intergroup relations is a long one, in particular on the consequences of contact between groups on the attitudes and behaviors of the members of the different groups. Originating in large part in the work of Gordon Allport and carried on by a long line of social scientists, much of this work has focused on the black-white dynamic (Allport 1954; see also Brown and Hewstone 2005; Pettigrew and Tropp 2006). More recently, however, ethnic diversity has opened the door to exploration of numerous combinations.

In its simplest form, the question is whether greater contact between different ethnic groups facilitates or impedes positive attitudes and friendly relations; evidence can be gathered to support both sides of this argument. Recent data reported by Eric Knowles and Linda Tropp, for example, suggest that for white Americans, greater exposure to Hispanics, as indexed by their numerical share of the neighborhood population, is associated with stronger white identities (2016). Yet research also indicates that although an increase in an immigrant group in a community can seem threatening to the native residents, those numbers also increase the probability of having contacts—some potentially favorable—with members of that immigrant group (Pettigrew, Wagner, and Christ 2010). More probing analyses suggest a variety of moderating conditions that can influence the outcome of intergroup contact; these conditions include equality of status between the two groups, the existence of common goals, experiences of cooperation, and institutional support (Tropp and Molina 2012). Another condition that has been identified in recent research is the importance of cross-group friendships (Pettigrew 1997). That is, the person who has a close friendship with a member of another ethnic group is more apt to have less prejudice and more liking for that group as a whole (Pettigrew and Tropp 2006; Davies et al. 2011).

Perhaps even more interesting, particularly in a multiethnic society such as ours, is evidence for a *secondary transfer effect* (Pettigrew 2009b). This effect is said to occur when contact with a member of a primary outgroup (for example, of whites with blacks) affects attitudes toward members of a different ethnic-racial group. In one recent exploration of this process, the attitudes of whites and blacks toward Indian and Mexican immigrants were assessed to see if they might be influenced by the extent of contact whites had with blacks, and vice versa (Jones-Correa et al. 2018; Marrow et al. 2018). As might be expected, the degree of direct contact that both whites and blacks had with each of the two immigrant groups was a primary determinant of their attitudes toward those groups. But in addition, mainly among U.S.-born white respondents, more frequent contact with blacks was associated with more welcoming attitudes toward both Indian and Mexican immigrants. Among U.S.-born black respondents, the pattern was more limited, showing evidence for secondary transfer effects for attitudes to Mexicans but not to Indians. Given differences in status positions and possible similarities or dissimilarities between particular combinations of groups, much more work is needed to map out exactly how primary and secondary transfer effects occur. It is clear, however, that in a multiethnic society, both history and current conditions can shape the course of intergroup relations and their consequences for identity development and change among immigrants and the native born.

The interactions that immigrants have with the U.S.-born groups they encounter have implications for their American identity as well. As Michael Jones-Correa and his colleagues discuss in their article in this issue, specific characteristics of the interactions matter (2018). For Mexican immigrants, interactions with both blacks and whites influence their identification as Americans; for Indian immigrants, by contrast, identifying as American is influenced only by the nature of their interactions with whites.

An additional caveat on the influence of intergroup interactions on identity patterns is a reminder that it is often the perception of conditions, rather than an objective tally, that shapes subsequent attitudes and behaviors. As Craig and Richeson report, not only does the actual percentage of racial minorities in a community influence whites' estimates of the discrimination that they and members of their group face, but so do their (not necessarily accurate) perceptions of those proportions (2018). Clearly the dynamics of intergroup contact are complex, characterized by numerous possible combinations of racial-ethnic groups and conditions of contact, not all of them marching in lockstep together. Yet, although overall consistency of patterns cannot be automatically assumed, evidence for the impact of interaction on identity processes is already convincing.

Panethnic Identities

The rise of Hispanic or Latino and Asian panethnicity, as noted, is a modern-day development, in that multiple ethnic groups have widened their boundaries to forge broader groupings and identities. Although Latinos and Asians remain strongly attached to their more specific ethnic or national identities, individuals allied with each panethnic group also often come together under the banner of panethnic identities, particularly in situations where cooperation allows them to exert political influence to common advantage. In general, as the historian George Fredrickson observes, to the "extent that the white or Anglo majority, nationally or locally, treats either Asians or Latinos as a single group and acts in ways that affect all or most of those so designated, panethnic identities . . . tend to emerge" (Foner and Fredrickson 2004, 7).

How are panethnic identities and intergroup relations connected? In the first place, relations among ethnic groups in the Asian or Latino panethnic category can influence panethnic identities. On one side, regular, positive interactions among members of different national-origin groups can encourage or fortify panethnic identities. This may be especially likely in institutional settings and local neighborhoods that have no dominant majority ethnic group, as in the Latino community of Corona in New York City's borough of Queens, where repeated interactions among residents in neighborhood arenas—from stores, churches, and senior centers to political groups—fostered an overarching Latino identity (Ricourt and Danta 2003; Espiritu 2013). Whatever the demographic configuration, collective organizing and political mobilization can encourage and strengthen panethnic identities among both Asian Americans and Latinos (see, for example, Okamoto 2014). On the other side are instances where divisive and conflictual relations among ethnic or national-origin groups reduce the salience or strength of panethnic identities, as when these groups compete for resources and desired positions, including political office. In the Sikh American case reported by Prema Kurien, a combination of factors in recent years, including discrimination experienced since September 11 and homeland political conflicts, have led to an emphasis on a Sikh American rather than Indian or South Asian identity, as well as a movement for Sikhs to be classified as a distinctive ethnic group by the U.S. census (2018).

The connection between panethnic identities and intergroup relations also may operate in the other direction: panethnic identities can affect intergroup relations. Most notably this happens when these identities provide the foundation for political mobilizations among ethnic groups, for example, when leaders of pan-Asian or pan-Latino organizations are able to appeal for support on the basis of panethnic allegiances. In other cases, panethnic identities support alliances with other panethnic or racial groups, such as the cooperation between Latino, Asian American, and black caucuses in state legislatures and city councils. More research is clearly needed on the consequences of panethnic identities for intergroup relations in communities and institutions as well as for political participation and organization (for political science analyses of the links between panethnicity and political attitudes and behavior, see Junn and Masuoka 2008; Lee 2008; Wong et al. 2011).

CONCLUSION

The massive immigration of the past half century has given rise to growing racial and ethnic diversity throughout the United States and led to striking shifts in the way that individuals, both immigrants and the native born, identify themselves and others. Indeed, the very categories used to define racial and ethnic similarities and differences, and the meanings attached to the categories, have undergone significant change.

We have focused on the past and present in the preceding pages, but have also speculated about the shape of racial and ethnic categories and identities in the years to come. Will any of the immigrant groups currently thought of as not white but not black, for example, come to be viewed as white—in other words, will the category white widen to include new strands? Or is it misleading to pose the question this way? Just as *white* meant something different a hundred years ago than it does today, so, too, the category *white* may become outmoded, or at least less salient, in the years ahead as new ways of thinking about racial and ethnic differences, and new racial divisions emerge, for example, a black-nonblack dichotomy, as some scholars speculate (see, for example, Lee and Bean 2010). In this scenario, Asians and most Hispanics, who start out in an in-between status, neither black nor white, could become part of a new nonblack or beige majority. Other social scientists suggest the possibility of a triracial stratification system, which in Eduardo Bonilla-Silva's version is made up of whites, honorary whites, and "collective blacks" (2004). The latter category, he proposes, would include, among others, dark-skinned Latino immigrants, West Indian and African immigrants, as well as Filipinos, Vietnamese and Laotians; honorary whites would consist of light-skinned Latinos, Japanese Americans, Korean Americans, Chinese Americans, Asian Indians, Middle Eastern Americans, and most multiracial Americans. Whatever the course of change, what seems clear is that some of the forces that operated in the past for the descendants of southern and eastern Europeans are unlikely to recur in the near future, such as an end to mass immigration or a huge expansion of higher education. Intermarriage, by contrast, is likely to be more significant in the coming years. Whereas in the past, Jews and Italians were transformed from races into white ethnics without undergoing alterations in phenotype, today, when the language of color is so prominent in racial discourse, intermarriage and the blurring of pigmentation and physical differences among mixed-race offspring are often predicted to be key agents of change. And though the kind of economic prosperity that occurred in the postwar years is not on the horizon today, the changing demography of the country—with fewer native whites in the working-age population and the labor market as the large cohort of baby boomers retires—is bound to create opportunities for some of the descendants of the post-1965 immigrants to move up the occupational ladder (Alba 2009; Alba and Foner 2015).

As we look ahead, additional research questions that can enhance our understanding of the links between immigration and racial and ethnic identities emerge. One broad question concerns how characteristics of different cities and other localities affect patterns of identity formation. Place matters, and a range of contextual features of cities—including the racial, ethnic, and class composition, and size of immigrant-origin as well as native white and minority populations and their relative political and economic standing—can influence the development of ethnic and racial identities. Another issue is how much it matters that one national-origin group may overwhelmingly dominate the immigrant population, as Mexicans do in many cities, and that a large proportion of them are also undocumented. Does being Mexican mean something different in Los Angeles, where Mexicans are around 40 percent of the immigrant population, versus New York

City, where they are only about 6 percent (Foner 2005; on views of Latinos in the U.S. South, see Brown et al. 2018). To take another example, the Haitian case suggests how other factors in an urban area—historical events shaping immigrant inflows and residential patterns—can affect the way an immigrant population is perceived. Haitians are a more highly stigmatized and visible group in Miami than in their other major area of settlement, New York City, in part because of distinctive features of Miami: the significant number of "boat people" who arrived there in the 1970s and 1980s and Haitians' association with their own distinctive neighborhood, Little Haiti, which has been home to many poorer Haitians as compared to New York City, where Haitians live in the same neighborhoods with English-speaking West Indians (Foner 2016).

To come back to a study mentioned earlier, how widespread are communities like those in Silicon Valley that Tomás Jiménez and Adam Horowitz studied, where traditional status rankings of ethnic and racial groups no longer hold (2013)? In their case study of a community that included only whites and large numbers of highly skilled Asians, whites are associated with mediocrity and Asians with the highest achievement, flipping the relative status of long-established native-born and immigrant groups. In general, what is the impact of living in ethnoburbs, advantaged suburbs where concentrations of well-off Asian families reside, for example, for the identities of those Asian immigrants and their children? And do other non-white immigrant-origin groups also occasionally find themselves near the top rather than near the bottom of their community hierarchy?

As immigrants have dispersed across the country in recent years and become less concentrated in traditional gateway cities, questions have arisen about the way so-called new destinations are distinctive contexts for immigrant incorporation (Singer 2014). These questions need to include ethnic and racial identities. Do whites, to raise just one issue, experience more group threat in new destinations where large numbers of Latino immigrants have recently moved into what had been virtually all-white communities, in contrast to traditional gateways that have long been accustomed to immigration and ethnoracial diversity? Do we need to consider the rate of change in a community as well as absolute numbers to fully understand the ways in which threat might operate? Also of relevance in the present political climate are the effects of local government policies impinging on unauthorized immigrants. Whereas some cities have developed migrant-inclusive policies, such as establishing sanctuary cities or developing municipal identification cards for use as identification by the unauthorized (de Graauw 2014), other communities have passed restrictive legislation designed to limit unauthorized immigrants' employment and residence or have actively worked with federal immigration enforcement to deport the unauthorized (Armenta 2017; Donato and Rodriguez 2014; Flores 2014; Menjivar and Kanstroon 2013). These responses, whether inclusive or exclusive, are likely to influence the ways that people define and understand their race and ethnicity and that of others.

Whatever the location, another set of questions relates to the range of social statuses and characteristics of those of immigrant origin as they affect the construction of racial and ethnic identities, that is, an intersectional perspective that emphasizes how race and ethnic identities are experienced in interaction with other identities such as gender and occupation (see, for example, Collins 2015). Legal status looms large given that one in four immigrants in the United States is undocumented. The common assumption that most Mexican immigrants are undocumented (only about half are and the number is declining) has contributed, as noted earlier, to negative views of *all* Mexican immigrants and questions about their right to be in the country. Just as we need to know more about the links between legal status and identities, education, social class, and rising inequality are also potentially important in influencing identities. More than a quarter of immigrants have a college degree, and the figure is higher for their U.S.-born children. How do educational and occupational achievements shape how Asian, Latino, and black immigrants identify themselves and how others identify them? These same issues of class and education can be raised for white identity as well, given emerging research showing links between class position and the importance of white identity (Stets and Phares 2016). A further intersection of potential significance is that of gender (Donato and Gabaccia 2015). Are there critical interactions among some of these demographic categories, such that, for example, gender might be more influential when considering some ethnic groups than others?

Finally, returning to the idea of change, we need to ask how identities might vary over the life course and differ by age and life stage. Even within the limited format of the U.S. Census and within a ten-year span, people have been found to change their choice of ethnic label, a finding particularly true for those who use a combination of categories at one of the two time points (Liebler et al. 2017). In this issue, Cynthia Feliciano and Rubén Rumbaut's research indicates that for some adult children of immigrants ethnic attachments become less central over the life course (2018). Other research shows how ethnic and racial identities vary between the first and second generation—for example, members of the U.S.-born second generation are more likely to adopt a hyphenated American identity than their immigrant parents and to be less attached to the national identity associated with their parents' country of origin (Portes and Rumbaut 2001, 165)—but we still have much more to learn about generational differences.

These are just some of the many questions that call for further study. As immigrants continue to enter and settle in the United States; as a huge second, and now third, generation descended from post-1965 immigrants grow up and take their place as adults in American society; and as political developments pose unpredictable challenges, understanding how immigrants and their descendants affect, and are affected by, the meanings attached to ethnoracial differences and their place in ethnoracial hierarchies are topics that should be high on our research agenda.

REFERENCES

Abrajano, Marisa, and Zoltan Hajnal. 2015. *White Backlash: Immigration, Race, and American Politics*. Princeton, N.J.: Princeton University Press.

Alba, Richard. 2009. *Blurring the Color Line: The New Chance for an Integrated America*. Cambridge, Mass.: Harvard University Press.

———. 2016a. "The Likely Persistence of a White Majority." *American Prospect* 27(1)(Winter): 67–71.

———. 2016b. "The Rise of Mixed Parentage: A Sociological and Demographic Phenomenon to Be Reckoned With." Paper prepared for RSF conference "What the Census Needs to Know to Improve Ethnic, Racial and Immigration Statistics." New York (December 9).

Alba, Richard, Brenden Beck, and Duygu Basaran Sahin. 2018. "The U.S. Mainstream Expands—Again." *Journal of Ethnic and Migration Studies* 44(1): 99–117.

Alba, Richard, and Nancy Foner. 2015. *Strangers No More: Immigration and the Challenges of Integration in North America and Western Europe*. Princeton, N.J.: Princeton University Press.

Allport, Gordon W. 1954. *The Nature of Prejudice*. Reading, Mass.: Addison-Wesley.

Appiah, Kwame Anthony. 2016. "The Diversity of Diversity." In *Our Compelling Interests: The Value of Diversity for Democracy and a Prosperous Society*, edited by Earl Lewis and Nancy Cantor. Princeton, N.J.: Princeton University Press.

Armenta, Amada. 2017. *Protect, Serve, and Deport: The Rise of Policing as Immigration Enforcement*. Berkeley: University of California Press.

Ashmore, Richard D., Kay Deaux, and Tracey McLaughlin-Volpe. 2004. "An Organizing Framework for Collective Identity: Articulation and Significance of Multidimensionality." *Psychological Bulletin* 130(1): 80–114.

Barker, Eugene C., William E. Dodd, and Henry Steele Commager. 1934. *Our Nation's Development*. Evanston, Ill.: Row, Peterson and Co.

Barrett, James, and David Roediger. 1997. "Inbetween Peoples: Race, Nationality, and the 'New Immigrant' Working Class." *Journal of American Ethnic History* 16(3): 432–45.

Benet-Martínez, Veronica. 2012. "Multiculturalism." In *The Oxford Handbook of Personality and Social Psychology*, edited by Kay Deaux and Mark Snyder. New York: Oxford University Press.

Bonilla-Silva, Eduardo. 2004. "From Bi-Racial to Tri-Racial: Towards a New System of Racial Stratification in the United States." *Ethnic and Racial Studies* 27(6): 931–50.

Bratter, Jennifer. 2016. "The Work in Progress of Analyzing Multiracial Populations? What the Census Bureau Needs to Know to Improve Statistics

About Multiple-Race People." Paper presented at RSF conference "What the Census Needs to Know to Improve Ethnic, Racial and Immigration Statistics." New York (December 9).

Brown, Hana E., Jennifer A. Jones, and Andrea Becker. 2018. "The Racialization of Latino Immigrants in New Destinations: Criminality, Ascription, and Countermobilization." *RSF: The Russell Sage Foundation Journal of the Social Sciences* 4(5): 118–40. DOI: 10.7758/RSF.2018.4.5.06.

Brown, Rupert, and Miles Hewstone. 2005. "An Integrative Theory of Intergroup Contact." *Advances in Experimental Social Psychology* 37:255–343.

Cheryan, Sapna, and Benoit Monin. 2005. "Where Are You Really From? Asian Americans and Identity Denial." *Journal of Personality and Social Psychology* 89(5): 717–30.

Chito Childs, Erica. 2005. *Negotiating Interracial Borders: Black-White Couples and Their Social Worlds.* New Brunswick, N.J.: Rutgers University Press.

Collins, Patricia. 2015. "Intersectionality's Definitional Dilemmas." *Annual Review of Sociology* 41(1): 1–20.

Cornell, Stephen, and Douglas Hartmann. 2004. "Conceptual Confusions and Divides: Race, Ethnicity, and the Study of Immigration." In *Not Just Black and White: Historical and Contemporary Perspectives on Race, Ethnicity, and Immigration,* edited by Nancy Foner and George Fredrickson. New York: Russell Sage Foundation.

Craig, Maureen A., and Jennifer A. Richeson. 2018. "Majority No More? The Influence of Neighborhood Racial Diversity and Salient National Population Changes on Whites' Perceptions of Racial Discrimination." *RSF: The Russell Sage Foundation Journal of the Social Sciences* 4(5): 141–57. DOI: 10.7758/RSF.2018.4.5.07.

D'Alisera, JoAnn. 2009. "Images of a Wounded Homeland: Sierra Leonean Children and the New Heart of Darkness." In *Across Generations: Immigrant Families in America,* edited by Nancy Foner. New York: New York University Press.

Davies, K., Linda R. Tropp, Arthur Aron, Thomas F. Pettigrew, and S. C. Wright. 2011. "Cross-Group Friendships and Intergroup Attitudes: A Meta-Analytic Review." *Personality and Social Psychology Review* 15(4): 332–51.

Deaux, Kay. 2015. "Social Identity in Sociology." In *International Encyclopedia of the Social & Behavioral Sciences,* 2nd ed., vol. 22, edited by James D. Wright. Amsterdam: Elsevier.

De Graauw, Els. 2014. "Municipal ID Cards for Undocumented Immigrants: Local Bureaucratic Membership in a Federal System." *Politics & Society* 42(3): 309–30.

Donato, Katharine M., and Donna Gabaccia. 2015. *Gender and International Migration: From the Slavery Era to the Global Age.* New York: Russell Sage Foundation.

Donato, Katharine M., and Leslie Ann Rodriguez. 2014. "Police Arrests in a Time of Uncertainty: The Impact of 287(g) on Arrests in a New Immigrant Gateway." *American Behavioral Scientist* 58(13): 1696–722.

Dowling, Julie. 2014. *Mexican Americans and the Question of Race.* Austin: University Texas Press.

Durand, Jorge, Edward Telles, and Jennifer Flashman. 2006. "The Demographic Foundations of the Latino Population." In *Hispanics and the Future of America,* edited by Marta Tienda and Faith Mitchell. Washington, D.C.: National Academies Press.

Edsall, Thomas. 2017. "Black People Are All Not 'Living in Hell.'" *New York Times,* April 27. Accessed January 5, 2018. https://www.nytimes.com/2017/04/27/opinion/black-people-are-not-all-living-in-hell.html.

Espiritu, Yen Le. 1992. *Asian American Panethnicity: Bridging Institutions and Identities.* Philadelphia, Pa.: Temple University Press.

———. 1997. *Asian American Men and Women.* Thousand Oaks, Calif.: Sage Publications.

———. 2013. "Panethnicity." In *The Routledge Handbook of Migration Studies,* edited by Steven Gold and Stephanie Nawyn. New York: Routledge.

Feliciano, Cynthia, and Rubén G. Rumbaut. 2018. "Varieties of Ethnic Self-Identities: Children of Immigrants in Middle Adulthood." *RSF: The Russell Sage Foundation Journal of the Social Sciences* 4(5): 26–46. DOI: 10.7758/RSF.2018.4.5.02.

Fischer, Claude. 2014. "Where Did 'Hispanics' Come From?" *Sociological Images,* March 29. Accessed January 5, 2018. https://thesocietypages.org/socimages/2014/03/29/where-did-hispanics-come-from.

Fiske, Susan T., and Tiane L. Lee. 2012. "Xenophobia and How to Fight It: Immigrants as the Quintessential 'Other'." In *Social Categories in Everyday Experience,* edited by Shaun Wiley, Gina

Philogène and Tracey A. Revenson. Washington, D.C.: American Psychological Association.

Fitzgerald, Frances. 1979. *America Revised*. Boston, Mass.: Little Brown.

Flores, Natalia M., and Yuen J. Huo. 2013. "'We' Are Not All Alike: Consequences of Neglecting National Origin Identities Among Asians and Latinos." *Social Psychological and Personality Science* 4(2): 143–50.

Flores, Rene D. 2014. "Living in the Eye of the Storm: How Did Hazelton's Restrictive Immigration Ordinance Affect Local Interethnic Relations?" *American Behavioral Scientist* 58(13): 1743–63.

Foner, Nancy. 2000. *From Ellis Island to JFK: New York's Two Great Waves of Immigration*. New Haven, Conn.: Yale University Press.

———. 2005. *In a New Land: A Comparative View of Immigration*. New York: New York University Press.

———. 2015. "Is Islam in Western Europe Like Race in the United States?" *Sociological Forum* 30(4): 885–89.

———. 2016. "Black Immigrants and the Realities of Racism: Comments and Questions." *Journal of American Ethnic History* 36(1): 63–70.

Foner, Nancy, ed. 2001. *Islands in the City: West Indian Migration to New York*. Berkeley: University of California Press.

Foner, Nancy, and George Fredrickson. 2004. "Immigration, Race, and Ethnicity in the United States: Social Constructions and Social Relations." In *Not Just Black and White: Historical and Contemporary Perspectives on Race, Ethnicity, and Immigration*, edited by Nancy Foner and George Fredrickson. New York: Russell Sage Foundation.

Fox, Cybelle, and Thomas Guglielmo. 2012. "Defining America's Racial Boundaries: Blacks, Mexicans, and European Immigrants: 1890–1945." *American Journal of Sociology* 118(2): 327–79.

Fredrickson, George. 2002. *Racism: A Short History*. Princeton, N.J.: Princeton University Press.

Gerstle, Gary. 2001. *American Crucible: Race and Nation in the Twentieth Century*. Princeton, N.J.: Princeton University Press.

Gleason, Philip. 1983. "Identifying Identity: A Semantic History." *Journal of American History* 69(4): 910–31.

Gonzales, Roberto G., and Steven Raphael, eds. 2017. "Undocumented Immigrants and Their Experience with Illegality." *RSF: The Russell Sage Foundation Journal of the Social Sciences* 3(4). DOI: 10.7758/RSF.2017.3.issue-4.

Guglielmo, Thomas. 2003. *White on Arrival: Italians, Race, Color, and Power in Chicago, 1890–1945*. New York: Oxford University Press.

Guterl, Matthew Pratt. 2001. *The Color of Race in America, 1900–40*. Cambridge, Mass.: Harvard University Press.

Hattam, Victoria. 2004. "Ethnicity: An American Genealogy." In *Not Just Black and White: Historical and Contemporary Perspectives on Race, Ethnicity, and Immigration*, edited by Nancy Foner and George Fredrickson. New York: Russell Sage Foundation.

Ho, Arnold K., Jim Sidanius, Daniel T. Levin, and Mahzarin R. Banaji. 2011. "Evidence for Hypodescent and Racial Hierarchy in the Categorization and Perception of Biracial Individuals." *Journal of Personality and Social Psychology* 100(3): 492–506.

Hochschild, Arlie. 2016. *Strangers in Their Own Land: Anger and Mourning on the American Right*. New York: New Press.

Hollinger, David. 2006. *Postethnic America: Beyond Multiculturalism*. New York: Basic Books.

Imoagene, Onoso. 2017. *Beyond Expectations: Second-Generation Nigerians in the United States and Britain*. Berkeley: University of California Press.

Itzigsohn, Jose. 2009. *Encountering Faultlines: Class, Race, and the Dominican Experience*. New York: Russell Sage Foundation.

Jacobson, Matthew Frye. 1998. *Whiteness of a Different Color: European Immigrants and the Alchemy of Race*. Cambridge, Mass.: Harvard University Press.

Jiménez, Tomás R. 2010. *Replenished Ethnicity: Mexican Americans, Immigration, and Identity*. Berkeley: University of California Press.

Jiménez, Tomás R., and Adam L. Horowitz. 2013. "When White Is Just Alright: How Immigrants Redefine Achievement and Reconfigure the Ethnoracial Hierarchy." *American Sociological Review* 78(5): 849–71.

Jones-Correa, Michael, Helen B. Marrow, Dina G. Okamoto, and Linda R. Tropp. 2018. "Immigrant Perceptions of U.S.-Born Receptivity and the Shaping of American Identity." *RSF: The Russell Sage Foundation Journal of the Social Sciences* 4(5): 47–80. DOI: 10.7758/RSF.2018.4.5.03.

Junn, Jane, and Rachel Masuoka. 2008. "Asian American Identity: Shared Racial Status and Political Context." *Perspectives on Politics* 6(4): 729–40.

Kasinitz, Philip. 1992. *Caribbean New York: Black Immigrants and the Politics of Race*. Ithaca, N.Y.: Cornell University Press.

Kasinitz, Philip, Juan Battle, and Ines Miyares. 2001. "Fade to Black? The Children of West Indian Immigrants in South Florida." In *Ethnicities*, edited by Rubén Rumbaut and Alejandro Portes. Berkeley: University of California Press.

Kasinitz, Philip, John Mollenkopf, Mary C. Waters, and Jennifer Holdaway. 2008. *Inheriting the City: The Children of Immigrants Come of Age*. New York / Cambridge, Mass.: Russell Sage Foundation / Harvard University Press.

Katz, Daniel, and Kenneth Braly. 1933. "Racial Stereotypes of One Hundred College Students." *Journal of Abnormal and Social Psychology* 28(3): 280–90.

Katznelson, Ira. 2005. *When Affirmative Action Was White*. New York: W. W. Norton.

Kibria, Nazli, Cara Bowman, and Megan O'Leary. 2013. *Race and Immigration*. Cambridge: Polity.

Klein, Olivier, Russell Spears, and Stephen Reicher. 2007. "Social Identity Performance: Extending the Strategic Side of SIDE." *Personality and Social Psychology Review* 11(1): 1–18.

Knowles, Eric D., and Kaiping Peng. 2005. "White Selves: Conceptualizing and Measuring a Dominant-Group Identity." *Journal of Personality and Social Psychology* 89(2): 223–41.

Knowles, Eric D., and Linda R. Tropp. 2016. "Donald Trump and the Rise of White Identity in Politics." *The Conversation*, October 20. Accessed January 5, 2018. http://theconversation.com/donald-trump-and-the-rise-of-white-identity-in-politics-67037.

Kurien, Prema. 2018. "Shifting U.S. Racial and Ethnic Identities and Sikh American Activism." *RSF: The Russell Sage Foundation Journal of the Social Sciences* 4(5): 81–98. DOI: 10.7758/RSF.2018.4.5.04.

Lash, Cristina L. 2018. "Making Americans: Schooling, Diversity, and Assimilation in the Twenty-First Century." *RSF: The Russell Sage Foundation Journal of the Social Sciences* 4(5): 99–117. DOI: 10.7758/RSF.2018.4.5.05.

Lee, Jennifer, and Frank Bean. 2010. *The Diversity Paradox: Immigration and the Color Line in Twenty-First Century America*. New York: Russell Sage Foundation.

Lee, Jennifer, and Min Zhou. 2014. "From Unassimilable to Exceptional: The Rise of Asian Americans and 'Stereotype Promise.'" *New Diversities* 16(1): 7–22.

———. 2015. *The Asian American Achievement Paradox*. New York: Russell Sage Foundation.

Lee, Taeku. 2008. "Race, Immigration, and the Identity to Politics Link." *Annual Review of Political Science* 11(1): 457–78.

Liebler, Carolyn A., Sonya Rastogi, Leticia E. Fernandez, James M. Noon, and Sharon R. Ennis. 2017. "America's Churning Races: Race and Ethnicity Response Changes Between Census 2000 and the 2010 Census." *Demography* 54(1): 259–84.

Livingston, Gretchen, and Anna Brown. 2017. *Intermarriage in the U.S. 50 Years After Loving v. Virginia*. Washington, D.C.: Pew Research Center.

Lopez, David, and Richard Stanton-Salazar. 2001. "Mexican Americans: A Second Generation at Risk." In *Ethnicities: Children of Immigrants in America*, edited by Rubén Rumbaut and Alejandro Portes. Berkeley: University of California Press.

Ludwig, Bernadette. 2013. "Liberians: Struggles for Refugee Families." In *One Out of Three: Immigrant New York in the Twenty-First Century*, edited by Nancy Foner. New York: Columbia University Press.

Major, Brenda, Alison Blodorn, and Gregory Major Blascovich. 2016. "The Threat of Increasing Diversity: Why Many White Americans Support Trump in the 2016 Presidential Election." *Group Processes & Intergroup Relations*, published online October 20, 2016. DOI: 10.1177/1368430216677304.

Marrow, Helen, Linda R. Tropp, Meta van der Linden, Dina Okamoto, and Michael Jones-Correa. 2018. "The Secondary Transfer Effect of Inter-Racial Contact on Whites and Blacks' Receptivity Toward Immigrants in the United States." Manuscript under review.

McCann, James A., and Michael Jones-Correa, eds. 2016. "Immigrants Inside Politics/Outside Citizenship." *RSF: The Russell Sage Foundation Journal of the Social Sciences* 2(3). DOI: 10.7758/RSF.2016.2.issue-3.

McDermott, Monica, and Frank L. Samson. 2005. "White Racial and Ethnic Identity in the United

States." *Annual Review of Sociology* 31(1): 245–61.

Menjívar, Cecilia, and Daniel Kanstroom. 2013. *Constructing Immigrant 'Illegality': Critiques, Experiences, and Responses*. New York: Cambridge University Press.

Model, Suzanne. 2001. "Where New York's West Indians Work." In *Islands in the City: West Indian Migration to New York*, edited by Nancy Foner. Berkeley: University of California Press.

Mora, Cristina. 2014. *Making Hispanics: How Activists, Bureaucrats & Media Constructed a New American*. Chicago: University of Chicago Press.

Morning, Ann, and Aliya Saperstein. 2016. "Generational Composition and Self-Identification of the U.S. Multiracial Population." Paper presented at the Russell Sage Foundation conference "What the Census Needs to Know to Improve Ethnic, Racial and Immigration Statistics." New York (December 9).

Okamoto, Dina G. 2014. *Redefining Race: Asian American Panethnicity and Shifting Ethnic Boundaries*. New York: Russell Sage Foundation.

Painter, Nell Irvin. 2016. "What Whiteness Means in the Trump Era." *New York Times*, November 12. Accessed January 5, 2018. https://www.nytimes.com/2016/11/13/opinion/what-whiteness-means-in-the-trump-era.html.

Park, Robert E., and Herbert A. Miller. 1921. *Old World Traits Transplanted*. New York: Harper.

Pettigrew, Thomas F. 1997. "Generalized Intergroup Contact Effects on Prejudice." *Personality and Social Psychology Bulletin* 23(2): 173–85.

———. 2009a. "Intergroup Contact Theory." *Annual Review of Psychology* 49(1): 65–85.

———. 2009b. "Contact's Secondary Transfer Effect: Do Intergroup Contact Effects Spread to Non-Participating Outgroups?" *Social Psychology* 40(2): 55–65.

Pettigrew, Thomas F., and Linda R. Tropp. 2006. "A Meta-Analytic Test of Intergroup Contact Theory." *Journal of Personality and Social Psychology* 90(5): 751–83.

Pettigrew, Thomas F., Ulrich Wagner, and Oliver Christ. 2010. "Population Ratios and Prejudice: Modelling Both Contact and Threat Effects." *Journal of Ethnic and Migration Studies* 36(4): 635–50.

Pew Research Center. 2015. *Multiracial in America: Proud, Diverse and Growing in Numbers*. Washington, D.C.: Pew Research Center.

Portes, Alejandro, and Rubén Rumbaut. 2001. *Legacies: The Story of the Immigrant Second Generation*. Berkeley: University of California Press.

Prewitt, Kenneth. 2013. *What Is Your Race? The Census and Our Flawed Efforts to Classify Americans*. Princeton, N.J.: Princeton University Press.

Ricourt, Milagros, and Ruby Danta. 2003. *Hispanas de Queens: Latino Panethnicity in a New York City Neighborhood*. Ithaca, N.Y.: Cornell University Press.

Robinson, Marilynne. 2017. "A Proof, a Test, an Instruction." *The Nation* 304(1): 16.

Rogers, Reuel. 2006. *Afro-Caribbean Immigrants and the Politics of Incorporation*. New York: Cambridge University Press.

Roth, Wendy. 2012. *Race Migrations: Latinos and the Cultural Transformation of Race*. Stanford, Calif.: Stanford University Press.

Rumbaut, Rubén. 2006. "The Making of a People." In *Hispanics and the Future of America*, edited by Marta Tienda and Faith Mitchell. Washington, D.C.: National Academies Press.

Schildkraut, Deborah J. 2011. *Americanism in the Twenty-First Century: Public Opinion in the Age of Immigration*. New York: Cambridge University Press.

Schildkraut, Deborah J., and Satia A. Marotta. 2018. "Assessing the Political Distinctiveness of White Millennials: How Race and Generation Shape Racial and Political Attitudes in a Changing America." *RSF: The Russell Sage Foundation Journal of the Social Sciences* 4(5): 158–87. DOI: 10.7758/RSF.2018.4.5.08.

Sears, David O., and Victoria Savalei. 2006. "The Political Color Line in America: Many 'Peoples of Color' or Black Exceptionalism?" *Political Psychology* 27(6): 895–924.

Singer, Audrey. 2014. "Metropolitan Immigrant Gateways Revisited, 2014." Washington, D.C.: Brookings Institution. Accessed January 5, 2018. https://www.brookings.edu/research/metropolitan-immigrant-gateways-revisited-2014.

Stets, Jan E., and Phoenicia Fares. 2016. "Gender Identity, Racial Identity, and Well-Being." Presented at 28th Annual Group Processes Conference. Seattle, Wash. (August 19).

Tehranian, John. 2010. *Whitewashed: America's Invisible Middle Eastern Racial Minority*. New York: New York University Press.

Tran, Van C., Jennifer Lee, Oshin Khachikian, and Jess Lee. 2018. "Hyper-selectivity, Racial Mobility, and the Remaking of Race." *RSF: The Russell Sage Foundation Journal of the Social Sciences* 4(5): 188–209. DOI: 10.7758/RSF.2018.4.5.09.

Tran, Van C., and Nicol Valdez. n.d. "Asian American Exceptionalism: Hyper-selectivity, Replenishment, and Second Generation Racial Mobility." Unpublished paper, Columbia University.

Tropp, Linda R., and Ludwin E. Molina. 2012. "Intergroup Processes: From Prejudice to Positive Relations Between Groups." In *The Oxford Handbook of Personality and Social Psychology*, edited by Kay Deaux and Mark Snyder. New York: Oxford University Press.

Tuan, Mia. 1998. *Forever Foreigners or Honorary Whites?* New Brunswick, N.J.: Rutgers University Press.

Vickerman, Milton. 2001. "Tweaking a Monolith: The West Indian Immigrant Encounter with 'Blackness.'" In *Islands in the City: West Indian Migration to New New York*, edited by Nancy Foner. Berkeley: University of California Press.

———. 2016. "Black Immigrants, Perceptions of Difference, and the Abiding Sting of Blackness." *Journal of American Ethnic History* 36(1): 71–81.

Vignoles, Vivian L. Forthcoming. "Identity: Personal and Social." In *Oxford Handbook of Personality and Social Psychology*, 2nd ed., edited by Kay Deaux and Mark Snyder. New York: Oxford University Press.

Wang, Jennifer, Camden Minervino, and Sapna Cheryan. 2013. "Generational Differences in Vulnerability to Identity Denial: the Role of Group Identification." *Group Processes & Intergroup Relations* 16(5): 600–17.

Wang, Wendy. 2012. *The Rise of Intermarriage: Rates, Characteristics Vary by Race and Gender*. Washington, D.C.: Pew Research Center.

Waters, Mary C. 1999. *Black Identities: West Indian Immigrant Dreams and American Realities*. Cambridge, Mass.: Harvard University Press.

———. 2014. "Nativism, Racism, and Immigration in New York City." In *Amsterdam and New York: Immigration and the New Urban Landscape*, edited by Nancy Foner et al. New York: New York University Press.

Waters, Mary C., and Philip Kasinitz. 2015. "The War on Crime and the War on Immigrants: Racial and Legal Exclusion in the Twenty-First Century United States." In *Fear, Anxiety, and National Identity: Immigration and Belonging in North America and Western Europe*, edited by Nancy Foner and Patrick Simon. New York: Russell Sage Foundation.

Watkins-Owens, Irma. 2001. "Early Twentieth Century Caribbean Women: Migration and Social Networks in New York City." In *Islands in the City: West Indian Migration to New York*, edited by Nancy Foner. Berkeley: University of California Press.

Wiley, Shaun, and Kay Deaux. 2011. "The Bicultural Identity Performance of Immigrants." In *Identity and Participation in Culturally Diverse Societies: A Multidisciplinary Perspective*, edited by Assaad E. Azzi, Xenia Chryssochoou, Bert Klandermans, and Bernd Simon. Chichester, UK: Wiley-Blackwell.

Wilkins, Clara L., Cheryl Kaiser, and Heather M. Reick. 2010. "Detecting Racial Identification: The Role of Phenotypic Prototypicality." *Journal of Experimental Social Psychology* 46(6): 1029–34.

Wollenberg, Charles. 1995. "'Yellow Peril' in the Schools." In *The Asian American Experience*, edited by Don Nakanishi and Tina Yamano Nishida. New York: Routledge.

Wong, Janelle, Karthick Ramakrishnan, Taeku Lee, and Jane Junn. 2011. *Asian American Political Participation: Emerging Constituents and their Political Identities*. New York: Russell Sage Foundation.

Wu, Ellen D. 2015. *The Color of Success: Asian Americans and the Origin of the Model Minority*. Princeton, N.J.: Princeton University Press.

Varieties of Ethnic Self-Identities: Children of Immigrants in Middle Adulthood

CYNTHIA FELICIANO AND RUBÉN G. RUMBAUT

This mixed-methods longitudinal study examines ethnic self-identity change from mid-adolescence to middle adulthood among a representative sample of adult children of immigrants first surveyed in 1992 in San Diego. Findings reveal the complexities of ethnic identity. Ethnic identity labels are often used interchangeably yet usually stabilize by middle adulthood. While the importance of ethnic identity often diminishes, immigrants' children in their late thirties express distinct ethnic identity formations, ranging from strong ethnic attachments to indifference, that vary within and between nativity and national-origin groups. Ethnic identities relate to political views and behaviors, interethnic friendships, and cultural practices, but not interethnic unions. Consistent with life course theory, results show how identities develop across nearly a quarter century, influenced by sociohistorical contexts and relationships with others.

Keywords: ethnic identity, second generation, immigrants, middle adulthood, life course

The study of the *new second generation*, framed as the most consequential legacy of contemporary immigration to the United States, is now more than twenty years old, and has generated a vibrant field of study.[1] Although the incorporation trajectories of the adult children of this immigration have been the subject of vigorous debates, the complexities of ethnic-panethnic identity formations in adult life are understudied.[2] The ethnic-panethnic identity outcomes of the adult children of immigrants—their meaning, importance, stability, or change—remain open questions, as does the nature of their interplay with other key aspects of incorporation processes, such as politics, family formation, and cultural practices.

Cynthia Feliciano is professor of sociology at the University of California, Irvine. **Rubén G. Rumbaut** is Distinguished Professor of Sociology at the University of California, Irvine.

© 2018 Russell Sage Foundation. Feliciano, Cynthia, and Rubén G. Rumbaut. 2018. "Varieties of Ethnic Self-Identities: Children of Immigrants in Middle Adulthood." *RSF: The Russell Sage Foundation Journal of the Social Sciences* 4(5): 26–46. DOI: 10.7758/RSF.2018.4.5.02. We thank Dr. Linda Borgen and Alma Nidia Garza for helpful research assistance and the Russell Sage Foundation for funding this research. Direct correspondence to: Cynthia Feliciano at felician@uci.edu, University of California, Irvine, Department of Sociology, 3151 Social Science Plaza, Irvine, CA 92697.

Open Access Policy: *RSF: The Russell Sage Foundation Journal of the Social Sciences* is an open access journal. This article is published under a Creative Commons Attribution-NonCommercial-NoDerivs 3.0 Unported License.

1. The *new second generation* refers to children of immigrants who have come to the United States since the 1960s. Although the term most often refers to U.S.-born children of immigrants, we use it here to also include those who migrated as children to the United States (see Portes and Rumbaut 2001).

2. We use the term *incorporation trajectories* to refer to adaptation paths and patterns over time.

Ethnic self-identities can be understood as "definitions of the situation of the self" (Rumbaut 2005). For children of immigrants, they can be conceptualized to emerge from the interplay of racial and ethnic labels and categories imposed by the external society and the ancestral attachments asserted by the newcomers. They may be hypothesized to vary across social situations, across developmental stages throughout the life course, and indeed across historical contexts. Previous studies have shed light into the ethnic self-identities of the growing second generation in adolescence and early adulthood, but we know little about how ethnic identities shift as individuals age beyond early adulthood, particularly in an extraordinarily diverse population whose immigrant parents have come largely from Asia and Latin America, differing significantly in their national, cultural, and class origins from the white Europeans whose incorporation in American life had dominated conventional narratives. No studies to date have examined ethnic identity change as children of immigrants transition from their teens and mid-twenties to their late thirties, and especially as they form unions (often ethnically mixed) and have children of their own to raise and socialize. Our longitudinal data from mid-adolescence into middle adulthood allowed us to apply a life course perspective to the development of ethnic identities among the 1.5 and second generations of children of immigrants, in which we considered how individuals' constructions of their identities are embedded within particular historical and sociogeographic contexts and linked to relationships with others (Elder, Johnson, and Crosnoe 2003).

Moreover, contextual influences on the definition and presentation of the self suggest that mixed-method work on ethnic identity should be an essential part of a comprehensive analysis. Survey instruments alone can explore neither the situational contexts in which ethnic self-identities may be differentially deployed nor the subjective meanings behind ethnic labels; yet how an ethnic identity is expressed in one's presentation of self can differ depending on the audience, and public expressions of identity may not correspond with private self-conceptions (Brunsma 2006). By combining quantitative and qualitative approaches to a longitudinal study encompassing a life span of more than two decades, we aim to enhance and contextualize our understanding of ethnic identity formations throughout the life course, and their connections to inter and intra-ethnic relationships, political orientations and behaviors, and cultural practices.

ETHNIC IDENTITIES AMONG CHILDREN OF IMMIGRANTS

Because ethnic identities necessarily invoke subjective feelings of group belonging and thus reveal boundaries between insiders and outsiders, the ethnic identifications of immigrants' children provide insight into the long-term incorporation trajectories of immigrant groups. According to Milton Gordon's influential framework, *identificational assimilation*, which he defines as the "development of a sense of peoplehood based exclusively on the host society," is one of the later stages of the assimilation process—indeed, arguably, its end point (1964, 71). Conventional accounts of ethnic identity shifts among descendants of European immigrants, conceived as part of a larger, linear process of assimilation, have pointed to the "thinning" of ethnic self-identities in the United States such that ethnic identity, for this population, has become an optional, leisure-time form of *symbolic* ethnicity (Alba 1990; Gans 1979; Waters 1990). However, such an outcome is possible only when accompanied by the absence of prejudice and discrimination in the core society (Gordon 1964; Waters 1990). In a context of perceived threats, persecution, discrimination, and exclusion, ethnic identity may not erode, but rather rise, in the form of reactive ethnicity (Rumbaut 2008). Reactive ethnicity is consistent with a psychological process of rejection-identification, when perceptions of prejudice lead to hostility toward the dominant group and identification with the minority group (Branscombe, Schmitt, and Harvey 1999). Indeed, Portes and Rumbaut found such a "thickening" of Mexican identity among adolescents in response to the passage of Proposition 187 in 1994, which, though never implemented, would have denied health care, public education, and social services to undocumented immigrants and their children in California, and required government employees to report suspected undocumented immigrants to the authorities (2001).[3]

However, assessing such possibilities among children of contemporary immigrants is complicated because no universally accepted definition of ethnic identity, nor shared understanding of its multiple dimensions, exists (Ashmore, Deaux, and McLaughlin-Volpe 2004; Phinney and Ong 2007). Self-labeling is one dimension of ethnic identity used widely in research on immigrants' children (Feliciano 2009; Fuligni, Witkow, and Garcia 2005). Based on responses to an open-ended question from the first wave of the Children of Immigrants Longitudinal Study, Rubén Rumbaut identified four types of self-labels among adolescents: national, hyphenated, plain American, and panethnic (1994). Although previous research on such outcomes reveals key insights, self-labeling captures just one dimension of a broad conceptualization of ethnic identity as "membership in a social group together with the value and emotional significance attached to that membership" (Taijfel 1981, 225). Moreover, studies find that ethnic minorities often use multiple labels in different situations, and that panethnic identities are often overlapping rather than distinct identities (Kasinitz et al. 2008; Dowling 2014).

ETHNIC IDENTITY CHANGE ACROSS THE LIFE COURSE

Adolescence is a crucial stage of life during which identities develop (Erikson 1968); and ethnic identity is assumed to stabilize by early adulthood (Phinney 1993). However, although previous studies show considerable change in ethnic identity among children of immigrants from early adolescence through early adulthood, researchers have not yet examined how ethnic identities shift from early to middle adulthood (Smith 2014; Feliciano 2009). From a life course perspective, lives are patterned by transitions (Elder, Johnson, and Crosnoe 2003). Thus, self-labels in middle adulthood, as well as the meaning and importance of ethnic identification, should be linked to those in earlier life stages, but may also shift as individuals transition further into adulthood and take on additional roles and identities as workers, spouses, and parents.

Moreover, a life course perspective emphasizes how development occurs within particular historical and social contexts (Elder 1998). Our focus is on immigrants' children born in the late 1970s, who were coming of age in San Diego during a time of relative inclusion. Unlike today's context, in which a high proportion of children of immigrants grow up in mixed legal status families, most parents in our sample arrived in the late 1970s and 1980s, including some who may have migrated without papers but were able to legalize through the Immigration Reform and Control Act of 1986. Thus, the overwhelming majority of our respondents who were not citizens by birth became naturalized U.S. citizens. Moreover, they grew up in a period when diversity was increasingly the accepted norm. From 1980 to 2015, California's Asian population grew from 5 percent to 14 percent, and the Latino population from 19 percent to 39 percent (Bohn et al. 2018). At the national level, the U.S. Census Bureau's decision in 2000 to allow identification as more than one race reflected an emerging consensus that individuals should be able to define themselves as they choose (Csizmadia et al. 2012).

Yet the political context was not uniformly inclusive. As mentioned, Mexican-origin immigrants' children often formed reactive ethnic identities in response to Proposition 187, passed during a core developmental period for the study respondents, from early to late adolescence (Portes and Rumbaut 2001). Moreover, a "Latino threat narrative" fueled by fears about Mexican immigrants and their descendants invading, taking over, refusing to assimilate, and posing a danger to the nation has long been evident in public discourse in the United States (Chavez 2008). Thus, we might expect children of Mexican immigrants' ethnic identities in middle adulthood to be more reactive than others, perhaps rejecting an American identity in favor of a panethnic or Mexican identity (Massey and Sánchez 2010). On the other hand,

---

3. Proposition 187 was halted by multiple lawsuits after passage and found unconstitutional by a federal court in 1997.

the respondents have diverse ethnic backgrounds, and the vast majority spent most of their lives in a multicultural California context, where anti-immigrant views do not dominate. Given the relatively accepting political and social climate for diversity, from a life course perspective, we may expect ample room for individual agency in ethnic identity development, leading to wide variations in ethnic identity formations even within ethnic groups.

ETHNIC IDENTITIES AND POLITICS, RELATIONSHIPS, AND CULTURAL PRACTICES

Ethnic identities are important because they signify boundaries between groups and thus potentially enduring divisions in society. However, as subjective attachments, ethnic identities may be only personally meaningful, unrelated to behaviors or beliefs. Few studies investigate how ethnic identities among children of immigrants are associated with attitudes or practices in other social realms, perhaps because existing studies focus on adolescents or young adults but the outcomes of most interest become most salient only in later stages of adulthood.

Political views and behaviors may be associated with ethnic identities. Although many suggest that the demographic shifts creating a more diverse electorate may lead to a more liberal and Democratic Party–affiliated population, Taeku Lee cautions against assuming that shared racial and ethnic identity labels correspond to group-based politics, arguing that the identity-to-politics link evident among African Americans may not apply to Asians or Latinos (2008). Others suggest that with identificational assimilation, differences in political views and behaviors by ethnic origins should decline (Alba, Beck, and Sahin 2017; Gordon 1964). Considering variation in ethnic identity attachments within ethnic groups may matter: immigrants' children who are less attached to their ethnic origins may differ in political affiliations, attitudes, and behaviors from those with strong ethnic attachments.

Like ethnic identity formations themselves, cross-ethnic and cross-racial friendships and romantic relationships offer insights into the strength of social boundaries (Kao and Joyner 2006; Qian and Lichter 2007). However, only limited research has examined how ethnic identity—conceived broadly as the strength of attachments and not only self-labeling—is associated with relationship formation. Jessica Vasquez's work is an exception; she finds that though Mexican Americans with "thinned ethnic attachments" often marry whites, bicultural identity often persists even within intermarriages (2011; Vasquez-Tokos 2017). Nevertheless, life course theory's emphasis on how individuals' lives are linked to significant others suggests that those with strong ethnic identities may be most likely to limit both close friendships and cohabiting or marital relationships to ethnic group members.

Few studies examine how ethnic identities relate to cultural practices among the second generation. Given that ethnic identity signals attachment to cultural heritages, we expect strongly ethnically identified respondents to incorporate cultural practices related to their parents' homeland into their lives, including passing on foreign languages to their children. However, Vasquez finds that Mexican Americans with strong emotional attachments to their ancestry often do not maintain cultural practices and language (2011). These questions have not yet been explored among second-generation adults from diverse ethnic backgrounds.

This study addresses three main questions. First, how do ethnic identities among immigrants' children change across the life course from adolescence to middle adulthood? Second, what types of ethnic identity formations are found in middle adulthood and how do these vary by gender, immigrant generation, and national origin? Third, are ethnic identities in middle adulthood associated with politics, relationships, and cultural practices? If so, how?

METHODS, SAMPLES, AND DATA COLLECTION

We rely on a mixed-methods analysis of survey and qualitative data drawn from a sample of original respondents from the Children of Immigrants Longitudinal Study (CILS), a longitudinal study of foreign-born and U.S.-born children with at least one immigrant parent and attending eighth or ninth grades in the San Diego City schools in the fall of 1991 (see Portes and Rumbaut 2001).[4]

The study used a school-based sampling frame to accurately represent the population of children of immigrants in San Diego younger than the age that they can legally drop out of school. Because the data are limited to the baseline sample drawn in San Diego, the findings cannot be generalized to the United States as a whole. However, San Diego is a large immigrant destination and a principal site of contemporary immigrant and refugee settlement.

Respondents were surveyed during four periods from early 1992 to early 2016: the first in spring 1992 (14.2 years old on average), the second in spring 1995 (17.2 years old), the third between 2001 and 2003 (mid-twenties), and the fourth between 2014 and 2016 (late thirties). The third phase included surveys from 1,480 respondents averaging 24.2 years old and in-depth, open-ended qualitative interviews conducted about a year after the survey with a representative subsample of 134 respondents. More than twelve years later (2014 to 2016), that subsample was tracked, and a full fourth wave of surveys and in-depth qualitative interviews conducted. We refer to each wave of data collection as T1, T2, T3, and T4, respectively. At T4, we completed 111 in-depth interviews (83 percent of the 134) with respondents in California and across the country (from Alaska to Atlanta and New York City), as well as Mexico, ranging in age from thirty-six to thirty-nine, with an average age of 37.2 years.[5] Table A1 provides a descriptive portrait of these respondents.

The interview format at T4 was flexible enough to delve deeply into the most important aspects of each person's experiences, while also allowing us to collect standard survey data to permit direct comparisons to their earlier responses. We analyzed the data using multiple methods. The data collected through closed-ended responses were combined with the existing CILS longitudinal data and analyzed using descriptive statistics. We analyzed the interview data with the assistance of Dedoose, a software program for analyzing qualitative and mixed-methods data, using the constant-comparison method.

Ethnic Identity Measures

Ethnic identity measures at T1, T2, T3, and T4 are based on the same open-ended question asked in each wave: "how do you identify? That is, what do you call yourself?" Examples include Asian, Hispanic, American, Mexican, Mexican American, Chicano, Latino, Filipino, Filipino American, Vietnamese, Vietnamese American, Lao, Lao American, Cambodian, and Cambodian American. In the surveys at T1, T2, and T3, respondents wrote in an open-ended response. In the T2 and T3 questionnaires, this question was followed by another, "how important is this identity to you?" with three options: "not important," "somewhat important," or "very important." In the in-depth interviews at T3 and T4, the same initial questions about ethnic self-identity and importance were asked but were followed by more in-depth discussion about identities, such as "do you always use this term to describe yourself?" and "What does being [ethnic identity label] mean to you?"

Following Rumbaut, we initially coded responses into five mutually exclusive ethnic identity labels: *American* includes those who responded only as American; *national* includes those who referred only to their or their parents' country of birth, such as Mexican; *hyphenated* includes those who combined the home country with an American identity, such as Filipino American; *panethnic* includes those who used a panethnic or racial label, such as Hispanic or Asian; and a last heterogeneous group included some who asserted mixed identities, such as Mexican Filipino or black Filipino, and others who did not respond in racial or ethnic

---

4. The original CILS study included a South Florida sample, who were not followed beyond early adulthood.

5. Systematic comparisons between the 111 interviewed in-depth and the full, original T1 survey respondents, along key variables (including age, gender, grade point average, family socioeconomic status, and so on) showed no sample attrition bias on any characteristic except, in one instance, national origin, which was by design because the T3 in-depth interviews intentionally included a larger sample of Chinese respondents to facilitate comparisons with other ethnic groups.

terms at all, such as human being (1994). Placing respondents in one category was not always straightforward. In open-ended interviews, respondents often mentioned more than one ethnic self-label (a finding we elaborate on later). In cases with multiple labels, we coded the most important or preferred label as the primary label. If this was unclear, we used the more specific label. For example, some stated that they were Hispanic and Mexican. Unless Hispanic was more important or preferred, their primary identity label was the national identity, Mexican. However, this coding scheme was used only for the first set of analyses to make comparisons across earlier waves of the study. We also conducted an inductive analysis of the qualitative data on ethnic identities, examining how and when multiple labels were used, and the subjective meaning of ethnicity. Through this process, we identified four distinct ethnic identity formation patterns, discussed in the following section.

Additional Variables
Respondents were asked several questions about politics (see table A1). First was whether they considered themselves politically conservative, moderate, or liberal. Most chose one of these options; several responded that they were socially liberal and fiscally conservative; and some refused to answer. Respondents were also asked whether they considered themselves Republican, Democratic, Independent, or Other; the four respondents who stated Other were recoded into a residual other–no answer category. U.S. citizens (93 percent by T4) were asked whether they voted in the 2012 election and for whom. All respondents were asked about political engagement beyond voting.

Respondents also provided their relationship histories and the ethnic background of their partners. For those currently or previously in a cohabiting or marital relationship, we coded whether the partner was a member of the same national-origin group, same panethnic group, white American, or another non-white ethnic group (for example, a Filipino married to a Chinese American would be coded as panethnic, and a Filipino married to a Mexican American would be coded as other non-white); we used the most recent partner for those with multiple partners. Respondents also provided the ethnic backgrounds of their close friends; we created a binary variable indicating whether they had close friends outside their panethnic group.

We examined cultural practices in two main ways. First, we coded thirteen categories from an open-ended question asking "what cultural practices of [your ethnic background] do you practice?" The most common responses were food (39 percent), language (20 percent), and holidays (19 percent). Only 18 percent replied "none." We created a categorical variable indicating whether respondents mentioned no practices, one, two, or three or more. We also asked a series of close-ended questions about language use with others and focus here on language with children (for those with children). We created a dichotomous measure indicating whether respondents speak about the same amount or more in a non-English language with their children. This outcome provides a window into language transmission to the next generation.

FINDINGS
Our first set of analyses focus on changes in ethnic identity labels; however, we find that outward expressions of identity fail to capture the complexities of ethnic identification. Further analyses of ethnic identity and salience revealed four types of ethnic identity formations, which vary by demographic characteristics and relate to politics, relationships with others, and culture.

Change in Primary Ethnic Identity Labels Across the Life Course
Like previous research at earlier life stages, we find that immigrants' children continue to most commonly use national (51 percent) and hyphenated (20 percent) ethnic labels as they age into middle adulthood. Panethnic (12 percent), mixed or other (13 percent), and especially plain American identity labels (3 percent) are used less often (see Portes and Rumbaut 2001; Tovar and Feliciano 2009). Figure 1 shows the percentage of respondents who changed their ethnic identity label across time (see also figure A1). About half changed ethnic identity labels in adolescence (T1 to T2) or the transi-

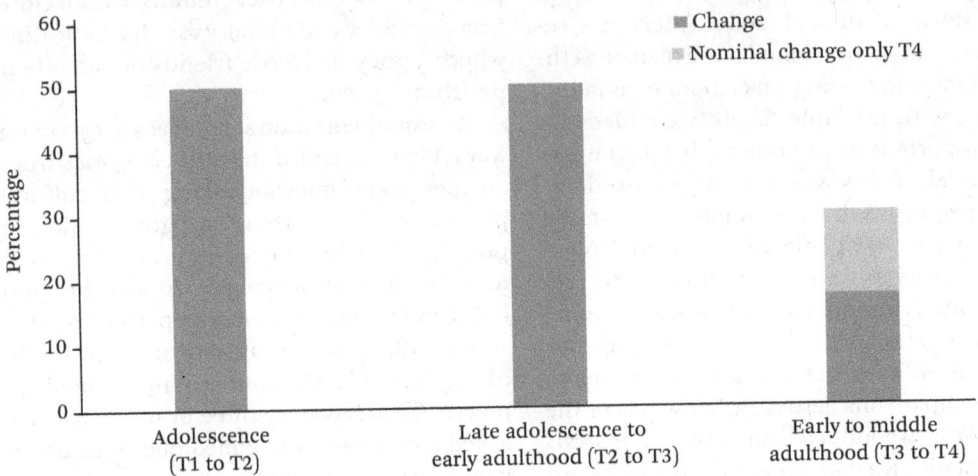

Figure 1. Percentage Who Change Ethnic Identity Label, by Life Course Stage

Source: Authors' analysis of data from the CILS-San Diego longitudinal in-depth sample, 1991–2016.

tion to adulthood (T2 to T3), but only 30 percent changed from early to middle adulthood, suggesting a crystallization of ethnic identity labels for most in adulthood. Across all four periods, the modal response was to use the same ethnic identity label. Twenty-six percent of respondents (n = 27) self-identified using the same ethnic identity label in response to an open-ended question from early adolescence to middle adulthood, revealing remarkable stability across more than twenty-two years. Of those who used the same ethnic identity label, 56 percent used a national term, 22 percent a hyphenated term, 19 percent a mixed term, and only one consistently a panethnic label. Another 33 percent used the same ethnic identity label at three of the four time points, again suggesting that stability is more common than fluidity. Only one respondent chose a different ethnic identity label each time.

Multiple Ethnic Identity Labels and Substantive Versus Nominal Change

Analyzing in-depth interview data at T3 and T4 allows us to examine whether different ethnic identity labels correspond to substantive differences in ethnic self-identification from early to middle adulthood. This analysis indicates that only 17 percent of the ethnic identity label change suggested by the quantitative data from T3 to T4 is meaningful, whereas nearly half of the change in ethnic labels is in name only (indicated by the shaded area of figure 1). Respondents often use ethnic identity labels interchangeably. For example, thirty-year-old Enrique, who migrated to San Diego as a four-year-old, explained: "I never changed my identity as far as I'm Hispanic, I'm Latino, I'm Mexican, I'm Mexican American."[6] Similarly, Anh, who migrated from Vietnam at age five, used some terms interchangeably. As a twenty-three-year-old woman, she identified as Vietnamese American, but at age thirty-six as Vietnamese. When asked whether she ever used different terms in different contexts, Anh responded, "Sometimes I'll just do Vietnamese and sometimes I'll do Vietnamese American."

Some respondents clearly articulated the contexts in which they used different terms. Enrique explained:

> "It just depends on who's asking me and how they're going about asking me . . . At my work . . . it's like, "Hey . . . what are you?" "I'm Mexican American." I wanna make sure they know I'm an American . . . If I was . . . just socializing, "Hey what are you?" "Oh, I'm

---

6. All names are pseudonyms.

Mexican." Because the conversation's not about your citizenship [or] your status."

Some Asian respondents similarly explained that they reserved hyphenated labels for white Americans and used national terms with Asians. For example, 1.5-generation Brian, who identified as Chinese American, said, "if it's ... an Asian person, I'll just say Chinese.... I'm more likely to say Chinese American if it's a ... a white ... person." He explained his reasoning by sharing a recent incident in which three older white people assumed that he did not speak English. For Brian and other Asians, a hyphenated American ethnic identity label served to combat a stereotype of Asian foreignness (Tuan 1999), whereas for Enrique and other Latino respondents, a hyphenated American identity combatted an undocumented immigrant stereotype.

The minority of respondents (16 percent) whose ethnic identity label in middle adulthood reflected a substantive change from early adulthood moved away from identities rooted in their or their parents' origin countries and toward Americanized identities, especially panethnic. For example, Kham, a thirty-six-year-old man who migrated at age twelve and previously identified strongly as Lao, identified solely as Asian. When asked, "what does it mean to say that you are Asian?" Kham explained, "the longer we live here ... we look at ourselves as being American now.... Everybody in our ... household became U.S. citizens ... we consider ourselves American."

Although Kham clearly distinguished between a panethnic identity (Asian) and his previous identity as Lao, it was more common for respondents to invoke panethnic labels in conjunction with national or hyphenated labels: only 12 percent used panethnic labels as their primary label, but another 34 percent mentioned panethnic labels. Several respondents noted that specific ethnic identity labels were rarely options on forms, or they did not think others were familiar with specific ethnic groups, so they would use a panethnic term, although their personal identity was more specific. For example, second-generation Vanna said, "I would just say Asian ... and ... in details I would say Cambodian." The use of panethnic terms on forms is consistent with our finding from T3 that 31 percent of respondents used a different ethnic identity label in the qualitative interview than they had on the written survey, and most who identified in panethnic terms on the survey used a national or hyphenated term in the interview.

Changes in Ethnic Identity Salience Across the Life Course

Ethnic self-labels are one aspect of identity, but we also considered whether ethnic identity changes in importance as immigrants' children age further into adulthood. Figure 2 shows that ethnic identity often becomes less important later in the life course. Although 64 percent of adolescents (T2) and 57 percent of young adults (T3) described their ethnic identity as very important, this proportion dropped to 41 percent by their late thirties (T4). These findings hold even among the fifteen respondents who consistently identified in national terms across all four waves: the number describing this identity as very important declined from eight in late adolescence, to six in early adulthood, to only three in middle adulthood (not shown).

Our qualitative findings suggest that the declining importance of ethnic identity reflects a shift in priorities as respondents age into new roles and identities. For example, thirty-seven-year-old Brian explained the declining importance of his Chinese American identity this way:

> when we were younger ... our ... sense of self or identity is ... tied with what the outside world sees you as.... And so, we all—the majority of my friends are Asian—had to figure out what that actually meant. It was a much more relevant and important topic back then. Now that we're all established professionals and ... we're married with kids and all this stuff... I'm never gonna say it's inconsequential or insignificant. But it's not one of the driving things. It doesn't define us anymore.

Brian's explanation is consistent with life course theory, which emphasizes how "changing lives alter developmental trajectories" (Elder 1998, 1), and how development is a lifelong

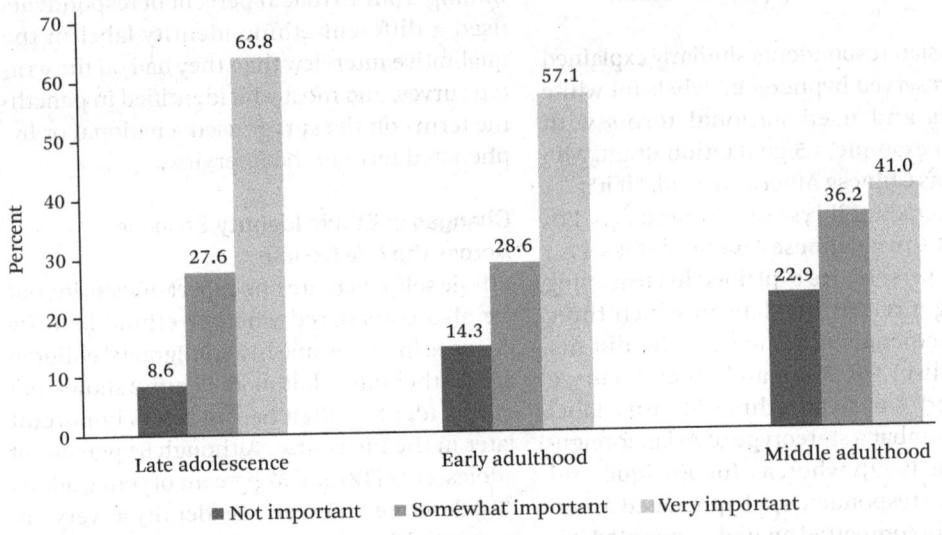

Figure 2. Importance of Ethnic Identity, Adolescence to Middle Adulthood

Source: Authors' analysis of data from the CILS-San Diego longitudinal in-depth sample, 1991–2016.
Note: One-way analyses of variance tests based on importance of identity as a 3-point scale show that differences across time are significant at the $p < .001$ level.

process shaped by relationships with significant others (Elder, Johnson, and Crosnoe 2003).

Ethnic Identity Formations in Middle Adulthood

Despite an overall pattern of decline in importance and the common use of multiple ethnic labels, inductive analyses of the qualitative interview data revealed substantial variation in the subjective meaning and importance of ethnic identification among adult children of immigrants in their late thirties. This analysis focused less on the label and more on the attachment to an ethnic identity, revealing four ethnic identity formations, as shown in table 1: a strong ethnic identity, a moderately important ethnic identity, an American-oriented ethnic identity, and a de-ethnicized identity (for variations by ethnic label, see table A2). Most respondents identified with an ethnic or pan-ethnic group and held this identity to be at least somewhat important.

Strong Ethnic Identity

The largest group of respondents (36 percent) expressed a strong ethnic identity, indicating that their ethnic background and associated culture was central to their personal identity. Vinh, a 1.5-generation woman, explained it this way: "I think being Vietnamese American is such a specific . . . experience that I think it is a defining part of—of my identity." Similarly, second-generation Elaine responded that her identity as Filipino is "very important . . . it's just the whole legacy thing . . . that's what I am. And that's all I've known to be." These respondents often described their ethnicity as a source of pride and a core part of themselves.

A few respondents, particularly Mexican-origin men, connected their pride in their ethnic identity to an awareness of negative stereotypes about their ethnic group and a hostile political climate—vivid examples of reactive ethnicity (Rumbaut 2005, 2008; Portes and Rumbaut 2014). Leo, who migrated as an infant and by age thirty-six had completed a master's degree, articulated how his strong ethnic identity was in part a response to hostile outside forces:

> For me it's very important to label me Mexican American because I wanna show people . . . two sides. I wanna show my parents

that . . . I'm proud of being Mexican. And the second aspect is, I wanna show . . . conservative people . . . we don't just come to this country and take advantage of it . . . I'm an immigrant . . . and I succeeded.

Expressions of strong ethnic identities do not correspond to rejections of American identities. Most with strong ethnic identities also clearly identify as American. For example, thirty-six-year-old Isabella emphasized her American identity along with her Mexican identity: "[My identity as Mexican American] is very important because my family is from Mexico and . . . they came here to be better, you know, for that American Dream . . . I'm proud, you know, to say that I'm Mexican, but I was born here, *so I am American*" (emphasis added).

Identifying as American, along with maintaining strong ethnic attachments, was not just common among the second generation who preferred hyphenated or American-based labels such as Mexican American or Chicano. For instance, 1.5-generation Anh recognized her dual identities: "[Identifying as Vietnamese] is very important because it's a huge part of me . . . [being Vietnamese American] is really important too . . . I do all the stereotypical American things."

Moderate Ethnic Identity
Other adult children of immigrants described their ethnic identity as somewhat important, but not central to who they are or their daily life. For example, second-generation Tara, whose parents migrated from Mexico and whose grandmother had migrated to Mexico from China, said, "I think it's important [to identify as Chinese Spanish] . . . I like to identify with my cultures . . . I'm not, like, adamant about it. But, you know, I think it's . . . important." Similarly, second-generation Jimmy said, "I don't think [being Indian] necessarily defines who I am . . . but it's something I want to always have some connection to."

Respondents with strong or moderate ethnic identities accounted for 69 percent of the sample, indicating that a substantial majority of immigrants' children maintain an attachment to an ethnic identity rooted in their homeland by middle adulthood. Nevertheless, 31 percent were not attached to their parents' homelands or their ethnic origins.

American-Oriented Identity
American-oriented respondents may respond to questions from others about their background with an ethnic identity label, but personally feel they are *really* American. This category, making up 14 percent of the total (sixteen cases), includes three respondents who identified solely as American as well as some who responded with varied ethnic labels. Mike, for example, whose father is white American and mother is from China, said that he is "Chinese and Irish" but that it is not important because "I don't really know either of those sides, so I'm American." He explained, "It's more that I identify myself as a courtesy to others." Mike suggests it is only because others want to classify him that he mentions ethnic origins beyond American.

Similarly, Trung, who came to the United States from Vietnam as an infant, explained that he identifies as Asian because "when you look at me, I'm not . . . the—physical embodiment of . . . an American . . . But I still consider myself an American since I lived here all my life and . . . this is where I call home." Trung and others like him suggested they would prefer to identify only as American but cannot because they do not appear white.

Others, like Thanh, who also came from Vietnam as a young child, asserted that a common American identity outweighs ethnic origins. Despite stating a Vietnamese identity in response to the question, Thanh also asserted that "[being Vietnamese is] not important . . . we're all Americans, I think. . . . Everyone's coming from different countries, so, the fact that I happen to be from Vietnam, not . . . a big deal, I don't think." Thanh alluded to how context—in this case, one in which diverse ethnic origins are common—shapes her identity. Similarly, Kim Cuc, who identified as plain "American," said that "living in San Diego you see a multicultural group of people." However, Kim Cuc's awareness of contextual variation is clear when she said, "in San Diego I'm part of [the American mainstream.] Outside of it, I'm not.

Table 1. Gender, Generation, and National Origin, by Ethnic Identity Formations in Middle Adulthood

	Strong	Moderate	American-Oriented	De-ethnicized	% Total	N
Overall	36	33	14	16	100	111
Gender[ns]						
Female	37	38	13	12	100	60
Male	35	27	16	22	100	51
Generation**						
1.5	31	26	16	26	100	61
2nd	50	39	6	6	100	36
2.5	21	50	29	0	100	14
Origin country*						
Mexican	50	29	4	18	100	28
Filipino	50	30	10	10	100	20
Vietnamese	43	0	43	14	100	14
Cambodian-Lao-Hmong	19	56	6	19	100	16
Chinese	10	50	0	40	100	10
Indian	0	50	0	50	100	4
South American	67	33	0	0	100	3
Mixed	25	38	38	0	100	16

Source: Authors' analysis of data from the CILS-San Diego longitudinal in-depth sample, 1991–2016.
Note: Pearson's chi-squared significance tests.
[ns] $p > .10$; *$p < .10$; **$p < .05$

I've been to states like Texas and Florida where they . . . look at me as an alien and they make it known."

De-ethnicized Identity
Like American-oriented respondents, those with de-ethnicized identities (16 percent, eighteen cases) are not attached to identities rooted in their origin country. Unlike those with American-oriented identities, however, these respondents expressed indifference toward ethnic and national identities in general. Although these respondents would respond (often with a specific national term) when asked, they said that ethnic background did not matter to them. For example, thirty-nine-year-old 1.5-generation Vanessa responded to a question about the importance of her identity this way: "[Being Filipino] is not really important. Like, I don't care. Like, I'm not like 'I'm proud! I have the—the sticker.' I'm like, no . . . I'm a person . . . it's not important to me." Individuals in this category suggested that their common humanity was more important than their ethnicity. For example, 1.5-generation Kye will tell people he is Chinese, but explained that

> your question . . . it's kind of hard for me to answer because . . . I kinda feel like the whole classification is . . . unnecessary. If we classify ourselves as humans, it makes everything so much easier . . . we don't need to pick apart our . . . identities . . . we're all one, one kind.

Similarly, Santi, a thirty-six-year-old second-generation male whose parents were from Mexico, identified as Hispanic but said, "I think it's more important to say I'm human . . . I think we're all mixed a little bit with something nowadays." Santi's comment suggests that growing up in a context in which mixed ancestries are commonplace has shaped his identity development.

Differences in Ethnic Identity Formations
Table 1 shows that ethnic identity formations do not vary significantly by gender, but, as expected, do vary by immigrant generation and

national origin. However, contrary to linear assimilation theories predicting that individuals who have lived in the United States longer would be most oriented toward American identities and away from ethnic identities, we find that in middle adulthood, U.S.-born respondents with two immigrant parents were the most strongly attached to their ethnic identities: 49 percent had a strong ethnic identity relative to the 32 percent of those who migrated as children.[7] These findings differ from earlier CILS research on adolescents and young adults showing ethnic identity was more salient for the foreign-born (Tovar and Feliciano 2009; Rumbaut 2005). Among the 2.5 generation (with one U.S.-born parent), the pattern is more consistent with a linear assimilation trajectory in that fewer expressed strong ethnic identities (21 percent), and more expressed American-oriented identities (29 percent).

With the caveat that the sample sizes for many groups are small, we note significant national-origin differences in ethnic identity formations. First, respondents with origins in Mexico (50 percent), the Philippines (50 percent), and Vietnam (43 percent) were most likely to express strong ethnic identities in middle adulthood, and the Chinese (10 percent) and East Indians (none) the least likely to do so. The Vietnamese sample was split: 43 percent also expressed American-oriented identities, versus only 4 percent of Mexicans, 10 percent of Filipinos, and 6 percent of Cambodians, Lao, and Hmong. Also, East Indians (50 percent) and Chinese (40 percent) were most likely to express de-ethnicized identities. Notably, none of the sixteen respondents whose parents came from different countries expressed de-ethnicized identities, and the same percentage (38 percent) expressed American-oriented or moderate ethnic identities.[8] Despite these national-origin differences, nearly all types of ethnic identity formations are found within each national-origin group, a finding that reinforces life course theory's principle of individual agency within structural contexts (Elder 1998).

Ethnic Identities and Politics, Relationships, and Culture

Are ethnic identity formations associated with other outcomes of interest, such as politics and family and cultural practices in middle adulthood? Table 2 considers whether these outcomes are significant correlates of ethnic identity formations. In terms of politics, the findings do not line up neatly with existing assumptions. First, we do not find that those with the strongest ethnic identities are the most liberal politically. The biggest differences are in the socially liberal, but fiscally conservative category: 31 percent of respondents with American-oriented identities held this political orientation versus only 6 percent of those with de-ethnicized identities and 8 percent of those with strong ethnic identities. Contrary to conventional assumptions of identity politics, more strongly ethnically identified respondents said that they were somewhat conservative (30 percent) than those with de-ethnicized (11 percent) or American-oriented (6 percent) identities did. Finally, those with de-ethnicized identities were much more likely to not express a political orientation at all (28 percent, versus only 0 to 3 percent among those with other identities), suggesting that individuals indifferent toward ethnicity are similarly apathetic about other aspects of identity and social life.

Ethnic identity formations and political party affiliations are also related. Somewhat as expected, individuals who express at least moderately strong ethnic identities are more likely than are those with de-ethnicized or American-oriented identities to identify as Democrats (58 and 70 percent versus 39 and 25 percent, respectively). American-oriented respondents are

---

7. Analyses restricted to only respondents with parents born in the same country reveal the same pattern of differences between the 1.5 and the second generation, as do analyses focused only on the two largest groups, Mexicans and Filipinos.

8. Those in the mixed category included seven with a white American parent and an Asian immigrant parent, four with a black American father and a Filipino immigrant mother, two with Filipino immigrant fathers and Mexican immigrant mothers, two with white American fathers and Mexican-born mothers, and one with a Mexican American father and Filippino immigrant mother.

Table 2. Ethnic Identity Formations in Middle Adulthood, by Political, Family, and Cultural Outcomes

	Strong	Moderate	American-Oriented	De-ethnicized
Political orientation, T4**				
Liberal	48	57	50	33
Moderate	10	8	13	17
Socially liberal, fiscally conservative	8	5	31	6
Conservative	33	24	6	17
Don't know/refused/don't think in those terms	3	5	0	28
	100%	100%	100%	100%
n	40	37	16	18
Political party, T4**				
Democrat	58	70	25	39
Independent	20	5	44	28
Republican	18	8	19	22
Other/none/no answer	5	16	13	11
	100%	100%	100%	100%
n	40	37	16	18
Voted in 2012 election? (U.S. citizens only), T4ns	72	69	73	69
n	39	33	15	16
Who voted for in 2012? (among those who voted), T4*				
Barack Obama	82	96	64	91
Mitt Romney or someone else	18	4	36	9
	100%	100%	100%	100%
n	28	23	11	11
Engaged politically beyond voting?, T4ns	28	24	25	6
n	40	37	16	18
Union formation, T4ns				
Single/never married or cohabited	15	22	25	33
Same ethnic group	43	35	31	17
Same panethnic group	10	19	25	17
White American	20	14	6	17
Other nonwhite group	13	11	13	17
	100%	100%	100%	100%
n	40	37	16	18
Has close friends outside of panethnic group**	64	65	88	44
n	39	37	16	18
Cultural practices, T4**				
None	8	11	53	29
1 mentioned	15	24	20	29
2 mentioned	38	38	13	29
3+ mentioned	40	27	13	12
	100%	100%	100%	100%
n	40	37	15	17

Table 2. (continued)

	Strong	Moderate	American-Oriented	De-ethnicized
Speaks non-English language with children?, T4**				
At least half non-English	54	32	11	18
n	28	31	9	11
Speaks non-English language with children?, bilinguals only, T4**				
At least half non-English	72	48	14	20
n	18	21	7	10

Source: Authors' analysis of data from the CILS-San Diego longitudinal in-depth sample, 1991–2016.
Notes: Pearson's chi-squared significance tests. Responses in percentages.
$^{ns}p > .10$; $*p < .10$; $**p < .05$

especially likely to identify as independents (44 percent, versus 5 to 28 percent of others).

In terms of political behaviors, we do not find significant differences in whether one voted in the 2012 presidential election. However, among those who voted in 2012, American-oriented respondents were least likely to vote for Barack Obama (64 percent versus 82 percent or higher among those with other ethnic identity formations). Although not statistically significant, that those lacking ethnic attachments were less likely to participate in politics beyond voting (6 percent versus 24 to 28 percent of others) is consistent with the earlier interpretation that a lack of attachments to ethnic identities extends to indifference in other social realms.

Beyond politics, ethnic identity may influence family and friendship formations and cultural practices. In particular, we might expect those who are strongly ethnically identified to marry and form friendships primarily within their ethnic group, practice cultural traditions, and pass on cultural practices, such as languages, to their children. However, differences by ethnic identity formations in interethnic unions are not substantial or statistically significant, nor always in the direction of theoretical expectations. For example, although a higher percentage of those with strong ethnic identities had partners who share their ethnic background than those with American-oriented identities (43 percent versus 31 percent), 20 percent of those with strong ethnic identities married or cohabited with white Americans, whereas only 6 percent of American-oriented respondents did. In terms of interethnic friendships, the findings are more consistent with existing theories. Respondents with strong or moderate ethnic identities were less likely than those with American-oriented identities to have close friends outside their panethnic group, although those with de-ethnicized identities were least likely to have close interracial friendships.[9]

The association between ethnic identities and cultural practices is consistent with existing theories: those who were not attached even moderately to their ethnic groups (especially American-oriented respondents) were less likely to mention any cultural practices related to their ethnic backgrounds. Those with strong ethnic identities were most likely to mention three or more cultural practices; moderately ethnic identified respondents fell in the middle.

Finally, for respondents who were parents, we considered whether ethnic identity formations related to speaking foreign languages with their children. Here we see a clear pattern: those who expressed strong (54 percent) and

9. Further analyses show that those with American-oriented identities were both more likely to have white American friends and more likely to have nonwhite friends of another panethnic group than those with strong or moderate ethnic identities, whereas de-ethnicized respondents more often had no close friends.

moderate (32 percent) ethnic identities were more likely than those with de-ethnicized (18 percent) or American-oriented (11 percent) identities to speak to their children at least half of the time in a language other than English. When we limited the sample to those who considered themselves bilingual, these differences are even more pronounced: 72 percent of bilinguals with strong ethnic identities spoke a non-English language to their children versus only 14 percent of American-oriented bilinguals. A strong ethnic identity relates to maintaining at least some cultural practices, including passing on a foreign language to children.

DISCUSSION AND CONCLUSIONS

Previous research has focused on self-identity expressions in the often volatile developmental stages of adolescence or early adulthood. This study is among the first to examine ethnic identity among immigrants' children as they age into the relatively stable life course stage of middle adulthood. Through our mixed-methods approach, we show the importance of incorporating in-depth qualitative interview data to understand the subjective meanings behind ethnic identity labels. Our data, drawn from a more representative sample than studies limited to snowball or convenience samples, suggests a wide range of ethnic self-identity formations among immigrants' children in middle adulthood. It is most common to have a strong ethnic identity; these adult children of immigrants indicated that identifying with their heritage or culture was a source of pride and a defining part of themselves. On the other hand, a significant portion of adult children of immigrants in our sample did not feel even moderately connected to an ethnic group, revealing de-ethnicized or American-oriented identities, which, in some cases, they lamented they could not fully claim because others wanted to classify them based on their nonwhite phenotype. Thus, although many adult children of immigrants fully embrace their ethnic identities, others feel constrained by a U.S. racial structure, which limits how much choice they have to assert a plain American identity or to not identify in ethnic or racial terms at all (Waters 1990; Song 2003; Waters 2001). Such diversity, which is evident even among those who respond with the same outward ethnic identity label (such as Filipino or Mexican), supports the life course perspective; previous research suggests that when structural constraints are loosened, in this case a multicultural historical context in which self-expression is encouraged, individuals can exert agency in choosing how to ethnically self-identify, but that structural constraints within historical contexts also shape development (Csizimadia et al. 2012; Elder et al. 2003).

We distinguish between ethnic identity labels (outward expressions of self-definitions) and ethnic identity formations (a subjective sense of ethnic belonging and its importance). We find that ethnic identity labels are used more consistently in adulthood than in adolescence, and overall, are much more stable than fluid. Moreover, measuring fluidity in ethnic identities based on survey responses (even to open-ended questions), misses the degree to which ethnic labels are used interchangeably. Consistent with previous research, our qualitative data show that immigrants' children often express different labels to different audiences in strategic ways, for example, to emphasize Americanness to a white native-born American, or to clarify one's national origin to an Asian American (Dowling 2014; Kasinitz et al. 2008). Like prior studies, we also find that adult children of immigrants tend to view panethnic terms, such as Hispanic or Asian, as broader groups, corresponding to official racial categories, which they layer over more specific ethnic identities (Itzigsohn and Dore-Cabral 2000; Kibria 2002; Lien, Conway, and Wong 2003; Okamoto 2014; Padilla 1985; Dowling 2014). Overall, our findings suggest that though the presentation of self-identifications to others may be contextually contingent, internal ethnic identities remain fairly consistent more often than not. However, whereas stability in ethnic self-labels was the more common pattern from early to middle adulthood, the importance of ethnic identity tended to diminish over this part of the life course as new social identities emerged.

Existing assimilation theories suggest two modes of ethnic self-identity formation. One view posits that the forging of a reactive ethnicity in the face of perceived threats, discrimination, and exclusion may account for the rise rather than the erosion of ethnicity over time (Rumbaut 2005, 2008; Portes and Rumbaut 2001, see also Massey and Sánchez 2010). This contrasts with the conventional account maintaining that descendants of European immigrants experienced a linear (if at times bumpy) process of assimilation, in which their ethnic self-identities thinned over time in the United States, such that ethnic identity became an optional, passive, leisure-time form of symbolic ethnicity (Alba 1990; Gans 1979; Waters 1990; see also Child [1943] 1970; Nahirny and Fishman 1965). Yet, our findings suggest that most adult children of Asian and Latin American immigrants in their late thirties developed ethnic identities in varied ways that fall somewhere in between these two poles. For instance, only a handful of respondents, all Mexican-origin men, conveyed a sense that their ethnic self-identities were primarily reactive, shaped by continuing awareness of discrimination, negative stereotyping, and a hostile political context. A much larger proportion of adult children of immigrants identified strongly with their parents' national origins or a combination of national origins and American identities because they maintained strong, positive, attachments to family and cultural practices that they associated with their ethnic origins. We must keep in mind, however, that respondents maintained strong ethnic attachments within a historical and social context they perceived as welcoming diversity and self-expression. Reactive ethnic identity formations may be more common in different historical and social contexts and among different ethnic groups facing more hostile political contexts—such as Sikh Americans facing post 9/11 backlash or the children of undocumented immigrants in today's political climate (on Sikh Americans, see Kurien 2018).

Although we find that ethnic identity formations vary significantly by national origin (for example, more Mexican-origin than Chinese-origin respondents identify strongly with their ethnicity), within each ethnic group we also find individuals attached to their ethnic identities and others not, such that the variation within each national-origin group is greater than the variation between them. Across all national-origin groups, we find a common pattern of difference by immigrant generation: those born in the United States with two immigrant parents being more likely than either the 1.5 or 2.5 generation to maintain strong ethnic identities into middle adulthood, and least likely to have American-oriented identities. Further, 1.5-generation adults in their late thirties were most likely to have de-ethnicized identities. The reasons behind these patterns are difficult to discern, but it may be that those who migrated as children are more aware of being disconnected from their origin country, and thus, by middle adulthood, are less likely to maintain those ethnic attachments. In contrast, the second generation may cling strongly to ethnic attachments to overcompensate for feeling they lack ethnic authenticity having been born in the United States. It may also be that immigrants who have crossed national borders themselves, even as children, may be more likely to downplay or "see through" the borders and boundaries implied by ethnic labels distinguishing *us* versus *them*. Exploring the sources of such variation further is a question for future research.

By examining ethnic identity among adult children of immigrants in their late thirties, who have often completed schooling, married, and formed families, we can consider the consequences of ethnic identity formation in ways previous studies have not. Of particular importance in today's context is how ethnic identity formations relate to political orientations and behaviors. We find that political views vary by ethnic identity formations, but in complex ways. For instance, those with strong ethnic identities were more conservative than those with American-oriented identities, which may relate to conservative religious views tied to ethnic backgrounds. However, this does not currently translate into affiliations with the Republican Party. In addition, respondents with American-oriented identities were more likely to express socially liberal, fiscally conservative political views than those with other ethnic identity formations, and more likely to identify as political independents. Ethnic identities do not appear to coincide with political engagement, including voting, except that adult children of immigrants with American-oriented identities were more likely to vote for someone else over Barack Obama in 2012 than those with any other ethnic identity formation. These findings challenge assumptions that the growing population of Latinos and Asians who are descendants of immigrants will constitute a monolithic voting block (Immigration Policy Center 2010), and instead reveal that political views, affiliations, and behaviors vary across the range of ethnic identity formations within these populations.

Like recent research on Mexican Americans, our findings do not support linear assimilation theories positing that those with stronger ethnic identities are more likely to marry within their ethnic group, or, conversely, that intermarrying leads to weaker attachments to ethnic identities (on Mexican Americans, see Vasquez-Tokos 2017). However, we do find that adult immigrants' children with stronger ethnic identities are more likely to have close coethnic friends, maintain cultural practices associated with their ethnic background, and speak with their children in a language other than English. This is not to say that retaining strong definitions of self as ethnic relate to patterns of behavior that are markedly distinct from those of nonethnic Americans. Indeed, most respondents also said that their everyday lifestyles and behaviors made them part of mainstream America. Nevertheless, our strongly ethnically identified respondents conveyed that their ethnicity and cultural practices made them unique, and as parents, some are at least attempting to transmit an important cultural element, language, to the next generation. Whether those efforts will be successful remains to be seen. Moreover, even though most bilingual adult children of immigrants with strong ethnic identities spoke a language other than English with their children, they constituted less than one-quarter of all parents in our sample.

Overall, this study suggests that ethnic identity formations among the second generation in middle adulthood are complex and varied. Although for some, attachments to an ethnic identity remain strong into their late thirties, for many, ethnic identity attachments begin to wane through the life course, as their social identities as parents, workers, or spouses become more central. Moreover, ethnic identities relate to political and social views and behaviors in complex, and often modest, ways. Future research should further explore the consequences of varied ethnic identities for the resilience or decline of ethnic boundaries into the next generation, as well as how ethnic identity formations vary in different historical and social contexts.

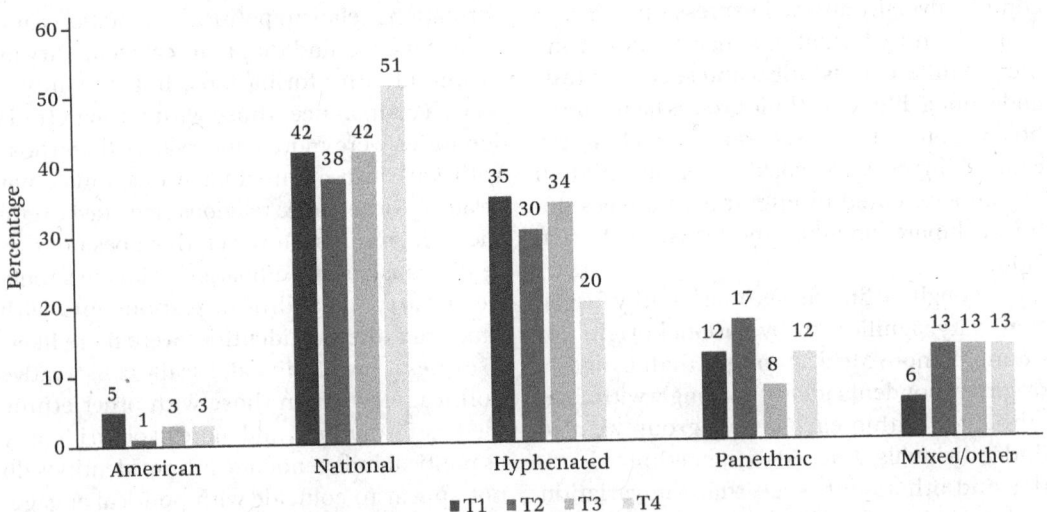

Figure A1. Ethnic Identity Labels, T1 to T4 (Percentages)

Source: Authors' analysis of data from the CILS-San Diego longitudinal in-depth sample, 1991–2016.

Table A1. The CILS T4 Subsample: A Portrait

Characteristic	N	%
Total	111	100.0
Gender		
Female	60	54.1
Male	51	45.9
Ethnicity		
Mexican	32	28.8
Filipino	27	24.3
Vietnamese	14	12.6
Cambodian-Lao-Hmong	16	14.4
Chinese	13	11.7
Asian American, other	6	5.4
Latin American, other	3	2.7
Age at T4 interview		
Thirty-six	31	27.9
Thirty-seven	38	34.2
Thirty-eight or thirty-nine	42	37.9
Generation		
1.5 (foreign born, came to the United States under age thirteen)	60	54.1
2.0 (U.S. born, both parents foreign born)	37	33.3
2.5 (U.S. born, one parent foreign born, one parent U.S. born)	14	12.6
Citizenship status		
U.S. citizen by birth	51	45.9
U.S. citizen by naturalization	52	46.9
Not a U.S. citizen	8	7.2
Marital status		
Married	62	55.9
Cohabiting	10	9.0
Single	24	21.6
Divorced, separated, other	15	13.5
How many children do you have?		
None	40	36.0
One	20	18.0
Two	28	25.2
Three	11	9.9
Four to five	12	10.8
Highest degree attained		
High school or vocational	38	34.2
Associate's (two-year degree) or three to four years (no degree)	13	11.7
Bachelor's (BA, BS)	37	33.3
Master's (MA, MS, MBA)	17	15.3
MD, JD, PhD	6	5.4

(continued)

Table A1. (continued)

Characteristic	N	%
Labor force status		
Employed full time	90	81.1
Employed part time	11	9.9
Unemployed and looking for work	5	4.5
Not in labor force (homemaker; disabled, unable to work)	5	4.5
Political orientation		
Liberal	54	48.65
Moderate	12	10.8
Strongly socially liberal, fiscally conservative	11	9.9
Conservative	26	23.4
Don't know, don't think in those terms	8	7.2
Political party affiliation		
Democrat	48	43.2
Independent	22	19.8
Republican	17	15.3
None, or no response	12	10.8
If U.S. citizen, registered to vote?		
Yes	86	83.5
No	17	16.5
Engaged politically beyond just voting?		
Yes	25	22.7
No	85	77.3
Are you bilingual?		
Yes	78	70.3
No (English only)	33	29.7

Source: Authors' analysis of data from the CILS-San Diego longitudinal in-depth sample, 1991–2016.

Table A2. Ethnic Identity Formations by Ethnic Identity Labels, Time 4 (Frequencies)

	Strong	American-Oriented	Moderate	De-ethnicized	N
American, unhyphenated	0	3	0	0	3
National, unhyphenated	22	1	24	10	57
Hyphenated American	14	3	4	0	21
Panethnic	1	4	2	7	14
Mixed or other	3	5	7	1	16
n	40	16	37	18	111

Source: Authors' analysis of data from the CILS-San Diego longitudinal in-depth sample, 1991–2016.

REFERENCES

Alba, Richard. 1990. *Ethnic Identity: The Transformation of White America.* New Haven, Conn.: Yale University Press.

Alba, Richard, Brenden Beck, and Duygu Basaran Sahin. 2017. "The U.S. Mainstream Expands–Again." *Journal of Ethnic and Migration Studies* 44(1): 99–117.

Ashmore, Richard D., Kay Deaux, and Tracy McLaughlin-Volpe. 2004. "An Organizing Framework for Collective Identity: Articulation and Significance of Multidimensionality." *Psychological Bulletin* 130(1): 80–114.

Bohn, Sarah, Dean Bonner, Caitrin Chappelle, Marisol Cuellar Mejia, Caroline Danielson, Alvar Escriva-Bou, Niu Gao, et al. 2018. "California's Future." San Francisco: Public Policy Institute of California. Accessed January 18, 2018. http://www.ppic.org/publication/californias-future/.

Branscombe, Nyla R., Michael T. Schmitt, and Richard D. Harvey. 1999. "Perceiving Pervasive Discrimination among African Americans: Implications for Group Identification and Well-Being." *Journal of Personality and Social Psychology* 77(1): 135–49.

Brunsma, David L. 2006. "Public Categories, Private Identities: Exploring Regional Differences in the Biracial Experience." *Social Science Research* 35(3): 555–76.

Chavez, Leo R. 2008. *The Latino Threat: Constructing Immigrants, Citizens, and the Nation.* Stanford, Calif.: Stanford University Press.

Child, Irvin L. (1943) 1970. *Italian or American? The Second Generation in Conflict.* New York: Russell & Russell.

Csizmadia, Annamaria, David L. Brunsma, and Teresa M. Cooney. 2012. "Racial Identification and Developmental Outcomes Among Black-White Multiracial Youth: A Review from a Life Course Perspective." *Advances in Life Course Research* 17(1): 34–44.

Dowling, Julie A. 2014. *Mexican Americans and the Question of Race.* Austin: University of Texas Press.

Elder, Glen H. 1998. "The Life Course as Developmental Theory." *Child Development* 69(1): 1–12.

Elder, Glen H., Monica K. Johnson, and Robert Crosnoe. 2003. "The Emergence and Development of Life Course Theory." In *Handbook of the Life Course*, edited by Jeylan T. Mortimer and Michael J. Shanahan. New York: Kluwer.

Erikson, Erik H. 1968. *Identity, Youth, and Crisis.* New York: W. W. Norton.

Feliciano, Cynthia. 2009. "Education and Ethnic Identity Formation Among Children of Latin American and Caribbean Immigrants." *Sociological Perspectives* 52(2): 135–58.

Fuligni, Andrew J., Melissa Witkow, and Carla Garcia. 2005. "Ethnic Identity and the Academic Adjustment of Adolescents from Mexican, Chinese, and European Backgrounds." *Developmental Psychology* 41(5): 799–811.

Gans, Herbert J. 1979. "Symbolic Ethnicity: The Future of Ethnic Groups and Cultures in America." *Ethnic and Racial Studies* 2(1): 1–20.

Gordon, Milton M. 1964. *Assimilation In American Life: The Role of Race, Religion, and National Origins.* New York: Oxford University Press.

Immigration Policy Center. 2010. *The New American Electorate: The Growing Political Power of Immigrants and their Children.* Washington, D.C.: American Immigration Council.

Itzigsohn, Jose, and Carlos Dore-Cabral. 2000. "Competing Identities? Race, Ethnicity and Panethnicity among Dominicans in the United States." *Sociological Forum* 15(2): 225–47.

Kao, Grace, and Kara Joyner. 2006. "Do Hispanic and Asian Adolescents Practice Panethnicity in Friendship Choices?" *Social Science Quarterly* 87(5): 972–92.

Kasinitz, Philip, John H. Mollenkopf, Mary C. Waters, and Jennifer Holdaway. 2008. *Inheriting the City: The Children of Immigrants Come of Age.* New York / Cambridge, Mass.: Russell Sage Foundation / Harvard University Press.

Kibria, Nazli. 2002. *Becoming Asian American: Second-Generation Chinese and Korean American Identities.* Baltimore, Md.: John Hopkins University Press.

Kurien, Prema. 2018. "Shifting U.S. Racial and Ethnic Identities and Sikh American Activism." *RSF: The Russell Sage Foundation Journal of the Social Sciences* 4(5): 81–98. DOI: 10.7758/RSF.2018.4.5.04.

Lee, Taeku. 2008. "Race, Immigration, and the Identity-to-Politics Link." *Annual Review of Political Science* 11(1): 457–78.

Lien, Pei-te, M. Margaret Conway, and Janelle Wong. 2003. "The Contours and Sources of Ethnic Identity Choices Among Asian Americans." *Social Science Quarterly* 84(2): 461–81. DOI: 10.1111/1540-6237.8402015.

Massey, Douglas S., and Magaly Sánchez. 2010. *Brokered Boundaries: Creating Immigrant Identity in Anti-Immigrant Times*. New York: Russell Sage Foundation.

Nahirny, Vladimir C, and Joshua A Fishman. 1965. "American Immigrant Groups: Ethnic Identification and the Problem of Generations." *Sociological Review* 13(3): 311–26.

Okamoto, Dina G. 2014. *Redefining Race: Asian American Panethnicity and Shifting Ethnic Boundaries*. New York: Russell Sage Foundation.

Padilla, Felix M. 1985. *Latino Ethnic Consciousness: The Case of Mexican Americans and Puerto Ricans in Chicago*. Notre Dame, Ind.: University of Notre Dame Press.

Phinney, Jean S. 1993. "A Three-Stage Model of Ethnic Identity Development in Adolescence." In *Ethnic Identity: Formation and Transmission among Hispanics and Other Minorities*, edited by Martha E. Bernal and George P. Knight. Albany: State University of New York Press.

Phinney, Jean S., and Anthony D. Ong. 2007. "Conceptualization and Measurement of Ethnic Identity: Current Status and Future Directions." *Journal of Counseling Psychology* 54(3): 271–81.

Portes, Alejandro, and Rubén G. Rumbaut. 2001. *Legacies: The Story of the Immigrant Second Generation*. Berkeley / New York: University of California Press / Russell Sage Foundation.

———. 2014. *Immigrant America: A Portrait*. 4th ed. Berkeley: University of California Press.

Qian, Zhenchao C., and Daniel T. Lichter. 2007. "Social Boundaries and Marital Assimilation: Interpreting Trends in Racial and Ethnic Intermarriage." *American Sociological Review* 72(1): 68–94.

Rumbaut, Rubén G. 1994. "The Crucible Within: Ethnic Identity, Self-Esteem, and Segmented Assimilation Among Children of Immigrants." *International Migration Review* 28(4): 748–94.

———. 2005. "Sites of Belonging: Acculturation, Discrimination, and Ethnic Identity Among Children of Immigrants." In *Discovering Successful Pathways in Children's Development: Mixed Methods in the Study of Childhood and Family Life*, edited by Thomas S. Weisner. Chicago: University of Chicago Press.

———. 2008. "Reaping What You Sow: Immigration, Youth, and Reactive Ethnicity." *Applied Developmental Science* 22(2): 1–4.

Smith, Robert Courtney. 2014. "Black Mexicans, Conjunctural Ethnicity, and Operating Identities: Long-Term Ethnographic Analysis." *American Sociological Review* 79(3): 517–48.

Song, Miri. 2003. *Choosing Ethnic Identity*. Cambridge: Polity Press.

Tajfel, Henri. 1981. *Human Groups and Social Categories: Studies in Social Psychology*. Cambridge: Cambridge University Press.

Tovar, Jessica, and Cynthia Feliciano. 2009. "'Not Mexican-American, but Mexican': Shifting Ethnic Self-Identifications Among Children of Mexican Immigrants." *Latino Studies* 7(2): 197–221.

Tuan, Mia. 1999. *Forever Foreigners or Honorary Whites? The Asian Ethnic Experience Today*. New Brunswick, N.J.: Rutgers University Press.

Vasquez, Jessica M. 2011. *Mexican Americans across Generations: Immigrant Families, Racial Realities*. New York: New York University Press.

Vasquez-Tokos, Jessica. 2017. *Marriage Vows and Racial Choices*. New York: Russell Sage Foundation.

Waters, Mary C. 1990. *Ethnic Options: Choosing Identities in America*. Berkeley: University of California Press.

———. 2001. *Black Identities: West Indian Immigrant Dreams and American Realities*. Cambridge, Mass.: Harvard University Press.

Immigrant Perceptions of U.S.-Born Receptivity and the Shaping of American Identity

MICHAEL JONES-CORREA, HELEN B. MARROW, DINA G. OKAMOTO, AND LINDA R. TROPP

Despite ideals grounding American identity in principles and ideas, most U.S. citizens continue to believe that they are rooted at least in part in ascriptive characteristics such as religion, race, or language. Research suggests that these views shape attitudes toward immigrants, and that nonwhite and non-Christian immigrants may therefore be less likely to feel American. Drawing on survey and interview data, this article examines the ways ascriptive characteristics shape immigrants' identification as American. Our results confirm the importance of particularly skin tone and language in shaping identification as well as the role of perceived welcome in tempering their negative impact. Such identification and perceptions have important consequences, increasing immigrants' likelihood of naturalization and decreasing their desire to return to their countries of origin.

Keywords: immigrant, Indian, Mexican, American identity, ascriptive characteristics, skin tone, religion, language, welcome

What constitutes American identity? Across disciplines, scholars have investigated whether American identity is grounded primarily in a set of principles and ideas—individualism, hard work, freedom, equality, and the rule of law—or in ethnonationalist traits such as language, skin color, native birth, and religion (Schildkraut 2014). Much of U.S. public and intellectual discourse signals that American identity should be thought of as the former—a civic culture revolving around the principles set out in the Constitution. Yet it is clear that in practice, a large majority of U.S. citizens continue to believe Americanness has its roots in at least some ascriptive characteristics (Citrin, Reingold, and Green 1990; Devos and Benaji 2005; Schildkraut 2011; Theiss-Morse 2009; Wong 2010).

Michael Jones-Correa is President's Distinguished Professor of Political Science and director of the Center for the Study of Ethnicity, Race, and Immigration at the University of Pennsylvania. **Helen B. Marrow** is associate professor of sociology at Tufts University. **Dina G. Okamoto** is Class of 1948 Herman B. Wells Professor in the Department of Sociology and director of the Center for Research on Race and Ethnicity in Society at Indiana University Bloomington. **Linda R. Tropp** is professor of social psychology at University of Massachusetts Amherst.

© 2018 Russell Sage Foundation. Jones-Correa, Michael, Helen B. Marrow, Dina G. Okamoto, and Linda R. Tropp. 2018. "Immigrant Perceptions of U.S.-Born Receptivity and the Shaping of American Identity." *RSF: The Russell Sage Foundation Journal of the Social Sciences* 4(5): 47–80. DOI: 10.7758/RSF.2018.4.5.03. Direct correspondence to: Michael Jones-Correa at mjcorrea@sas.upenn.edu, University of Pennsylvania, Department of Political Science, 214 Stiteler Hall, Philadelphia, PA 19104; Helen B. Marrow at helen.marrow@tufts.edu; Dina G. Okamoto at dokamoto@indiana.edu; and Linda R. Tropp at tropp@psych.umass.edu.

Open Access Policy: *RSF: The Russell Sage Foundation Journal of the Social Sciences* is an open access journal. This article is published under a Creative Commons Attribution-NonCommercial-NoDerivs 3.0 Unported License.

The specific definitions of Americanness among the U.S. born has profound downstream implications for domestic minority groups and larger processes of nation-building, but also for the foreign born who have immigrated to the United States. Through the assimilation process, many immigrants move progressively closer to the American mainstream over time and generations, regardless of whether they pursue that outcome intentionally (Alba and Nee 2003; NASEM 2015). However, even if these immigrants take on an American national identity defined in terms of language, skin color, birthplace, or religion, it may not be an easy fit for them. Given that the large majority—85 percent according to the 2010 Census—of the forty-one million immigrants currently residing in the United States are neither European nor white, and for the most part arrive without speaking English and perhaps also practicing a religion other than Christianity, most contemporary first-generation immigrants may not conform to the characteristics that the U.S. born attach to being American (on the census, Grieco et al. 2012). In addition, more immigrant newcomers have recently begun settling in areas, such as the Southeast, where local residents may be less likely to see new immigrants as "one of us" (Marrow 2011a, 2011b; Massey 2008; Winders 2013).

Research on American identity suggests the attitudes of the U.S. born toward immigrants are shaped by immigrants' ascriptive characteristics (Kinder and Kam 2009; Theiss-Morse 2009; Wong 2010), and that nonwhite and non-Christian immigrants may therefore be less likely to feel American (Devos and Benaji 2005; Huynh, Devos, and Smalarz 2011; Masuoka and Junn 2013). In a separate strand of literature, mainly in sociology, scholars also emphasize the importance of the surrounding "contexts of reception" in facilitating or hindering immigrant integration patterns in the United States (Portes and Rumbaut 2014). Undoubtedly the context to which immigrants arrive, alongside immigrants' characteristics, has a role in their developing sense of Americanness. In this literature, these contexts tend to be defined broadly, highlighting how factors such as governmental policies, labor markets, and other key social institutions, as well as public opinion, can be either more or less receptive to immigrant newcomers, and how such receptivity in turn can shape immigrants' downstream outcomes as well as their feelings of belonging or exclusion within a polity (see, for example, Bloemraad 2006; de Graauw 2016).

In this article, we bring together these two approaches, examining how receptivity toward immigrants might moderate well-established relationships between immigrants' ascriptive characteristics and their patterns of identification as American. We also advance existing research in two novel ways. First, we add *legal status* to the list of ascriptive characteristics typically analyzed by scholars of American identity, given that legal status has emerged as a key axis of social stratification since the mid-1980s (Gonzales 2015; Massey 2007; Massey and Sánchez 2010; NASEM 2015). Second, we extend existing analyses of contexts of reception down to the interpersonal level, reasoning that immigrants may experience receptivity or lack of it not only in their encounters with large institutions or via generalized public opinion, but also as their daily encounters and interactions with U.S.-born blacks and whites in their communities, from whom they receive signals about whether they "belong" (see, for example, on education, Gonzales 2015; on law and media, Menjívar 2016; on policing, Menjívar and Bejarano 2004; Williams 2015).

Our focus on the interpersonal level of receptivity is not meant to discount the larger and more institutional levels of context of reception highlighted in the literature. Rather, we intend to provide a useful extension of that literature, noting that existing research focused on individual-level attitudes and behaviors toward immigrants tends to pay attention to negative or restrictive ones rather than positive or welcoming ones. This is the case despite recent growth in local initiatives designed to encourage the U.S. born to welcome immigrants (Welcoming America 2017), and new scholarship demonstrating how welcoming attitudes and behaviors play key roles in facilitating downstream immigrant integration processes and outcomes (see Fussell 2014; Jones-Correa 2011; Okamoto and Ebert 2016; Phelps et al. 2013; Tropp et al. 2018).

This research draws on a new representative

survey and follow-up interviews conducted with South Asian Indian and Mexican immigrants, two groups positioned very differently in U.S. social and economic life. We gathered these data in two major metropolitan areas in the United States, Atlanta and Philadelphia, both of which have seen their populations grow increasingly diverse through immigration over the last several decades. Our survey data include measures of both immigrant groups' ascriptive characteristics (including their English-language ability, religion, and skin tone), their legal status, their perceptions of the (non) welcoming-ness of their interactions with the U.S. born (both whites and blacks), and finally, the strength of their identification as American. We find that for both Mexican and Indian immigrants, the perception of more welcoming treatment by U.S.-born whites softens the relationship between their darker skin tone and lesser English-language ability and weaker American national identification. For Mexican immigrants, but not Indian, the perception of more welcoming treatment by U.S.-born blacks has a similar effect. Examining some of the downstream effects of American identity, immigrants' identification as Americans, along with their ascriptive characteristics (mitigated by their sense of welcome), shapes their likelihood of naturalizing as U.S. citizens and their intentions of returning to their countries of origin.

Our results confirm the importance of some ascriptive characteristics—particularly skin tone and language—in shaping immigrants' identification as American, and highlight the role of perceived welcome among contemporary immigrants in tempering the negative impact of these characteristics. Together, immigrants' identification as American and their perceptions of being welcomed appears to strengthen their attachment to the polity despite the barriers posed by their ascriptive characteristics.

LITERATURE REVIEW

We briefly review three interrelated literatures: the views of the U.S. born of American identity and its effect on immigrant identification as American, the importance of the individual level contexts of reception in shaping immigrants' American identity, and the effects of identification as American on immigrants' adoption of U.S. citizenship and their expression of a desire to return to their country of origin.

Views of Americanness and Immigrants' Identifications as "American"

A number of surveys have asked respondents about what elements constitute being a "true" American (Citrin, Reingold, and Green 1990, Schildkraut 2007a; Theiss-Morse 2009). The General Social Survey, for example, asks respondents how much they believe that a number of characteristics—such as ancestry, being born in the United States, having American citizenship, speaking English, and respecting American institutions and laws—define being American. Despite widespread acceptance that the Constitution and respect for rule of law are important aspects of being American, surveys consistently find that speaking English is also considered a necessary condition. In addition, a substantial percentage of the U.S. born feel that being born in the United States and being Christian are as well (Citrin, Reingold, and Green 1990; Schildkraut 2011, 2007b; Theiss-Morse 2009; Wong 2010).

Race also appears to matter, in that some ethnic groups are perceived as more American than others, European Americans in particular (Huynh, Devos, and Smalarz 2011). In fact, a number of studies demonstrate that Americanness is attributed more to European immigrants than to African Americans, Asian Americans, or Latinos, regardless of which definition of Americanness respondents use (Devos and Banaji 2005; Devos, Gavin, and Quintana 2010; Huynh, Devos, and Altman 2015; Theiss-Morse 2009). This linking of American identity to a set of ascriptive characteristics privileging whiteness leads to an implicit (and sometimes explicit) ranking of the U.S. born over the foreign born, U.S. citizens over noncitizens, and European immigrants over their non-European counterparts (Hafsa and Devos 2014). It is not surprising, then, that scholars have found that the U.S. born often conceive of nonwhite immigrant newcomers as *them* rather than *us*, reinforced by the psychological tendency to favor one's in-group (Kinder and Kam 2009; Wong

2010). Thus, the more ascriptively similar immigrants are to U.S.-born whites in regard to race, the more likely they may eventually be accepted as American, as *one of us*.

The way in which American identity is defined and understood has more than symbolic effects; it also has consequences for immigrant integration or exclusion through its impact on the development of attitudes among the U.S. born toward policy. Que-Lam Huynh, Thierry Devos, and Hannah Altman's experimental study suggests that agreeing with the notion of European ancestry as more typically American is a significant predictor of antiminority policy attitudes (2015, 466). Jack Citrin and his colleagues, relying on survey data, reach similar conclusions in reference to immigrants' outgroups: U.S.-born Americans who see national identity through an ethnic lens hold more negative views of both immigrants and immigration policy (Citrin, Reingold, and Green 1990; Citrin and Wright 2009). Likewise, Elizabeth Theiss-Morse finds that though white respondents who identify most strongly as American are more likely to provide aid to other Americans, they largely do so for people they consider to be like themselves—that is, those who are also defined as part of the prototypical American in-group (2009; see also Wong 2010).

The well-established links between American identity and ascriptive characteristics such as language, Christianity, and whiteness, suggest not only that the U.S. born may have difficulty seeing many contemporary immigrant newcomers as truly American, but also that recent immigrants may find it difficult to feel truly American. Drawing on a set of small-group experimental studies eliciting participants' identification as Americans, Devos and Mazharin Benaji conclude that "subgroups may differ in the ease with which they are included in a superordinate identity," and that the "propensity to equate American with White may *facilitate the integration of ethnic and American identities* for White Americans but *not* for members of groups excluded from the national identity" (2005, 464, emphasis added). Huynh and her colleagues reach similar conclusions, as do Massey and Sánchez, who find that many Latino immigrants living in the current anti-immigrant political context are hesitant to express an American identity, often citing feelings of being discriminated against for not speaking English or not being born in the United States (Huynh, Devos, and Altman 2015; Massey and Sánchez 2010). According to Theiss-Morse, it is precisely these ethnic minorities, some foreign born but others who are members of domestic minority groups, who are deemed the most undeserving, helped the least, and defined as marginal to the American body politic (2009). Consequently, Huynh and her colleagues argue that members of ethnic minority groups are aware of negative stereotypes and the skepticism with which their American identities will be viewed, leading them to question their belonging in the United States (2011; see also Gast and Okamoto 2016; Massey and Sánchez 2010; Masuoka and Junn 2013; Rydell, Hamilton, and Devos 2010). Nonetheless, most of these studies focus on the U.S. born (how they define American identity, how they see immigrants within that vision) or on immigrants' perceptions of belonging at large (how they feel included in or, more typically, excluded from the bounds of American identity). Few studies have direct measures of immigrants' micro-level contact experiences with the U.S. born, including how they interpret these relations and what the attendant consequences for their patterns of national identification might be.

In addition, although existing scholarship on American identity has focused on race, religion, nativity, and language as the key components of an ethno-national conception of Americanness, it has not adequately examined the role of legal status. Currently, the United States has approximately eleven million undocumented immigrants, more than half of them from Mexico, eliciting "strong cultural anxieties" (Citrin and Wright 2009) and charged rhetoric alleging the need to "uphold the law" (Brettell and Nibbs 2010). Illegality, rather than being an attribute of individual migrants, has become a status marker ascribed onto entrants arriving without documentation (Bean, Brown, and Bachmeier 2015; De Genova 2002). Several scholars argue that it now operates as a key axis of social stratification in the United States (Gonzales 2015; Massey and Sánchez 2010; NASEM 2015). Undocumented immigrants, for example, are consistently viewed more negatively in public opinion polls than their legal counterparts (Espenshade and Calhoun 1993; Espenshade and Hempstead 1996; Fussell 2014; Suro 2009). In these ways, illegality is likely to be a key ascriptive characteristic shaping the perception toward the U.S. born of immigrant newcomers, and in turn, of immigrants' sense of belonging within U.S. society today (Masuoka and Junn 2013). In the language of immigrant incorporation, we might even conceive of illegality as a characteristic ascribed onto some new immigrant arrivals via a negative, such as unwelcoming or hostile, context of reception (Portes and Rumbaut 2014).

Contexts of Reception: U.S.-Born Welcome to Immigrants

At the same time, we assert that positive receptivity toward immigrants on the part of the U.S. born may play an important role in offsetting these relationships between immigrants' ascriptive characteristics and their willingness to identify as American. Our emphasis on welcoming-ness emerges from new research demonstrating how policies and institutions can signal inclusion as well as exclusion—for instance, by implementing multiculturalism policy at the national level (Bloemraad 2006) or employment, identity card, health, and community policing strategies at the local level (for example, de Graauw 2016; Marrow 2012; Marrow and Joseph 2015). Several recent studies have drawn attention to the types of inclusionary processes occurring within specific institutional contexts (Calvo, Jablonska-Bayro, and Waters 2017; Gast and Okamoto 2016; Huang and Liu 2017; Mallet, Calvo, and Waters 2017; Williams 2015). Such studies suggest that welcoming policies and practices can bolster immigrants' incorporation outcomes both symbolically and materially. New government policies and official events have even been established in cities across the country to highlight the value of welcoming immigrants into local communities (Jones-Correa 2011; Welcoming America 2017).

Still, to date most of these studies focus on receptivity at the level of law and policy, or operationalized as broad public opinion, overlooking the importance of understanding receptivity in terms of how immigrants engage with and feel welcomed by U.S.-born individuals they encounter in their local social environments.[1] This is surprising, as there is considerable evidence that individual-level contact—defined as face-to-face interactions between members of different groups—can meaningfully contribute to improving intergroup attitudes (Pettigrew and Tropp 2011). It is also surprising given the much larger body of research that clearly suggests, in the opposite direction, that negative encounters with the U.S. born, sometimes conceptualized as perceptions of discrimination, increase immigrants' sense of exclusion from the polity (Kasinitz et al. 2008; Massey and Sánchez 2010).

Indeed, recent research has found that, among the U.S. born, having more frequent contact with immigrants predicts greater tendencies to welcome immigrants even after demographic characteristics, perceived discrimination, and contextual exposure to immigrants are controlled for (Tropp et al., forthcoming). Moreover, contact is often used as a strategy to build connections between immigrant and U.S.-born communities and to enhance immigrant integration (Bergmann 2016). In these ways, we expect that the extent to which immigrants perceive that the interactions they have with the U.S. born are positive and welcoming—as opposed to negative and unwelcoming or hostile—is likely to increase their feelings of belonging and of being American. It is even possible, in our view, that such feelings of belonging might attenuate negative impacts of ascriptive characteristics on American identity, such as nonwhite race, non-Christian religion, or lack of English fluency.

Correlates of American Identity: Citizenship and Return

Immigrants' identification as American has more than a symbolic importance. Social scientists have demonstrated that the adoption of a national identity—or feeling American—matters for other outcomes in several ways. For

---

1. Elizabeth Fussell, for one, has called for migration scholars to pay greater attention to intergroup contact in their studies of incorporation processes and public opinion (2014).

one, it shapes support for redistributive policies, which tend to garner more support if they are perceived as applying to "deserving" individuals who are already members of the community as opposed to "undeserving" members located outside it, a boundary drawn in part along ascriptive lines (Theiss-Morse 2009; Wong 2010; Fox 2011). Second, the adoption of a national identity matters for civic and political engagement. Deborah Schildkraut finds, for example, that identifying as American is significantly and positively correlated with individuals' trust in government, trust in law enforcement, and expectations of obligation to the polity (2007b; also see Theiss-Morse 2009; Wong 2010).

Immigrants' identification as Americans thus likely shapes key decisions they make to orient themselves both toward and away from their American host communities and the national *we*. Immigrants who do not fall neatly within the boundaries of American identity because of their ascriptive characteristics may not only be less likely to identify as American. They may also, as a consequence, be less likely to adopt U.S. citizenship—a key form of attachment to the nation—or more likely to indicate a desire to permanently return to their countries of origin—an indicator of a non-U.S. orientation. Thus, if immigrants' perceptions of the welcoming-ness of the U.S.-born Americans turn out to mitigate negative relationships between their ascriptive characteristics and their identification as American, then we might also expect the results to have implications for their subsequent choice of acquiring citizenship or returning to their countries of origin.

DATA

We explore these questions drawing on a new representative survey and follow-up semistructured interviews conducted with two first-generation immigrant groups in Atlanta and Philadelphia, two major U.S. metropolitan areas.

Group Selection

We chose to study South Asian Indian and Mexican immigrant groups for three reasons. First, they are currently the largest two immigrant groups in the nation as well as in each of these two metro areas (Chakravorty, Kapur, and Singh 2017; Portes and Rumbaut 2014; Zong and Batalova 2016; Atlanta Regional Commission 2015; Singer et al. 2008). Second, they exemplify, in stark relief, the bifurcation of skills and economic status that is arguably the core feature of post-1965 U.S. immigration patterns (Alba and Nee 2003; Portes and Rumbaut 2014). Whereas Mexicans are seen as a quintessential low-status group (Massey 2007; Perlmann 2005; Bean, Brown, and Bachmeier 2015; Telles and Ortiz 2008), South Asian Indians are viewed as a quintessential high-status one, often even a model minority (Chakravorty, Kapur, and Singh 2017; Lee and Zhou 2015; Nee and Holbrow 2013; Sandhu 2012).[2] Such pointed differences in the two immigrant groups' socioeconomic positioning shape the host society's reactions to them, driving, for example, the general American perception that all Mexicans are poorly educated and heightening the fear of many Americans that Mexicans will never assimilate (see, for example, Huntington 2004). Indians' socioeconomic standing helps drives U.S. perceptions that Indians, like all Asian immigrants, are well educated, smart, and talented, improving Americans' views about Asian immigrants relative to other nonwhite groups (Jiménez and Horowitz 2013; Samson 2013). Indeed, Asian immigrants as a group are generally typified much more positively than Hispanic-Latinos ones in the public realm (Pew Research Center 2015).

Third, Mexicans and Indians vary in their constellations of other ascriptive status markers that the literature on American identity shows U.S.-born Americans connect to American identity—namely language, skin tone, religion—as well as legal status. Mexican immi-

---

2. The sociologists Jennifer Lee and Min Zhou even characterize Mexican and Indian immigrants in the United States today as dually hypo-selected and hyper-selected, respectively. That is, whereas Indian immigrants have educational levels not only well above the nonmigrant population of India they leave behind but also above the U.S. population, Mexican immigrants have the inverse. Their mean college degree rate is less than that of the nonmigrant population in Mexico and they are poorly educated compared with the U.S. born, both whites and blacks (2015, 31).

grants have not only less education and more employment in lower-skilled sectors of the economy, but also less English-language proficiency and, after decades of intensifying border and interior immigration enforcement, very high levels of undocumented status (Bean, Brown, and Bachmeier 2015; Massey 2013; Massey, Durand, and Malone 2002; NASEM 2015; Telles and Ortiz 2008). Today, Mexicans are the group most strongly affected by and associated with undocumented status (Baker and Rytina 2013; García 2017; Jiménez 2010; Massey and Sánchez 2010). In skin tone, Mexican immigrants in the United States tend to self-report all along the continuum from lighter to darker, reflecting the ethnic diversity within Mexico itself (Villareal 2010; Sue 2013); a few are even able to "pass" as black in the U.S. context (Jones 2012; Vaughn 2005; Vaughn and Vinson 2007).

In contrast, considered as a single group Indian immigrants are "doing very well" (Leonard 2007). A relatively low proportion are undocumented, though some reports suggest the number has been increasing since the 1990s (Rangaswamy 2000, 2007; Baker and Rytina 2013). They are residentially dispersed within metropolitan areas, many residing in well-heeled suburbs or ethnoburbs, largely among white Americans, where scholars see their children well poised to achieve upward mobility (Lee and Zhou 2015; Mishra 2016; Zhou and Bankston 2017). Still, they too exhibit significant internal variation—by factors such as social class, caste, citizenship, legal status, language, and even their regions of origin within India depending on when and in which wave they arrived. In fact, some scholars even suggest they are a highly "divided" (Mishra 2016) or even an economically and regionally "polarized" community, characterized by "extremes at two ends" (Chakravorty, Kapur, and Singh 2017).

By religion, non-Hindu minority groups, especially Sikhs and Christians, are overrepresented in the diaspora relative to their proportions in the general population in India; most survey estimates put the proportion of Hindus among all Indian Americans at somewhere between 45 and 76 percent (Kurien 2001, 2006). One recent national survey estimated that Hindus constitute about half of all Indian Americans (51 percent), followed by Christians (18 percent), Muslims (10 percent), Sikhs (5 percent) and others (Pew Research Center 2012). Some scholars note that religion is increasing in salience for Indian immigrants, in response to both the aftermath of the September 11 terrorist attacks in the United States in 2001 and the rise of neo-Hindu (Hindutva) nationalistic politics in India since the 1980s (Kurien 2001, 2006; Mishra 2016). Turban-wearing Sikhs and Muslims have been subject to the most intense anti-Islamic and racial targeting since 9/11, following an intense "racialization of religion" in the United States in recent years (Kalita 2003; Joshi 2006).

Skin tone among Indian immigrants is a complex topic. On the one hand, Indian immigrants can be mistaken for Mexican, Native American, or black in the U.S. context (George 1997; Kurien 2001). Sangay Mishra argues that skin color and phenotype result in all Indian immigrants being mistaken for Muslims or Arabs, not just Mexicans or Native Americans—especially if they are male and especially in public spaces where the encounters they have with other groups are fleeting and anonymous (2016). Indeed, some Indian immigrants have recently been attacked and killed based on their skin color and perceived "outsiderness" (Kumar 2017). But according to Mishra and Susan Koshy (1998), many middle-class Indian immigrants and their organizations still tend to emphasize class and ethnicity over race or skin tone. Lower-class immigrants, on the other hand, in tandem with students and intellectuals, take a race- and color-conscious approach, even arguing that a race-blind approach is itself akin to white racism. Either way, Koshy points out many Indian immigrants express confusion about their racial identities not only in India, but also in the United States (1998).

In sum, Mexican and Indian immigrants make good comparison groups for this study because they occupy vastly different places in the U.S. social and economic hierarchy. This is likely to lead to their being perceived quite differently by the U.S. born, as well as to different contact experiences with the U.S. born in everyday life. Because of their higher socioeconomic status, Indian immigrants clearly have more opportunities to live and work alongside

U.S.-born whites than Mexican immigrants, who are more segregated. Greater intergroup contact could lead to more favorable relations between Indians and U.S.-born whites in particular, though Indian immigrants' relative success and darker skin tone may also provoke feelings of threat among whites (see Hochschild and Weaver 2007; Hochschild, Weaver, and Burch 2012; Jiménez and Horowitz 2013; Samson 2013). For their part, Mexican immigrants may experience less frequent and less positive contact with U.S.-born groups because of their lower socioeconomic status as well as their lower English-language ability and higher likelihood of residing in the United States without documents. Because of this status, they may also have more frequent contact with U.S.-born minorities, such as African Americans, than Indian immigrants do.

At the same time, Indian immigrants, who are predominantly Hindu, Sikh, and Muslim, might have greater difficulties in making their religious practices intelligible to the U.S.-born Christian majority (Pew Research Center 2010). Because of this, despite being more linguistically isolated and having lower socioeconomic status, on average, Mexican immigrants are more likely to share religious practices with U.S.-born communities than Indian immigrants are, and their participation in local congregations alongside the U.S. born could facilitate cross-ethnic contact and encourage positive intergroup attitudes. Taken together, these two immigrant groups provide a unique opportunity for examining how language, skin tone, religion, and legal status influence identification as Americans. Their perceptions of welcome by the U.S. born, both on their own and interacting with the visible marker of skin tone, has important consequences for the strength of their American identity, and downstream implications for the two groups' decisions to naturalize or return to their countries of origin.

Selection of Metropolitan Areas

We conducted our study of these four groups in Philadelphia and Atlanta for both theoretical and demographic reasons. To give us some purchase on understanding the dynamics of contact in the context of our four groups (particularly among immigrants and the U.S. born), we selected places with sizable populations of U.S.-born blacks and whites, and significant contemporary immigration streams from India and Mexico.[3] Politics and social interactions in both metropolitan areas are profoundly shaped by the long history of black-white relations, which history provides the context for immigrant reception and intergroup relations. This suggests as well that immigrant relations with the U.S. born are best distinguished between interactions with whites and blacks separately. Despite similarities, Philadelphia and Atlanta also diverge in important ways. The political contexts of the two metro areas may shape intergroup interactions with the Georgia legislature, for instance, passing several laws targeting the state's undocumented population, and Philadelphia having declared itself a "sanctuary city," directing city agencies to avoid asking residents about their legal status (Frey 2001; Hansen 2005; Creighton and Katz 2007; Odem 2008). In short, although the four groups in the study are represented in both metropolitan areas, differing regional contexts may also help shape differing perceptions of American identity for immigrants.

---

3. Both metropolitan areas are approximately the same size (five to six million people each) and have racialized black-white histories that have been reshaped by recent immigrant arrivals. Although Philadelphia has had a more constant history of immigration than Atlanta, it is only since the 1980s that both metro areas have become home to diverse streams of post-1965 immigrants. Respectively, these new migration streams have transformed Philadelphia into a "re-emerging" immigrant gateway and Atlanta into a major new "emerging" immigrant gateway (Singer 2004; Singer et al. 2008). Indians and Mexicans constitute the two largest immigrant groups in both areas (for more demographic and historical detail, see tables A1 and A2), and Mexican and Indian immigrants play similar roles in both local economies—Mexicans a predominantly low-skilled, labor migrant group, and Indians primarily a highly skilled, professional one. Both groups show a pattern of greater suburban settlement and are more geographically dispersed than African Americans (Creighton and Katz 2007; Odem 2008). Taken together, these commonalities afford us an excellent opportunity to examine interactions among our four target groups in both metro areas.

Survey and Qualitative Interviews

The Study of Immigrants and Natives in Atlanta and Philadelphia (SINAP) was fielded in 2013 by telephone, yielding interviews with 2,006 respondents, approximately five hundred from each group.[4] In addition, interviews with a subsample of Mexican and Indian immigrants were conducted face to face.[5] To be eligible for inclusion in the study, respondents had to be at least eighteen years old and reside in one of ten counties in the Philadelphia or Atlanta metropolitan areas. Respondents who identified as white or black had to indicate that they were born in the United States, and survey respondents who identified as Mexican or Indian had to indicate that they were born in Mexico or India, respectively.[6] The study's in-depth semi-structured interviews were conducted in 2014 with recontacted survey respondents and with additional snowball sampling where necessary. The research team interviewed 249 individuals, with approximately thirty interviews from each target group in each site.

The study generated a wide array of demographic and other data. Beyond determining their age, racial and ethnic background, place of residence, and place of birth, survey respondents were asked to report their gender and political ideology, and—as indicators of socioeconomic status—their level of education, employment status, and homeownership. Sample characteristics from the survey are summarized for respondents from each group in table A1, and additional characteristics are tabulated for immigrant groups only in table A2.

A key dependent variable in our analyses is strength of identification as American: "In general, how strongly do you think of yourself as American? Very strongly, somewhat strongly, not very strongly, or not at all?" with the response categories ranging from 0 (not at all) to 3 (very strongly). This is a common measure of American national identity used in a number of other studies, which we supplement with novel data on individual respondents' experiences and perceptions of their intergroup contact experiences among both the U.S. born and immigrants. This affords us insight into how immigrants' individual-level interactions with the U.S. born (both white and black) might moderate the relationships between their ascriptive characteristics, legal status, and strength of their adoption of American national identity, and beyond that how that American identity may relate to naturalization and desires to return to their sending countries.

This study takes advantage of the unique characteristics of these data, in particular their attention both to ascriptive status markers among the foreign born, including legal status, and to perceptions of interactions occurring among the U.S. born and foreign born to build on prior work on the predictors of American identity. We looked first to the qualitative in-

---

4. Telephone interviews were conducted in English and Spanish for Mexican respondents, and in English for respondents from the other three groups. U.S.-born white and black samples were drawn through random-digit dialing (RDD) of landlines and cell phone numbers to minimize selection bias, in conjunction, for blacks, with an oversampling of high-density census tracts, based on American Community Survey (ACS) block-group level estimates. SINAP employed a stratified sampling design for the Mexican and Indian foreign-born samples, drawing a random sample, using surname dictionaries, from cell phone and landline lists, in conjunction with an oversampling of high-density census tracts based on ACS block-group level estimates of Mexican and Indian residential concentration.

5. Two hundred of the five hundred Mexican immigrants and forty-eight of the 503 Indian immigrants completed the surveys in face-to-face interviews rather than over the telephone. Because of the characteristics of respondents differed somewhat by mode of interview (by gender, education and employment), we controlled for mode of interview in our models.

6. The survey component had a response rate of 20 percent for all households with whom contact was made [AAPOR Response Rate 4, $(I+P)/((I+P) + (R+NC+O) + e(UH+UO))$], and a cooperation rate of 90 percent for all respondents contacted who also met our eligibility criteria [AAPOR Cooperation rate 4, $(I+P)/((I+P)+R)$]. Altogether, 2,006 individuals—including 503 U.S.-born whites, 502 U.S.-born blacks, 500 Mexican immigrants, and 501 Indian immigrants—responded to the survey, half of each sample being drawn from each of the two metropolitan areas.

terviews to see immigrants and the U.S. born discuss Americanness in their own words. Respondents were not prompted to talk about how they thought being American meant to them; the findings we discuss were a part of larger conversations about relations between immigrants and the U.S. born. The excerpts touching on American identity very much support the existing literature. In their conversations, respondents perceive and display a very strong association between immigrants' ascriptive characteristics, particularly race and language and American identity, and less legal status or religion. Because we saw these patterns upheld by our qualitative data, we then tested whether immigrants' ascriptive characteristics (including legal status) shaped the likelihood that Mexican and Indian foreign-born respondents identify as American on our larger quantitative sample. Third, we included positive receptivity ("feeling welcomed") as a moderating variable, seeking to test whether our immigrant respondents' perceptions of the valence of their interpersonal encounters with U.S.-born blacks and whites changes these relationships. Finally, we examined whether and how Mexican and Indian foreign-born respondents' identification as American affected their acquisition of citizenship and plans to return to their countries of origin.

FINDINGS

We present two sets of empirical findings. The first, based on extensive in-depth interviews with immigrant and U.S.-born respondents in both Atlanta and Philadelphia, highlights the intersection of immigrants' American identity with certain ascriptive characteristics. The second, drawing on survey data, echoes the themes emerging from the interviews, to suggest that language and skin tone, in particular, shape immigrants' identification as American. In turn, their identification as American, moderated by their ascriptive characteristics, shapes immigrants' adoption of U.S. citizenship, and their desire to return to their countries of origin.

Qualitative Interviews

Our qualitative in-depth interviews with U.S.- and foreign-born residents in the Atlanta and Philadelphia metropolitan areas help illustrate some of the dynamics highlighted in earlier survey-based research. In particular, the interviews point to the ways in which Mexican and Indian immigrants do perceive barriers to being seen and treated as fully American, particularly by race and language. In one interview, for instance, an Indian immigrant man in Montgomery County, Pennsylvania, expressed his dismay at being questioned about where he and his parents were from:

RESPONDENT: I mean, it's a really weird question to ask because *what about me looks like I have not grown up here?* [emphasis added] You know, it's not the way I dress. I don't speak with an Indian accent. There's nothing that would give that impression that my parents would be [from] anywhere other than where their parents are—in this country. And so that's completely being based on something very superficial—not even superficial like the way you're dressed. It's something...

INTERVIEWER: Related to, do you think, skin color?

RESPONDENT: Yeah—I mean, *what else could it be?* [emphasis added] You know, I don't speak with an Indian accent at all. I mean, I have a completely American accent and I speak like an American. . . . I mean, the thing that bothers me is that why would I be anything else? Why am I being thought of anything other than as American as this person? And why do they feel that it's okay to ask me that? I mean assume—there was so much assumption in that that was just very irritating and has set me on this whole journey where if I'm not American, what am I? Because I have grown up thinking I am American. And all of a sudden, I feel like I'm being surrounded by people that don't think that.

The questions this respondent was asked reminded him that despite the absence of any accent, the way he looks—including his skin tone and perhaps other markers of phenotype—place him apart. This raised subtle doubts for him about his ability to be fully accepted as American, even as he has always "grown up thinking" that he was, and despite not feeling that he had another comparable identity to adopt instead.

In another interview, an Indian immigrant woman living in Chester County, Pennsylvania, was upset that her son, while playing with other children, had a boy say this to him:

RESPONDENT: "I don't like you all people here you should go back to your country." My son, he was not born in India and came here. So he thinks of himself as American. But other people don't treat him that way *because of his skin color*. [emphasis added]

This respondent worried that her son, despite having grown up in the United States and thinking of himself as American, will never be fully accepted as American, mainly because of his race and skin tone. Like the earlier respondent, this could potentially lead him to question his identity and attach to it less strongly in the future.

In our interviews, the U.S. born perceive the role of ascriptive characteristics in setting the boundary between Americans and immigrants as well. A U.S.-born African American woman interviewed in Philadelphia, for example, highlighted the additional role of language in excluding many immigrants from the boundaries of American identity:

RESPONDENT: I find that Americans are taken aback when people are speaking another language—I mean, people are communicating in another language—generally, Americans are. But for some reason—I don't know whether it's being terribly self-conscious that "They're speaking another language, are they talking about me," kind of thing.... I listen because it's interesting to me, but I find that other people... Americans—English-speaking... I mean, [native-] born Americans... seem to be taken aback by the fact that people are speaking another language in front of them as though somehow "This is America—you're supposed to speak English here."

Language, this woman noted, is what many U.S. born latch onto as the primary marker of insider-ness versus foreignness, thus potentially excluding some new immigrants from the boundaries of American identity.

Other interview respondents echoed these findings in different ways. Some of the U.S. born agreed that Americans fear immigrants, and did not see them as belonging to the country or being able to be American. In the words of one U.S.-born white woman living in Cobb County, Georgia, this sentiment was applied mostly to Hispanics (including Mexican immigrants):

RESPONDENT: There are so many negative attitudes about Hispanic people with this whole immigration thing, [that] people are coming in and they're taking our jobs and all that stuff. I think that's just pervasive in the way people talk about [Hispanics]... *That you don't belong here, or that this is America and you're not American.* [emphasis added]

In turn, our interview data also suggest that many of the immigrant respondents are attentive to such exclusion by natives. One Mexican immigrant respondent living in Philadelphia even argued against it, claiming that he had every much a right to think of this as his country as persons born in the United States do: "[I like] to live together with [different] people, and also... to get along with them. Why? For the simple reason that... very possibly *this is my country, like it is theirs*."[7]

Taken together, the interview excerpts provide a sense of the key fault lines between those included and those excluded from being considered fully American. In particular, they highlight language and skin tone as markers that exclude and potentially erode both Indian and Mexican immigrants' identifications as Americans; by contrast, lack of legal status and religion did not emerge in the interview data to the same degrees. Interestingly, some of these excerpts highlight critical negative in-

---

7. Translated by the authors. The original Spanish is "Respondent: [Me gusta] convivir con la gente y al mismo tiempo, este... llevarme con ellos. ¿Por qué? Por la sencilla razón de que... posiblemente este es mi país como el de ellos."

teractions between the native and foreign born, in which the latter's national identities are policed or called into question during interpersonal interactions. We therefore move on to explore how race, language, and other ascriptive status characteristics might serve as potential barriers to Mexican and Indian immigrants' adoption of American identity more fully in our survey data in the next section. Here we also give more attention to the potential role of immigrants' perceptions of welcome from the native born, to the extent that perceived welcome (as opposed to perceived unwelcome, hostility, or discrimination) may result in stronger (as opposed to weaker) American identification, and consequently, perhaps also greater citizenship acquisition or weaker desires to return to their countries of origin.

Multivariate Analyses Predicting American Identity

Do the significant ascriptive barriers that our immigrant interview respondents perceive to being considered by the U.S. born as fully American hold up in our larger SINAP survey sample? The multivariate models we present here are ordered logistic regression models, with the strength of respondents' *identification as American* serving as the dependent variable, response categories ranging from 0 (feeling not at all American) to 3 (very strongly American).[8]

American Identity
Three variables capture immigrants' alignment with widely held ascriptive definitions of American identity: respondents' *knowledge of English* (coded 0 to 3, a self-assessed measure ranging from knowing no English to being fluent in English),[9] *religion* (coded as a dummy variable, 1 being Christian), and *skin tone* (coded 1 to 7, a self-assessed measure of skin tone, from lighter to darker skinned).[10] We also asserted that *current undocumented status* could also be considered, under the current restrictive policy environment, an additional ascriptive dimension of American identity. We included a dummy variable coded 1 if the respondent was currently undocumented and 0 indicating otherwise.

Perceptions of Welcome
The model included two variables gauging respondents' perceptions of being welcomed—one by U.S.-born whites and the other by U.S.-born blacks. Respondents from each ethnic group was asked "Overall, when you think about [whites/blacks] in [greater Philadelphia/Atlanta], how often do you feel welcomed by them?" The response categories ranged from not feeling welcomed at all to feeling very welcomed, coded 0 to 3.[11]

---

8. The analyses use weighting to account for differences in age and sex of our sample relative to the actual distribution of these traits across the Philadelphia and Atlanta metropolitan areas.

9. Daniel Hopkins finds that it is immigrants' attempts at speaking English, not their language ability or accent, that is positively assessed by the U.S. born (2014). Unfortunately, SINAP does not include immigrants' self-assessment of their accent in English, so the effects of accent could not be included as part of this analysis.

10. Self-assessed skin tone is not the same as race. Although U.S.-born blacks and whites might more easily be assigned racial categories, immigrant Indians and Mexicans are not so easily categorized. Eighty-three percent of Indian respondents, for instance, chose Asian–South Asian as their race, the next largest group (9 percent) opting for Some Other Race. Among Mexican respondents, 71 percent chose Some Other Race as their preferred racial category, the next largest cohort, 14 percent, opting for white. The mean evaluation of self-assessed race also differed meaningfully across groups. The variable was coded from 1 to 7, running from lighter to darker skinned, yielding a mean for U.S.-born whites of 2.3 and for blacks of 4.5. The median response for both immigrant groups was closer to that of U.S. blacks than to that of U.S. whites. For Mexican immigrants it was 3.8, for Indians 4.3. The difference in median skin tone across the four groups is significant at $p < .00$.

11. In robustness checks not shown here, we added measures of perceived similarity to U.S.-born whites and to U.S.-born blacks, anticipating the possibility that respondents' perceived welcome simply reflects their feelings of similarity or dissimilarity with other groups. The addition of these additional controls was not significant, and did not change the results presented here.

Control Variables

Age, gender (male coded 1), and percent life in the United States (calculated as time spent in the United States divided by age) were included as control variables because attachments to the United States vary by age and length of time in the United States (Schildkraut 2011; Theiss-Morse 2009), and because there are indications that immigrants' attachment to the country of reception, and their desire to return to their countries of origin, vary by gender (Jones-Correa 1998). The model also included a dummy variable to indicate whether the interview was conducted over the phone or face to face to control for differences in mode of interviewing that introduced some variation in sampling, which could be reflected in the results.[12]

Collinearity tests indicated that the variables included in the model are in no danger of being collinear.[13] We estimated the model for all immigrant respondents together, and then separately for each immigrant group (Indian and Mexican). As an additional robustness check, we ran the models first including demographic characteristics only, then with demographic and ascriptive characteristics included, and then added welcoming variables. In addition, to check whether the effects of immigrants' perceptions of welcome by U.S. blacks and whites was affected by respondents' self-assessed skin tone, we ran the models including these interaction terms. The full models, both with and without interaction terms, are shown in table 1. Additional models—showing reduced models, are presented in table A4. The results are generally consistent across the models.

Results from the ordered logit models indicate that ascriptive attributes do indeed shape both immigrant groups' likelihood of identifying as American. For each immigrant group, only one of the demographic controls is significant; Indian respondents are likely to identify more strongly as American if they are older, whereas Mexican immigrants are more likely to identify as American if they are men. The results presented in table 1 also indicate that only one of the ascriptive attributes—knowledge of English—shapes both immigrant groups' likelihood of identifying as American (though for Mexican immigrants the effect of language ability is marginally significant). Our results indicate that English-language ability is associated with a stronger identification as American. For Mexican immigrants, self-assessed skin tone is a significant predictor of American identity as well. Holding the other variables in the model at their means, the predicted probability of feeling very strongly American increases 48 percentage points from those immigrants who indicated they spoke little or no English, to those who reported they spoke English very well. Mexican immigrants who assessed their skin tone as very dark (7 on a scale of 1 to 7) were 12 percentage points less likely to identify strongly as American than those who thought of themselves as having a very light skin tone (for this and other calculations of predicted probabilities, see table 2).

These results from the analysis of the survey data reinforce our qualitative findings. Knowledge of English, alongside age and gender, shapes Indian immigrants' national identifications, and both knowledge of English and skin tone shape that of Mexican immigrants. For neither group was undocumented status or religion a significant predictor of respondents' strength of American identification. Although perhaps surprising, this finding mirrors our qualitative interview data, in which few immigrant respondents referenced legal status or religion in reference to feeling excluded from American identity.

Other results from the model indicate the perception of being welcomed by the U.S. born is positive and significant for both Indian

---

12. See note 5: Two hundred Mexican immigrants and forty-eight Indian immigrants completed the surveys face to face rather than by telephone. We controlled for mode of interview in our models.

13. We used the *collin* postestimation package in STATA to check for multicollinearity. *Collin* calculates both the variance inflation factor for each variable in the model, and variable tolerance, defined as 1/VIF, to check on the degree of collinearity, the degree to which a variable could be considered as a linear combination of other independent variables. None of the VIF scores for the variables in the model came close to the level (10) at which we would be concerned about collinearity in the model. The mean VIF for the variables in the model is 1.66.

Table 1. Effects of Ascriptive Characteristics and Welcome on Immigrants' Identification as American

	All Immigrants	Mexicans	Indians
Demographics			
Age	0.035***	-0.008	0.036***
	(0.010)	(0.018)	(0.010)
Gender	0.353	0.571*	0.347
	(0.246)	(0.285)	(0.255)
Percent life in United States	0.337	-1.260	0.368
	(0.574)	(0.960)	(0.584)
Education	-0.210	0.810	-0.238
	(0.175)	(0.138)	(0.186)
Married	-0.053	0.130	-0.035
	(0.329)	(0.295)	(0.346)
Children	-0.098	0.050	-0.100
	(0.095)	(0.243)	(0.096)
Face to face	-0.750*	-0.012	-0.862*
	(0.380)	(0.352)	(0.416)
Metro	0.554*	-0.419	0.552
	(0.237)	(0.279)	(0.243)
Mexican	-1.566*	—	—
	(0.737)		
Ascriptive characteristics			
Undocumented	-0.174	0.039	-0.192
	(0.526)	(0.261)	(0.604)
Skin tone	0.019	-0.352*	0.058
	(0.151)	(0.168)	(0.160)
Christian	0.685	-0.105	0.700
	(0.641)	(0.300)	(0.670)
English fluency	0.732**	0.440	0.755**
	(0.257)	(0.234)	(0.271)
Welcome			
Welcomed by whites	0.587**	0.366*	0.607*
	(0.194)	(0.169)	(0.203)
Welcomed by blacks	0.125	0.395*	0.113
	(0.189)	(0.164)	(0.199)
N	699	382	317
Pseudo R	.14	.08	.13

Source: Authors' calculations based on SINAP 2013 data (Jones-Correa et al. 2013).
Note: Ordered logistic regression is used to estimate model. Standard errors are in parentheses.
* $p<.05$; ** $p<.01$; *** $p<.001$

and Mexican immigrants, confirming that it does help mitigate the negative relationships between skin tone, language, and American identity. However, its effects play out somewhat differently for the two groups. Mexican immigrants' attachment to an American identity was shaped positively and significantly by their sense of being welcomed by both U.S.-born whites and blacks, whereas Indian immigrants' identification was largely shaped by their interactions only with whites, which were positive and significant in the model. Feeling welcomed often by U.S.-born whites increased the probability of Mexican immigrants' identifying as

Table 2. Changes in Predicted Probabilities

Variable	Prob at Min	Prob at Max	Change Min to Max
Predicted probability of feeling "very strongly" American, for Mexican and Indian immigrants			
Age ***	0.22	0.77	0.55
Mexican (min=Mexican) *	0.48	0.12	−0.36
Metro (min=Atlanta) **	0.34	0.47	0.13
English **	0.16	0.64	0.48
Welcomed by whites **	0.24	0.76	0.52
Predicted probability of feeling "very strongly" American, for Mexican immigrants			
Gender (min=male) *	0.04	0.07	0.03
Skin tone *	0.14	0.02	−0.12
English ~	0.05	0.17	0.12
Welcomed by whites *	0.05	0.19	0.14
Welcomed by blacks *	0.06	0.22	0.16
Predicted probability of feeling "very strongly" American, for Indian immigrants			
Age ***	0.23	0.78	0.55
Metro (min=Atlanta) *	0.35	0.48	0.17
English **	0.16	0.65	0.49
Welcomed by whites *	0.24	0.49	0.11
Predicted probability of being a U.S. citizen, Mexican and Indian immigrants			
Age (eighteen to ninety-four) ***	0.37	0.99	0.62
Married (min=unmarried) *	0.96	0.89	−0.12
Percent life in United States (4 to 100) ***	0.21	1	0.79
Identification as American *	0.63	0.93	0.3
Predicted probability of possible return to country of origin, Mexican and Indian immigrants			
Gender (min=female) **	0.04	0.14	0.1
Percent life in the United States*	0.28	0.02	−0.26
Undocumented (undoc =1) ***	0.1	0.02	−0.08

Source: Authors' calculations based on SINAP 2013 data (Jones-Correa et al. 2013).
* $p<.05$; ** $p<.01$; *** $p<.001$

very strongly American by 14 percentage points, but feeling welcomed by U.S.-born blacks increased it by 16 percentage points. For Indian immigrants, feeling often welcomed by whites increased the probability they identify as very strongly American by 11 percentage points.

The results presented are evidence that immigrant respondents experience at least some significant ascriptive barriers to being considered by the U.S. born as fully American, judged primarily by language and skin tone, a finding that dovetails with our qualitative findings. Second, these results show a significant positive relationship between immigrants' perception of being welcomed by the U.S. born and their identification as American. Together, these findings suggest that welcome by the U.S. born may help mitigate some of the negative effects of immigrants' ascriptive characteristics on their feelings of attachment to their identity as

Americans, in line with our expectations (though the results shown in table 1 do not show any significant effects of interactions between skin tone and welcome, at least with respondents' identification as American as the dependent variable).

Multivariate Analyses Predicting Citizenship and Return

We now direct our attention to whether immigrants' identification as American is in turn correlated with their decisions to take on U.S. citizenship, or their plans to eventually return to their countries of origin. In many ways, the models presented in this section mirror the design of the models. The dependent variable for the first model is *citizenship* (coded as a dummy variable, 1 indicating acquisition of U.S. citizenship). For the second model, the dependent variable is respondents' *plans to return to their country of origin* (also coded as a dummy variable, 1 indicating a desire to eventually return to live in the country of origin). Because the dependent variables are binary, we estimated logit models. Age, gender, percent life in the United States are included as control variables along with a dummy variable to indicate whether the interview was conducted over the phone or face to face. As before, variables capturing immigrants' alignment with widely held ascriptive definitions of American identity—respondents' knowledge of English, religion, and skin tone—are included in the models, as well as variables gauging respondent' perceptions of being welcomed by U.S.-born whites and U.S.-born blacks.[14] Finally, American identity is included as a possible predictor of acquisition of *citizenship*. Because the option of citizenship is available only to those immigrants with the appropriate documents, undocumented migrants are not included in that model even though they are included in the second model for *plans to return*. Both models were run for both immigrant groups together, and then separately for each immigrant group (Asian Indian and Mexican). The results for citizenship acquisition are presented in table 3.[15]

As indicated in table 3, for all immigrants, and in the models run separately for both South Asian Indian and Mexican immigrants, age and the percentage of their lives spent in the United States are, unsurprisingly, both significant, positive predictors of acquiring U.S. citizenship. Our results also show that some of the ascriptive characteristics of immigrants matter in shaping their decision to acquire U.S. citizenship. For Mexican immigrants, for example, knowledge of English is significant, with an effect separate from time in the United States (which is controlled for in the model). The negative effects of immigrants' ascriptive characteristics are mitigated, however, by the perceived welcome of whites and blacks. Welcome by whites and blacks is significant, an indicator that they serve to counter the effects of the relationship between ascriptive characteristics and citizenship, just as they did for immigrants' identification as American. However, some of the direction of the effects are counterintuitive: the results indicate that immigrants' perceived welcome by blacks is positively associated with acquisition of citizenship, but immigrants perceived welcome by whites is negatively associated with naturalization as U.S. citizens. These findings are clarified by the interactions between welcome and skin tone in the model, which show that the effects of perceptions of welcome by whites on citizenship acquisition shifts depending on the self-assessed skin tone of the respondent. Darker-skinned respondents who perceived greater welcome by whites were also more likely to have become U.S. citizens. This was the case for both Mexican and Indian immigrants. Among Indian immigrants indicating they have a darker skin tone, however, a greater perceived wel-

---

14. As a robustness check not shown here, we included measures of perceived similarity to respondents, again anticipating the possibility that respondents' perceived welcome simply reflects their feelings of similarity or dissimilarity with other groups. These controls were not significant and their inclusion no effect on the results presented here.

15. As an additional robustness check, we ran the models first including demographic characteristics only, then with demographic and ascriptive characteristics included. These results are presented in table A5. The results are stable across the two sets of results (table 3 and table A5).

Table 3. Effects of Ascriptive Characteristics and Welcome on the Acquisition of Citizenship

	All Immigrants		Mexicans		Indians	
Demographics						
Age	0.103***	0.105***	0.066*	0.043	0.036***	0.109***
	(0.027)	(0.027)	(0.029)	(0.029)	(0.010)	(0.028)
Gender	0.029	0.082	0.160	0.021	0.347	0.122
	(0.399)	(0.433)	(0.498)	(0.535)	(0.255)	(0.461)
Percent life in United States	7.740***	9.209***	3.010*	5.157***	0.368	9.469***
	(1.170)	(1.310)	(1.218)	(1.462)	(0.584)	(1.411)
Education	0.085	0.049	0.058	0.129	−0.238	0.053
	(0.248)	(0.258)	(0.195)	(0.194)	(0.186)	(0.279)
Married	−1.301*	−1.761**	0.283	0.716	−0.035	−1.939**
	(0.577)	(0.637)	(0.532)	(0.564)	(0.346)	(0.702)
Children	−0.324	−0.060	0.119	0.227	−0.100	−0.029
	(0.170)	(0.197)	(0.501)	(0.504)	(0.096)	(.0197)
Face to face	−0.538	0.731	0.533	1.450*	−0.862*	0.809
	(0.625)	(0.710)	(0.557)	(0.652)	(0.416)	(0.760)
Metro	−0.020	−0.800	−0.210	0.207	0.552	−0.093
	(0.370)	(0.386)	(0.506)	(0.486)	(0.243)	(0.399)
Mexican	1.204	−2.390	—	—	—	—
	(1.020)	(1.272)				
Ascriptive characteristics						
Skin tone	0.204	−1.731	0.043	−0.708	−0.192	−1.657
	(0.184)	(0.996)	(0.229)	(0.564)	(0.604)	(1.049)
Christian	−1.303	−1.667*	−1.838*	−1.208	0.058	−1.675*
	(0.779)	(0.806)	(0.718)	(0.886)	(0.160)	(0.825)
English fluency	−0.351	−0.621	1.305**	1.348**	0.700	−0.749
	(0.301)	(0.363)	(0.415)	(0.441)	(0.670)	(0.403)
American identification	0.722**	0.858**	−0.555	−0.543	0.755**	0.899**
	(0.261)	(0.269)	(0.295)	(0.284)	(0.271)	(0.285)

(continued)

Table 3. (continued)

	All Immigrants		Mexicans		Indians	
Welcome						
Welcomed by whites	0.052	−6.983**	−0.556	−2.600*	0.607*	−7.241**
	(0.413)	(2.193)	(0.351)	(1.124)	(0.203)	(2.371)
Welcomed by blacks	−0.343	2.829*	0.368	0.192	0.113	3.190*
	(0.413)	(1.264)	(0.323)	(0.852)	(0.199)	(1.381)
Interactions						
Welcome Wh 1 x Skin tone	—	1.519	—	1.850*	—	1.114
		(1.138)		(0.791)		(1.218)
Welcome Wh 2 x Skin tone	—	4.350***	—	−0.029	—	4.537**
		(1.215)		(0.726)		(1.321)
Welcome Wh 3 x Skin tone	—	4.212**	—	1.806*	—	4.382**
		(1.237)		(0.893)		(1.321)
Welcome Bl 1 x Skin tone	—	−0.662	—	−0.369	—	−0.691
		(0.923)		(0.691)		(1.061)
Welcome Bl 2 x Skin tone	—	−1.984*	—	0.592	—	−2.238*
		(0.890)		(0.790)		(0.965)
Welcome Bl 3 x Skin tone	—	−2.128*	—	−0.146	—	−2.348*
		(0.928)		(0.726)		(1.000)
N	511	511	209	209	302	302
Pseudo R	.40	.37	.30	.30	.39	.39

Source: Authors' calculations based on SINAP 2013 data (Jones-Correa et al. 2013).
Note: Logistic regression is used to estimate model. Standard errors in parentheses.
* *p*<.05; ** *p*<.01; *** *p*<.001

come from U.S.-born blacks was negatively associated with U.S. citizenship. Strength of American identity for its part predicts naturalization in the model for both groups together and for South Asian Indian immigrant respondents separately, but falls just over the .05 significance threshold for Mexican immigrant respondents. The key takeaway here is that although ascriptive characteristics do appear sometimes to affect the decision to acquire U.S. citizenship, and American identity has a positive association with citizenship among both immigrant groups, the role of welcome is complicated by skin tone.

In table 4, we present the results of six additional logit models predicting immigrant respondents' plans to return to their country of origin.[16] The results indicate that for Indian immigrants, intent to return declines over time in the United States but remains significantly greater for men than for women. Here again, the findings indicate that certain ascriptive characteristics shape immigrants' decision making: specifically, undocumented migrants, both Mexican and Indian, are significantly less likely to indicate a desire to return to their countries of origin. Among Indian immigrants, those with darker skin tones were also significantly less likely to say they would consider a return to India. For Indian immigrants, the perception of being welcomed by U.S.-born whites also mattered, because welcome is negatively associated with the desire to return. Taking the analysis a step further, the models with interactions between perceived welcome by whites and skin tone indicate that Indian immigrants with darker skin tones who were welcomed by U.S.-born whites were significantly less likely to indicate that they planned on returning to India. Perceived welcome by U.S.-born blacks had no effect on immigrants' decision to return. Identification as American mattered for Mexican immigrants in particular: strength of American identity was negatively associated with an indication of return. The larger narrative here, then, is that ascriptive characteristics like skin tone and legal status play a role in shaping immigrants' decisions to stay in the United States or return to their countries of origin, but this is mitigated by their perceptions of welcoming by whites (but not blacks) and their identification as Americans.

DISCUSSION AND CONCLUSION

The findings here support earlier, foundational work indicating that conceptions of American identity are very much shaped by ascriptive characteristics (Kinder and Kam 2009; Schildkraut 2007b, 2011; Theiss-Morse 2009; Wong 2010). Our findings also add to a significant literature focused on how Americans of non-European descent are marginalized by these ascriptive notions of identity (Cheryan and Monin 2005; Devos and Banaji 2005; Huynh, Devos, and Altman 2015; Huynh, Devos, and Smalarz 2011; Mukherjee, Molina, and Adams 2012; Pehrson and Green 2010). Here, we extend these lines of research by providing an empirical test of how immigrants' varying ascriptive characteristics, including legal status, influence their adoption of an American identity.

Moreover, this article provides a more nuanced take on the importance of immigrants' context of reception, with important theoretical and empirical implications. Sociologists of immigration have long argued that a receiving country's "context of reception" shapes new immigrants' incorporation paths and identity formation (Portes and Rumbaut 2014). This concept, though, has rarely been operationalized at the individual level. Cumulative interpersonal contacts arguably form the local context of reception as much or more than the broader policy or structural contexts that have been the focus in the literature thus far. Our findings demonstrate how the adoption of American identity is indeed moderated by immigrants' perceptions of their interactions with U.S.-born residents, in particular by their perceptions of welcome by U.S.-born whites and blacks. That is, although ascriptive characteristics (namely, race and skin tone and language) appear to raise barriers to being considered and consid-

---

16. As an additional robustness check, we ran the models first including demographic characteristics only, then with demographic and ascriptive characteristics included. These results are presented in table A6. The results are stable across the two sets of results (table A4 and table A6).

Table 4. Plans to Return to Country of Origin, Mexican and Indian Immigrants

	All Immigrants	Mexican Respondents	Indian Respondents
Demographics			
Age	-0.015	0.018	-0.017
	(0.016)	(0.026)	(0.018)
	-0.019	0.028	-0.020
	(0.019)	(0.024)	(0.021)
Gender	1.292**	0.944	1.350**
	(0.433)	(0.371)	(0.472)
	1.347**	-0.063	1.450**
	(0.451)	(0.368)	(0.494)
Percent life in United States	-3.063*	-1.829	-3.111*
	(1.272)	(1.117)	(1.368)
	-2.956	-2.383	-2.971*
	(1.282)	(1.309)	(1.363)
Education	0.227	0.170	0.246
	(0.250)	(0.154)	(0.277)
	0.152	0.218	0.151
	(0.256)	(0.156)	(0.268)
Married	-0.419	0.134	-0.485
	(0.613)	(0.422)	(0.675)
	-0.334	0.118	-0.406
	(0.663)	(0.404)	(0.728)
Children	-0.074	0.340	-0.089
	(0.249)	(0.412)	(0.297)
	-0.046	0.338	-0.041
	(0.293)	(0.418)	(0.370)
Face to face	-1.391	-0.084	-1.480
	(0.791)	(0.435)	(0.943)
	-1.460	0.049	-1.66
	(0.913)	(0.425)	(1.171)
Metro	-0.804	-0.271	-0.837
	(0.420)	(0.366)	(0.435)
	-0.794	-0.448	-0.845
	(0.434)	(0.381)	(0.463)
Mexican	1.445	—	—
	(1.185)		
	1.132		
	(1.377)		
Ascriptive characteristics			
Undocumented	-1.728	-0.571	-14.69***
	(0.387)	(0.369)	(0.520)
	-1.602***	-0.730	-15.52***
	(0.431)	(0.429)	(0.669)
Skin tone	0.201	0.224	0.206
	(0.244)	(0.204)	(0.262)
	-1.208	-0.216	-13.19***
	(0.843)	(0.430)	(2.197)
Christian	1.250	-0.158	1.260
	(0.898)	(0.935)	(0.925)
	1.150	-0.493	1.145
	(0.937)	(1.010)	(0.956)

	(1)	(2)	(3)	(4)
English	-0.020	-0.057	0.100	-0.016	-0.085
	(0.327)	(0.337)	(0.262)	(0.360)	(0.371)
Identification as American	-0.233	-0.349	-0.593**	-0.211	-0.332
	(0.243)	(0.245)	(0.203)	(0.255)	(0.270)
Welcome					
Welcomed by whites	-0.246	-3.133	0.041	-0.294	-15.68***
	(0.399)	(1.662)	(0.215)	(0.436)	(3.153)
Welcomed by blacks	0.369	1.732	-0.323	0.440	2.532
	(0.380)	(1.568)	(0.229)	(0.428)	(2.085)
Interactions					
Welcome Wh 1*Skin tone	—	1.748	—	—	14.15***
		(0.898)			(2.545)
Welcome Wh 2*Skin tone	—	2.754**	—	—	15.09***
		(0.968)			(2.471)
Welcome Wh 3*Skin tone	—	2.244*	—	—	14.56***
		(1.145)			(2.519)
Welcome Bl 1*Skin tone	—	-0.040	—	—	-0.541
		(0.654)			(0.980)
Welcome Bl 2* Skin tone	—	-1.244	—	—	-0.156
		(0.814)			(0.958)
Welcome Bl 3*Skin tone	—	-0.879	—	—	-1.226
		(1.074)			(1.246)
N	642	642	357	285	285
Pseudo R	.15	.20	.09	.17	.22

Source: Authors' calculations based on SINAP 2013 data (Jones-Correa et al. 2013).

Note: Logistic regression is used to estimate model. Standard errors in parentheses.

* $p<.05$; *** $p<.01$; *** $p<.001$

ering oneself American, perceptions of more welcoming individual-level interactions with the U.S. born can counter this, making both Indian and Mexican immigrants more likely to feel more strongly American.

Results from the multivariate analyses indicate that certain of immigrants' ascriptive characteristics—particularly language and skin tone—shape their identification as Americans. Darker-skinned immigrants and those with less knowledge of English are less likely to identify as American, even among immigrant groups that are very different across many other dimensions, corroborating findings by Schildkraut (2007b). Religion and legal status did not shape American identity, even for immigrants from two groups whose experiences are profoundly shaped by their marginalization by legal status (Mexicans) and their differences from the mainstream along religious lines (South Asian Indians). Aristide Zolberg and Long Witt Woon maintain that language, not religion, is the main dividing line between insiders and outsiders in the United States (1999). Our findings here suggest that language has not lost its relevance.

Although ascriptive characteristics shape immigrants' adoption of a national identity, perceptions of welcome also shape the likelihood that the foreign born identify as American. Here, however, the effects of *who* the foreign born feel welcomed by plays out differently for South Asian Indian and Mexican immigrants. Mexican immigrants' attachment to an American identity is shaped by their interactions with both native-born whites and blacks, whereas that of Indian immigrants is largely shaped by their interactions only with whites. Immigrants' class positions and how these influence both occupational and residential choices in a highly segregated American society likely account for these differences (Lee and Zhou 2015). Indian immigrants are more likely to consider white U.S.-born residents as their relevant peer group; Mexican immigrants, though their relationships with both whites and blacks might be more fraught, see both as relevant.

Similarly, our findings indicate differences in Indian and Mexican immigrants' decisions to adopt U.S. citizenship and to weigh a return to their countries of origin. Identification as American significantly influences Indian immigrants' decisions to become citizens. Mexican immigrants with a stronger attachment to an American identity are significantly more likely to indicate they plan to stay in the United States rather than return to their country of origin. The differences in results here may say less about the differences in effects of American identity for Mexican and Indian immigrants than they do about the relative distribution the options in these two groups: the large majority of Indian respondents having already adopted U.S. citizenship, and an equally large majority of Mexican respondents being, at one time or currently, undocumented (for details, see table A2). In any case, being undocumented or darker skinned diminishes immigrants' desire for return. Certainly, our findings here indicate that for both groups identification as Americans shapes further choices and behaviors, orienting them both toward and away from the United States.

This research opens important new lines of inquiry into immigrant incorporation and the micro-foundations of the context of reception, underlining the importance of the role that immigrants' ascriptive characteristics play in their adoption of national identities, and the ways in which this can be tempered by their interactions with the native born, particularly immigrants' sense of feeling welcomed. Certainly, some aspects of this study bear further exploration—looking more closely, for instance, at other measures of immigrants' positive and negative interpersonal interactions with the native born—but a critical area will be comparative research into the micro-level dynamics of incorporation in other settings, and in other countries. At a time when ascriptive aspects of national identities seem to be increasingly emphasized across a number of industrialized economies, it may be helpful to recognize that national attachments are also formed at the local level, through positive individual-level interactions between people, immigrants and U.S. born.

Table A1. SINAP Survey Sample Characteristics

	U.S.-Born Whites	U.S.-Born Blacks	Mexican Immigrants	Indian Immigrants
Total	N=503	N=502	N=500	N=501
Metropolitan area				
Atlanta	N=250	N=252	N=250	N=250
Fulton County (including Atlanta city)	10%	18%	10%	14%
Clayton County	4	6	6	2
Cobb County	14	7	8	10
DeKalb County	8	14	8	6
Gwinnett County	13	6	18	18
Philadelphia	N=253	N=250	N=250	N=251
Philadelphia County (including Philadelphia city)	12%	35%	29%	11%
Bucks County	9	3	1	12
Chester County	8	2	16	6
Delaware County	9	6	1	7
Montgomery County	13	3	3	14
Gender				
Male	47%	45%	48%	54%
Female	54	55	52	46
Age				
Range	18–94	18–90	18–82	18–91
Mean	49	46	35	45
Education				
Eighth grade or less	0%	1%	25%	0%
Some high school	4	5	21	0
High school degree/GED	20	23	40	6
Some college	24	36	11	14
Four-year college degree	30	20	3	25
Graduate degree	23	14	1	53
Employment status				
Full or part time	58%	55%	64%	71%
Not employed	42	45	36	29
Pre-tax annual household income				
Mean	$91,788	$62,555	$32,761	$114,483
Median	80,000	50,000	20,000	100,000
Home ownership				
Home owner	72%	55%	21%	75%
Rent or other	28	45	79	25
Political ideology				
Strong conservative	14%	8%	14%	3%
Moderate conservative	20	10	28	14
Neither, or don't think of self in these terms	34	53	40	43
Moderate liberal	21	17	11	27
Strong liberal	12	11	8	13

(continued)

Table A1. (*continued*)

	U.S.-Born Whites	U.S.-Born Blacks	Mexican Immigrants	Indian Immigrants
Religion				
Catholic	25%	8%	79%	1%
Protestant (Evangelical or other)	41	53	7	3
Jewish	7	0	0	0
Muslim	1	5	1	5
Hindu	0	0	0	79
Other (including Buddhist, Jain, Sikh)	12	21	5	8
No religious affiliation or no belief in God	14	14	8	5
Skin tone (1=very light; 7=very dark)				
(1) Very light	38%	3%	4%	1%
(2)	24	4	9	2
(3)	17	9	11	10
(4) Medium	15	43	62	56
(5)	3	20	10	21
(6)	2	11	2	7
(7) Very dark	1	10	2	2
Mean	2.31	4.45	3.79	4.24
Mode of survey				
Telephone	N=0	N=0	N=300 (60%)	N=455 (90%)
Face to face	N=503	N=502	N=200 (40%)	N=48 (10%)
Language of survey				
English	N=503	N=502	N=114 (23%)	N=501
Spanish			N=386 (77%)	

Source: Authors' calculations based on SINAP 2013 data (Jones-Correa et al. 2013).
Note: Percentages are valid percentages and do not include missing data.

Table A2. Additional SINAP Survey Sample Characteristics for Mexican and Indian Immigrants

	Mexican Immigrants	Indian Immigrants
Total	N=500	N=501
Years living in the United States		
Range	3–46	1–55
Mean	16	21
Decade of arrival		
Before 1980	3%	20%
1980s	13	16
1990s	36	34
2000–2013	48	30
Percent of life spent in United States		
Mean	47%	47%
Citizenship status		
Not a U.S. citizen	78%	21%
U.S. citizen	23	79
Years since becoming a U.S. citizen		
Range	0–32	0–48
Mean	11	15
Legal status		
Currently undocumented	36%	1%
Ever undocumented	62	3
English language proficiency		
Not at all	9%	1%
Just a little	43	4
Pretty well	30	30
Very well	17	66
State/territory of origin		
Mexico (top five states)[a]		
Guanajuato	15%	
Guerrero	13	
Puebla	10	
Federal district (state or city)	10	
Jalisco	9	
India (top five states)		
Gujarat		24%
Maharashtra		13
Kerala		9
Andhra Pradesh		8
Delhi (union territory)		8

Source: Authors' calculations based on SINAP 2013 data (Jones-Correa et al. 2013).
Note: Percentages are valid percentages and do not include missing data.
[a] Mexican immigrant respondents who reported their state or territory of origin hailed from twenty-nine of the thirty-one states in Mexico, plus the Mexico state or city federal district. Indian immigrant respondents who reported their state or territory of origin hailed from twenty-eight of the twenty-eight states and seven union categories that existed in India in 2013.

Table A3. Descriptive Statistics for Variables in the Models

Variable	Observations	Mean	Standard Deviation	Min	Max
American ID	1,981	2.2	1.02	3	0
Age	1,985	43.8	16.6	18	94
Gender (male = 1)	2,016	0.48	0.5	0	1
Percent life in United States	1,776	0.77	0.3	0.04	1
Education	1,930	4.07	1.5	0	1
Married	2,016	0.52	0.5	0	1
Children	2,016	0.4	0.49	0	1
Face-to-face interview	2,016	0.12	0.33	0	1
Metro (Atlanta = 1)	2,016	0.5	0.5	0	1
Undocumented	2,016	0.13	0.34	0	1
Skin tone	2,000	3.71	1.45	1	7
Christian	2,016	0.7	0.46	0	1
English	986	2.09	0.92	0	3
Welcomed by whites	1,973	2.16	0.88	0	3
Welcomed by blacks	1,965	2.06	0.92	0	3

Source: Authors' calculations based on SINAP 2013 data (Jones-Correa et al. 2013).

Table A4. Identification as American, Reduced Models

	All Immigrants		Mexicans		Indians	
Demographics						
Age	0.287**	0.033***	−0.010	0.000	0.029**	0.034***
	(0.009)	(0.009)	(0.018)	(0.019)	(0.010)	(0.010)
Gender	0.462*	0.489*	0.646*	0.527	0.456	0.490*
	(0.227)	(0.232)	(0.287)	(0.299)	(0.234)	(0.024)
Percent life in	1.099*	0.452	−0.296	−1.197	1.124*	0.482
United States	(0.540)	(0.547)	(0.892)	(0.973)	(0.549)	(0.557)
Education	−0.160	−0.201	0.234	0.120	−0.045	−0.230
	(0.142)	(0.174)	(0.141)	(0.147)	(0.151)	(0.190)
Married	−0.080	−0.073	0.042	0.047	−0.056	−0.056
	(0.311)	(0.317)	(0.289)	(0.307)	(0.325)	(0.332)
Children	−0.159	−0.147	0.074	0.023	−0.164	−0.150
	(0.103)	(0.094)	(0.250)	(0.259)	(0.104)	(0.095)
Face to face	−1.420	−1.096	−0.322	−0.274	−1.512**	−1.209**
	(0.412)	(0.400)	(0.350)	(0.351)	(0.445)	(0.442)
Metro	0.549*	0.603	−0.551	−0.478	0.550*	0.604*
	(0.229)	(0.228)	(0.268)	(0.293)	(0.234)	(0.233)
Mexican	−1.670***	−1.826	—	—	—	—
	(0.413)	(0.735)				
Ascriptive characteristics						
Undocumented	—	−0.398	—	−0.052	—	−0.445
		(0.555)		(0.262)		(0.636)
Skin tone	—	0.005	—	−0.300	—	0.035
		(0.149)		(0.158)		(0.158)
Christian	—	0.619	—	−0.197	—	0.634
		(0.619)		(0.250)		(0.645)
English fluency	—	0.727**	—	0.520*	—	0.741**
		(0.242)		(0.237)		(0.255)
N	729	713	393	385	336	328
Pseudo R	.10	.11	.02	.04	.09	.11

Source: Authors' calculations based on SINAP 2013 data (Jones-Correa et al. 2013).
Note: Ordered logistic regression is used to estimate model. Standard errors in parentheses.
* $p<.05$; ** $p<.01$; *** $p<.001$

Table A5. Acquisition of Citizenship, Reduced Models

	All Immigrants		Mexicans		Indians	
Demographics						
Age	0.102***	0.110***	0.278	0.068*	0.104***	0.112***
	(0.023)	(0.280)	(0.028)	(0.028)	(0.023)	(0.025)
Gender	−0.184	−0.101	0.614	0.329	−0.193	−0.107
	(0.332)	(0.389)	(0.469)	(0.495)	(0.340)	(0.401)
Percent life in United States	7.510***	7.721***	4.610**	3.084**	7.539***	7.809***
	(1.090)	(1.145)	(1.392)	(1.228)	(1.120)	(1.185)
Education	−0.023	0.003	0.265	0.081	−0.039	−0.076
	(0.200)	(0.241)	(0.206)	(0.201)	(0.209)	(0.254)
Married	−0.924	−1.307*	0.262	0.381	−0.949	−1.361*
	(0.534)	(0.552)	(0.514)	(0.569)	(0.551)	(0.575)
Children	−0.367*	−0.264	0.626	0.247	−0.375*	−0.271
	(0.164)	(0.159)	(0.527)	(0.495)	(0.168)	(0.163)
Face to face	0.769	0.701	0.726	0.809	0.742	0.647
	(0.556)	(0.633)	(0.444)	(0.505)	(0.574)	(0.657)
Metro	0.044	0.011	−0.599	−0.447	0.052	0.004
	(0.319)	(0.371)	(0.411)	(0.504)	(0.324)	(0.382)
Mexican	−2.566***	−1.156	—	—	—	—
	(0.714)	(1.073)				
Ascriptive characteristics						
Skin tone	—	0.215	—	−0.035	—	0.196
		(0.187)		(0.220)		(0.228)
Christian	—	−1.316	—	−1.465*	—	−1.343
		(0.828)		(0.698)		(0.846)
English fluency	—	−0.308	—	1.273**	—	−0.358
		(0.307)		(0.416)		(0.317)
American identity	—	0.670**	—	−0.610*	—	0.694**
		(0.252)		(0.308)		(0.262)
N	552	524	221	211	331	313
Pseudo R	.35	.40	.21	.29	.35	.40

Source: Authors' calculations based on SINAP 2013 data (Jones-Correa et al. 2013).
Note: Logistic regression is used to estimate model. Standard errors in parentheses.
* $p<.05$; ** $p<.01$; *** $p<.001$

Table A6. Return to Country of Origin, Reduced Models

	All Immigrants		Mexican Respondents		Indian Respondents	
Demographics						
Age	-0.250	-0.013	0.016	0.017	-0.026	-0.014
	(0.016)	(0.016)	(0.022)	(0.025)	(0.016)	(0.016)
Gender	1.250**	1.356**	-0.066	0.114	1.317**	1.421**
	(0.423)	(0.431)	(0.349)	(0.376)	(0.459)	(0.471)
Percent life in United States	-3.474**	-3.110*	-1.366	-1.885	-3.532**	-3.155*
	(1.077)	(1.217)	(1.015)	(1.127)	(1.125)	(1.292)
Education	0.277	0.190	0.201	0.166	0.292	0.199
	(0.021)	(0.240)	(0.150)	(0.153)	(0.231)	(0.264)
Married	-0.091	-0.353	0.099	0.102	-0.127	-0.403
	(0.588)	(0.602)	(0.392)	(0.420)	(0.633)	(0.661)
Children	-0.086	-0.094	0.175	0.283	-0.093	-0.112
	(0.174)	(0.220)	(0.377)	(0.412)	(0.187)	(0.261)
Face to face	-1.274*	-1.296	-0.268	-0.890	-0.133	-1.360
	(0.594)	(0.683)	(0.380)	(0.442)	(0.686)	(0.820)
Metro	-0.704	-0.858*	-0.326	-0.228	-0.717	-0.890*
	(0.383)	(0.421)	(0.305)	(0.363)	(0.396)	(0.437)
Mexican	1.953**	1.195	—	—	—	—
	(0.616)	(1.124)				
Ascriptive characteristics						
Undocumented	—	-1.676***	—	-0.491	—	-14.61***
		(0.366)		(0.378)		(0.497)
Skin tone	—	0.211	—	0.208	—	0.219
		(0.242)		(0.213)		(0.261)
Christian	—	1.380	—	-0.249	—	1.410
		(0.879)		(0.952)		(0.903)
English fluency	—	0.074	—	0.102	—	0.099
		(0.340)		(0.256)		(0.376)
American identity	—	-0.232	—	-0.679**	—	-0.214
		(0.225)		(0.209)		(0.239)
N	677	665	369	360	308	295
Pseudo R	.14	.15	.03	.08	.14	.17

Source: Authors' calculations based on SINAP 2013 data (Jones-Correa et al. 2013).
Note: Logistic regression is used to estimate model. Standard errors in parentheses.
* $p<.05$; ** $p<.01$; *** $p<.001$

REFERENCES

Alba, Richard D., and Victor Nee. 2003. *Remaking the American Mainstream: Assimilation and Contemporary Immigration*. Cambridge, Mass.: Harvard University Press.

Atlanta Regional Commission. 2015. "A Regional Snapshot of Ethnic Populations: Foreign-Born, Hispanic-Latinos & Asians." Atlanta, Ga.: New Voices, Global Atlanta Snapshots.

Baker, Bryan, and Nancy Rytina. 2013. "Estimates of the Unauthorized Immigrant Population Residing in the United States: January 2012." *Population Estimates*, March. Washington: U.S. Department of Homeland Security, Office of Immigration Statistics.

Bean, Frank D., Susan K. Brown, and James D. Bachmeier. 2015. *Parents Without Papers: The Progress and Pitfalls of Mexican American Integration*. New York: Russell Sage Foundation.

Bergmann, Jonas. 2016. "Building Contact Between Immigrants and Host Communities Is Vital to Integration—And Should Be a Central Goal of the UN Summit on Refugees and Migrants." World Bank. Accessed March 14, 2018. http://blogs.worldbank.org/peoplemove/building-contact-between-immigrants-and-host-communities-vital-integration-and-should-be-central.

Bloemraad, Irene. 2006. *Becoming a Citizen: Incorporating Immigrants and Refugees in the United States and Canada*. Berkeley: University of California Press.

Brettell, Caroline B., and Faith G. Nibbs. 2010. "Immigrant Suburban Settlement and the 'Threat' to Middle Class Status and Identity: The Case of Farmer's Branch, Texas." *International Migration* 49(1): 1–30.

Calvo, Rocio, Joanna M. Jablonska-Bayro, and Mary C. Waters. 2017. "Obamacare in Action: How Access to the Health Care System Contributes to Immigrants' Sense of Belonging." *Journal of Ethnic and Migration Studies* 43(12): 2020–36.

Chakravorty, Sanjoy, Devesh Kapur, and Nirvikar Singh. 2017. *The Other One Percent: Indians in America*. New York: Oxford University Press.

Cheryan, Sapna, and Benoit Monin. 2005. "'Where Are You *Really* From?' Asian Americans and Identity Denial." *Journal of Personality and Social Psychology* 89(5): 717–30.

Citrin Jack, Beth Reingold, and Donald P. Green. 1990. "American Identity and the Politics of Ethnic Change." *Journal of Politics* 52(4): 1124–54.

Citrin, Jack, and Matthew Wright. 2009. "Defining the Circle of We: American Identity and Immigration Policy." *The Forum* 7(3): 1–20.

Creighton, Matthew, and Michael Katz. 2007. "Immigrants and Suburbs: Growth and Distribution in Greater Philadelphia, 1970–2000: A Tract-Level Analysis." *Philadelphia Migration Project* working paper. Philadelphia: University of Pennsylvania.

De Genova, Nicholas. 2002. "Migrant 'Illegality' and Deportability in Everyday Life." *Annual Review of Anthropology* 31(1): 419–47.

de Graauw, Els. 2016. *Making Immigrant Rights Real: Non-Profits and the Politics of Integration in San Francisco*. Ithaca, N.Y.: Cornell University Press.

Devos, Thierry, and Mazharin R. Banaji. 2005. "American = White?" *Journal of Personality and Social Psychology* 88(3): 447–66.

Devos, Thierry, Kelly Gavin, and Francisco J. Quintana. 2010. "Say 'Adios' to the American Dream: The Interplay Between Ethnic and National Identity Among Latino and Caucasian Americans." *Cultural Diversity and Ethnic Minority Psychology* 16(1): 37–49.

Espenshade, Thomas J., and Charles A. Calhoun. 1993. "An Analysis of Public Opinion toward Undocumented Immigration." *Population Research and Policy Review* 12(3): 189–224.

Espenshade, Thomas J., and Katherine Hempstead. 1996. "Contemporary American Attitudes Toward U.S. Immigration." *International Migration Review* 30(2): 535–70.

Fox, Jonathan. 2011. "Indigenous Mexican Migrants." In *Beyond La Frontera: The History of US-Mexico Migration*, edited by Mark Overmyer-Velázquez. New York: Oxford University Press.

Frey, William H. 2001. "Census 2000 Shows Large Black Return to the South, Reinforcing the Region's 'White-Black' Demographic Profile." *Population Studies Center* research report no. 01–473. Ann Arbor: University of Michigan, Institute for Social Research.

Fussell, Elizabeth. 2014. "Warmth of the Welcome: Attitudes Toward Immigrants and Immigration Policy in the United States." *Annual Review of Sociology* 40(1): 479–98.

García, San Juanita. 2017. "Racializing 'Illegality': An Intersectional Approach to Understanding How Mexican-Origin Women Navigate an Anti-Immigrant Climate." *Sociology of Race and Ethnicity* 3(4): 474–90.

Gast, Melanie Jones, and Dina G. Okamoto. 2016. "Moral or Civic Ties? Deservingness and Engagement among Undocumented Latinas in Non-Profit Organizations." *Journal of Ethnic and Migration Studies* 42(12): 2013–30.

George, Rosemary Marangoly. 1997. "'From Expatriate Aristocrat to Immigrant Nobody': South Asian Racial Strategies in the Southern California Context." *Diaspora: A Journal of Transnational Studies* 6(1): 31–60.

Gonzales, Roberto G. 2015. *Lives in Limbo: Undocumented and Coming of Age in America*. Berkeley: University of California Press.

Grieco, Elizabeth M., Yesenia D. Acosta, G. Patricia de la Cruz, Christine Gambino, Thomas Gryn, Luke J. Larsen, Edward N. Trevelyan, and Nathan P. Walters. 2012. *The Foreign Born Population in the United States: 2010*. American Community Survey Reports. Washington: U.S. Department of Commerce.

Hafsa, Mohamed, and Thierry Devos. 2014. "Shades of American Identity: Implicit Relations between Ethnic and National Identities." *Social and Personality Psychology Compass* 8(12): 739–54.

Hansen, Art. 2005. "Black and White and the Other: International Immigration and Change in Metropolitan Atlanta." In *Beyond the Gateway: Immigrants in a Changing America*, edited by Elzbieta M. Gozdziak and Susan F. Martin. Lanham, Md.: Lexington Books.

Hochschild, Jennifer L., and Vesla Weaver. 2007. "The Skin Color Paradox and the American Racial Order." *Social Forces* 86(2): 643–70.

Hochschild, Jennifer L., Vesla Weaver, and Traci Burch. 2012. *Creating a New Racial Order: How Immigration, Multiracialism, Genomics, and the Young Can Remake Race in America*. Princeton, N.J.: Princeton University Press.

Hopkins, Daniel J. 2014. "The Upside of Accents: Language, Inter-Group Difference and Attitudes Toward Immigration." *British Journal of Political Science* 45(3): 1–27.

Huang, Xi, and Cathy Yang Liu. 2017. "Welcoming Cities: Immigration Policy at the Local Government Level." *Urban Affairs Review* 75(3): 433–42.

Huntington, Samuel P. 2004. *Who Are We: The Challenges to America's National Identity*. New York: Simon and Schuster.

Huynh, Que-Lam, Thierry Devos, and Hannah R. Altman. 2015. "Boundaries of American Identity: Relations Between Ethnic Group Prototypicality and Policy Attitudes." *Political Psychology* 36(4): 449–68.

Huynh, Que-Lam, Thierry Devos, and Laura Smalarz. 2011. "Perpetual Foreigner in One's Own Land: Potential Implications for Identity and Psychological Adjustment." *Journal of Social and Clinical Psychology* 30(2): 133–62.

Jiménez, Tomás R. 2010. *Replenished Ethnicity: Mexican Americans, Mexican Immigrants, and Identity*. Berkeley: University of California Press.

Jiménez, Tomás, and Adam Horowitz. 2013. "When White is Just Alright. How Immigrants Redefine Achievement and Reconfigure the Racial Ethnic Hierarchy." *American Sociological Review* 78(5): 849–71.

Jones, Jennifer A. 2012. "Blacks May Be Second Class, but They Can't Make Them Leave: Mexican Racial Formation and Immigrant Status in Winston Salem." *Latino Studies* 10(1–2): 60–80.

Jones-Correa, Michael. 1998. "Different Paths: Gender, Immigration and Political Participation." *International Migration Review* 32(2): 326–49.

———. 2011. "All Immigration Is Local: Receiving Communities and Their Role in Successful Immigrant Integration." Washington, D.C.: Center for American Progress.

Jones-Correa, Michael, Helen B. Marrow, Dina G. Okamoto, and Linda R. Tropp. 2013. "Study of Immigrants and Natives in Atlanta and Philadelphia (SINAP)." *Philadelphia-Atlanta*. Accessed January 21, 2018. http://philadelphia-atlanta.weebly.com.

Joshi, Khyati. 2006. *New Roots in America's Sacred Ground: Religion, Race, and Ethnicity in Indian America*. New Brunswick, N.J.: Rutgers University Press.

Kalita, S. Mitra. 2003. *Suburban Sahibs: Three Immigrant Families and Their Passage from India to America*. New Brunswick, N.J.: Rutgers University Press.

Kasinitz, Philip, John H. Mollenkopf, Mary C. Waters, and Jennifer Holdaway. 2008. *Inheriting the City: The Children of Immigrants Come of Age*. Cambridge, Mass. / New York: Harvard University Press / Russell Sage Foundation.

Kinder, Donald R., and Cindy Kam. 2009. *Us and Them: Ethnocentric Foundations of American Opinion*. Chicago: Chicago University Press.

Koshy, Susan. 1998. "Category Crisis: South Asian Americans and Questions of Race and Ethnicity." *Diaspora* 7(3): 285–320.

Kumar, Amitava. 2017. "Being Indian in Trump's America." *New Yorker*, March 22.

Kurien, Prema. 2001. "Religion, Ethnicity, and Politics: Hindu and Muslim Indian Immigrants in the United States." *Ethnic and Racial Studies* 24(2): 263–93.

———. 2006. "Multiculturalism and "American" Religion: The Case of Hindu Indian Americans." *Social Forces* 85(2): 723–41.

Lee, Jennifer, and Min Zhou. 2015. *The Asian American Achievement Paradox*. New York: Russell Sage Foundation.

Leonard, Karen Isaksen. 2007. "India." In *The New Americans: A Guide to Immigration Since 1965*, edited by Mary C. Waters and Reed Ueda with Helen B. Marrow. Cambridge, Mass.: Harvard University Press.

Mallet, Marie L., Rocío Calvo, and Mary C. Waters. 2017. "'I Don't Belong Anymore': Undocumented Latino Immigrants Encounter Social Services in the United States." *Hispanic Journal of Behavioral Sciences* 39(3): 267–82.

Marrow, Helen B. 2011a. *New Destination Dreaming: Immigration, Race, and Legal Status in the Rural American South*. Stanford, Calif.: Stanford University Press.

———. 2011b. "Race and the New Southern Migration, 1986 to the Present." In *Beyond La Frontera: The History of US-Mexico Migration*, edited by Mark Overmyer-Velázquez. New York: Oxford University Press.

———. 2012. "Deserving to a Point: Unauthorized Immigrants in San Francisco's Universal Access Healthcare Model." *Social Science & Medicine* 74(6): 846–54.

Marrow, Helen B., and Tiffany D. Joseph. 2015. "Excluded and Frozen Out: Unauthorised Immigrants' (Non)Access to Care after Us Health Care Reform." *Journal of Ethnic and Migration Studies* 41(14): 2253–73.

Massey, Douglas S. 2007. *Categorically Unequal: The American Stratification System*. New York: Russell Sage Foundation.

———, ed. 2008. *New Faces in New Places: The Changing Geography of American Immigration*. New York: Russell Sage Foundation.

———. 2013. "America's Immigration Policy Fiasco: Learning from Past Mistakes." *Dædalus: Journal of the American Academy of Arts & Sciences* 142(3): 1–15.

Massey, Douglas S., and Magaly R. Sánchez. 2010. *Brokered Boundaries: Immigrant Identity in Anti-Immigrant Times*. New York: Russell Sage Foundation.

Massey, Douglas S., Jorge Durand, and Nolan J. Malone. 2002. *Beyond Smoke and Mirrors: Mexican Immigration in an Era of Economic Integration*. New York: Russell Sage Foundation.

Masuoka, Natalie, and Jane Junn. 2013. *The Politics of Belonging: Race, Public Opinion and Immigration*. Chicago: University of Chicago Press.

Menjívar, Cecilia. 2016. "Immigrant Criminalization in Law and the Media: Effects on Latino Immigrant Workers' Identities in Arizona." *American Behavioral Scientist* 60(5–6): 597–616.

Menjívar, Cecilia, and Cynthia Bejarano. 2004. "Latino Immigrants' Perceptions of Crime and Police Authorities in the United States: A Case Study from the Phoenix Metropolitan Area." *Ethnic and Racial Studies* 27(1): 120–48.

Mishra, Sangay. 2016. *Desis Divided: The Political Lives of South Asian Immigrants*. Minneapolis: University of Minnesota Press.

Mukherjee, Sahana, Ludwin Molina, and Glenn Adams. 2012. "National Identity and Immigration Policy: Concern for Legality or Ethnocentric Exclusion?" *Analyses of Social Issues and Public Policy* 12(1): 21–32.

National Academies of Sciences, Engineering, and Medicine (NASEM). 2015. *The Integration of Immigrants into American Society*, edited by Mary C. Waters and Marisa Gerstein Pineau. Washington, D.C.: National Academies Press.

Nee, Victor, and Hilary Holbrow. 2013. "Why Asian Americans Are Becoming Mainstream." *Dædalus: The Journal of the American Academy of Arts & Sciences* 142(3): 65–75.

Odem, Mary E. 2008. "Unsettled in the Suburbs: Latino Immigration and Ethnic Diversity in Metro Atlanta." In *Twenty-First Century Gateways: Immigrant Integration in Suburban America*, edited by Audrey Singer, Susan W. Hardwick, and Caroline B. Brettell. Washington, D.C.: Brookings Institution Press.

Okamoto, Dina G., and Kim Ebert. 2016. "Group Boundaries, Immigrant Inclusion, and the Politics of Immigrant-Native Relations." *American Behavioral Scientist* 60(2): 224–50.

Pehrson, Samuel, and Eva Green. 2010. "Who We Are and Who Can Join Us: National Identity Content and Entry Criteria for New Immigrants." *Journal of Social Issues* 66(4): 695–716.

Perlmann, Joel. 2005. *Italians Then, Mexicans Now: Immigrant Origins and Second-Generation Progress, 1890 to 2000.* New York: Russell Sage Foundation.

Pettigrew, Thomas F., and Linda R. Tropp. 2011. *When Groups Meet: The Dynamics of Intergroup Contact.* New York: Psychology Press.

Pew Research Center. 2010. "Public Remains Conflicted Over Islam." Washington, D.C.: Pew Forum on Religion & Public Life and Pew Research Center for the People & the Press. Accessed January 21, 2018. http://pewresearch.org/pubs/1706/poll-americans-views-of-muslims.

———. 2012. "Asian Americans: A Mosaic of Faiths." Washington, D.C.: Pew Research Center.

———. 2015. "Modern Immigration Wave Brings 59 Million to U.S., Driving Population Growth and Change Through 2065." Washington, D.C.: Pew Research Center.

Phelps, Joshua M., Reidar Ommundsen, Salman Turken, and Pal Ulleberg. 2013. "Intergroup Perception and Proactive Majority Integration Attitudes." *Social Psychology* 44(3): 196–207.

Portes, Alejandro, and Rubén G. Rumbaut. 2014. *Immigrant America: A Portrait*, 4th ed. Berkeley: University of California Press.

Rangaswamy, Padma. 2000. *Namaste America: Indian Immigrants in an American Metropolis.* University Park: University of Pennsylvania Press.

———. 2007. "South Asians in Dunkin' Donuts: Niche Development in the Franchise Industry." *Journal of Ethnic and Migration Studies* 33(4): 671–86.

Rydell, Robert J., David L. Hamilton, and Thierry Devos. 2010. "Now They Are American, Now They Are Not: Valence as a Determinant of the Inclusion of African Americans in the American Identity." *Social Cognition* 28(2): 161–79.

Samson, Frank. 2013. "Multiple Group Threat and Malleable White Attitudes Towards Academic Merit." *Du Bois Review* 10(1): 233–60.

Sandhu, Sabeen. 2012. *Asian Indian Professionals: The Culture of Success.* El Paso, Tex.: LFB Scholarly Publishing.

Schildkraut, Deborah. 2007a. "Defining American Identity in the 21st Century: How Much 'There' Is There?" *Journal of Politics* 69(3): 597–615.

———. 2007b. *Press ONE for English: Language Policy, Public Opinion, and American Identity.* Princeton, N.J.: Princeton University Press.

———. 2011. *Americanism in the Twenty-First Century: Public Opinion in the Age of Immigration.* Cambridge: Cambridge University Press.

———. 2014. "Boundaries of American Identity: Evolving Understandings of 'Us'." *Annual Review of Political Science* 17(1): 441–60.

Singer, Audrey. 2004. "The Rise of New Immigrant Gateways." Washington, D.C.: Brookings Institution. Accessed May 3, 2018. https://www.brookings.edu/research/the-rise-of-new-immigrant-gateways/.

Singer, Audrey, Domenic Vitiello, Michael Katz, and David Park. 2008. "Recent Immigration to Philadelphia: Regional Change in a Re-Emerging Gateway." Washington, D.C.: Brookings Institution, Metropolitan Policy Program.

Sue, Christina A. 2013. *Land of the Cosmic Race: Race Mixture, Racism, and Blackness in Mexico.* New York: Oxford University Press.

Suro, Roberto. 2009. "America's Views of Immigration: Evidence from Public Opinion Surveys." Transatlantic Council on Migration, Migration Policy Institute. Accessed March 14, 2018 https://www.migrationpolicy.org/pubs/TCM-USPublicOpinion.pdf

Telles, Edward E., and Vilma Ortiz. 2008. *Generations of Exclusion: Mexican Americans, Assimilation, and Race.* New York: Russell Sage.

Theiss-Morse, Elizabeth. 2009. *Who Counts as an American?: The Boundaries of National Identity* Cambridge: Cambridge University Press.

Tropp, Linda R., Dina G. Okamoto, Helen B. Marrow, and Michael Jones-Correa. 2018. "How Contact Experiences Shape Welcoming: Perspectives from U.S.-Born and Immigrant Groups." *Social Psychology Quarterly*, published online March 23, 2018. DOI: 10.1177/0190272517747265.

Vaughn, Bobby. 2005. "Afro-Mexico: Blacks, Indígenas, Politics, and the Greater Diaspora." In *Neither Enemies Nor Friends: Latinos, Blacks, Afro-Latinos*, edited by Anani Dzidzienyo and Suzanne Oboler. New York: Palgrave Macmillan.

Vaughn, Bobby, and Ben Vinson III. 2007. "Unfinished Migrations: From the Mexican South to the American South—Impressions on Afro-Mexican Migration to North Carolina." In *Beyond Slavery: The Multilayered Legacy of Africans in Latin America and the Caribbean*, edited by Darién J. Davis. Lanham, Md.: Rowman & Littlefield.

Villareal, Andrés. 2010. "Stratification by Skin Color in Contemporary Mexico." *American Sociological Review* 75(5): 652–78.

Welcoming America. 2017. "Welcoming Week: Connecting Neighbors, Serving Communities." Atlanta, Ga.: Welcoming America. Accessed January 21, 2018. https://www.welcomingamerica.org/programs/welcoming-week.

Williams, Linda M. 2015. "Beyond Enforcement: Welcomeness, Local Law Enforcement, and Immigrants." *Public Administration Review* 75(3): 433–42.

Winders, Jamie. 2013. *Nashville in the New Millennium: Immigrant Settlement, Urban Transformation, and Social Belonging.* New York: Russell Sage Foundation.

Wong, Cara. 2010. *Boundaries of Obligation in American Politics: Geographic, National and Racial Communities.* New York: Cambridge University Press.

Zhou, Min, and Carl L. Bankston III. 2017. "Growing Up Under the Shadow of the Model Minority: Diverse Experiences of the Children of Asian Immigrants." Paper presented at the "Children of Immigrants in New Places of Settlement" Conference, American Academy of Arts and Sciences. Cambridge, Mass. (April 19–21).

Zolberg, Aristide, and Long Witt Woon. 1999. "Why Islam Is Like Spanish: Cultural Incorporation in Europe and the United States." *Politics and Society* 27(1): 5–38.

Zong, Jie, and Jeanne Batalova. 2016. "Mexican Immigrants in the United States." *Migration Information Source*, March 17. Accessed January 21, 2018. https://www.migrationpolicy.org/article/mexican-immigrants-united-states.

Shifting U.S. Racial and Ethnic Identities and Sikh American Activism

PREMA KURIEN

This article brings a historical and transnational perspective to the changing identities of immigrants and their census categorization, and emphasizes the role of immigrant political activism in identity change. The focus is on Sikh Americans, the oldest South Asian group in the United States, and on three periods when Sikh Americans rallied to change their identity. Early in the twentieth century, Sikhs mounted legal and political campaigns to obtain U.S. citizenship by claiming Aryan roots. Subsequently, attacks against Sikhs in India beginning in 1984 led to a movement to disavow an Indian identity. Finally, a post-9/11 backlash against men with turbans and beards sparked a campaign to be recognized as an American religious group as well as an ethnic group distinct from Indian Americans.

Keywords: Sikh Americans, religion, majority and minority status, race and ethnic identity, South Asians, citizenship

Michael Omi and Howard Winant point out that racial classification in the United States has been, from its inception, an inherently political project (2015). Race and ethnicity categories in the census are part of the "nation-making process" in which the state delineates the groups that belong to the national community (Jung 2015). The literature on racial and ethnic categorization in the United States examines the meanings associated with what has been called "corporeal distinction," or with national ancestry and cultural heritage (Omi and Winant 2015, 107). It focuses on the ways these factors are shaped by individual or group-level circumstances intersecting with state structures and civil society. In other words, this literature concentrates almost entirely on conditions within the United States: on the U.S. racial system or structure (Jung 2015), how immigrants undergo the process of "racial acculturation" to this structure (Roth 2012), and on the micro-level racial fluidity that some individuals can achieve within this system (Saperstein and Penner 2012).

Prema Kurien is professor and chair of sociology, as well as the founding director of the Asian/Asian American Studies program at Syracuse University.

© 2018 Russell Sage Foundation. Kurien, Prema. 2018. "Shifting U.S. Racial and Ethnic Identities and Sikh American Activism." *RSF: The Russell Sage Foundation Journal of the Social Sciences* 4(5): 81–98. DOI: 10.7758/RSF.2018.4.5.04. The research for this article was conducted as part of two larger projects funded by a Woodrow Wilson International Center Fellowship, a Carnegie Corporation grant (#D09048), two National Science Foundation grants (SES-1323881 and SES-1528344), and grants from Appleby Mosher and PARCC at Syracuse University. Direct correspondence to: Prema Kurien at pkurien@maxwell.syr.edu, Department of Sociology, Maxwell 302, Syracuse University, Syracuse, NY 13244.

Open Access Policy: *RSF: The Russell Sage Foundation Journal of the Social Sciences* is an open access journal. This article is published under a Creative Commons Attribution-NonCommercial-NoDerivs 3.0 Unported License.

The introduction of the *transnational turn* in U.S. immigration studies, however, cautions us about the danger of methodological nationalism, or the assumption that key social and political forces are contained or confined by the nation-state (Basch et al. 1994; Wimmer and Schiller 2002). In the case of immigrant identities in the United States, homeland or other international factors can play an important role in how groups are categorized. Sociopolitical developments between majority and minority groups in host countries due to global events can bring about shifts in group identification. In other words, the process of immigrant identity change may not simply be a result of individual immigrants assimilating to, or struggling with, the domestic racial system. It is often an outcome of group-based political mobilization shaped by transnational factors. Finally, the two processes—transnationalism and immigrant political mobilization—can intersect and interact. A change in the relationship between majority and minority groups in the country of origin may lead groups classified under the same ethnoracial category in the host country to self-identify and mobilize in different ways. These changes, as well as other global events, can affect groups differently within the United States, resulting in new patterns of activism around identity and categorization.

This article develops these theoretical arguments by focusing on Sikhs, an ethnoreligious group originating in the Punjab region of South Asia, which has been very active in the U.S. public sphere around racial, ethnic, and religious rights over the past hundred years. (Punjab was partitioned between India and Pakistan in 1947.) South Asians have been classified in a number of ways in the U.S. Census from 1910 to 1980 (Das Gupta 2006, 32–33; Haney López 1996). Sikhs are the earliest group of South Asian migrants to North America and dominated the migration from British India at the turn of the twentieth century. This migration was concentrated on the west coasts of Canada and the United States.

Because the census does not have a religion category, we do not have an accurate estimate of how many Sikhs live in the United States at the current time. According to Pew Research Center estimates, at least two hundred thousand Sikhs lived in the United States in 2012. This compares with around 1.6 million Hindus, who make up 51 percent of the Indian American population (Pew Research Center 2015). However, Sikh groups argue that the more accurate number of Sikhs in the country is between five hundred thousand to one million.[1] In the postcolonial period, Sikhs in South Asia have been largely concentrated in the state of Punjab in northwest India and made up only 1.7 percent of the Indian population as a whole in 2011; Hindus were 79.8 percent of the Indian population in the same period. Many observant Sikh men, and some women, maintain their unshorn hair in a turban (men also maintain unshorn beards and mustaches) and carry a ceremonial dagger (usually hidden under clothing), as these are articles of faith in the Sikh tradition. These visible symbols of religion have made Sikhs particularly vulnerable to discrimination and racial attacks, one reason for Sikh American activism. But this does not explain why Sikhs have redefined their racial and ethnic identities several times over the past hundred years, which is the focus of this article.

This article demonstrates the impact of global and transnational factors on the identities of immigrants and even the American-born generation. It also showcases the active role of racial and ethnic groups in contesting and trying to change imposed identity categories. Specifically, it traces the shifting racial and ethnic identities of Sikh Americans, focusing on three periods when they rallied to change their racial-ethnic identities. The first period of activism was in the early decades of the twentieth century when Sikhs mobilized as Indians with Aryan roots to gain access to U.S. citizenship. They also began to link their racial discrimination in North America to their status as British colonial subjects. Consequently, they rallied as

---

1. Part of this argument rests on the fact that Sikhs are greatly overrepresented in the diaspora and comprised 34 percent of the Indian population in Canada in 2001, more than the Hindu population from India which was 27 percent (Lindsay 2001). In England and Wales, Sikhs are almost as many as Hindus (732,429 versus 817,000 in the 2011 census).

Indian patriots around a militant Indian nationalist movement. Discrimination against Sikhs in India during and after Indian independence in 1947, and attacks against Sikhs in India beginning in 1984, however, led to the rise of a Sikh separatist movement. This in turn led to a campaign by many Sikh Americans, in the second period of activism, to disavow an Indian identity and mobilize as Sikh nationalists. The third period came in the wake of September 11, 2001. A post-9/11 backlash against men with turbans and beards sparked a movement to be recognized as an American religious group deserving of accommodations for its articles of faith, as well as an ethnic group distinct from Indian Americans in the U.S. census.

FACTORS SPURRING MOBILIZATION AROUND RACE AND ETHNICITY

Racial and ethnic categories in the U.S. census were developed in the late 1700s because race and color were the basis for citizenship and legal status (Anderson 2002, 269–71). Two hundred years later, after civil rights laws were passed, the census became a tool to measure racial disparities and allocate funds to reduce these disparities as well as for election redistricting in the wake of the 1965 Voting Rights Act. A federal measure, Directive 15, adopted in 1977, led to the adoption of the ethnoracial pentagon of five categories—white, black, Hispanic, Asian or Pacific Islander, American Indian or Alaskan Native—still used today with some modifications. Although the state obviously plays an important role in racially and ethnically classifying groups, we should also examine how and why immigrants challenge census categories, and the role that developments in the home countries can play in promoting these campaigns.

In their seminal book, *Nations Unbound*, Linda Basch and her coauthors argue that many immigrants are "transmigrants," individuals who "take actions, make decisions, and develop subjectivities and identities embedded in networks of relationships that connect them simultaneously to two or more nation-states" (1994, 7). Other researchers have also demonstrated that in the contemporary period, many countries, parties, and groups have begun to recognize the value of harnessing the political capital of their diasporas to advance particular domestic and international agendas (Lyons and Mandaville 2012; Varadarajan 2010). This type of work has challenged the container model of the nation-state, and shown that we cannot understand the experiences and activism of ethnic groups by solely focusing on national processes. Most literature on transnationalism argues that it wanes over generations (Levitt and Waters 2002). This perspective, however, has also been recently challenged by research showing that the second and later generations can continue to maintain special ties with the ancestral homeland (Azuma 2017).

Paul Schor presents an interesting discussion of several mobilizations around American census categories by immigrants that were impacted by developments in their home countries (2005). For instance, the Mexican government and Mexican American organizations mobilized to challenge the new category "Mexican race" introduced in the 1930 Census—until then, Mexicans had been classified as white (Schor 2005, 92–93).[2] Another example is the case of immigrant organizations representing national minorities in central and eastern Europe who mobilized, due to the rise of nationalist sentiments in Europe, to have their mother tongue used to classify their populations in the 1910 census instead of birthplace. Some Jewish groups attempted to have Jews classified as Hebrews in the same census to distinguish them from other central and eastern European immigrants (Schor 2005, 94–95).[3]

Although ethnicity is usually understood as referring to national background, majority and minority status within the country of origin can profoundly affect the attitude of immigrant groups toward their homeland state and con-

---

2. The Census Bureau backed down at this time but later disagreements about the "race" of Mexicans led to the mobilization of Latinos around a separate census category that defined them on the basis of language and ethnicity, rather than race (Prewitt 2013, 76).

3. Although this attempt was not successful, Jews came to be distinguished from other Europeans as Yiddish speakers when the mother tongue question was introduced in 1910 (Schor 2005, 94).

sequently ethnic identity and political activism in host countries. Majority and minority groups usually have very different histories, political interests, and social concerns in their homelands given that the culture of the dominant group often tends to be institutionalized as the national culture, marginalizing minority groups (Gurr 2000; Wimmer 1997). In an earlier research project, I found that Hindu and Muslim Indian immigrants in the United States had very different conceptions of Indianness tied to their majority and minority positions in India, and were mobilizing to influence American and Indian politics in line with their respective definitions of national identity (Kurien 2001). Traumatic events in the homeland affecting minority groups may be memorialized within communities and can lead to ethnic solidarity and mobilization in host countries. For instance, the Armenian genocide in Turkey in 1915 became the catalyst for Armenian Americans to lobby Congress to obtain official commemoration of the event and to demand cuts in aid to Turkey (Paul 2000, 31). Likewise, Sarah Wayland discusses the activism of Sri Lankan Tamil Canadians against the atrocities committed on the Tamils—a minority group in Sri Lanka—by the Sri Lankan state, for recognition as a distinct group, and in support of a separate Tamil Eelam state (2004).

Discrimination against minority groups in host countries can result in the development of what has been called "reactive ethnicity" (Portes and Rumbaut 2001, 284) or "rejection-identification" (Branscombe, Schmitt, and Harvey 1999)—in other words, stronger ethnic identification as a self-defense mechanism against marginalization, and attempts to separate from the majority group. In their study of Christian and Muslim Arab Americans in the Detroit region in the post–September 11 period, Kristine Ajrouch and Amaney Jamal find that Arab Christians were more likely to identify as white when compared with Arab Muslims (2007). Arab Muslims, they argued, demonstrated a greater tendency to distance themselves "from the mainstream," perhaps due to experiences of being "othered" and discriminated against (2007, 873). Rejection-identification can also lead to group-based activism. Fiona Barlow and her co-authors find that Māori respondents who perceived race-based rejection in Australia were motivated to increase their support for political action for Māori rights (Barlow et al. 2012).

METHODS

This article draws on material from two larger projects. The first examined the activism of a variety of national Indian American advocacy organizations, and a second, ongoing project, focuses on South Asian community formation and mobilization in some regions of the United States and Canada (the larger New York City, San Francisco, Vancouver, and Toronto areas). Both projects used a variety of methods of data collection: interviews with leaders, activists and lay community members, some participant observation, and an examination of archival material, internet websites, YouTube videos of talks and conferences, e-newsletters of organizations, and a variety of secondary sources such as newspaper, magazine, and internet articles. Sikhs are one of the most active groups that I studied in both projects. In this article, I draw on interviews with twenty-four Sikh American leaders, activists, and community members, both first and second generation, out of a total of fifty-four interviews with Sikh Americans for both projects together, conducted between 2007 and 2017. Any names of individuals, when used, have been changed to protect their identity. The names of the organizations have been retained.

EARLY SOUTH ASIAN MIGRATION TO NORTH AMERICA

Sikhs from rural Punjab were the dominant group of immigrants from British India to North America in the early decades of the twentieth century for three reasons. First, economic conditions in the Punjab had worsened under British colonial land policies (Oldenburg 2002). The region also experienced droughts, famines, and epidemics during this period, triggering an outmigration in search of work (Jensen 1988, 24). Second, many Sikh men were in the British army. The British took over the Punjab region after a long and bitter struggle with Maharaja Ranjit Singh, the founder of the Sikh Empire (Gould 2006, 77–78). They were so impressed with the military skills of the Maharaja's Sikh warriors that they designated Sikhs a "martial race" and heavily recruited them into the British army (Dirks 2001, 178–80).[4] The British encouraged Sikh orthodoxy. Separate Khalsa Sikh, initiated Sikhs who maintain articles of faith, regiments were formed and the leaders of these regiments were rewarded by the British with honorary titles and material rewards to ensure their loyalty (Sohi 2014, 18). Sikhs were strong supporters of the British Empire in the nineteenth century: Sikh regiments were considered to be an elite unit of the British army and served around the world. A Sikh representative in Ottawa in 1908, protesting a discriminatory travel ban on the group, described Sikhs in the following way: "We are British subjects, of proven loyalty . . . With the name Sikh is linked up fidelity and loyalty to the Empire . . . The Sikh has always been ready in the past to give willing service to the Empire" (quoted in Gill 2014, 24).

The roots of the Sikh settlement in North America can be traced to the celebration of Queen Victoria's Diamond Jubilee in 1897, when a Sikh regiment based in India was sent to London to attend the rituals. In returning to India via Canada, they learned about the work opportunities on the Pacific coasts of Canada and the United States and some returned seeking work (McMahon 2001, 9). The final factor that gave Sikhs an advantage over men of other religions from Punjab were their religious networks. Sikhs had *gurdwaras* (temples) all along the long route from Punjab to North America, including in Hong Kong, where migrants had to break journey, often for weeks. The *gurdwaras* provided free lodging and one free meal a day, which was useful for wayfarers (Jensen 1988, 27).

A second, smaller group of migrants from India in the early decades of the twentieth century was made up of educated anticolonial leaders, both Sikh and non-Sikh, from urban areas, who left India to escape British surveillance and to find safer bases from which to organize a nascent independence movement. Many of them came as students to the United States to enroll in universities and learn about the U.S. political system (Sohi 2014, 21–22). The University of California in Berkeley was an important hub because the tuition was low and finding work nearby was possible (McMahon 2001, 29). But Indian students were also to be found in many other universities around the country.

EARLY SIKHS ON THE PACIFIC WEST COAST: FROM SUPPORTERS OF THE BRITISH EMPIRE TO ANTICOLONIAL INDIAN NATIONALISTS

Between 1901 and 1910, 5,762 immigrants, mostly Sikh, from Punjab in British colonial India arrived in Northern California (Gould 2006, 90). About an equal number arrived in British Columbia in Canada over the same period. Sikhs faced a variety of citizenship restrictions and exclusion acts in North America and mobilized against them. This mobilization became intertwined with a militant *Ghadar* (mutiny) Indian nationalist movement as they realized that the British, instead of providing support to its citizens, had condoned and supported the exclusion acts.

Punjabi communities in the United States and Canada were close-knit and movement across the border was relatively easy at the time. After the Continuous Journey Regulation of 1908 in Canada (requiring migrants to arrive in Canada through a direct ship voyage that in practice targeted Indians and prevented their migration) several thousand moved down to the Pacific West coast of the United States (Johnston 2014, 18). Around 85 to 90 percent of the Punjabi immigrants in the first decade of the twentieth century were Sikh, even though Sikhs made up only around 13 percent of the population of Punjab (McMahon 2001, 10; Sohi 2014, 8). Punjabi Muslims were the second largest religious group among the early West Coast immigrants, followed by Punjabi Hindus. But they were all identified in the United States as Hindoos or Hindus, the term then used for inhabitants of India, which was also called Hindustan, or the land of the Hindus. The early immigrants worked in lumber mills, railroad construction, and later in agriculture (McMahon 2001, 19).

---

4. In fact, the British were able to defeat the first major anticolonial rebellion in India in 1857, primarily because of the support of Sikh regiments (Jensen 1988, 6).

Sikh immigrant workers faced anti-Asian mobilization in both Canada and the United States. A Japanese and Korean Exclusion League formed in 1905 in both San Francisco and Vancouver by white labor union leaders was renamed the Asiatic Exclusion League by 1907 to include Indians among the groups that it opposed (Jensen 1988, 44). In 1907, a series of race riots directed against Indian immigrants by white workers took place along the North American West Coast. The first took place in Bellingham, Washington, soon to be followed by others in Seattle, Everett, Vancouver, and parts of California. The 1908 Canadian law banning Indian migrants emboldened officials in the United States to take their own measures against the "Hindu invasion" of Northern California (107). Immigration officials in San Francisco used a "likely to become a public charge" clause beginning in 1909 to exclude a large number of Indians seeking entry into the United States, leading to a steep decline in the number of Indian immigrants in the United States, from 1,710 in 1908, down to 377 in 1909 (111). Despite these small numbers, in 1910, a U.S. immigration commission issued a report on Indian immigrants, describing them as "the least desirable race of immigrants thus far admitted to the United States" and as "unassimilable" (cited, 141). In 1912, American immigration officials were also able to pressure steamship companies to stop selling tickets to Indian laborers intending to travel to the American West Coast (147).

As Indians became aware that the discriminatory laws against them in Canada and the United States had been passed with the approval and support of the British, they realized that they could not turn to their British-ruled home country for support against discrimination in North America (Sohi 2014, 27). Anticolonialists started to link the discrimination that Indians were facing in North America with their colonial status in India. One older male Sikh interviewee in Northern California, Dilraj Singh, a descendant of an early Sikh anticolonial leader, talked about how the white mobs attacking Indians in Bellingham had called them slaves and coolies. According to Dilraj, Indian immigrants were "discriminated as slave Indians since they were not from an independent, free country. They were from a country . . . under British rule." Anticolonial leaders began to mobilize Indians in North America against British rule, calling for a revolution in India like the American Revolution (Sohi 2014, 66). They warned the British colonialists that racial discrimination experienced by Indians within the territories of the British Empire—referring to Canada—could foment revolution in India (Sohi 2014, 34). They started several anticolonial periodicals that they sent to India and to Indian communities around the world. One of the important goals of these publications was to turn Sikhs in India against the British by telling them about the Canadian exclusion acts targeting them (Johnston 2014, 24; Sohi 2014, 53).

A group of nationalistic Indian students formed the Hindustan Association of the United States in Oregon in May 1913 (Jensen 1988, 173, 179–80). Later that year, they established the Hindustan Ghadar Party for Indian independence in Oregon, with its headquarters in San Francisco (Sohi 2014, 57). Although the Ghadar movement was active in both Canada and the United States, it was based in the United States, in part because of America's history of fighting a war against Britain and gaining independence, a link that Ghadar leaders also emphasized in their speeches to members of the wider American society (Sohi 2014, 66–68; Jensen 1988, 94–95). The party aimed to get its message out through the publication and dissemination of a weekly newspaper, the *Ghadar*, and a volume of poetry composed and written by Sikh workers, *Ghadar-di-gunj*, Echoes of Mutiny (Sohi 2014, 59–60). Both were mailed (or sent through individual travelers) to South Asian communities in North America and other countries, and to India.[5] In 1914, the 376 Punjabi (mostly Sikh) passengers of a ship, the *Komagata Maru*, sailing directly from India to Canada (to challenge the Continuous Journey Regulation) were not even allowed to disembark in Vancouver and were sent back to India,

---

5. The newspaper periodically carried the following advertisement: "Wanted – Brave soldiers to stir up Ghadar in India / Pay – Death / Prize – Martyrdom / Pension – Liberty / Field of battle – India" (Jensen 1988, 183).

many to face death or imprisonment. This incident angered Sikhs on the North American Pacific Coast and led to several thousand Ghadar supporters leaving North America for India to launch an Indian independence movement. By mid-1915, the British had managed to crush the movement and put India under martial law. Some Ghadarites were sentenced to death and others were imprisoned or confined to their home villages (Buchignani, Indra, and Srivastiva 1985, 64; Sohi 2014, 163–64).

U.S. RACIAL STATUS: FROM HINDU CAUCASIANS TO NONWHITE ALIENS

In the United States, the racial status of early Indian migrants, and consequently, their eligibility for citizenship (then conferred only on "free white persons" and people of African descent), was not settled until 1923. Drawing on colonial scholarship that classified upper-caste Indians as Aryans, part of the Indo-European people originating from the Caucasus who had migrated to India several thousand years earlier (Trautmann 1997), Indian immigrants in the United States, (mostly Sikhs at the time) argued that as upper-caste Indians, they were Aryans and therefore Caucasians, and consequently eligible for citizenship. Between 1908 and 1922, around sixty-nine Indians received citizenship in various states in the United States. In California alone, at least seventeen Indian men were granted citizenship during this period (Jensen 1988, 255).

Bhagat Singh Thind, whose name is associated with a famous legal case that denied him—and subsequently other Indians—citizenship, was a turban-wearing Sikh who had come to the United States in 1913 for higher education. He was active in the Ghadar movement (Coulson 2015, 15–22). In the middle of his studies at the University of California, Berkeley, he joined the U.S. army to fight in World War I (the first turbaned Sikh to serve in the U.S. army) and was honorably discharged in 1918 when the war ended. He initially received U.S. citizenship, but it was revoked a few months later. In 1919, Thind filed a court case to challenge the revocation. Following on the Ozawa case, in which a Japanese American plaintiff had been denied citizenship on the grounds that although he might be white, he was not Caucasian, Thind's lawyers argued that as a high-caste Hindu of the Aryan race from north India, Thind was of Caucasian descent and therefore eligible for U.S. citizenship. They made the case that the caste system in India prevented interracial marriages in India, like the racial system did in the United States, ensuring the Aryan racial purity of upper-caste Indians (Haney López 1996, 149; Coulson 2015, 26). In 1923, British-born Justice George Sutherland delivered the unanimous Supreme Court decision that though Thind might be Caucasian, he was not white as commonly understood in the United States and western Europe, and was therefore not eligible for citizenship. Doug Coulson argues that the U.S. Supreme Court denied Thind citizenship under pressure from the British government because of Thind's involvement in the Ghadar movement (2015).[6] Many Indians in the United States were stripped of their citizenship after this ruling. Because a 1913 California Alien Land Law prohibited "aliens ineligible for citizenship" from owning or holding long-term leases on agricultural land, Asian exclusionists in California also took the opportunity to deprive Indians of the land they owned (Jensen 1988, 265).

FROM NONWHITE ALIENS TO SUCCESSFUL LOBBYISTS FOR CITIZENSHIP AND INDIAN INDEPENDENCE

These restrictions stimulated and reinforced Sikh involvement in Indian nationalist activism. Dalip Singh Saund, who eventually became the first Asian American in Congress (1957–63), was an early Sikh immigrant to California who came in 1920 to study at the University of California, Berkeley. In his autobiogra-

---

6. In 1917, exclusionists in the United States were successful in getting the U.S. government to pass an Immigration Act that included a literacy test and the demarcation of an Asiatic Barred Zone. As a result, the legal immigration of most Asians, including Sikhs, into the United States was prohibited. However, students were still permitted into the country and others were able to enter illegally through Mexico (McMahon 2001, 15). The Immigration Act of 1924 finally excluded all Asians from immigrating into the United States.

phy he wrote of that time, "All of us were ardent nationalists and we never passed up an opportunity to expound on India's rights" (Saund 1960, 38). Seeking allies in the U.S. Congress, Indian leaders in the United States were able to convince important Americans that the support of the people of India for America was "key to victory over Japan" in World War II (Gould 2006, 334), leading the Roosevelt administration to establish an India section of the Office of Strategic Services (predecessor to the Central Intelligence Agency) in 1943 to forge alliances with anticolonial leaders in India (Gould 2006, 377). Two organizations—the Indian League, and the National Committee for Indian Freedom—were active in Washington, D.C., in the 1930s and 1940s, supported financially by the Sikh-based organization on the West Coast, the Indian National Congress Association of India established by Dalip Singh Saund (Jacoby 2007, 251). A Sikh, J. J. Singh based in New York, elected president of the Indian League in 1939, played a leadership role in the mobilization of American support for India's independence and citizenship rights for Indians in the United States. Through J. J. Singh's close connection with Representatives Clare Booth Luce of Connecticut and Emanuel Celler of New York (Gould 2006, 394), he was able to influence them to introduce the Luce-Celler Act in 1946 in Congress which granted citizenship to Indians, restored the citizenship rights for those who had obtained it prior to the *Thind* case, and permitted a quota of one hundred immigrants from India to the United States every year.

POST-1965 SIKH IMMIGRANTS IN THE UNITED STATES: FROM OTHER RACE TO ASIAN INDIAN

Most contemporary Sikh Americans are post-1965 immigrants. After the passage of the 1965 Immigration act, Sikhs in the United States were able to sponsor their relatives from India. Others arrived in the United States for higher education or for work in professional fields. After the independence of India in 1947, the U.S. Census classified all people of Indian background, including Sikhs, in the Other Race category in 1950 and 1960 and identified them as Asiatic Indian or Hindu. In 1970, however, the U.S. census reclassified people "having origins in the Indian subcontinent" as white. By this time, the civil rights laws had come into effect and census data were used to measure and track discrimination against groups. A 1975 report by the Ad Hoc Committee on Racial and Ethnic Definitions of the Federal Interagency Committee on Education, describes how people from the Indian subcontinent presented a problem to the committee as it deliberated about how to classify groups for the 1970 census.

The question at issue was whether to include them in the minority category Asian because they came from Asia and some are victims of discrimination in this country, or to include them in this category [Caucasian-white] because they are Caucasians, though frequently of darker skin than other Caucasians. The final decision favored the latter. (Trotter and Michael 1975, 4–5)

On learning of this decision, an Indian American organization, the Association of Indians in America (AIA), formed in 1967, mobilized, starting from the mid-1970s to make the argument that Indians in the United States should be included under the category of "Asian" as they had been in the 1917 Asiatic Exclusion Act, and that they experienced discrimination. Through their efforts, AIA leaders introduced a new census category, Asian Indian, for the census of 1980, and obtained minority status for Indian Americans (and consequently Sikhs) as Asians from 1980 on (Dutta 1982).

Although Sikhs self-identified as Indians at this time, an early Sikh immigrant who came to the United States to study in the 1960s described how the turban worn by many Sikh men made them stand out. "When we came here, we were out and out Indians, you know. The identity of the Sikh was forced upon us when the local people looked on us turbaned people as different. So, we were Indians at heart, and Sikhs by our looks." Because of the turban, other interviewees told me that Sikh American men faced some "hostility and backlash" during the 1979–1980 Iranian hostage crisis "because people associated Sikhs with Ayatollah Khomeini, because he wore a turban." Issues connected with the turban and beard led Sikh Americans to form an organization—the Sikh Council of North America—in 1979 to unite at the national level to combat discrimination.

SIKHS IN INDEPENDENT INDIA: FROM PARTITION TO 1984

For someone to understand the shift in Sikh attitudes toward the Indian state and an Indian identity between the 1940s and the 1980s, some background on developments in India is necessary. The partition of India in 1947 into India and Pakistan came as a major blow to Indian nationalists in the United States who had mobilized for an undivided India. Sikhs were particularly badly affected because Punjab was divided between India and Pakistan, Pakistan getting a much bigger portion than India. Several sacred sites and sites important to Sikh history remained in Pakistan and Sikhs living in the Punjab region of Pakistan had to move to Indian Punjab.

Toward the end of the colonial period, Sikh leaders in India mobilized for a separate state for Sikhs called Khalistan because they realized that the Muslim demand for a separate state was being seriously considered. To pacify Sikhs, Indian nationalist leaders promised them special consideration. In 1946, Nehru was quoted as saying, "The brave Sikhs of Punjab are entitled to special consideration [and] I see nothing wrong in an area and a set up in the north wherein the Sikhs can also experience the glow of freedom" (K. Singh 2005, 291). Gandhi and Nehru are also said to have assured Sikhs that the Indian constitution would be framed in such a way that minority communities like Sikhs would be provided adequate protection. However, the final constitution document created a strongly centralized political structure, which the two Sikh representatives strongly opposed (S. H. Singh 1949). Again, Article 25 classified Sikhs—as well as Jains and Buddhists—as Hindus and refused to acknowledge that theirs was a separate religion. Consequently, the two Sikh representatives in the Constituent Assembly refused to ratify and sign the Indian constitution (P. Singh 2005, 914), a fact that Khalistan activists in the contemporary period have seized upon.

In the 1950s, Indian states were carved out based on language but the Indian government was initially reluctant to grant a separate Punjabi language state for Sikhs given concerns about creating a state based on religion. In 1966, after a victory for India in the 1965 Indo-Pakistani War, due in good part to the support of Sikhs, however, the Indian Punjab region was divided into three states—Punjab, Haryana, and Himachel Pradesh—and a Punjabi-majority state was created. However some of the specific ways that the division took place were not to the liking of Sikhs. Tension also arose about the division of the river water running through the region, with Sikhs arguing that the Hindu states of Himachal Pradesh and Haryana were favored over Sikh-dominated Punjab. These issues led to Sikh mobilization and a demand for "an autonomous region" within India where Sikhs and Sikhism could flourish. When the central government, by this time with Indira Gandhi as prime minister, proved intransigent on all of these demands, a secessionist Khalistan movement developed for a separate homeland for Sikhs free of Indian control. In the early 1980s, some Khalistan leaders turned to violence and militancy.

Sikh discontent regarding discrimination against them and the Punjab region by the Indian central government came to a head on June 5, 1984, when Indira Gandhi ordered troops into their sacred Golden Temple (the center of Sikh spiritual and political authority) in the northern Indian city of Amritsar to rout out militants. Several thousand Sikh pilgrims were in the temple because it was the day of an important Sikh religious festival. Several hundreds, possibly thousands, of pilgrims were trapped in the complex and killed in the attack. A few months later, on October 31, 1984, Indira Gandhi was assassinated by two of her Sikh bodyguards in Delhi, setting off anti-Sikh violence in Delhi and other cities in north India. Several thousand Sikhs were killed. Allegations circulated that key figures of the ruling Congress Party had been involved in the massacres and that the attacks were well organized, but no action was taken against the perpetrators. Political repression against Sikhs in Punjab suspected of being supporters of Khalistan continued for another decade, leading to the detention, torture, and disappearance of tens of thousands of Sikh men (Chima 2010, 3; Human Rights Watch 2007).

THE IMPACT OF 1984 ON SIKH AMERICANS

Although Sikh Americans were classified and identified as Indian after Indian independence, the described developments in India led Sikhs to believe that they were being systematically marginalized and treated as second-class citizens. The events of 1984 stunned the Sikh community around the world and proved a watershed moment, bringing together even those who had until then not been involved with the Sikh community. As one of my interviewees poignantly narrated, "We never thought, I never thought that a massacre would happen in India . . . we were part of India, we defended India, we spilt our blood in India for India, you know." North American Sikhs held a large convention in Madison Square Garden in New York City on July 28, 1984—this was after the invasion of the Golden Temple but before the large-scale anti-Sikh attacks in north India. An estimated 2,500 attended and formed a World Sikh Organization to represent Sikhs in Canada, the United States, and Britain; at present the organization survives only in Canada. The leaders called for Sikhs supporting the Indian government "to disassociate themselves from that regime" (Howe 1984). There were many calls for Khalistan at the convention but the final resolution defined it broadly as a place where Sikhs could "enjoy the 'glow of freedom'" that Nehru had promised.

Sikhs in Canada and the United States mobilized to monitor events in India and to organize marches and protests in front of the Indian consulates and the United Nations in New York City. The Sikh Foundation, founded in the San Francisco Bay area in 1967, hired a public relations team and prepared a full-page advertisement for newspapers in New York City, Washington, D.C., San Francisco, and Los Angeles.[7] Through the help of the public relations team, Sikh commentators appeared on many radio and television shows and programs and also went to Washington, D.C., to educate Congress "about the civil war against Sikhs happening in India" in the words of one of my interviewees. Sikhs were successful in obtaining support from some Republicans in Congress, including Senator Jesse Helms (R-NC) and U.S. Representative Dan Burton (R-IN, founding member and co-chair of the Pakistani Caucus) who spoke about human rights violations in India in the Congress on a regular basis. In the post-1984 period, a variety of Khalistani organizations were formed in the United States, including the Council of Khalistan (founded in 1986) and a Khalistan Affairs Center (founded in 1991), both with offices in Washington, D.C. In New York City, most Sikhs stopped attending the annual India Day Parade after 1984 and from 1986 on organized a separate Sikh Day Parade.

In the meantime, the Indian government undertook its own propaganda campaign. A book written by two well-known Toronto-based Canadian journalists makes the claim, based on reports from the reputed *India Today* magazine, that India had posted a number of "intelligence operatives" in North America from 1982 onward "to hijack" or discredit the Sikh separatist movement.[8] Several older Sikh American men I interviewed seemed to be aware of this given that they talked about "plants" by the Indian government being placed in Sikh communities. As one elderly man explained, "The thing is that, even before '84, I think, because of the Ghadar movement from USA, Sikhs have always been considered radicals by the Indian government." After the attack on the Golden Temple, the Indian government produced a video defending the raid and minimizing the damage on the temple and the casualties from the attack, as well as a glossy magazine prais-

---

7. See Sikh Foundation International, "The Sikhs of India are much like the American colonists of 1776," July 2011, http://www.sikhfoundation.org/wp-content/uploads/2011/07/Preserving_Lives_1984/1984_Full_Page_advertisement.pdf, accessed January 23, 2018. The ad was discussed in an interview with Sarinder Singh Kapany about the 1984 attacks (see 1984 Living History, "Narinder Singh Kapany," February 28, http://www.1984livinghistory.org/2014/02/28/narinder-singh-kapany, accessed January 23, 2018).

8. The book focused on the investigation into the 1985 Air India disaster, when a plane originating in Canada was blown up, allegedly by Sikh Canadian Khalistan supporters, killing all on board.

ing the contributions of Sikhs to India and denouncing Sikh separatists, both of which were sent to Sikh communities in North America and to key American and Canadian Hindus (Kashmeri and McAndrew 2005, 45, 49). These efforts further enraged Sikhs in North America.

Several interviewees mentioned that the events of 1984 also created tensions with Hindus with whom, until that time, they had had fairly close and cordial relations. An older Sikh man from California told me, "I actually had a lot of Hindu friends . . . what happened in 1984 definitely created a wedge between the two communities . . . it took a long time to heal." Another issue that a large number of interviewees mentioned was that many Sikhs stopped identifying as Indian after the events of 1984. A second-generation man in his thirties said, "I was raised in a context, and this was part of my training earlier as a teen, where I was taught, we are Sikhs, we are Punjabis, we are not Indians, the Indian state has suppressed our community, and we ought to reject that identity." Similarly, another young Sikh man remarked,

> I mean essentially . . . what's clear among most Americans [Sikhs] with whom I interact is that Indian identity is just not part of the equation . . . strangers come up to us in the streets all the time, especially with the turban and the beard, and they'll ask, you know, where are you from? Sometimes they'll say oh, are you from India? And I know many people including people in my own family who would say no, I'm not from India, I'm from Punjab. You know, just refuse to be identified with the Indian state.

A young woman emphasized,

> For me, it was about my identity being primarily Sikh, and not Indian. I mean, I just always saw myself as Sikh . . . I was well educated at a young age about the events of '84, and feel quite strongly about that to this day. I've always identified as Sikh, and as American. I have not identified with the Indian state.

As the anti-Sikh violence abated in India in the mid-1990s, support for an armed Khalistani movement among immigrant Sikhs in North America gradually dwindled, though some pockets of support remain. Consequently, scholars like Giorgio Shani refer to Khalistan in the contemporary period as a "*deterritorialized* imagined community" or, like Cynthia Mahmood, as "political critique" (Shani 2008, 143 [emphasis in the original]; Mahmood 2014). Some of my respondents seemed to agree with this characterization. An older Sikh man described it this way: "this demand for Khalistan and our disowning India, it's, it's really a form of protest." However, from my interviews it seemed that Khalistan meant different things to different people. Here is a Sikh American graduate student articulating what he thinks Khalistan means for the U.S. Sikh community today:

> I think a better way to think about the Khalistani movement is that . . . most Sikhs think that they got dicked over when partition happened and that Sikhs didn't get their fair share. And I think in general they would like to see a space in which Sikhism would be able to flourish in India. I don't think people are super crazy about wanting their own nation-state, but they understand that because of the historical processes around postcolonialism, that Sikhism has been corrupted. And the Punjab is not a place in which Sikhism is allowed to flourish and spread its wings as far as it can go. So in that sense most Sikhs are Khalistani in that they wish for a space in which Sikhism can flourish. And they all hate the Indian government: everybody hates the Indian government.

Many interviewees who talked about Khalistan (the issue did not come up in all the interviews) did seem to see it as a protest movement against the Indian state that emphasized Sikh self-determination rather than an actual separatist movement. These individuals, mostly second-generation Sikh Americans, pointed to the variety of ways that organizations formed by individuals of their generation had been mobilizing around discrimination against Sikhs by the Indian state, without mentioning the issue of Khalistan.

For instance, an organization, Ensaaf, formed in 2004 by second-generation Sikh

Americans in the Bay area, has been working in Punjab to "end impunity and achieve justice for mass state crimes . . . by documenting abuses, bringing perpetrators to justice, and organizing survivors."[9] The organization's oral history and video testimonies project has collected two hundred oral histories about disappearances and extrajudicial killings in Punjab between 1984 and 1995. A variety of Sikh American organizations formed by second-generation Sikh Americans mobilized around the thirtieth anniversary of the events of 1984. An organization called Saanjh in the San Francisco Bay Area came up with the idea of creating a video archive of interviews with Sikhs around the world about their memories and experiences of 1984.[10] Another organization, The Surat Initiative, collaborated with Ensaaf to create a 2014 Remembrance Project, posting a historical item linked to 1984 every day through the whole of 2014.[11] In September 2014, when the newly elected Indian prime minister, Narendra Modi, was visiting the United States, Sikh Coalition—yet another organization formed by second-generation Sikh Americans—and Ensaaf organized a congressional hearing focusing on the alleged collusion of Indian politicians from the Congress Party in the 1984 anti-Sikh violence and the lack of indictments against the perpetrators of that violence. All of these organizations have kept the issue of anti-Sikh violence and discrimination alive, educating the younger generations and some members of the wider society about these issues, and seeking justice for the victims.

In contrast to the quoted interviewees, others felt the Khalistan movement continued to be about establishing a Sikh political territory. One graduate student who had read Shani's 2008 book on Sikh nationalism, for example, said it was "absurd" to argue that Sikh nationalism is no longer tied to territory. "Because how could people be shouting these slogans [for Khalistan] at the Sikh Day Parade, and then not pointing to Punjab?" He felt that Khalistan was still a simmering issue within the Sikh American community, although not a focus of many Sikh American organizations in the post–September 11 period. The young man however, pointed me to a Sikh American organization, Sikhs for Justice, that was working with the United Nations for Khalistan.

Sikhs for Justice was formed in 2009 in New York City largely by immigrant Sikh lawyers in response to the lack of justice for the "genocide" of Sikhs in India after the death of Prime Minister Indira Gandhi. The organization, which now has representatives in Canada as well, gained publicity within the Indian American community by filing human rights violations lawsuits under the Alien Tort Claims Act, eventually dismissed by U.S. courts, against two prominent Indian Congress leaders alleged to have been involved in the anti-Sikh attacks of 1984 who were visiting the United States.

In 2015, influenced by the Scottish independence referendum of the previous year, the organization launched a Referendum 2020 movement, seeking to build support from Sikhs around the world for "India-occupied Punjab" to become an independent country (Nibber 2015). The goal is to hold an unofficial referendum in 2020 among Sikh communities in India and around the world to find out the level of support for Khalistan. If the majority supports Khalistan, the organization plans to work with the United Nations to hold an official referendum and, the group hopes, to achieve independence. In a YouTube video of a 2015 Sikh community event held in Toronto on April 9 to educate people about the referendum, a second-generation activist for Sikhs for Justice from Toronto speaking in English and some Punjabi (most speeches were by immigrants and were in Punjabi), addressed the "youth," explaining the goals and rationale of the referendum:

Sikhs for Justice's goal is an independent Punjab, whether it is called Khalistan, whether it is given any other name, we want a state that is based on Sikh principles that looks out for

9. "A Mission to End Impunity," *Ensaaf*, http://www.ensaaf.org, accessed January 24, 2018.

10. The 1984 Living History Project, http://www.1984livinghistory.org, accessed January 24, 2018.

11. "The 1984 Remembrance Project," *The Surat Initiative*, http://www.thesuratinitiative.com/social-justice-project/1984-remembrance-project, accessed January 24, 2018.

Sikh issues, and Sikh people. We want our home and we want our home back, which we chose to give to the Indians in 1947.[12]

Describing India as "the occupying power," he argued that every year, Indians "steal 80 billion dollars from Punjab [referring to the river waters], I want to make it clear, steal $80 billion every year from *your* pocket." At the end of his speech, he introduced Karen Parker, a U.S.-based attorney specializing in human rights law, as a person who had liaised with the United Nations to help a variety of groups achieve independence, and who had "single-handedly, brought the world's most oppressive regimes to their knees." In her presentation, Parker outlined the five principles of self-determination of the United Nations, advised her audience on how Sikhs could make a case under each of the five principles, and promised her support to Sikhs for their self-determination movement.[13] A similar event with many of the same speakers (including Karen Parker) was held in California on August 17, 2015.[14]

THE IMPACT OF 9/11: MOBILIZING AS AN AMERICAN RELIGIOUS AND ETHNIC MINORITY

A second watershed moment for American Sikhs came on September 11, 2001, when they became the targets of hate crimes in the United States. This also coincided with the coming-of-age of the second generation, who took the lead in forming organizations to obtain public recognition and civil rights for Sikh Americans as a distinct American religious minority. Turban-wearing Sikhs became particularly vulnerable to hate crimes after September 11 because they have been often mistaken for Osama bin Laden followers. The first fatality of the 9/11 backlash in the United States was a Sikh, Balbir Singh Sodhi of Arizona, who was killed on September 15, 2011, by a man who thought Sodhi was a Muslim. In describing how Sikhs were affected immediately after 9/11, a young activist from the Richmond Hill area of Queens (a neighborhood with a large Sikh settlement) spoke of a Sikh man walking down the street who was beaten by baseball bats by a bunch of young white men. "So that was a shocker to everybody. We thought we were safe in Richmond Hill after India [referring to the anti-Sikh violence in north India] and now this was happening to us." Another young man told me of hearing about "someone getting shot on 57th Street because of their turban and the police not registering a case. And the community was not taken seriously by law enforcement and also the media and politicians." The "horrible, burning platform of 9/11" led to the formation of new Sikh advocacy organizations in the United States and the refocusing of others. The Sikh Coalition, one of the major U.S. Sikh advocacy organizations, was formed in the weeks after 9/11. Discussing its founding, Amrita Kaur argued that the need had been urgent:

> Because it was such a big tragedy that occurred. And Sikhs were being impacted and targeted so, so deeply and so violently, that, you know, people took six months off work, and . . . stopped going to school . . . they spent a lot of time addressing these issues because they just felt like they couldn't do any other work.

A Sikh organization, SMART (Sikh Mediawatch and Resource Taskforce), formed in 1996 to represent Sikhs in the media, changed its focus to civil rights issues after 9/11 and renamed itself SALDEF (Sikh American Legal Defense and Education Fund) in 2004. Yet another Sikh American organization, United Sikhs, originally created in 1999 to help the underprivileged in New York City's borough of Queens, also changed its mission after 9/11 to focus on international issues of concern to the Sikh diaspora.

---

12. Elsewhere he refers to the fact that because the Sikh representatives did not sign the Indian constitution, Punjab was never really legally a part of India.

13. TAG TV Community Roundup, "'2020 Referendum Conference' by Sikhs for Justice," April 9, 2015, https://www.youtube.com/watch?v=tbXQr3lx_cl, accessed January 24, 2018.

14. Sikhs for Justice Channel, "Watch 'Referendum 2020'—Conference Live Broadcast from California," August 16, 2015, https://www.youtube.com/watch?v=44TIVVcSJyU, accessed January 24, 2018.

The activities of the national Sikh American advocacy organizations have focused on educating the wider public about Sikhs, mobilizing around their civil and religious rights, and drawing attention to hate crimes. SALDEF developed programs to, among other things, educate and train law enforcement personnel about the cultural and religious heritage of Sikh communities. Sikh Coalition and SALDEF also worked on educating the Transportation Security Administration at airports about the rights of Sikhs around their symbols of faith, the Sikh turban and *kirpan* (ceremonial dagger), to ensure that Sikh air travelers were not harassed.

Given the lack of knowledge about Sikhism in the United States, an important task facing Sikh American organizations has been to educate Americans about the Sikh religion. The Sikh Coalition and SALDEF now have short presentations on Sikhs and Sikhism on their websites, have organized Sikh awareness presentations in schools and educational institutions around the country, and have funded public service media messages to demystify the Sikh turban and beard. These organizations have also been very active in the educational arena to influence the way their religious histories and traditions are presented in U.S. school textbooks—and, indeed, to have these histories and traditions presented in the first place. They have been able to get Sikh content included in the curriculum in Texas, California, New York, New Jersey, and Idaho. A 2014 study by the Sikh Coalition found that Sikh children disproportionately experienced bullying in schools around the country.[15] Consequently, working with schools to combat negative stereotypes and address bullying has been an important task of the Sikh Coalition.

Sikh advocacy organizations have been particularly active around religious accommodation rights. Although turbaned Sikhs have been banned from joining the U.S. armed forces since the 1980s, due to the activism of second-generation Sikh leaders, individual exceptions were made in 2009 for three Sikhs who were allowed to join the army and maintain their beards, turbans, and *kirpans*. Four other Sikh men were granted religious accommodations in 2016 and allowed to serve with their articles of faith. In early 2017, the U.S. army made it easier for religious accommodations to be provided for new recruits by allowing them to be approved at the brigade level. Sikh activists have also mobilized around the right of Sikhs to maintain their symbols of faith in the workplace and have been successful in getting Workplace Religious Freedom Acts introduced in New York City and California. Finally, Sikh American groups successfully mobilized to sponsor a float at the New Year's Rose Bowl Parade every year since 2014.

Hate crimes against turban-wearing Sikhs are an ongoing problem. The 2012 shooting attack on a Sikh temple in Wisconsin by a white supremacist killed five Sikhs and wounded many others. More recently, Sikh activists told me that hate crimes in the United States against Sikhs had escalated after the Paris and San Bernardino terrorist attacks. Sikh American advocacy organizations have mobilized to bring attacks against Sikhs to the attention of authorities, and in 2013 the FBI agreed to track those against Sikhs as well as Hindus and Arabs.

The events of 1984 and 2001 also led to a movement by Sikh American organizations to have Sikhs classified as a separate ethnic group, distinct from Indian Americans, in the 2010 U.S. census. In Britain, the House of Lords ruled in 1983 that Sikhs were an ethnic group and could therefore receive legal protection against discrimination for their articles of faith under the Race Relations Act of 1976 (Singh and Tatla 2006, 133). Using that precedent, United Sikhs, with the support of SALDEF, the Sikh Coalition, and other Sikh organizations, petitioned the Census Bureau to create a separate Sikh category in the census and to count them as an ethnicity, challenging the Census Bureau practice of counting Sikhs as Asian Indians even if they marked the Other Race category and wrote in Sikh on the census form. The Sikh organiza-

---

15. More than 50 percent of Sikh children (versus 32 percent of all American schoolchildren) reported being bullied. The figure for turbaned Sikhs was even higher, 67 percent. Many indicated that they were attacked because they were labeled as terrorists.

tions argued that this change was important because American Sikhs fit the classification of a minority under international law, that the U.S. category of race should also include ethnicity and the right to self-define that ethnicity, that the U.S. Sikh population remains invisible and undercounted because of the lack of a separate census category, and finally, that Sikhs have been victims of hate crimes and discrimination particularly after 9/11 but that these issues cannot be properly documented or prosecuted unless Sikhs are recognized as a separate ethnic group.[16] This campaign was not successful, but United Sikhs urged Sikhs in the United States not to check Asian Indian but to write in Sikh under the Other Race category (not the Other Asian category) for the 2010 census arguing that it was still important to do this because the Census Bureau reviews the write-in forms, and that a large number of write-ins may ultimately result in the bureau being more receptive to the demand in the future.[17]

CONCLUSION

An examination of Sikh American activism over more than one hundred years demonstrates how and why racial and ethnic classifications, as well as identifications, can change due to the interaction between international events (including developments in the home countries) and those in host countries, and the role of religion, particularly religious minority status in this process.

The three-way relationship between the United States, Canada, and Britain played an important role in the development of discriminatory policies against people from the Indian subcontinent in North America and helped shape how Sikhs in the United States identified themselves and mobilized to further their interests. The 1908 Canadian act banning further Indian immigration was passed with the approval of American and British authorities (Jacoby 2007, 91; Sohi 2014, 27). Anti-immigrant groups in the United States used the 1908 Canadian law to develop similar policies in Northern California. For their part, Indian nationalist leaders moving across the Canadian and U.S. borders worked to link the degrading treatment of Sikhs in North America to their status as the colonial subjects of the British Empire. Leaders of the movement for citizenship rights in the United States—such as Bhagat Singh Thind, Dalip Singh Saund, and J. J. Singh—were strong Indian patriots, also working for Indian independence from the United States. Early Sikh immigrants used Western ideas about an Aryan homeland in the Caucasus (from which originated a migration to Europe and India) to argue that they were racially related to white Europeans and therefore deserving of citizenship. However British worries about the development of the Ghadar movement in the United States shaped the U.S. Supreme Court's *Thind* decision, leading Indians to be reclassified from white to nonwhite alien, which meant that they lost their citizenship rights and their land holdings. The argument that Indians were Caucasians was resuscitated by a census agency after the passage of civil rights legislation in the 1960s to argue that Indian Americans should not be brought under the protection of this legislation and should be classified as white. The Japanese attack on Pearl Harbor and the entry of the United States into World War II helped change the position of Indian immigrants in this country. Needing Indian support for the war against Japan, the American administration and the Congress became more sympathetic to the cause of Indian independence and the demand for citizenship for Indians in the United States.

Later developments in India as well as in the United States led the group to stress their identity as Sikhs rather than Indians. Although Sikhs were officially classified as Asian Indians by the U.S. government, discrimination against them in India led many Sikh Americans to dissociate from an Indian identity after the events of 1984. Tensions with Middle Eastern coun-

---

16. Minority Rights Group International, "Memorandum Regarding the Tabulation of Sikh Ethnicity in the United States Census," accessed January 24, 2018, http://www.unitedsikhs.org/petitions/Memo%20re%20Sikh%20Ethnicity.pdf.

17. United Sikhs, "Census 2010 Sikh American Census Campaign FAQ," http://www.unitedsikhs.org/Press Releases/census_FAQ_final_2_3.10.10.pdf, accessed January 24, 2018.

tries, culminating in the attacks of September 11, 2001, gave rise to hate crimes against Sikh American men with turbans and beards, continuing to the present, resulting in mobilizations led by second-generation Sikh Americans to obtain recognition and rights as an American religious minority. Making claims based on the 1983 ruling by the House of Lords in Britain identifying Sikhs as an ethnic group entitled to receive protection against discrimination, some Sikh American organizations have been trying to get Sikhs defined as an ethnic group in the U.S. census distinct from Asian Indians.

Minority status in the home and host country has been an important factor in the construction and changes in Sikh American identity. In India, Sikhs went from being a privileged minority under the British to a discriminated-against minority after the end of colonial rule. In the United States, race and the presence and visibility of external articles of faith such as the turban and unshorn beard have led to the intertwining of racial and religious discrimination against Sikhs. In the United States, despite the official disestablishment of religion, Protestant Christianity long dominated the public square and the nation is now commonly conceived of as Judeo Christian (Torpey 2010). Consequently, minority religious groups are motivated to mobilize to educate the wider society about their religion, challenge stereotypes, and obtain recognition and rights for their beliefs and practices.

Rejection-identification, or the embrace of a strong Sikh identity in response to discrimination, has been another factor shaping Sikh activism. The collective memory of the traumatic 1984 attacks against Sikhs in India provided a rallying point for diasporic Sikh mobilization, followed by the post-9/11 attacks in the United States. The second generation has been organizing by welding together Sikhi (Sikh theology) and their knowledge of the American system. Many of the activists are lawyers, having gone to law school to pursue social justice activism. Consequently, they were well positioned to take leadership of Sikh advocacy after the events of September 11, 2001.

What lessons does the Sikh American experience have for theories of immigration and identity? The analysis of Sikh American identity and activism brings out the importance of examining how international events and connections between countries, as well as the transnational links that immigrant groups forge or maintain, can play a role in the development of American racial and ethnic identities. It shows the need to adopt a historical perspective to understand identity, demonstrating the significance of the colonialism project and its legacies for the development of racial categories. We also see that often changes in identity come about as a result of immigrant political activism. Consequently, it is essential that we do not overlook immigrant agency in this process. Finally, this study makes clear that racial and ethnic classification and self-identification may be much more dynamic than we have previously understood.

REFERENCES

Ajrouch, Kristine, J., and Amaney Jamal. 2007. "Assimilating to a White Identity: The Case of Arab Americans." *International Migration Review* 41(4): 860–79.

Anderson, Margo J. 2002. "Counting by Race: The Antebellum Legacy." In *The New Race Question: How the Census Counts Multiracial Individuals*, edited by Joel Perlmann and Mary C. Waters. New York: Russell Sage Foundation.

Azuma, Eiichiro, 2017. "The Lure of Military Imperialism: Race, Martial Citizenship, and Minority American Transnationalism During the Cold War." *Journal of American Ethnic History* 36(2): 72–82.

Barlow, Fiona, K., Chris G. Sibley, and Matthew J. Hornsey. 2012. "Rejection as a Call to Arms: Inter-racial Hostility and Support for Political Action as Outcomes of Race-Based Rejection in Majority and Minority Groups." *British Journal of Social Psychology* 51(1): 167–77.

Basch, Linda, Nina Glick Schiller, and Cristina Szanton Blanc. 1994. *Nations Unbound: Transnational Projects, Postcolonial Predicaments, and Deterritorialized Nation-States*. Amsterdam: Gordon and Breach.

Branscombe, Nyla R., Michael T. Schmitt, and Richard D. Harvey. 1999. "Perceiving Pervasive Discrimination Among African Americans: Implications for Group Identification and Well-Being."

Journal of Personality and Social Psychology 77(1): 135–49.

Buchignani, Norman, and Doreen M. Indra, with Ram Srivastiva. 1985. *Continuous Journey: A Social History of South Asians in Canada.* Toronto: McClelland and Stewart Ltd. in association with the Multiculturalism Directorate, Department of the Secretary of State, and the Canadian Government Publishing Centre, Supply and Services, Canada.

Chima, Jugdep S. 2010. *The Sikh Separatist Insurgency in India: Political Leadership and Ethnonationalist Movements.* New Delhi: Sage Publications.

Coulson, Doug. 2015. "British Imperialism, the Indian Independence Movement, and the Racial Eligibility Provisions of the Naturalization Act: United States v. Thind Revisited." *Georgetown Journal of Law & Modern Critical Race Perspectives* 7(1): 1–42.

Das Gupta, Monisha. 2006. *Unruly Immigrants: Rights Activism, and Transnational South Asian Politics in the United States.* Durham, N.C.: Duke University Press.

Dirks, Nicholas B. 2001. *Castes of Mind: Colonialism and the Making of Modern India.* Princeton, N.J.: Princeton University Press.

Dutta, Manoranjan. 1982. "Asian Indian Americans: Search for an Economic Profile." In *From India to America: A Brief History of Immigration, Problems of Discrimination, Admission and Assimilation,* edited by Siripati Chandrasekhar. La Jolla, Calif.: Population Review.

Gill, Parmbir Singh. 2014. "A Different Kind of Dissidence: The Ghadar Party, Sikh History, and the Politics of Anticolonial Mobilization." *Sikh Formations* 10(1): 23–41.

Gould, Harold A. 2006. *Sikhs, Swamis, Students, and Spies: The India Lobby in the United States, 1900–1946.* New Delhi: Sage Publications.

Gurr, Ted R. 2000. *Peoples Versus States: Minorities at Risk in the New Century.* Washington, D.C.: United States Institute for Peace.

Haney López, Ian. 1996. *White by Law: The Legal Construction of Race.* New York: New York University Press.

Howe, Marvine. 1984. "Sikh Parley: 'We Are United: We Are Angry." *New York Times,* July 29. Accessed January 4, 2017. http://www.nytimes.com/1984/07/29/world/sikh-parley-we-are-united-we-are-angry.html.

Human Rights Watch. 2007. *Protecting the Killers: A Policy of Impunity in Punjab, India.* Vol. 19, no. 14(C). Fremont, Calif. / New York: Ensaaf / Human Rights Watch. Accessed January 24, 2018. https://www.hrw.org/report/2007/10/17/protecting-killers/policy-impunity-punjab-india.

Jacoby, Harold, S. 2007. *History of East Indians in America: The First Half-Century Experience of Sikhs, Hindus, and Muslims,* 2nd ed. Amritsar: B. Chattar Singh Jiwan Singh.

Jensen, Joan M. 1988. *Passage from India: Asian Indian Immigrants in North America.* New Haven, Conn.: Yale University Press.

Johnston, Hugh J. M. 2014. *The Voyage of the Komagata Maru: The Sikh Challenge to Canada's Colour Bar.* Vancouver: UBC Press.

Jung, Moon-Kie. 2015. *Beneath the Surface of White Supremacy: Denaturalizing US Racisms Past and Present.* Palo Alto, Calif.: Stanford University Press.

Kashmeri, Zuhair, and Brian McAndrew. 2005. *Soft Target: The Real Story Behind the Air India Disaster,* 2nd ed. Toronto: James Lorimer & Company.

Kurien, Prema. 2001. "Religion, Ethnicity, and Politics: Hindu and Muslim Indian Immigrants in the United States." *Ethnic and Racial Studies* 24(2): 263–93.

Levitt, Peggy, and Mary C. Waters. 2002. *The Changing Face of Home: The Transnational Lives of the Second Generation.* New York: Russell Sage Foundation.

Lindsay, Colin. 2001. "The East Indian Community in Canada." Catalogue no. 89-621-XIE, No. 4. Ottawa: Statistics Canada. Accessed January 24, 2018. http://www.statcan.gc.ca/pub/89-621-x/89-621-x2007004-eng.pdf.

Lyons, Terrence, and Peter Mandaville. 2012. *Politics from Afar: Transnational Diasporas and Networks.* New York: Columbia University Press.

Mahmood, Cynthia Kepley. 2014. "'Khalistan' as Political Critique." In *The Oxford Handbook of Sikh Studies,* edited by Pashaura Singh and Louis E. Fenech. Oxford: Oxford University Press.

McMahon, Susanne. 2001. *Echoes of Freedom: South Asian Pioneers in California, 1899–1965.* Berkeley: University of California, Center for South Asian Studies.

Nibber, Gurpreet Singh. 2015. "Referendum 2020? Khalistan Divides, Unites, Sikhs Abroad." *Hindustan Times,* August 4, 2015. Accessed January 5, 2017. http://www.hindustantimes.com/punjab

/referendum-2020-khalistan-divides-unites-sikhs-abroad/story-QBlfntRdW0zF7kVpw9XgmN.html.

Oldenburg, Veena. 2002. *Dowry Murder: The Imperial Origins of a Cultural Crime.* New York: Oxford University Press.

Omi, Michael, and Howard Winant. 2015. *Racial Formation in the United States,* 3rd ed. New York: Routledge.

Paul, Rachel Anderson. 2000. "Grassroots Mobilization and Diaspora Politics: Armenian Interest Groups and the Role of Collective Memory." *Nationalism and Ethnic Politics* 6(1): 24–47.

Pew Research Center. 2015. *America's Changing Religious Landscape.* Washington, D.C.: Pew Research Center. Accessed January 24, 2018. http://www.pewforum.org/2015/05/12/americas-changing-religious-landscape.

Portes, Alejandro, and Rubén G. Rumbaut. 2001. *Legacies: The Story of the Immigrant Second Generation.* Berkeley: University of California Press.

Prewitt, Kenneth, 2013. *What Is Your Race? The Census and Our Flawed Efforts to Classify Americans.* Princeton, N.J.: Princeton University Press.

Roth, Wendy D. 2012. *Race Migrations: Latinos and the Cultural Transformation of Race.* Stanford. Calif.: Stanford University Press.

Saperstein, Aliya, and Andrew M. Penner 2012. "Racial Fluidity and Inequality in the United States." *American Journal of Sociology* 118(3): 676–727.

Saund, Dalip Singh. 1960. *Congressman from India.* New York: E. P. Dutton.

Schor, Paul. 2005. "Mobilizing for Pure Prestige? Challenging the Federal Census Ethnic Categories in the USA (1850–1940)." *International Social Science Journal* 57(183): 89–101.

Shani, Giorgio. 2008. *Sikh Nationalism and Identity in a Global Age.* New York: Routledge.

Singh, Gurharpal, and Darshan Singh Tatla. 2006. *Sikhs in Britain: The Making of a Community.* New York: Zed Books.

Singh, Khushwant. 2005. *A History of the Sikhs,* vol. 2: *1839–2004.* Delhi: Oxford University Press.

Singh, Pritam. 2005. "Hindu Bias in India's 'Secular' Constitution: Probing Flaws in the Instruments of Governance." *Third World Quarterly* 26(6): 909–926.

Singh, Sardar Hukam. 1949. *Constitutional Assembly Debates: Official Report, 1946–1950.* Vol. XI, p. 753, 21 November 1949, Speech. Delhi: Parliament of India.

Sohi, Seema. 2014. *Echoes of Mutiny: Race, Surveillance and Indian Anticolonialism in North America.* New York: Oxford University Press.

Torpey, John. 2010. "A (Post-) Secular Age? Religion and the Two Exceptionalisms." *Social Research* 77(1): 269–96.

Trautmann, Thomas, R. 1997. *Aryans and British India.* Berkeley: University of California Press.

Trotter, Virginia, Y., and Bernard Michael. 1975. *Report of the Ad Hoc Committee on Racial and Ethnic Definitions of the Federal Interagency Committee on Education.* Washington, D.C.: Federal Interagency Committee on Education.

Varadarajan, Latha. 2010. *The Domestic Abroad: Diasporas in International Relations.* New York: Oxford University Press.

Wayland, Sarah. 2004. "Ethnonationalist Networks and Transnational Opportunities." *Review of International Studies* 30(3): 405–26.

Wimmer, Andreas. 1997. "Who Owns the State: Understanding Ethnic Conflict in Post-Colonial Societies." *Nations and Nationalism* 3(4): 631–65.

Wimmer, Andreas, and Nina Glick Schiller. 2002. "Methodological Nationalism and Beyond: Nation-State Building, Migration, and the Social Sciences." *Global Networks* 2(4): 301–34.

Making Americans: Schooling, Diversity, and Assimilation in the Twenty-First Century

CRISTINA L. LASH

How do schools teach American identity in light of immigration-driven diversity? This ethnographic study focuses on everyday nation-making at Castro Middle School, located in a city transformed by immigration. Building on theories of bidirectional assimilation, I show how assimilation can produce new definitions of Americanness more recognizable to immigrant communities, facilitating their national identification. At Castro, bidirectional assimilation supported African American students' descriptions of Americans in multicultural terms and their own identification as American. Assimilation between the school and the larger Latino and Asian student populations, however, was limited because of a binary racial paradigm that excluded them from the national community. This study thus nuances the role of race as a barrier in the assimilation process, particularly as it unfolds in schools.

Keywords: assimilation, immigration, national identity, American identity, school diversity

For the past thirty years, the United States has witnessed the highest rates of immigration to the country since the late nineteenth century, the current wave consisting primarily of immigrants from Latin America and South and East Asia. The result is that nearly a quarter of all students in U.S. classrooms are either immigrants or children of immigrants, many of whom speak a language other than English at home (Gándara 2013). The fastest-growing group is Latino school-age children, of whom 8 percent are foreign born, 52 percent are U.S. born with immigrant parents, and 40 percent are part of the third-plus generation of Latino Americans (Ruggles et al. 2017).[1] These demographic and cultural shifts have raised new questions about the role of schools in the Americanization process. Specifically, how do schools teach American identity in the context of immigration-driven diversity?

The details of how schools "make" nationals have been remarkably undertheorized within the sociology of education literature (Waldinger 2007), despite the prominent role of schools in the Americanization process (for exceptions, see Banks 2008; Olsen 2000). Yet

Cristina L. Lash is a doctoral candidate at the Stanford Graduate School of Education.

© 2018 Russell Sage Foundation. Lash, Cristina L. 2018. "Making Americans: Schooling, Diversity, and Assimilation in the Twenty-First Century." *RSF: The Russell Sage Foundation Journal of the Social Sciences* 4(5): 99–117. DOI: 10.7758/RSF.2018.4.5.05. Sincere thanks are due to the National Academy of Education/Spencer Foundation, the Research Institute of Comparative Studies in Race and Ethnicity, the Stanford Graduate School of Education, and the Stanford Office of the Vice Provost for Graduate Education for sponsoring this research. Direct correspondence to: Cristina L. Lash at cristinalash@stanford.edu, 485 Lasuen Mall, Stanford, CA 94305.

Open Access Policy: *RSF: The Russell Sage Foundation Journal of the Social Sciences* is an open access journal. This article is published under a Creative Commons Attribution-NonCommercial-NoDerivs 3.0 Unported License.

1. Author's calculations based on the American Community Survey 2016 sample.

such analyses are increasingly imperative as the changing demographies of the nation have become a source of growing conflict across the country. The current political climate shows a rise in white nativism and hate crimes against immigrants, people of color, Muslims, and LGBT (lesbian, gay, bisexual, transgender) members, including a significant spike in the days immediately following the election of Donald Trump as president of the United States on November 8, 2016 (Federal Bureau of Investigation 2016; Miller and Werner-Winslow 2016). On top of already fierce debates and protests over the ethnic content of the U.S. history curriculum, such as in Arizona and Texas in 2010 and in Colorado in 2014, the recent rise in national intergroup conflict points to the challenge facing schools to teach American identity within a demographically and culturally shifting nation, and the need for research to examine these dynamics in context.[2]

This article thus focuses on the everyday ways that schools teach middle school students what it means to be American in the context of immigration-driven diversity and presents findings from an ethnographic study of Castro Middle School, a diverse school in a city profoundly shaped by immigration. It reveals how American nationals and foreigners are "made" at Castro through direct classroom instruction, school events and programming, and daily interactions between peers, teachers, and staff.

The findings illustrate how efforts to reduce the ethnic distance between schools and their minority student populations may be explained as a process of two-way assimilation, whereby both mainstream institutions and immigrant communities undergo ethnic change and become more alike (Alba and Nee 2003; Jiménez 2017). Through this process of assimilation, a social context emerges in which a "true American" includes the cultural attributes of particular ethnic minority groups, facilitating the national identification of minority students and their definition of *American* in multicultural terms. Race, however, remains a significant barrier in the assimilation process (Portes and Zhou 1993). At Castro, the staff's desire to reproduce a multicultural nation was significantly limited by a black-white racial binary paradigm in which race and diversity were conceived almost exclusively in terms of blacks and whites (Perea 1997). Thus, although Castro staff consciously reduced the ethnic distance between the school and their small African American population, they did little to reduce the ethnic distance with their much larger Latino and Asian student populations, limiting the process of bidirectional assimilation.

SCHOOLING, ASSIMILATION, AND NATION-MAKING

According to the political scientist Elizabeth Theiss-Morse, national members are able to recognize each other based on social boundaries that define the prototypical or core national (2009; see also Miller 1995). These social boundaries are often based on ascriptive characteristics, including race, ethnicity, and language (Theiss-Morse 2009; Smith 1991; Anderson 1983), but may also be based on more civic attributes and political beliefs, such as liberalism and individualism (Smith 1991; Smith 1997). This mutual recognition is necessary for nationals to believe they belong together as a group, though they will never meet most of their compatriots (see also Anderson 1983). As the political theorist David Miller notes, "nations are not aggregates of people distinguished by their physical or cultural traits, but communities whose very *existence* depends upon mutual recognition" (1995, 23, emphasis added). How nationals imagine the social boundaries of the national community often influences which people or groups receive the full benefits and protections of the state and full rights of membership within the national polity (Anderson 1983). Yet the existing literature on national identity has done little to explain how children learn the boundaries of the nation in the first place or the social processes

---

2. In 2010 in Tucson, Arizona, protesters fought a ban on ethnic studies curriculum. Marches and rallies in Austin, Texas, the same year similarly opposed the school board's decision to change ethnic content in the U.S. history curriculum. In 2014 in Denver, Colorado, debates and protests ensued over the school board decision to limit topics in U.S. history that emphasized race, class, and ethnicity, which were argued to be un-American.

that lead to eventual national identification, including assimilation.

Assimilation is, in fact, a process of ethnic change whereby "foreigners" become nationals even as the characteristics of a national may change (Waldinger 2003, 2007). Moreover, the image of the core national in large part directs both the Americanization and assimilation processes for minority and immigrant groups.

Classic theories of assimilation have treated it as a process of cultural subtraction, whereby the ethnic elements of the individual are stripped away and replaced with Anglo European cultural and linguistic norms (Gordon 1964; Park and Burgess 1921; Donato 1997). Indeed, the common school movement led by Horace Mann in the late nineteenth century was in many ways designed to assimilate European immigrants from Germany, Ireland, Italy, and Poland into a common American culture, and to make American citizens who would serve the new republic (Tyack 1967; Labaree 1997). These European immigrants were eventually racialized as white as social acceptance in antebellum America became defined by a shared hatred toward and distance from African Americans (Ignatiev 1995; Roediger 1991). As the boundaries of the American mainstream became more defined by whiteness, these boundaries were enforced through structural racism in American institutions, including the Chinese Exclusion Act of 1882, Jim Crow policies of the South, and the segregated "Mexican schools" of the American Southwest.

The early assimilation scholars Robert Park and Ernest Burgess believed that race, and specifically whiteness, determined who was able to assimilate into a common American culture and who was not (1921). Although assimilation was seen as fully possible for white ethnic groups, it was (at best) only partially possible for nonwhite groups, including African Americans and the Japanese. Latinos were also viewed as racial outsiders who would never blend into the mainstream (Donato 1997). Later theories of assimilation emerging in the mid- and late twentieth century—including those forwarded by Milton Gordon (1964) and Alejandro Portes and Min Zhou (1993)—similarly described the core group (or upwardly mobile sector) of American society as white and middle-class, and it was into this culture that immigrants were presumed to assimilate. Notably, these theories share the assumption that the boundaries of the American mainstream are normative and based on roughly the same ethnocultural features, rather than socially constructed and contested (Anderson 1983). Only the immigrant community is presumed to undergo cultural change as it moves toward a fixed point of Americanness.

Sociologists have recently shifted on this point, suggesting a more dynamic construction of the nation that is shaped by both immigrant communities and the host society (Alba and Nee 2003; Jiménez 2017). Richard Alba and Victor Nee, for example, argue that assimilation is a bidirectional process of ethnic change experienced by both the host society and the immigrant community, leading to an overall decline of ethnic distinction (2003). Rather than presume that the mainstream is fixed as white or middle class, the authors suggest that bidirectional assimilation takes into account changes made within mainstream institutions (such as schools, organizations, churches) as they also evolve toward a common culture with ethnic minorities. Yet Alba and Nee do not develop national identity as an independent construct within their conceptual model. Although they describe how immigrants become part of and eventually change the American mainstream, they do not distinguish between the mainstream (defined primarily by the dominant group) and the imagined national community (Waldinger 2003). Tomás Jiménez similarly describes assimilation as a relational (or give and take) process of cultural change between the host society and immigrant community over time, but adds that the host society has changed their understanding of American national identity as a consequence of long-term immigration (2017). Still, this research leaves open the question of whether these shifts in national perceptions are shared by immigrants and their descendants, or how these new perceptions of Americanness shape their national identification.

This research thus provides an important conceptual bridge between assimilation theory and social theories of national identity. I argue that through this process of relational or two-way assimilation between immigrant communities and the host society, the social boundaries of the nation may change and a new definition of a core national (or "true American") may emerge that is more similar to immigrant communities. This new image of an American is also more recognizable to immigrant groups, thus allowing them to more easily see themselves as fellow members of the national community and identify as American. This article focuses on the interrelated processes of assimilation and national identity formation within the context of schools—key nationalizing institutions. My analysis highlights the specific mechanisms of assimilation within schools that allow for this mutual recognition to occur (or not), and how these processes shape students' national identification.

Education scholars have previously analyzed assimilation as a process of change occurring only among immigrants and their descendants (Ogbu and Simons 1998; Brown 2004; Yoon, Simpson, and Haag 2010), rather than as bidirectional change with the host society. Moreover, critical scholars within education have strongly critiqued assimilation because of its long association with ethnic erasure and positioning whiteness and standard English as the cultural norm (Ladson-Billings 1999; Valenzuela 1999). What has been missing is an analysis of how, over time, schools can also undergo ethnic change to become more like the minority communities they serve.

The closest theories that describe a cross-fertilization between student and school cultures come from the scholarship on culturally responsive teaching (CRT) and critical multicultural education (CME) (Ladson-Billings 1995, 1999; Sleeter 2012). CRT and CME are paradigms that construct racially and ethnically marginalized students as valuable contributors of knowledge whose diverse experiences are assets to student learning. CRT and CME also have an explicit antiracism, social justice agenda that prioritizes equity and inclusion in school programming and structures. One of the underlying assumptions of CRT is the belief that the degree of ethnocultural mismatch (or ethnic distance) between students and their teachers, curriculum, and school culture profoundly influences student achievement, motivation, and sense of belonging at their school. Despite the lack of any specific blueprint for how teachers should reduce this ethnic distance, as they are expected to tailor their instruction to the identities of the children in their seats, a primary focus of CRT and CME has been to provide diverse students with access to a range of multicultural curricula and academic learning tools that reflect their cultural identities.

Staff efforts to reduce the ethnic distance with their students—for example, through CRT, hiring teachers of similar ethnic backgrounds to the students, or having school assemblies to celebrate the accomplishments of various ethnic groups—are, in fact, indicators of bidirectional assimilation between the students and their schooling institution, resulting in an overall decline of ethnic distinction. By reconceptualizing such school practices through the lens of assimilation, the link between these practices and the emergence of new models of Americanness within schools comes into clearer focus.

Although CRT assumes that schools will be responsive to the ethnic and cultural identities of students within the local context, some evidence indicates that school reform since the civil rights era has predominately focused on the experiences of African Americans, giving far less attention to the incorporation of other racial groups, including Latino and Asian subgroups (Donato 1997). The education historian Rubén Donato argues that the experience of African Americans and their struggle for civil rights has dominated U.S. historical memory and often serves as the frame of reference for current discussions in education reform (1997). Thus, Latinos and Asians are largely left out of the historical record of civil rights, erasing the agency of these communities in desegregation and advocacy for bilingual education and culturally appropriate curriculum. According to the legal scholar Juan Perea, these historical omissions are evidence of a black-white racial binary paradigm that dominates the racial discourse within the United States (1997). In this paradigm, race in America is constructed primarily or exclusively in terms of blacks and whites. It limits the sets of problems that may be recognized in racial discourse, and creates significant distortions in the way people learn to view Latinos and Asians, including perpetuating negative stereotypes. The relative absence of Latino and Asian subgroups from local histories and U.S. history curriculum further relegates the contributions and longtime struggles of these communities to insignificance and, ultimately, leaves teachers with fewer resources to apply CME to a wider range of cultural identities (Menchaca 1995; Oboler 1997; Yosso 2002).

At Castro Middle School, a black-white racial paradigm among the staff limited their ability to reproduce the image of a multicultural nation among students and incorporate Latino and Asian–Pacific Islanders at the school. The staff described their use of CRT and multicultural education as guided by their desire to celebrate national diversity, promote tolerance and inclusion, and recognize injustice on the basis of race, income, and sexuality. Yet, in practice, the staff framed racial diversity as almost exclusively blacks and whites. Thus, although educators reduced the ethnic distance between the school and their small African American student population, they did not assimilate with the much larger Latino and Asian–Pacific Islander population. The findings further reveal that where Latino and Asian–Pacific Islander students were not provided a model of Americanness that was recognizable to them (that is, reflected their racial, ethnic, or linguistic identity), these students commonly defaulted to the hegemonic definition of American as white and English monolingual.

METHODOLOGY

Drawing from prior research on national identity, I operationalized the construct of national identity to include values and beliefs (such as democracy and individualism), cultural practices and traditions (such as holidays and festivals), ethnoracial and linguistic boundaries (how nationals distinguish themselves from foreigners based on ethnic, racial, and linguistic categories), and common myths and heroes (such as famous battles and political leaders) (Smith 1991; Theiss-Morse 2009).

To document the everyday practices of nation-making in schools, I conducted seven months of ethnographic fieldwork in Castro Middle School during the 2014–2015 school year (Fox and Miller-Idriss 2008).[3] I selected Castro for its geographic location in Bridgeview, a city in California that has been dramatically transformed by immigration. Between 1970 and 1990, Bridgeview changed from a predominately white working-class city with a small African American population to a primary destination for immigrant families from Latin America and Asia. By 2010, its Latino population had grown to 40 percent, and Asians and Pacific Islanders made up another 25 percent. The diverse students at Castro well represent the changing demographics of the larger city. Most of the students are U.S.-born children of immigrants. Their families represent an array of national origins, including Mexico, Honduras, Guatemala, China, the Philippines, Iraq, Saudi Arabia, and Fiji. The majority of students are Latino (55 percent) and predominately of Mexican descent. Approximately 25 percent are Asian or Pacific Islander, and include a fast-growing Filipino population. Of the remainder, 10 percent are African American and 7 percent are white. Test score data from the California Department of Education show that Asian and Filipino students significantly outperform Latino, Pacific Islander, and African American students at Castro and in the school district. In 2014–2015, 76 percent of students were low-income and eligible for free or reduced-price lunch.

Although the socially diverse demographics and large second-generation student population of Castro are increasingly characteristic of schools located in urban centers across the country, the ethnic diversity of the Castro staff far exceeds that of the national teaching force.[4] Among the twenty-seven staff members, including the administration, teachers, and parent outreach coordinator, the ethnoracial composition was roughly 56 percent white, 19 percent African American, 11 percent Latino, and 11 percent Asian–Pacific Islander. The diversity of the staff and students (including the limited pres-

---

3. I use pseudonyms for the school name, city name, and all names of respondents to protect anonymity.

4. The educator workforce nationally is roughly 80 percent white (U.S. Department of Education 2016).

ence of white students), and the progressive social politics of the local region made Castro a theoretically generative case to study how American identity is constructed within a school where we would strongly predict a multicultural national narrative to emerge. Although not generalizable in a statistical sense, the findings from this study also provide a sharper lens on how, within other school contexts with pronounced diversity, the process of assimilation can lead to a new shared image of national identity between the host society and immigrant community.

My methodology included participant observations three days a week at Castro, documenting how American identity was constructed during class lessons, in the curriculum, and through the social relations and structures of the school. This included observations in three eighth-grade U.S. history classrooms and three English-language arts (ELA) classrooms. The principal recommended the three teachers who taught both ELA and history for the study, and these teachers volunteered to participate. One ELA and history class served English learners (ELs) only, allowing me to assess whether American identity was constructed differently for EL students and mainstream students. I conducted additional participant observations in the cafeteria, main office, and on the schoolyard, as well as at various school events (performances, assemblies, staff meetings, and so on). I took photographs of school posters, murals, flyers, and notices as further evidence of the school's institutional culture.[5]

I conducted semistructured interviews with thirteen school staff members to ascertain the dominant model of American identity on campus, and the role of the school and local community in shaping this model. My respondents included nine seventh- and eighth-grade ELA and history teachers, the principal, assistant principal, academic counselor, and family outreach coordinator. School personnel shared their thoughts on the meaning of American identity in the twenty-first century and discussed how the social context of the school and local community influenced their pedagogy, programming, and organizational decisions.

Finally, I conducted semistructured individual interviews with thirty-five eighth-grade students (ages twelve through fourteen) from the observed ELA and history classes to assess how peer interactions, school structures, and classroom lessons shaped how students conceptualized American identity.[6] I selected consented student respondents that represented the different ethnic, racial, and generational status groups at the school. The final interview sample included seventeen Latino, nine black, four Asian-Pacific Islander, one white, and four other or mixed-race students representing a range of ethnicities, including Mexican, African American, Nigerian, Honduran, Saudi Arabian, Filipino, and Chinese. Nineteen of these students were males, sixteen were females. Most were second-generation immigrants, but the African American students had typically been in the country for at least three generations. Four students were immigrants. All interviews with students and staff were transcribed verbatim.

Using NVivo software, I coded, analyzed, and triangulated these data sources using a modified grounded theory approach (Charmaz 1995), guided by how national identity has previously been operationalized in the literature (that is, values and beliefs, cultural practices and traditions, ethnoracial and linguistic boundaries, and common myths and heroes). I specifically drew on Theiss-Morse's social theory of national identity to determine which characteristics were used by the staff to describe core na-

---

5. A note on positionality, within classrooms, I alternated between being a quiet observer and engaging directly with students. Occasionally I served as a teaching assistant, made copies, and tutored. With the students, I positioned myself as a trusting adult keenly interested in their experience, but not a formal staff member. My identity as a Mexican American with an immigrant mother and my experience growing up in urban communities were often points of connection with the students and helped build rapport and openness in our conversations.

6. All students were given a consent form to return with the signature of their parent or guardian in order to participate in the interview. I informed students that their participation was voluntary and would not affect their academic evaluation in any way.

tionals, peripheral nationals, and foreigners (2009). I then analyzed how the school reproduced their model of a core national in their efforts to reduce the ethnic distance with their minority students (evidence of assimilation). Finally, I assessed whether the students reproduced the school's model of a true American and how this shaped their national identification.

STAFF DEFINITIONS OF AMERICAN IDENTITY

Interviews with the Castro teachers and administrators showed that the staff shared a similar vision of the American nation.[7] They described America as a land of great opportunity and freedom, including being a place where teachers could present multiple perspectives on American history, rather than a strictly Eurocentric perspective. They also described America as a diverse nation with respect to race, ethnicity, religion, and sexuality, noting that this diversity of culture is what makes the country great. Some staff members directly tied the nation's diversity to the country's long history of immigration. In general, the teachers and administration felt strongly about helping students learn and celebrate national diversity by incorporating curricula that was responsive to their students' own cultural identities.

The views of Mr. Freeman, an African American ELA teacher in his mid-forties, capture that of other staff members in this regard. He believed that the school should include ELA and history curricula that reflects the diverse identities of the students within Castro and the nation.

> I really am a firm believer that teachers in this day and age with our changing population, not only in California but all across the United States, really need to be culturally sensitive, respectful and use materials that reflect the classroom. If we are truly a melting pot and every culture has something to contribute to the American experience, then why not use authors that have contributed and to show that to our students. So I've—we've read materials from Latino—Latino and Latina authors, we've read materials from Asian authors, Chinese, Japanese, Filipino authors. So I've tried to look at the population of my class and bring in materials that reflect, you know, their contribution to America.

Many of the staff expressed wanting to challenge the view that American history belongs to only white Americans by bringing in culturally responsive curricula. Ms. Fisher, for example, was a white teacher in her late fifties, and had taught English and history at the school for more than fifteen years. When asked what lessons from American history she hoped her students would remember in five years, she responded,

> I've written quite a bit of curriculum about minorities represented in history and so when I go back and I look at some of the things we've done and some of the things we'll do in the future, it's always that—that they see people similar to them represented in history. So that would be the thing that I would like them to remember . , . that all of them represent history. It's not just the rich white guys, which is what the books do a lot of times.

In addition to acknowledging the nation's diversity, the staff described the unequal treatment of different social groups in the United States as a result of historic oppression and ongoing racism. Their examples of national injustice included recent events in Ferguson, Baltimore, and New York where unarmed black men were killed by police officers, rising anti-immigrant sentiment, and the struggle for marriage equality for gay couples. The staff therefore wanted to help students develop a critical understanding of the nation that acknowledged both diversity and inequality, and to prepare students to better embody America's values of acceptance, inclusion, and equality for all.

---

7. I use American to refer to the people of the United States or the sociopolitical community that defines the nation (Anderson 1983). I recognize that the Americas include two full continents, despite the colloquial usage of America or Americans to describe the people of the United States.

FROM THEORY TO PRACTICE: LIMITED ASSIMILATION AT CASTRO

Although the Castro staff outwardly expressed a desire to create the image of a multicultural, multiracial America at the school, in practice, celebrating diversity nearly always meant celebrating blackness and the contributions of African Americans, rather than the broader ethnic representation of the school. Though African American students made up only 10 percent of the student population, the staff almost exclusively reduced the ethnic distance between the school and the African American students. Consequently, they neither constructed a national image that included Latino or Asian Americans, nor did they assimilate with their much larger Latino and Asian–Pacific Islander student population.

Bidirectional assimilation with African Americans was visible at both the school and district level. For example, a major effort within the school district was the African American Achievement Initiative (AAAI), which prioritized strengthening family engagement for African American parents at their local school sites, ensuring teachers were trained in implementing culturally and linguistically responsive pedagogy, and creating a school climate that was inclusive of African Americans. Schools were responsible for hosting two AAAI meetings a year, yet at Castro, numerous after-school events and assemblies throughout the school year were specifically dedicated to engaging African American parents and acknowledging African American students for their success in academic subjects, elective courses, sports, and school citizenship. These events were held either in the library in the center of campus, or in the multipurpose room, which served as the prime location for all-school events. According to the principal, AAAI events and similar school initiatives were equity-driven in an attempt to address the ongoing achievement gap between black students and Asian students at the school.

Castro staff also reduced the ethnic distance with their African American students through school-wide events and contests. In celebration of Black History Month (February in the United States), the students in the leadership class put up a large poster-mural of African American heroes in the cafeteria that included activists, philosophers, and scientists. The school administration also organized a mandatory assembly to celebrate Black History Month that began with a photomontage of African American figures and the principal leading students in singing the black national anthem. Students from the drama class performed monologues from speeches by Malcolm X, Booker T. Washington, Rosa Parks, and Martin Luther King Jr. The STEP team performed several routines, and the school counselor presented awards for a schoolwide contest for the best essay and art project that focused on the contributions of African Americans.[8] Notably, no other heritage months were celebrated at Castro during the school year.[9]

Beyond STEP, other aspects of African American culture and identity were reflected in Castro's art and music, as well as in the school visual environment. On the outside walls of campus buildings and the inside walls of classrooms were murals of African American figures, including a mural outside the music class of jazz legend Louis Armstrong. One classroom had two large artistic renderings of African American civil rights leaders Martin Luther King Jr. and Bayard Rustin hanging in the front of the room for the entire school year.

Assimilation with African Americans was also visible at the classroom level. In eighth-grade history and English classes throughout the year, teachers led lessons on the accomplishments of black Americans, including showing videos about the lives of baseball champion Jackie Robinson, the Freedom Riders of the civil rights movement, and transgender actress Laverne Cox. Teachers also assigned projects in which students had to research famous black writers, scientists, philosophers, and activists and present these figures to the

---

8. Stepping is a dance form historically associated with the African American community that involves using the body to make rhythms using a combination of clapping, footsteps, and spoken word.

9. The staff did not, for example, arrange school events to celebrate Hispanic-Latino Heritage Month (September 15 through October 15) or Asian Pacific American Heritage Month (May).

class. Students learned about leading abolitionist Harriet Tubman; hip-hop and rap artist Tupac Shakur; Barbara Jordan, the first African American woman in the U.S. House of Representatives; and Madam C. J. Walker, actress and entrepreneur of the early twentieth century. In two eighth-grade history classes, teachers showed episodes from the 1970s television miniseries *Roots,* describing the history of African Americans in the United States from the perspective of descendants of African slaves. Students also read literature by African American authors in their ELA classes, including *Bronx Masquerade* by Nikki Grimes, a story about identity, belonging, and poetry told from the perspective of black and Latino youth in the inner city.

In short, the Castro staff used critical multicultural education—specifically, Afro-centric programming, practices, and curricula—that effectively reduced the ethnic distance between the schooling institution and the African American students. Moreover, the staff created a context in which African Americans were "true Americans," despite ongoing inequality. Black Americans were projected as valuable members of both the national and school community and were incorporated into a diverse model of the American nation.

In sharp contrast to the African American students, the Castro staff made little effort to reduce the ethnic distance between the school and the Latino, Asian, or Pacific Islander students, despite the fact that these groups together made up the vast majority of the student population. The contributions of Latino and Asian Americans were entirely absent from school assemblies, events, and the school visual environment. While numerous classroom walls displayed imagery of African American figures, they did not display similar imagery of Latino or Asian Americans. Nor were there student groups or clubs like the STEP team that reflected the musical or dancing traditions of other ethnic groups. Interviews with the staff suggested that in the past, a Polynesian dance club had briefly existed at the school and performed at the school talent show, but at the time of data collection, this group was essentially defunct and received little, if any, attention from the administration.

Although Latino families represented the majority of students at the school, these parents were not meaningfully incorporated into the activities of Castro. Many of the Latino parents had immigrated to the United States from Mexico and Central America and were Spanish-dominant, yet few staff members spoke Spanish at the school. One of these was Ms. Morales, the parent outreach coordinator who worked only part time at Castro. She organized a variety of educational workshops, English classes, and translation services for parents. However, informal conversations with Ms. Morales and Latino students suggested that she was one of the few staff members Latino parents interacted with at the school. Whereas activities with African American parents through AAAI took place in the center of campus, close to the administrative offices, activities for Latino parents were typically held in The Parent Center/Centro de Padres, which was located in a bungalow at the edge of the school campus. It was rare to see Latino parents in other areas of the school; the exception being the main office, where parents typically went to handle disciplinary issues with their child.[10]

At the classroom level, assimilation with Latino and Asian communities was also notably absent. In seven months of observations at the school, only twice did staff members provide curriculum that included a prominent Latino figure. On one occasion, the date was May 5, popularly known in the United States as Cinco de Mayo, a holiday originating in Mexico celebrating the defeat of the French by the Mexican army at the Battle of Puebla. This holiday has since become popularized in the United States as a day to celebrate a stereotypical, cartoon version of Mexican culture—including wearing *panchos* and *sombreros* and drinking Mexican beer—and has largely been detached from its historic significance. On this day, one of the ELA teachers, Ms. Fisher, began class this way:

10. Although parents' legal status may have affected their engagement at school, particularly among undocumented parents, it was largely unknown to the staff and was not collected for this study. That said, the staff typically included undocumented immigrants in their imagined vision of the national community.

Ms. Fisher: We're going to talk about César Chávez today. Why today?
Ava: (enthusiastically raises her hand) Because it's Cinco de Mayo!
Sonia: What?
Ava: Cinco de Mayo.
Ms. Fisher: That's right. So we're going to spend some time talking about him.

Ms. Fisher proceeded to have a discussion with the students about economic injustice, then showed a video on César Chávez, noted migrant labor activist.

Several things were noteworthy about this event. First, Ms. Fisher did not explain the significance of Cinco de Mayo, including its origin as a Mexican holiday that was then appropriated by Americans. By contrast, on Saint Patrick's Day in March, both the mainstream and EL teachers showed multiple videos in class explaining the historical origins and meaning of the holiday to Irish Americans. Second, despite the complete lack of connection between César Chávez and Cinco de Mayo, this was the only day during the school year that Ms. Fisher chose to focus on a Latino figure, specifically a Mexican American figure. César Chávez thus became a tokenized representation of Mexican culture more broadly, rather than a meaningful model of a Mexican American hero.

The only other occasion in which a Latino figure was mentioned in class was during a final assignment for U.S. history in which students had to choose a historical figure to research and portray for a living museum. The teacher, Ms. Walker, gave students a list of American figures to choose from (or they could research another figure), which included mostly white American and some African American figures. Also on this list was Pancho Villa, a controversial figure from the Mexican Revolution. When I asked Ms. Walker whether the class had discussed Pancho Villa during the school year, possibly on a day when I was not on-site, she responded that they had not covered him in the curriculum, but that she wanted to include "someone from their culture." Indeed, Pancho Villa was a popular pick among the Latino boys in several of her classes. As one Mexican American boy explained on his poster, he selected Pancho Villa precisely because he was "the same culture." However, this event highlighted the trivialization of Mexican culture at Castro. Rather than integrate multiple models of Mexican American or other Latino American heroes into the curriculum, as the teachers had done with African Americans, Ms. Walker chose a Mexican national to represent Latino identity. Consequently, in this class, the only option available to represent a Latino was to be a foreigner.

Asian Americans and other ethnoracial groups were even more absent from classroom curricula than Latino Americans. On no occasion was an Asian American hero discussed in school curricula or programing. Moreover, several history teachers skipped the limited content provided in the U.S. history textbook that acknowledged the longtime presence of Chinese and Mexican communities in the country.[11] This included chapters addressing Chinese immigrants and the Chinese Exclusion Act, the settlements and culture of Mexican *Californios* in the early 1800s, and the Mexican-American War. Although teachers regularly face difficult choices about which content to cover in a school year, as well as institutional constraints around these choices (for example, test-based accountability), these notable exclusions effectively erased the early contributions and struggles of Asians and Latinos in the United States.

One teacher, Ms. Fisher, made some effort to educate her students about "other" (non-

---

11. The textbook used throughout the school district was *United States History: Independence to 1914*, published by Holt Rinehart & Winston (2006). Teachers described having a great deal of autonomy regarding which classroom materials they used as long as they met the state content standards for the eighth grade. This meant that the teachers' reliance on textbooks varied a great deal, but was more common for teaching history than ELA. In California at the time of data collection, teachers were accountable to standards released in 1998 before the arrival of new Common Core standards. The standards expected students to know about Mexican settlements of the early 1800s, the outcomes of the Mexican-American War on the lives of Mexican Americans today, and immigration to the northeast, but they make no mention of any Asian immigrants.

Christian) religions and holidays, including a lesson on Chinese New Year, yet the accompanying classroom discussions and assignments had the effect of distancing Chinese culture from American culture. Ms. Fisher began the lesson by telling the class, "Today you're going to write an essay about whether you should celebrate Chinese New Year or American New Year to work on your argumentative writing." She then passed out an article with two passages for the students to read. One passage was about celebrating the New Year in America and the other was about celebrating the New Year in China. After reading the passages aloud as a class, Ms. Fisher prepped the students on how to write their essays.

MS. FISHER: You need to choose one. [American New Year or Chinese New Year]
CARLOS: I thought you could choose both.
STEVEN: Yeah.

Without addressing these comments, Ms. Fisher went on to explain her model for writing the essay. Yet, as this brief exchange shows, the students disagreed with the premise of the assignment, which made them choose which holiday to celebrate as opposed to being able to celebrate both holidays, traditions, and cultures. In reality, many Chinese Americans in the United States celebrate Chinese New Year and the New Year on January first, and many non-Chinese Americans participate in Chinese New Year celebrations. The assignment, however, presented a forced choice: in essence, students could either be Chinese or American, but not both. Celebrating Chinese New Year thus turned into a marker that you were *not* American.

To summarize, although the staff made targeted efforts to include African Americans as true Americans within the national imaginary and to reduce the ethnic distance between these students and the school, the same could not be said for other ethnoracial groups at Castro, including Latino or Asian students. Using pedagogical strategies in line with CME and CRT, the staff directly challenged the hegemonic construction of true Americans as exclusively white and of European descent. However, when they attempted to incorporate Latino or Asian identities within the school, they reproduced a token or essentialized representation of these identities or constructed them as foreign. It was thus not surprising that when Castro students were asked during their interviews to describe Americans, they in many ways reproduced the boundaries of American identity that were reflected in school practices and curricula.

ASSIMILATION AND STUDENT NATIONAL IDENTIFICATION

This article began with the assumption that becoming American happens through the process of assimilation. I therefore expected that bidirectional assimilation would support the national identification of immigrant and minority groups by creating a modified image of a core national that was more ethnically similar to these groups and thus more easily recognizable. At Castro, interviews with eighth-grade students showed that African American students were indeed more likely than other ethnic groups to reproduce the multicultural national narrative put forth by the school staff that included African Americans specifically. They also more strongly identified as American themselves. However, in this same context, where Latinos and Asians were rarely depicted as American nationals or were absent from the national narrative altogether, Latino, Asian, and Pacific Islander students predominately reproduced the ethnocultural image of Americans as white and English monolingual that is prevalent in mainstream media and policy (Linton 2009; Gándara and Hopkins 2010). Based on this definition of Americanness, Latino and Asian-Pacific Islander respondents typically separated their American English identity from their ethnic minority-language identity, or did not identify as American at all.

AFRICAN AMERICAN STUDENT PERCEPTIONS OF AMERICANS

African American students at Castro generally believed that America is a multiracial society that offers freedoms and opportunities not available in other countries. Consistent with the staff's views, they also believed that diversity, tolerance, and multiculturalism were national values, despite the country's ongoing struggle with racism.

Lucas's description of Americans well exemplifies the common view among the African American students, specifically that Americans are a diverse people of many backgrounds and cultures, rather than a fixed, homogeneous culture. His own mixed ethnic identity as African American and Fijian reflects this diversity.

> I would describe [Americans] as, you know, they're diverse in culture, like they're not just one. They're like, they can be Italian and German, like especially with the . . . Caucasian people, like they're not just one. They're not just German, specifically. They're like Italian, Irish and so forth and so on. And like with Hispanic people, they're not just Hispanic, they're El Salvadorian and Puerto Rican and Spaniard. So it's, you know, it's just a mix of cultures with everybody. They're not just one particular thing.

African American students also commonly suggested that to be American is to be accepting of all people, regardless of cultural background, and to reject prejudice. Concurrently, African American students often attributed their strong identification as Americans to the fact that they shared these national values. The views Levi expressed typify those of many of his African American peers, who like him, grew up in the highly diverse community of Bridgeview. I asked Levi to describe the values he thought were important to Americans and later whether he identified as American himself.

> LEVI: Important values . . . Especially in America, you shouldn't be really judgmental of everyone, because everyone is so different and you can't really . . . You have to be accepting of people.
> [. . .]
> AUTHOR: How about for yourself personally, do you think of yourself as American?
> LEVI: Yeah, I think of myself as American.
> AUTHOR: How come?
> LEVI: How come? I mean, I feel the culture. I'm really accepting of all people. Unless, you know, like you have some bad thoughts, like you're prejudiced about people basically. Like you don't like that person because they believe in this, or they have that skin color but . . . yeah . . . I mean, you can't really live in this country if you're not really accepting of different kinds of people. That's what I believe.

Beyond diversity and acceptance, African American students described other aspects of American culture and disposition, including that Americans are smart, loud, dress a certain way, enjoy sports, like to party, like to be "outside the box," walk with swagger and conviction, know how to behave in certain social environments, and have knowledge of American history and heroes. Notably, they also discussed that Americans are free to be who they choose, say what they want, and (with the exception of breaking the law) do what they want, which they believed was not possible in many other countries. These freedoms were also important to their identification as American and their sense of national pride. Brandon, for example, discussed how his daily freedoms and opportunities made him feel American and set Americans apart from people in other countries.

> AUTHOR: So how about for yourself personally, do you think of yourself as American?
> BRANDON: Yeah.
> AUTHOR: How come?
> BRANDON: Because I was born in the U.S. and lived in the U.S. all my life and I have the freedom to do what I want and when I wanna do it.
> AUTHOR: Are you proud of, or, how proud of you are you being American?
> BRANDON: Very, because some people are born not American, and probably going through hell, so for me to be American and living a good life, it makes me happy because some people don't even—can't even do most of the things I do every day. They have to suffer so . . .
> AUTHOR: Sure, what are some things that you feel like you do every day that other people don't get?
> BRANDON: Fast food, basketball practice, hanging out with friends, homework, talking on

the phone. Most people can't do that every day.

An important distinction between African American students and other students at Castro was that African American students rarely used ethnocultural descriptors to define Americans, including race or language. Only one student mentioned race as a defining feature of Americans, but as a measure of inclusion rather than exclusion. This student, Olivia, said that her racial identity as African American is what made her feel American. She also used the example of African Americans overcoming slavery to exemplify that Americans (broadly) are strong and smart. African American students also rarely used English to describe fellow nationals. Nearly all of them saw value in learning multiple languages and believed this should be required of all Americans. In their view, one's identity as a true American was based less on specific ascriptive attributes, and more on pluralism, acceptance across social differences, and freedoms. Based on these definitions, African American students strongly identified as American.[12]

LATINO AND ASIAN–PACIFIC ISLANDER STUDENT PERCEPTIONS OF AMERICANS

In contrast to the African American students, Latino and Asian–Pacific Islander students most often described Americans in ethnocultural terms, specifically as white and English monolingual. They also commonly conflated their national, racial, and linguistic identities, unlike their African American peers.

Latino and Asian–Pacific Islander students generally believed that true Americans—whom they sometimes referred to as American Americans or full Americans—speak English, do not speak another language, and do not have an accent. The majority of these students also described Americans as white, explicitly noting their white or light skin, blond hair, and blue eyes. They used these ascriptive features to construct a social boundary that determined who was also partially American and who was foreign.

Emilio's view captures this position well. Like most of the Latino and Asian–Pacific Islander students at the school, Emilio is bilingual and a U.S.-born child of immigrant parents. He grew up in Bridgeview but his parents are from Mexico. Here Emilio uses a combination of race, language, and accent to distinguish full Americans from others.

AUTHOR: Do you think you can tell when someone is not American?
EMILIO: I think everyone says this—that it's because of your color and your accent.
AUTHOR: What do you mean by color?
EMILIO: Usually everyone is white. My friends that are American, fully American, they're all white. They're usually not tanned. They have light hair, like light brown or blonde. Their accent is full-on English. They don't have an accent.

This definition of American in terms of English and whiteness strongly affected the national identification of Latino and Asian–Pacific Islander students and their relationship to school. Although most Latino and Asian–Pacific Islander students identified as American to some degree, their connection to American identity predominately came from their identity as English speakers. This also meant that Latino and Asian–Pacific Islander students felt American when they were in settings where they mostly spoke English, including at school. Conversely, they felt less American or not American when they spoke Spanish, Tagalog, or Mandarin, or when they were in an environment where minority languages were dominant, usually at home or with their family. Roughly half of the Latino respondents described being split as both Mexican and American for this very reason, rather than identify-

---

12. The one white student interviewed for this project, Kaylee, had a similar view of Americans as the African American students. Kaylee described Americans in terms of their freedoms and rights, and specifically referenced the struggle of African Americans for freedom as an exemplar for why Americans nationally have the freedoms they do. She said she learned about these freedoms from videos in history class, including a video on the Freedom Riders of the civil rights movement.

ing as a hybrid Mexican American identity. Their American side was their English-speaking, school-going side, and their Mexican side was their Spanish-speaking family side.

Laura's interview best demonstrates the feelings of many Latino students. Laura is a second-generation Mexican American and a bilingual English-Spanish speaker. Here she explains her split identity as half American and half Mexican:

LAURA: I feel that I am half and half because a large proportion of my life revolves around being American because I speak a lot of English, and because the community around me is mostly people who live in here and who speak this language. But then, there's always the other half of my family . . . they speak Spanish. We usually have that. . . . how would you explain it? Not so much belief, but it's the culture we share together. So half—like my life usually revolves around the American side, but then I have some parts of my life where it's the Mexican and I talk and I'm used to being in like a Spanish-speaking community and I have the stereotypical Spanish food and those kinds of things.
AUTHOR: Got it. So, which aspects of your life do you feel like the American side revolves around?
LAURA: School, education. That's the large part, a large proportion of my life.
AUTHOR: Yeah.
LAURA: That's like my number one thing. . . . Because it's English, because . . . we're usually taught that.

Laura's association between her English identity and her American identity was common among the Latino and Asian respondents. Indeed, studies of American identity among immigrant and second-generation minority groups have found a similar association between American identity and English (Lippi-Green 2012), and between this association and schooling (Olsen 1997; Olsen 2000). Notably, students like Laura have learned to compartmentalize their American English identity and their ethnic Spanish identity. Much like the activity when students had to choose between celebrating American New Year and Chinese New Year, the interviews with Latino students suggest that many have internalized a forced separation between their ethnic and national selves. Yet instead of choosing one or the other, most Latino students felt an attachment to both. At the same time, they saw this hyphenated or split identity as an indication that they were not fully American.

For Latino and Asian–Pacific Islander students who defined American identity in terms of both English and whiteness, these students either struggled to identify as American or did not identify as American at all, including those who were U.S. born. In their view, whiteness functioned as yet another boundary that prevented them from seeing themselves as full Americans. Take Sam, for example, a second-generation Chinese American who struggled with this issue. When first asked to describe Americans, Sam characterized them as white and blond. He then elaborated that you could tell Asians and Hispanics were not American because they "look different than white people." I later asked Sam whether he identified as American. He responded this way:

SAM: Yeah, I think.
AUTHOR: Okay, how come?
SAM: Because I was born here and. . . . I don't know. I don't know. I'm not sure.
AUTHOR: You're not—okay, so what makes you not sure?
SAM: Because my parents are a different race, yeah.
AUTHOR: Okay. You're saying they are a different race. What are you referring to?
SAM: Errrr, I don't know.
AUTHOR: That they're—that they're Chinese or that they're Asian?
SAM: They're Asian.

Sam questioned his identity as American because of his family's racial background. In his view, to be American is to be white, and as he and his parents are Asian, he cannot be a true American, despite the fact that he was born in the United States. This same feeling was shared by U.S.-born Latinos, as well as Filipino immigrants who similarly defined Americans in terms of whiteness. Whereas English fluency provided an avenue for these students to at least partially identify as American, race served as an impenetrable boundary that prevented these students from identifying as core nationals.

Even Julie, a mixed-race Pacific Islander and white student whose family had been in the United States for over three generations, similarly described "straight Americans" (true Americans) as white and rejected identifying as American herself: "I don't personally think I'm an American because like, I'm like mixed with so many different cultures.... I don't think I'm just straight American, like straight white people. I'm mostly Pacific Islander, and so that's why I like, tend to not think that I'm American."

Julie preferred to identify as Islander or Hawaiian and distanced herself from Americans she felt were both homophobic and prejudiced against nonwhite groups. Her perspective is particularly illuminating because it shows that an ethnocultural description of Americans extended well into the fourth generation of Asian–Pacific Islander students, suggesting that this description does not necessarily disappear with more generations in the United States.

Latino and Asian–Pacific Islander students thus viewed the American nation in fundamentally different ways from African American students, largely because of their different perceptions of how race and language were social boundaries to national inclusion. These views may be partially explained by the dramatic difference in the way Latinos, Asians, and African Americans were included within the national imaginary of the school. African Americans were consistently constructed as core members of the national mainstream and the achievements of African American students were celebrated. This provided an image of Americans that was more ethnically similar to the African American students, enabling them to more easily recognize themselves as members of the nation (Miller 1995). However, Latinos and Asians were almost entirely left out of the national image constructed by the staff, mirroring the relative absence of these communities from the historical memory of the nation (Donato 1997). Thus, Latino and Asian students were less able to recognize their fuller cultural selves in the national community, and often reproduced a definition of Americanness based primarily on English-speaking ability.

DISCUSSION AND IMPLICATIONS

This article illustrates the role of bidirectional assimilation in shaping both shared notions of national identity and national identification. I theorized that bidirectional assimilation can produce a modified definition of a core national that is more ethnically similar to immigrant and minority groups, facilitating the identification of these groups as American. I showed empirically how this relationship plays out within one of the most important institutions in the Americanization process: schools. Although many factors contribute to how children imagine the nation, the role of schools in shaping national perceptions should not be underestimated.[13] In schools, students learn the nation's values (freedom, democracy, equality), the common language, and the history of the country and its people. Thus, although findings from this study are not generalizable statistically, they show how new shared notions of Americanness can emerge through the process of assimilation within highly diverse schools.

In the case of Castro Middle School, staff efforts to reduce the ethnic distance between the school and African American students were guided by their image of the nation as multicultural and racially diverse, which they wished to reproduce among students. However, observational data showed that in practice, bidirectional assimilation at Castro was limited by a racial paradigm that constructed race and diversity in America as almost exclusively limited to the experiences of blacks and whites (Perea 1997). Thus, while the staff reduced the ethnic distance with their small African American student population through school programming, events, and curricula that highlighted the ex-

---

13. Other factors may include parent background, local politics, and dominant portrayals of Americans in the media and policy. However, little empirical research has actually explored how these other factors shape the national perceptions of children.

periences and culture of African Americans, they did not assimilate with their much larger Latino and Asian student populations. Latino and Asian identities were notably absent from the national community within the school. On the few occasions when they were included in curriculum, they appeared in an essentialized or foreign form, as in the examples of César Chávez and Pancho Villa.

This disparity in representation may be partly due to the limited availability of alternative racial frames within the American national imaginary and mainstream institutions. The history of slavery, the national trauma of the Civil War, and the iconography of the civil rights movement have profoundly shaped the racial discourse and historical memory of the country. The lack of shared national memories and mainstream curriculum materials that acknowledge the contributions of nonblack minority groups means educators have limited resources to construct a national image that challenges a black-white racial binary paradigm, even in a school like Castro, where staff members take a race-conscious approach to school inclusion.

Despite these disparities in practice, assimilation between the school and African American students at Castro was shown to support their national identification. The staff constructed African Americans as true Americans, despite ongoing racism in the country. This image enabled African American students to more easily recognize themselves as core nationals and to identify as such. These findings contradict those of Theiss-Morse's national study of American identity, which showed that strong American identifiers were more likely to define prototypical Americans in ethnocultural terms and black respondents were more likely to consider themselves atypical Americans relative to other racial groups (2009). This study suggests that theories of national identity must take into account the potential of assimilation to shift the definition of a prototypical American away from an ethnocultural model and toward a model that reflects the identities of historically marginalized groups. In local contexts where this is the case, ethnic minorities—including African Americans—may more likely view themselves as typical Americans.

In contrast to the African American students at Castro, Latino and Asian–Pacific Islander students more often reproduced an ethnocultural model of Americanness, defined primarily as English monolingual and white. This definition led many of the Latino and Asian students to either split their national and ethnic identity into two non-overlapping parts (such as English American and Spanish Mexican), or to reject an American identification outright. These findings are consistent with studies of ethnic and national identity among Latino and Asian students in college (Devos, Gavin, and Quintana 2010; Cheryan and Monin 2005), second-generation Latino and Asian Americans (Bloemraad 2013; Lash 2017), and high school immigrants of various backgrounds (Olsen 1997) that found similar associations between American identity, English, and whiteness. We might predict that these associations would disappear with more time in the United States and more exposure to American multiculturalism. Yet the interview with Julie (fourth-generation Pacific Islander white student) suggests that, rather than a marker of students' newcomer status, ethnocultural descriptions of Americans are more likely a reflection of the history of colonialism and the continuing racialization of Latino and Asian groups as Other, inferior, or foreign (Tuan 1998; Oboler 1997; Kim 1999). Still, the persistence of the ethnocultural narrative among the Latino and Asian students at Castro is noteworthy given the school's concerted efforts to construct a national image that was inclusive of African Americans.

Certainly the ethnocultural model of the nation has deep roots in U.S. history and continues to be reproduced at the macro-level of mainstream media, language policy, and anti-immigrant policies (Linton 2009; Gándara and Hopkins 2010; Chavez 2008), as well as at the meso-level of school practice (Olsen 1997; Lippi-Green 2012; Pérez Huber 2011; Crawford 2000). It is therefore possible that the school's message of national diversity was not enough to counter the hegemonic ethnocultural narrative from being reproduced among Latino and Asian students, particularly given that these students were not presented with a model of Americanness that included their ethnic or racial identities at the school. Scholarship from sociolinguistics further suggests that the strong association between standard English and whiteness (Bucholtz 2001) effectively positions African Americans as distorters of English or not "true English-speakers" (Lippi-Green 2012). This may explain why Latino and Asian students who described true Americans primarily in terms of English did not include African Americans in their description, especially given the staff's regular enforcement of standard English as the linguistic norm of the school. More research is needed to explore whether Latino or Asian students have a more pluralist view of the nation and stronger national identification if they attend a school with a more critical language ideology or more expansive view of national diversity.

Although this study confirms the ongoing significance of race in the assimilation process, it provides important nuance to the existing literature on this point. Sociologists have posited that race may be a barrier to the incorporation of immigrants within the host society, but largely characterized the host society (or at least the upwardly mobile sector) as white, Anglo, and middle class (Gordon 1964; Portes and Zhou 1993). My findings reveal that even in a local context where the American mainstream included blackness, race still presented a barrier to the incorporation of Latino and Asian students. This study also complicates Portes and Zhou's argument that interaction with native-born youth of the inner city and ties to African American culture will necessarily lead to downward assimilation and a rejection of mainstream America (1993). The findings from Castro suggest that were mainstream institutions to construct an image of the nation that includes African American identity, this would support a positive American identification among these youths.

Finally, this research shows how the process of assimilation and the outcome of national identification are both influenced by local definitions of the mainstream. The findings demonstrate that district policies, school leadership, the ethnic composition of students and staff, and the politics of the local community all shape how the boundaries of the nation are reproduced among youth, as well as how the assimilation process unfolds at the institutional and group level. Future research should continue to explore assimilation in context, providing important nuance to existing quantitative scholarship.

This study carries a number of implications for schools and classrooms as they navigate a changing national terrain. How we define ourselves as a nation and whom we see ourselves becoming as a result of the influence of immigration has significant implications for national educational standards, language policy decisions, textbook and curriculum design, and teacher education and professional development. Findings from this study may therefore guide policymakers, curriculum designers, and practitioners toward creating a national narrative that is inclusive of our increasingly diverse population. At the micro level, this study also illuminates the conscious and unconscious ways that school staff members transmit messages to students about who does and does not belong in the nation. As student's sense of belonging is significantly linked to academic achievement and motivation (Osterman 2000), the findings suggest that educators should ensure their model of national inclusion aligns with school practices at the organizational, programmatic, and curricular level, as well as in daily interactions with students. Educators must also reflect on how their model of diversity may exclude students from full membership in the national community based on race, language, or culture.

REFERENCES

Alba, Richard, and Victor Nee. 2003. *Remaking the American Mainstream: Assimilation and Contemporary Immigration*. Cambridge, Mass.: Harvard University Press.

Anderson, Benedict. 1983. *Imagined Communities: Reflections on the Origin and Spread of Nationalism*. London: Verso.

Banks, James A. 2008. "Diversity, Group Identity, and Citizenship Education in a Global Age." *Educational Researcher* 37(3): 129–39.

Bloemraad, Irene. 2013. "Being American/Becoming American: Birthright Citizenship and Immigrants' Membership in the United States." *Studies in Law, Politics and Society* 60(1): 55–84.

Brown, Bryan A. 2004. "Discursive Identity: Assimilation into the Culture of Science and Its Implications for Minority Students." *Journal of Research in Science Teaching* 41(8): 810–34. DOI:10.1002/tea.20228.

Bucholtz, Mary. 2001. "The Whiteness of Nerds: Superstandard English and Racial Markedness." *Journal of Linguistic Anthropology* 11(1): 84–100.

Charmaz, Kathy. 1995. "Grounded Theory." In *Rethinking Methods in Psychology*, edited by Jonathan A. Smith, Rom Harré, and Luk Van Langenhove. London: Sage Publications.

Chavez, Leo R. 2008. *The Latino Threat: Constructing Immigrants, Citizens, and the Nation*. Stanford, Calif.: Stanford University Press.

Cheryan, Sapna, and Benoît Monin. 2005. "'Where Are You Really From?': Asian Americans and Identity Denial." *Journal of Personality and Social Psychology* 89(5): 717–30. DOI:10.1037/0022-3514.89.5.717.

Crawford, James. 2000. *At War with Diversity: US Language Policy in an Age of Anxiety*. Tonawanda, N.Y.: Multilingual Matters.

Devos, Thierry, Kelly Gavin, and Francisco J. Quintana. 2010. "Say 'Adios' to the American Dream? The Interplay Between Ethnic and National Identity Among Latino and Caucasian Americans." *Cultural Diversity & Ethnic Minority Psychology* 16(1): 37–49. DOI:10.1037/a0015868.

Donato, Rubén. 1997. *The Other Struggle for Equal Schools: Mexican Americans during the Civil Rights Era*. Albany: State University of New York Press.

Federal Bureau of Investigation. 2016. "Hate Crime Statistics, 2015." Washington: U.S. Department of Justice. Accessed January 24, 2018. https://ucr.fbi.gov/hate-crime/2015.

Fox, Jon E., and Cynthia Miller-Idriss. 2008. "Everyday Nationhood." *Ethnicities* 8(4): 536–63.

Gándara, Patricia. 2013. "Meeting the Needs of Language Minorities." In *Closing the Opportunity Gap: What American Must Do to Give Every Child an Even Chance*, edited by Prudence L. Carter and Kevin G. Welner. Oxford: Oxford University Press.

Gándara, Patricia, and Megan Hopkins, eds. 2010. *Forbidden Language: English Learners and Restrictive Language Policies*. New York: Teachers College Press.

Gordon, Milton. 1964. *Assimilation in American Life: The Role of Race, Religion and National Origins*. Oxford: Oxford University Press.

Ignatiev, Noel. 1995. *How the Irish Became White*. New York: Routledge.

Jiménez, Tomás R. 2017. *The Other Side of Assimilation: How Immigrants Are Changing American Life*. Berkeley: University of California Press.

Kim, Claire Jean. 1999. "The Racial Triangulation of Asian Americans." *Politics and Society* 27(1): 105–38.

Labaree, David F. 1997. "Public Goods, Private Goods: The American Struggle over Educational Goals." *American Educational Research Journal* 34(1): 39–81.

Ladson-Billings, Gloria J. 1995. "Toward a Theory of Culturally Relevant Pedagogy." *American Educational Research Journal* 32(3): 465–91.

———. 1999. "Preparing Teachers for Diverse Student Populations: A Critical Race Theory Perspective." *Review of Research in Education* 24(1): 211–47.

Linton, April. 2009. "Language Politics and Policy in the United States: Implications for the Immigration Debate." *International Journal of the Sociology of Language* 2009(199): 9–37.

Lash, Cristina L. 2017. "Defining 'American' in the Context of Immigration: A Case Study of Helping Hands Elementary." *Ethnic and Racial Studies* 40(6): 871–90. DOI: 10.1080/01419870.2016.1250933.

Lippi-Green, Rosina. 2012. *English with an Accent: Language Ideology, and Discrimination in the United States*, 2nd ed. New York: Routledge.

Menchaca, Martha. 1995. *The Mexican Outsiders: A Community History of Marginalization and Discrimination in California*. Austin: University of Texas Press.

Miller, Cassie, and Alexandra Werner-Winslow. 2016. "Ten Days After: Harassment and Intimidation in the Aftermath of the Election." Montgomery, Al.: Southern Poverty Law Center. Accessed January 24, 2018. https://www.splcenter.org/sites/default/files/com_hate_incidents_report_2017_update.pdf.

Miller, David. 1995. *On Nationality*. Oxford: Oxford University Press.

Oboler, Suzanne. 1997. "'So Far from God, So Close to the United States': The Roots of Hispanic Homogenization." In *Challenging Fronteras: Structuring Latina and Latino Lives in the U.S.*, edited by Mary Romero, Pierrette Hondagneu-Sotelo, and Vilma Ortiz. New York: Routledge.

Ogbu, John U., and Herbert D. Simons. 1998. "Voluntary and Involuntary Minorities: A Cultural-Ecological Theory of School Performance with Some Implications for Education." *Anthropology & Education Quarterly* 29(2): 155–88.

Olsen, Laurie. 1997. *Made in America: Immigrant Students in Our Public Schools*. New York: The New Press.

———. 2000. "Learning English and Learning America: Immigrants in the Center of a Storm." *Theory into Practice* 39(4): 196–202.

Osterman, Karen F. 2000. "Students' Need for Belonging in the School Community." *Review of Educational Research* 70(3): 323–67.

Park, Robert, and Ernest W. Burgess. 1921. "Chapter 11: Assimilation." In *Introduction to the Science of Sociology Including the Original Index to Basic Sociological Concepts*, 3rd ed. Chicago: University of Chicago Press.

Perea, Juan F. 1997. "The Black/White Binary Paradigm of Race: The 'Normal Science' of American Racial Thought." *California Law Review* 85(5): 1213–58.

Pérez Huber, Lindsay. 2011. "Discourses of Racist Nativism in California Public Education: English Dominance as Racist Nativist Microaggressions." *Educational Studies* 47(4): 379–401.

Portes, Alejandro, and Min Zhou. 1993. "The New Second Generation: Segmented Assimilation and Its Variants." *Annals of the American Academy of Political and Social Science* 530(1): 74–96.

Roediger, David R. 1991. *The Wages of Whiteness: Race and the Making of the American Working Class*. New York: Verso.

Ruggles, Steven, Katie Genadek, Ronald Goeken, Josiah Grover, and Matthew Sobek. 2017. *Integrated Public Use Microdata Series: Version 7.0* [dataset]. Minneapolis: University of Minnesota. 10.18128/D010.V7.0.

Sleeter, Christine E. 2012. "Confronting the Marginalization of Culturally Responsive Pedagogy." *Urban Education* 47(3): 562–84.

Smith, Anthony. 1991. *National Identity*. London: Penguin Books.

Smith, Rogers. 1997. *Civic Ideals: Conflicting Visions of Citizenship in U.S. History*. New Haven, Conn.: Yale University Press.

Theiss-Morse, Elizabeth. 2009. *Who Counts as American? The Boundaries of National Identity*. New York: Cambridge University Press.

Tuan, Mia. 1998. *Forever Foreigners or Honorary Whites? The Asian Ethnic Experience Today*. New Brunswick, N.J.: Rutgers University Press.

Tyack, David, ed. 1967. *Turning Points in American Educational History*. Waltham, Mass.: Blaisdell.

U.S. Department of Education. 2016. "State of Racial Diversity in the Educator Workforce." Washington: Government Printing Office. Accessed January 24, 2018. https://www2.ed.gov/rschstat/eval/highered/racial-diversity/state-racial-diversity-workforce.pdf.

Valenzuela, Angela. 1999. *Subtractive Schooling: U.S.-Mexican Youth and the Politics of Caring*. Albany: State University of New York Press.

Waldinger, Roger. 2003. "Foreigners Transformed: International Migration and the Remaking of a Divided People." *Diaspora* 12(2): 247–72.

———. 2007. "The Bounded Community: Turning Foreigners into Americans in Twenty-First Century L.A." *Ethnic and Racial Studies* 30(3): 341–74.

Yoon, Bogum, Anne Simpson, and Claudia Haag. 2010. "Assimilation Ideology: Critically Examining Underlying Messages in Multicultural Literature." *Journal of Adolescent and Adult Literacy* 54(2): 109–18.

Yosso, Tara J. 2002. "Toward a Critical Race Curriculum." *Equity & Excellence in Education* 35(2): 93–107.

The Racialization of Latino Immigrants in New Destinations: Criminality, Ascription, and Countermobilization

HANA E. BROWN, JENNIFER A. JONES, AND ANDREA BECKER

This article analyzes patterns in Latino immigrant racialization in the U.S. South. Drawing on a unique dataset of more than 4,200 news stories from the region, we find that Latino immigrants face multifaceted racialization in the news media and that this racialization shares substantive similarities with African American racialization processes. The most dominant negative characterizations of Mexican and Latino immigrants focus on their perceived criminal tendencies. Claims of Latino criminality apply implicitly coded racial language about black criminality to new Latino arrivals. A close qualitative analysis of these trends reveals an ongoing cycle of racialization in which immigration foes challenge Latino or Mexican immigrants as criminal elements and immigration advocates respond with charges of racism and discrimination. Supplemental analyses from four African American newspapers suggest that black elites perceive Latinos as sharing a common experience of racial discrimination at the hands of whites.

Keywords: race, immigration, South, Latinos, criminalization, racialization

Due in large part to immigration, the Latino share of the U.S. population has increased dramatically in recent years. Latinos now make up 16 percent of the U.S. population, accounting for half of the nation's growth demographic in the past decade (Passel, Cohn, and Lopez 2011). By 2050, demographers project that the Latino population will have doubled to more than one hundred million (Krogstad 2015). Thanks to these transformations, a vigorous debate has

---

Hana E. Brown is associate professor of sociology at Wake Forest University. **Jennifer A. Jones** is assistant professor of sociology at the University of Notre Dame. **Andrea Becker** is a PhD student in sociology at Vanderbilt University.

© 2018 Russell Sage Foundation. Brown, Hana E., Jennifer A. Jones, and Andrea Becker. 2018. "The Racialization of Latino Immigrants in New Destinations: Criminality, Ascription, and Countermobilization." *RSF: The Russell Sage Foundation Journal of the Social Sciences* 4(5): 118–40. DOI: 10.7758/RSF.2018.4.5.06. The authors would like to thank Felicia Arriaga, Ann Hollingsworth, Christina Lawrence, Robert Reece, and Nura Sediqe for their research assistance. Funding for this research was provided by a Russell Sage Presidential Authority Award (#88-14-05) and grants from the National Science Foundation (SES-1728780), University of Notre Dame, and Wake Forest University. The first two authors are equal co-authors, listed in alphabetical order. Direct correspondence to: Hana E. Brown at brownhe@wfu.edu, Department of Sociology, Wake Forest University, Box 7808, 1834 Wake Forest Rd., Winston-Salem, NC 27109; Jennifer A. Jones at jjones23@nd.edu, Department of Sociology, University of Notre Dame, 749 Flanner Hall, Notre Dame, IN 46556; and Andrea Becker at andrea.beccker @vanderbilt.edu, Department of Sociology, Vanderbilt University, PMB 351811, Nashville, TN 37235.

Open Access Policy: *RSF: The Russell Sage Foundation Journal of the Social Sciences* is an open access journal. This article is published under a Creative Commons Attribution-NonCommercial-NoDerivs 3.0 Unported License.

emerged about the role that Latino immigrants occupy in the U.S. racial hierarchy (Bonilla-Silva 2004; Chavez 2008; Lee and Bean 2004). Will Latinos join African Americans as collective minorities? Are they assimilating into whiteness? Or will Latinos occupy a distinctive racial position between whites and African Americans? These questions have taken on particular importance in the U.S. South, a region long characterized by stark black-white divisions and now home to the fastest growth Latino population in the nation (Kochhar, Suro, and Tafoya 2005).

Most work on these questions draws either from large-scale analyses of survey data (Frank, Akresh, and Lu 2010; Golash-Boza 2006) or on qualitative case studies focused on a single locale (Marrow 2011; Ribas 2015). Recognizing that the media are a critical site of racial formation (Omi and Winant 1994) and an important aspect of the context of reception (Menjívar 2016), we analyze patterns in Latino immigrant racialization in Southern news coverage. Our analyses of immigrant racialization draw from a unique dataset of more than 4,200 news stories from 2003 to 2013 from eight newspapers across four new destination states: Alabama, Georgia, Mississippi, and North Carolina.

Results indicate that Latino immigrants face multifaceted racialization in the news media and that this racialization is, in key ways, consistent in substance and form with that faced by African Americans. Rather than focus on immigrants as economic threats, the most dominant negative characterizations of Mexican immigrants and of Central and South American immigrants focus on their perceived criminal tendencies. Moreover, claims of Latino criminality apply implicitly coded racial language about black criminality to new Latino arrivals (Alexander 2012; Mendelberg 2001). Our results further suggest that pro-immigration forces also racialize Latinos, albeit differently. Despite much evidence that immigrants use economic arguments to make claims for various rights (Deckard and Browne 2016), we find that an equally if not more common argument made to defend Latino immigrants in Southern newspapers is that they face racism and discrimination. The writers, editorial board members, and political figures making these arguments routinely draw parallels between immigration enforcement efforts and the South's historic commitment to racial inequality, Jim Crow, and segregation. A close qualitative analysis of these trends reveals an ongoing cycle of racialization in which immigration foes challenge Latino or Mexican immigrants as criminal elements, and immigration advocates respond with charges of racism and discrimination. Supplemental analyses of 476 news stories from the largest African American newspapers in these states reveal that these newspapers portray immigrants much more positively than mainstream newspapers do. Our results further suggest that African American political and cultural elites perceive Latinos as sharing a common experience of racial discrimination at the hands of whites.

These findings suggest that, at this historical juncture, Latinos are not uniformly assimilating into whiteness. Rather, in key ways, Latinos in the South face racialization as collective minorities. Our results also suggest a need for renewed attention to the role that the social distinctions of place play in shaping ideas about race. Moreover, they indicate that making sense of the racially transformative effects of immigration requires a nuanced understanding of the racialization process. Existing research largely emphasizes explicit micro patterns of immigrant racial self-identification and macro patterns of state ascription (but see Mora 2014). Although important, this focus neglects the effects that pro-immigration forces, meso-level organizations, and implicit racial appeals have on immigrants' place in and adjustment to U.S. race relations and racial hierarchies.

RACIALIZATION, IMMIGRATION, AND NEW IMMIGRANT DESTINATIONS

Over the course of U.S. history, racial dynamics and immigration trends have been closely intertwined (Calavita 2007; Lee 2002; Molina 2013). Immigration patterns not only affect individual and collective self-identification, they influence intergroup relations, racial hierarchies, and racialized public policies (Lee and Bean 2004, 2012). Contemporary questions about Latino racialization emerge from this broader entanglement of racial formation processes and immigration trends and settlement patterns.[1]

To assess the effect of immigration on racial formation requires a foundational recognition of the socially constructed nature of racial categories and groups. Racial meanings vary from society to society as well as overtime within a particular geographic and social context. These shifts arise in part due to racialization processes that make racial distinctions and schemas "common sense—a way of comprehending, explaining, and acting in the world" (Omi and Winant 1994, 60). Racialization, in Frantz Fanon's formulation of the term, referred to colonialism's erasure of intragroup differences and its imposition of racial categories onto previously distinct groups (2004). Today, racialization "signals the processes by which ideas about race are constructed, come to be regarded as meaningful, and are acted upon" (Murji and Solomos 2005, 1).

Race and stratification scholars generally concur that racialization involves the mutually constitutive processes of ascription and identification (Brodkin 1998; Brown and Jones 2015; Nobles 2000). Ascription involves the application of arbitrary and usually phenotypic characteristics to lump together individuals into a meaningful social category. This process creates a common sense assumption of shared characteristics used to legitimate specific patterns of resource allocation and exploitation (Lacayo 2017). The identificational element of racialization involves acceptance of this designation, often for mobilization or identity construction (Espiritu 1993; Okamoto and Mora 2014; Omi and Winant 1994).

U.S. research on racialization has focused heavily on black-white racial dynamics, but racial formation involves groups such as Latinos as well. Since at least the mid-nineteenth century, Latino racialization patterns have shifted in response to political, legal, and demographic actions (Jimenez 2009; Mora 2014; Oboler 1995; Portes and Rumbaut 2001; Rodriguez 2000; Rumbaut 2011; Sommers 1991). The 1848 Treaty of Guadalupe Hidalgo classified Mexican-origin people as legally white regardless of ancestry. However, this classification did not translate into social acceptance as whites (Gutiérrez 1995; Haney-Lopez 1997; Montejano 1987). As a result, the first half of the twentieth century involved constant social and political negotiations over the racial status of Latin American and Caribbean origin individuals. Latin American and Caribbean origin peoples in the United States found themselves alternately subject to Jim Crow, segregation, and exclusion on the one hand, and the beneficiaries of resource access and protections not afforded to African Americans and Asian Americans on the other, depending on origin, phenotype, and location of settlement (FitzGerald and Cook-Martin 2014; Hattam 2007; Ngai 2005). The racial positioning of Mexican Americans in particular varied by geography, by time period, and even by institutional setting (Fox and Guglielmo 2012).

After the passage of the 1965 Immigration Act, migration from Latin American countries swelled, and Latino identity and racialization took on new political significance. Motivated in part by a desire to eliminate legalized racial discrimination in both civil rights and immigration law, the law shifted the allocation of visas. With few visas available to immigrants from the Western hemisphere, Latinos, especially Mexicans and Central Americans, became further connected in the collective imaginary to "illegal" or undocumented immigration. In the 1990s and 2000s, various geopolitical and economic shifts such as the North American Free Trade Agreement set off unprecedented migration flows, marking an explosive period of Latino population growth in the United States that was compounded by high fertility rates among U.S.-based Latinos (Massey, Durand, and Malone 2003).

This period also witnessed a fundamental shift in the settlement patterns of Latino individuals in the United States. Thanks to new economic opportunities and heightened immigration enforcement in some traditional des-

---

1. Whether Latinos constitute a race is much debated. We argue that Latinos experience racializing processes that homogenize a diverse population, institutionalize categories in a status hierarchy, and unevenly distribute resources along those lines (Browne and Odem 2012, 322).

tinations, Latino immigrants began settling in large numbers in small towns and suburbs across the nation (Massey 2008; Singer, Hardwick, and Brettell 2008). Southeastern states such as Georgia and North Carolina saw massive increases in their Latino and foreign-born populations and now rank in the top ten in terms of states with the highest population of unauthorized immigrants (Massey 2008; Singer 2004; Singer, Hardwick, and Brettell 2008). These demographic transformations raise old questions about Latino racialization but in a new context—the U.S. South. Given that racial dynamics in the South have largely revolved around black-white relations and inequalities, what position do Latinos occupy in the region's racial landscape? Some hypothesize that Latinos will join African Americans as collective minorities (Jones 2012; Smith 2014). Others highlight the possibility that Latinos will assimilate into whiteness (Alba 2016; Alba and Islam 2009; Gans 2017; but see Vargas 2015) or occupy a distinctive and possibly elevated racial position between whites and blacks (Bonilla-Silva 2004; Frank, Akresh, and Lu 2010; Gans 1999; Alba and Islam 2009; Lee and Bean 2004; Marrow 2011).

To address this question, a collection of pathbreaking researchers have examined emergent racial dynamics on the ground in new immigrant destinations like the U.S. South. Focused largely on the early 2000s or periods prior, these studies present evidence of black-brown tensions, conflict, and distancing. Although both blacks and whites at the time perceived Latinos as outsiders, African Americans did so thanks in part to perceptions of resource competition and long histories of interracial hostility and resource competition (LeDuff 2000; Marrow 2011; Ribas 2015; Rich and Miranda 2005; Stuesse 2009). These results provide empirical support for the view that Latinos occupy a racial middle. However, this interpretation depends on whether distancing is understood as a short-term mobility strategy used by immigrants throughout history to avoid association with blacks or a more lasting triangulated position in which Latinos are neither accepted by whites nor demoted to collective blacks (Kim 1999; Roediger 2006). Further, shifts in immigration enforcement priorities and racial politics in the mid-2000s may have altered Latino racial incorporation trajectories since these earlier studies were conducted (Jones 2012; Marrow 2017; Williams 2016). Indeed, in the South today, traditional indicators of racial incorporation, such as intermarriage rates and residential segregation patterns, show clear similarities between blacks and Latinos, suggesting possible shifts in racialization processes on the ground in recent years (Frey 2015; Lofquist et al. 2012).[2]

Existing studies on these questions draw largely on in-depth ethnographic research that provides a nuanced and powerful picture of emergent race relations in individual communities. Although these are essential contributions to our understanding of the racializing facets of immigration, the emphasis on individual community relations offers limited insights into the broader context in which the dynamics of racialization and intergroup relations occur, suggesting a need for cross-regional work. Moreover, because few of these studies account for cultural and institutional discourses, further work is required to understand the broader practices that drive ascriptive racialization and the location of Latinos in the racial hierarchy (Chavez 2008; Chavez 2012; Mora 2014; Santa Ana 2002). This gap in the research is consequential not only because ascription is an essential component of racialization, but also because it plays an important role in shaping race relations and social policy (Browne, Deckard, and Rodriguez 2016; McConnell 2011).

Because the news media are an important part of the context of reception (Menjívar 2016), media analysis provides a useful opportunity to address these gaps. As Eileen McConnell notes, the mass media actively construct metaphors, ideologies, and beliefs about nonwhites in the United States, often emphasizing a narrow range of negative topics that link racial mi-

---

2. Out-marriage rates for blacks and Latinos are similarly low in the four states under study here (Lofquist et al. 2012). Hispanic and black residential segregation rates are also similar, with Hispanic-white segregation indices revealing increasing segregation in recent years (Frey 2015).

norities with social problems (2011). This focus shapes public perceptions of nonwhites as racialized nuisances and social threats. News media shape both conscious and unconscious biases about immigrants and racial minorities (Haney-Lopez 1997; Kaufmann 2003). For example, the media have powerfully shaped popular understandings of African Americans, portraying them as dangerous outsiders, predators, and public menaces. These portrayals occur at rates that are disproportionate to the actual crime rate among African Americans, arise in both fictional and nonfictional contexts, and perpetuate stereotypes of pervasive criminality and social threat (Chiricos and Eschholz 2002; Dixon and Linz 2000b; Smiley and Fakunle 2016). The media in traditional immigrant destinations have also constructed Latinos and immigrants as existential threats to U.S. culture and the nation-state (Chavez 2008; De Genova and Ramos-Zayas 2003; McConnell 2011; Rodriguez 2000; Santa Ana 2002). Such representations characterize Latinos as unassimilable, foreign, and an economic threat.

These media characterizations are not mere expressions of grievances. They shape the ideologies and social understandings of local residents toward racial groups and toward immigration (Brown 2013; Domke 2000; Flores 2003; Hopkins 2010). Because the media construct and disseminate cultural frames that give meaning to critical issues, they play a crucial role in the racialization process and in immigration politics (Gilens 1999; Menjívar 2016; Rodriguez 2018). They also shape the attitudes of bureaucrats, and policymakers who shape opportunities and access for these groups, closing off opportunities for incorporation and upward mobility (Dunaway, Branton, and Abrajano 2010; Sohoni and Mendez 2014). Examining newspaper coverage in Oregon, José Padín argues that news media play a critical role in shaping what he calls the "climate of new immigrant reception," asserting that the media frames Latinos relationally, positioning them according to a set of normative racialized codes that are used to distinguish or establish similarities to other groups (2005). Such processes are deeply implicated in the construction of local racial hierarchies and in the identity formation of Latinos, who may decide to contest or accept this new set of ascriptive meanings and definitions assigned to them (Dávila 2012; Mora 2014).

DATA AND METHODS

To assess Latino racialization in new destinations, we conducted a news media content analysis of more than 4,200 news stories from 2003 to 2013 from eight newspapers across the South. The use of newspapers to analyze public discourse is a long-standing trend in the social sciences. In recent years, newspaper circulation has decreased, suggesting that newspaper framing may have less public impact than previously. That said, ample evidence suggests that that declining print subscriptions are counterbalanced by increases in online subscriptions and readership (Mitchell and Rosenstiel 2012). Studies also reveal that the content and framing of mainstream print, online, and social media news sources are relatively similar (Janssen 2010; O'Neill et al. 2015; Smith 2005). Given these trends and parallel framing processes, print media sources continue to present useful data for the analysis of cultural framing and public discourse.

We analyzed newspapers from four Southern states: Alabama, Georgia, Mississippi, and North Carolina.[3] As table 1 shows, these four states have witnessed rapid growth in their Latino and foreign-born populations since 1990 (Migration Policy Institute 2012). Using Access World News Database and the online archives of the *Jackson Clarion-Ledger*, we randomly sampled news stories per year from 2003 to 2013 from each of the two largest newspapers in each state. To create these samples, we searched for articles including the term *immigra* and retained only those that discussed immigration-related issues in the United States. We then sampled from the eligible stories to retain fifty

---

3. The eight newspapers are the *Jackson Clarion-Ledger*, the *Biloxi Sun-Herald*, the *Birmingham News*, the *Mobile Press-Register*, the *Atlanta Journal-Constitution*, the *Augusta Chronicle*, the *Charlotte Observer*, and the *Raleigh News and Observer*.

Table 1. Foreign-Born Population and Change by State, 1990–2010

Region	1990 Estimate	2000 Estimate	2010 Estimate	1990 to 2010 Percent Change
United States	19,767,316	31,107,889	21,419,957	8.4
Alabama	43,533	87,772	168,596	287.3
Georgia	173,126	577,273	942,959	444.7
Mississippi	20,383	39,908	61,428	201.4
North Carolina	115,077	430,000	719,137	524.9

Source: Migration Policy Institute 2012.

stories per state per year for analysis. We did so by taking every Nth story, where N equaled the number of eligible stories that year divided by fifty.

After compiling the dataset, we used Dedoose, a cloud-based qualitative content analysis software, to code these stories. All codes with less than 80 percent intercoder reliability were dropped from the analysis. The average for the retained codes was 98 percent agreement. The coding scheme included codes for racial labels, immigrant country or region of origin, speaker characteristics, positive and negative characterizations of immigrants, and article type and date. In addition to this specified analysis, we used the full universe of news stories on immigration (approximately twenty-three thousand stories) to construct broader histories of immigration and immigration policy in each state to provide context for the study. We supplemented this analysis with content analysis of immigration-related stories published in the one of the largest African American newspapers from each state.[4] Following the same sampling and coding procedures as for the mainstream newspapers, we compiled and analyzed a dataset of 476 additional news stories from the African American newspapers. In what follows, we present results first from the mainstream newspapers, highlighting trends in reporting of immigrants over time. We follow that discussion with results from the African American newspapers.

LATINO RACIALIZATION IN MAINSTREAM NEWSPAPERS

Results reveal consistent patterns in the characterizations of immigrants in mainstream newspapers in the U.S. South. Table 2 presents descriptive statistics for the most frequently occurring themes for each code category. Overall, news stories contained slightly more negative characterizations of immigrants than positive ones. Approximately 31 percent of stories contained at least one negative characterization; 29 percent characterized immigrants positively. The relative balance between positive and negative characterizations may well reflect the long-standing journalistic practices of seeking multiple competing viewpoints to demonstrate "objectivity" (Schudson 1981; American Press Association 2017). Our results suggest, however, that even if journalistic norms encourage reporters to balance both negative and positive viewpoints on immigrants, the substance of these viewpoints varies in important ways. Immigration advocates and opponents used distinct portrayals of immigrants that reveal complex and contested debate about the specific characteristics of immigrants worthy of discussion.

The most common negative claim about immigrants emphasized the perceived criminal tendencies of noncitizens; economic threat claims were far less common. Nearly 60 percent of the negative arguments made about immigrants involved judgments about immigrants' involvement in criminal activities or their crim-

---

4. These newspapers include the *Jackson Advocate*, the *Birmingham Times*, the *Atlanta Daily World*, and the *Charlotte Post*. Only the *Atlanta Daily World* is publicly available for our entire period, from 2003 to 2013. We acknowledge these limitations when discussing our data from these newspapers.

Table 2. Descriptive Statistics for Key Codes

Code	Total (N)	Frequency
Article type		
Letter to editor	320	0.08
News reporting	2,857	0.68
Opinion	1,033	0.25
Total articles in category[a]	4,208	1.00
Immigrant country or region		
Central or South America	125	0.03
Mexico	864	0.21
Vietnam	73	0.02
Total articles in category[a]	1,527	0.36
Negative immigrant		
Crime	779	0.19
Drain collective resources	367	0.09
Steal jobs	194	0.05
Total articles in category[a]	1,323	0.31
Positive immigrant		
Hard work	401	0.10
Make collective resources	318	0.08
Racism or discrimination	582	0.14
Total articles in category[a]	1,227	0.29
Race		
Asian	104	0.02
Black	428	0.10
Latino or Hispanic	982	0.23
Total articles in category[a]	1,245	0.30
Speaker		
Federal official or politician	384	0.09
State, local elected official	535	0.13
Advocacy, service, nonprofit	464	0.11
Immigrant member of public	365	0.09
Total articles in category[a]	1,590	0.38

Source: Authors' compilation.
[a] *Total* is the total number of articles with codes for that category. Because an article might have references to multiple subcodes within a category, totals are not the sum of all subcodes for the code category.

inal predispositions. This argument is exemplified by a 2005 piece in the *Raleigh News and Observer*, which reported on crimes involving local immigrants. The article noted that "Eight illegal immigrants from Honduras pleaded guilty Tuesday to federal charges related to a multistate scheme to steal and resell more than $2.5 million worth of baby formula and over-the-counter drugs" (Weigl 2005). An article from the *Jackson Clarion-Ledger* in Mississippi similarly highlighted the fact that the perpetrator of a local crime was an undocumented immigrant: "A police report shows the suspect in the Wheaton hit-and-run is Jaime Martinez, an illegal immigrant wanted for a homicide in Mexico, who was driving a borrowed 1997 white Cadillac" (Apel 2011). Like constructions of African Americans, these news stories portray im-

Figure 1. Crime Claims by Year and Violent Crime Rate

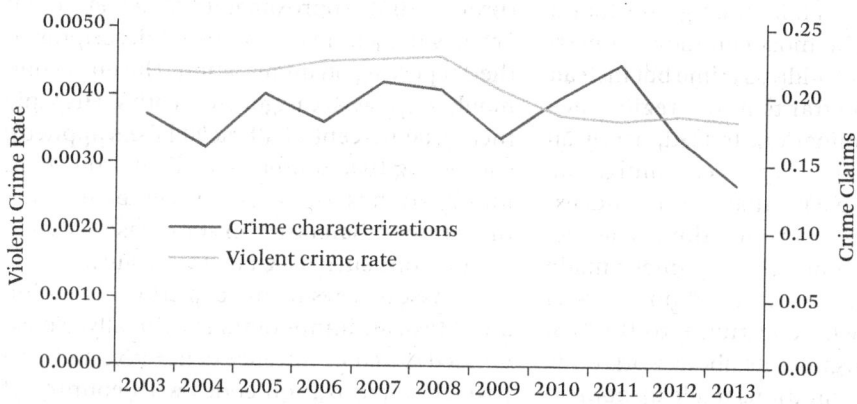

Source: Authors' calculations.

migrants as dangerous menaces. Further, media elites opted for language and contextual associations that depict illegal status as a criminal violation, despite the fact that unauthorized presence in the United States is a civil, not a criminal, infraction. Although illegality could be framed as a bureaucratic, legal, or administrative issue, by and large the news media chose to frame illegality as a form of criminality. These discussions of crime dwarfed the other negative stereotypes about immigrants, despite the fact that crime rates for immigrants and in immigrant-heavy areas are consistently lower than in other areas (Ewing, Martinez, and Rumbaut 2016; Nowrasteh 2015; Rumbaut 2009). Indeed, as figure 1 shows, the prevalence of criminality claims in our data do not reflect any shifts in the crime rate in these four states under the study period.[5] Although crime characterizations rose and fell between 2003 and 2013, the violent crime rate trend remained stable from 2003 to 2008 and gradually declined between 2008 and 2013. Moreover, the largest spike in crime characterizations in 2011 occurred despite a dip in the violent crime rate the same year.

The crime characterization was so dominant in our data that the second most frequent negative characterization of immigrants (that they drain collective resources) constituted only 28 percent of all negative characterizations. A story from Georgia typified the "drain collective resources" argument when it reported that residents in the state "want the law to clear the state of illegal immigrants, who they say are taking advantage of Georgia's schools, hospitals and workplaces, draining public funds as they take jobs that could help the unemployed" (Schneider 2011). Only 15 percent of articles contained the claim that immigrants steal jobs from citizens, despite prior scholars pointing to economic threat as a dominant anti-immigrant sentiment (Wilson 2001; Deckard and Browne 2016; Fryberg et al. 2012). A news story from Raleigh, North Carolina, conveyed this argument in a 2011 story on opposition to immigration. The story quoted Ron Woodward, president of an North Carolina–based advocacy group called N.C. Listen, as saying, "If we had half of those people here illegally and those jobs were freed up, that's 100,000 Americans today that would have a job that don't have one . . . That would be a great improvement" (Barrett 2011). That the steal jobs argument appears so rarely in the data is surprising given the wealth of academic and public attention to the presumed economic costs of immigration to American-born workers (Newton 2000; Simon and Sikich 2007; Stuesse 2009; Wright, Levy, and Citrin 2015).

Although negative and positive characterizations appeared at similar frequencies in our

---

5. The trends in crime rates are not driven by a single state. In Alabama, the per capita violent crime rate remained the same from 2003 to 2013, but in the other three states it declined over the same period.

sample, positive characterizations and countervailing arguments about immigrants took a variety of forms. The most common counterpoint offered did not address crime but instead asserted that immigrants in the region face racism and discrimination. Indeed, nearly 50 percent of stories that portrayed immigrants positively made the case that immigrants experience racism or discrimination.[6] The second most common positive argument made about immigrants characterized noncitizens as hard workers who contribute to the U.S. economy. These arguments about work ethic and economic contributions made up approximately 33 percent of all positive arguments made about immigrants. The third most common positive argument (26 percent) identified immigrants as contributors to the public good or as individuals who make collective resources from which others benefit. Around 14 percent of positive claims argued that immigrants have strong family values or that immigrant children are deserving members of society. If immigration opponents attempted to steer public discourse toward the assumed criminality of immigrants, supporters focused instead on racism and discrimination and on work ethic.

To understand media trends in immigration coverage, we also examined the countries of origin noted for those immigrants discussed in the mainstream newspapers. Country of origin proved an important device for writers in framing their arguments about immigration. A full 36 percent of news articles noted immigrants' country or region of origin. Of these articles, 57 percent focused on immigrants from Mexico, an unsurprising trend given the demographics of the newly arrived noncitizen population in these states. No other region or country of origin made up more than 8 percent of the total. Because public and media discourse about immigration also relies at times on racialized framing to make arguments about immigrants, we also coded for the use of racial labels in immigration-related news coverage (Brown 2013). Approximately 30 percent of all articles used at least one racial descriptor in their reporting on immigration. The most commonly used racial category was Latino-Hispanic (nearly 80 percent of all racial labels applied), suggesting that Southern media discourse on immigration is overwhelming centered on Latinos rather than other, in some cases, sizable populations such as Asian Americans.

To assess news media depictions of Latino and Mexican immigrants specifically, we examined the co-occurrence of negative and positive characterization codes with country of Mexican origin and Latino-Hispanic race codes (see figures 2 and 3). First, we examined the most common negative characterizations made in articles that discuss Mexican immigrants. Surprisingly, only 15 percent of negative immigrant characterizations in our data set asserted that Mexicans newcomers steal jobs or otherwise threaten the economic stability of nonimmigrants.[7] Rather than highlight the economic effects of immigration, the most common attacks levied against Mexican immigrants during this period characterized these newcomers as criminals. Nearly two-thirds of all negative characterizations in these stories labeled Mexican immigrants as perpetrators of crime. These stories took multiple forms, including news reporting on individual instances of criminal activity perpetrated by noncitizens, groups of immigrants implicated in gang activity and the illegal drug trade, and undocumented immigrants as inherently criminal due to their unauthorized status. Consider the following quote from a 2011 *Augusta Chronicle* story:

> U.S. Attorney Ed Tarver said Wednesday that 51-year-old Oscar Lazo and 35-year-old Eva Ramos were charged with conspiring to sell the stolen identities of U.S. citizens and harboring illegal immigrants. Prosecutors also charged Maurcio Cruz and Manuel Cruz—

---

6. Racism or discrimination claims appear at similar rates in Alabama, Mississippi, and North Carolina (around 50 to 52 percent of all positive claims and 14.1 percent to 16.6 percent of all stories) but are slightly less common in Georgia (36 percent of all positive codes and 38 percent of all published stories).

7. By contrast, the most frequently made negative claim in stories about Middle Eastern immigrants involved terrorism; Southeast Asian immigrants were chided for their lack of English skills.

Figure 2. Negative Characterizations of Immigrants

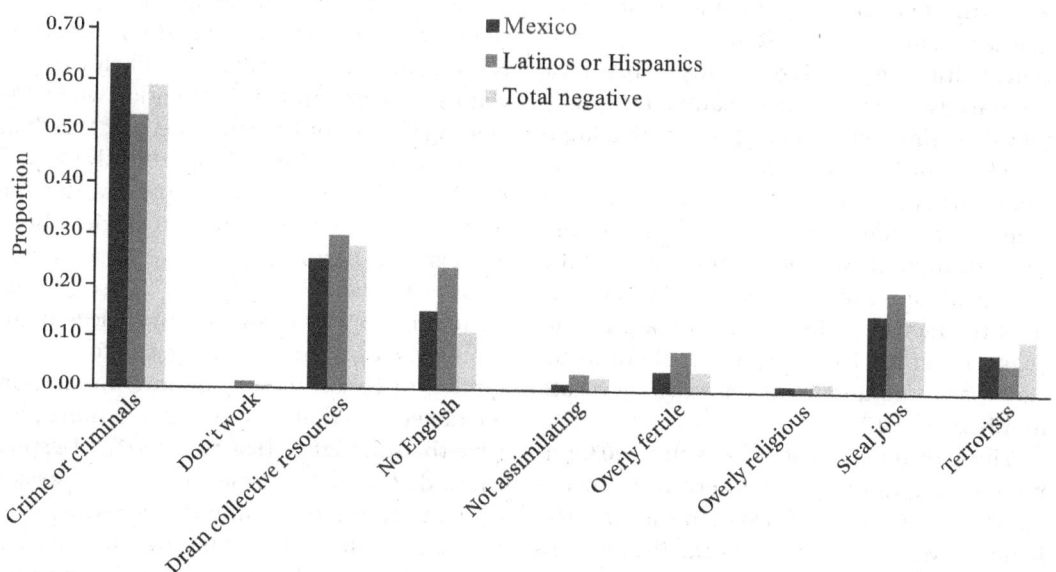

Source: Authors' calculations.

Figure 3. Positive Characterizations of Immigrants

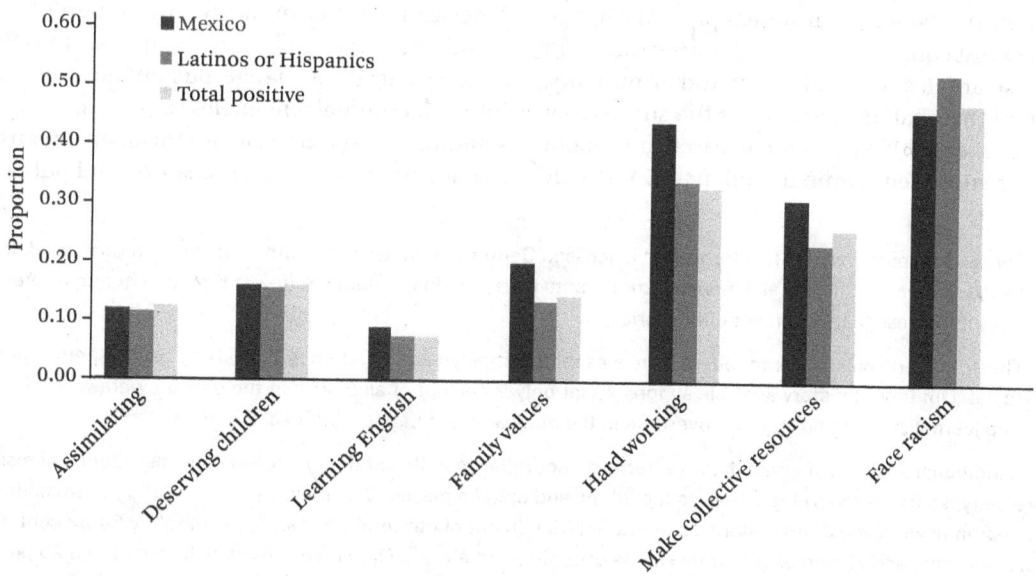

Source: Authors' calculations.

both citizens of Mexico—with using the stolen identities to get hired at the restaurant. (*Augusta Chronicle* 2011)

As is typical in the data, this story not only reports on law-breaking activities by Mexican immigrants, but also stresses the criminal schemes hatched by those immigrants.

Whereas the most common negative characterization of Mexican immigrants focused on criminal tendencies and activities, the two most common positive characterizations emphasized immigrants' hard work and strong work ethic (44 percent) or claimed that immigrants face racism and discrimination (46 percent).[8] Although the aggregate measures show the hard work and racism claims as equally prevalent, time-series analyses reveal that arguments about Mexicans' work ethic were most common in the earlier years of our sample, and racism-discrimination arguments remain consistently high. In only one year (2006), did the hard work argument appear more frequently than the racism or discrimination argument, suggest that the latter argument about Mexicans was more dominant than the aggregate numbers reveal.[9]

These results indicate that, since 2003, immigration discourse in Southern news media has crystallized around two themes: the criminality of Mexican immigrants and the discriminatory treatment these immigrants face.[10] But are these discussions primarily about race or primarily about country of origin? To answer that question, we examined characterizations of Latinos-Hispanics in our dataset (see figures 2 and 3). Results reveal similar patterns. Again, the most common negative characterization in these articles involved crime and criminality. More than half (53 percent) of the stories that discussed Latinos also made assertions about their supposed criminal tendencies. Virtually the same proportion of stories with positive characterizations (47 percent) argued that Latinos face ongoing racism and discrimination. Notably, news stories were more likely to make claims of racism and discrimination when discussing Latinos or Hispanics (52 percent) than when discussing Mexicans specifically (46 percent). Arguments about immigrant work ethic were also far more common in stories about Mexicans (44 percent) than in stories about Latinos or Hispanics (34 percent). These linguistic distinctions may signal differences in an ethnic versus a racial framing, the former intended to construct and denote population characteristics that are cultural and more positive than the latter (Hattam 2007).[11] Despite these distinctions, these findings suggest a deep racialization of immigration discourse in the news media, with media coverage focused on constructions of Latino criminality and anti-Latino racism.

In at least three respects, this media characterization of Latino newcomers parallels the long-standing associations between African Americans and criminality (Alexander 2012; Mendelberg 2001). First, the emphasis in our data on Latinos as dangerous outsiders with inherent criminal tendencies mirrors the long-standing characterization of African Americans as dangerous outsiders, predators, and public

---

8. These same patterns hold for stories that discussed Central American immigrants. We do not report this data because references to Central American immigrants were rare in our data set (fewer than two hundred references total or less than 5 percent of all stories).

9. These shifts do not appear to reflect increases in the employment of Latino journalists by newspapers in our data set. Our story-by-story analysis suggests that only 2 percent of all stories in the dataset were written by Latino journalists, with no increase overtime in the publication of Latino-authored pieces.

10. Additional analyses suggest these patterns do not reflect significant differences in code distribution across article types (news reporting, letters to the editor, and opinion pieces). The majority of crime and racism codes appear in news stories. News stories constituted 68 percent of our total sample. Approximately 64 percent of racism claims and 72 percent of crime claims occur in news stories. Opinion pieces, which constituted 25 percent of the sample, contained 33 percent of the racism codes and 23 percent of the crime codes. Both codes are underrepresented in letters to the editor. A breakdown of results by state shows that these trends are not driven by a single state. Rather, trends appear regionally.

11. Whether there is an analytic distinction between *race* and *ethnicity* is heavily debated (see Brown and Jones 2015). Here, we follow panethnicity researchers and colloquial usage in treating national-origin labels as *ethnic*, in contrast to *panethnic* or *racial* labels that homogenize diverse national origin groups (Okamoto and Mora 2014). In using the terms *racial* and *ethnic* in this fashion, we do not suggest a clear analytical distinction between the two concepts but rather argue that the two concepts conjure different "associative chains" that produce distinct discourses in the United States (Hattam 2007)

Figure 4. Crime and Racism Claims by Year in Mainstream Newspapers

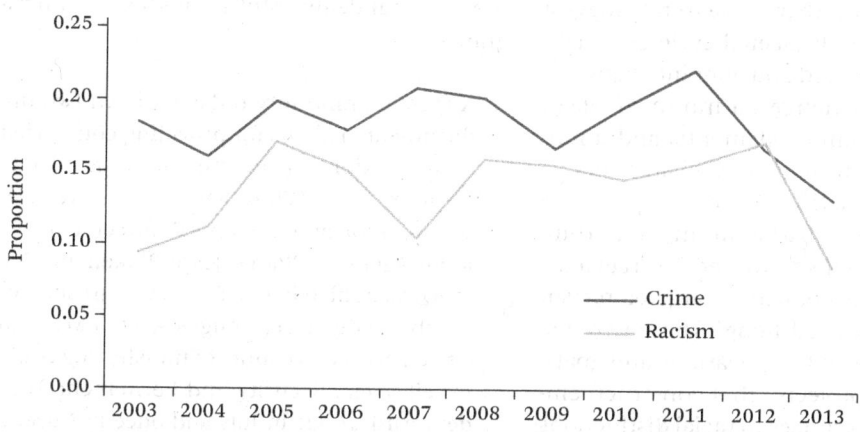

Source: Authors' calculations.

menaces (Russell-Brown 2008; Alexander 2012). Second, just as assumptions of black criminality often precede any actual criminal actions (Yancy 2016), news coverage of Latinos in our data typically assume criminality on the basis of a civil violation: unauthorized presence. Third, media portrayals of African American and Latino crime are disproportionate to the actual levels of crime committed by those groups (Dixon and Linz 2000a).

Our results further suggest that Latino racialization originates not only from critics of immigrants who characterize Latinos and Mexicans as criminals but also from pro-immigration forces. Rather than make pro-immigrant arguments grounded in economic or human rights claims (Bloemraad, Silva, and Voss 2016; Deckard and Browne 2016; Fujiwara 2005; Lawlor 2015), immigration news stories more often asserted that immigrants, Latinos and Mexicans in particular, faced widespread racism and discrimination. The writers, editorial board members, and political figures making these arguments routinely drew parallels between immigration enforcement efforts and the South's historic commitment to racial inequality, Jim Crow, and segregation. For example, in a column focused on immigration, Sid Salter of the *Jackson Clarion-Ledger* dispelled common myths about Latino immigrants and argued, "Now that a measure of progress has been made in race relations between blacks and whites in Mississippi, it seems some among us are encouraging new avenues for racism and bigotry, and adding a side order of misplaced nationalism" (Salter 2003). Another article in the same newspaper quoted Bill Chandler, a Mississippi immigration advocate, as saying, "[Anti-Latino racism] is the same kind of racism that has been perpetuated against African Americans for years" (Crisp 2010).

Time-series data show that these two racializing arguments (that of Latino criminality on one hand and of racial discrimination on the other) are not independent of each other. As figure 4 shows, these arguments about racism and discrimination rise and fall in tandem with criminality assertions. More specifically, both Latino criminality and racial discrimination claims rise and then decline from 2004 to 2006. Criminalization arguments rise again in 2007, followed closely by a steep increase of racial discrimination arguments the following year. This parallel relationship continues throughout the period of analysis—declining slowly after 2007, rising again between 2010 and 2012, and declining steeply through to 2013.

Although these claims rise and fall concurrently, our data suggest that different actors make each argument. News stories highlighting the criminality of Mexicans and Latinos most commonly quoted state and local government officials, whereas those focused on racism and discrimination relied most often on reports from representatives from advocacy and nonprofit organizations that serve local immigrants. Taken together, these trends suggest an ongoing and multifaceted cycle of racialization in which elected and appointed government officials challenge Latino or Mexican immigrants as criminal elements, and immigration advocates respond with charges of racism and discrimination. As counterpoints to racializing claims of Latino immigrant criminality, publishers choose to feed this racialization by citing claims of Latino-targeted racism and discrimination. Although these two discourses have different implications and goals, both are "racial projects" that construct, emphasize, and give primacy to racial distinctions between Latinos and other groups (Omi and Winant 1994).

AFRICAN AMERICAN NEWSPAPERS

Do the same patterns present in African American newspapers in the region? To answer this question, we turn to results from our content analysis of immigration-related stories published in four African American newspapers. Slightly different patterns are evident. First, although positive and negative characterizations of immigrants appeared at the relatively same frequency in the mainstream newspapers (31 percent and 29 percent, respectively), African American newspapers portrayed immigrants in strikingly more positive terms. African American newspapers published more than twice as many positive characterizations of immigrants than negative. Approximately 15 percent of stories in the database contained at least one negative characterization versus 33 percent containing positive characterizations. Although the balance of positive and negative characterizations differed from the mainstream press, the content of immigration characterizations was quite similar.

As in the mainstream press, the most common negative characterization of immigrants was the argument that immigrants perpetuate crime. Negative arguments made up only 15 percent of the total stories, but nearly 60 percent of the negative arguments about immigrants in African American newspapers involved judgments about immigrants' involvement in criminal activities or their criminal dispositions. For instance, the *Birmingham Times* published a story in 2010 that reported on the criminal dealings of local Mexican immigrants:

> A federal grand jury today indicted two undocumented aliens for providing counterfeit identification documents, announced U.S. Attorney Joyce White Vance and Bureau of Immigration and Customs Enforcement Resident Agent in Charge Jesse Blakeman. The indictment filed in U.S. District Court charges Adalberto de la Cruz-Angeles, 42, a Mexican citizen, with two counts of transferring counterfeit Social Security and Permanent Resident cards, once in July and once in November. (*Birmingham Times* 2010)

Although the African American papers focused on the supposed criminal tendencies and behaviors of immigrants, they differed from the mainstream papers in their secondary focus on immigrants as an economic burden. The claim that immigrants steal jobs appeared in approximately 39 percent of the articles that negatively characterized immigrants. Assertions that immigrants drain collective resources appeared in 21 percent. These articles typically asserted that immigrants drained public coffers by virtue of their overrepresentation in local prisons, their mental and physical health issues, and their reliance on various welfare programs. These claims echo popular arguments that African Americans see immigrants, particularly Latinos, as their direct competition for resources and employment (McClain et al. 2006). Rather than appearing as a dominant narrative in the African American press, however, these arguments represented only a small proportion of the total articles in the newspapers under study. The economic threat claims were also concentrated in the early years of our sample, peaking in 2006 and tapering off by 2008 (see figure 5).

Despite commonly made claims about conflict between Latinos and African Americans, our results reveal that positive characterizations of immigrants, Latinos in particular, far outpaced negative ones in the African American press. Consider the following excerpt from the *Atlanta Daily World* in 2006. The author of the article included a quote from a nationally re-

Figure 5. Steal Jobs Claims by Year in African American Newspapers

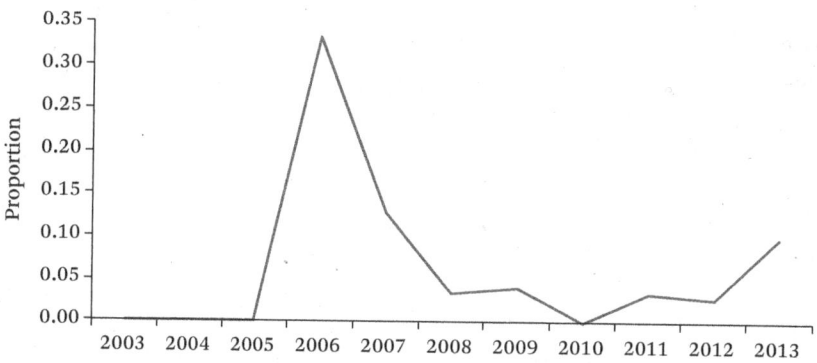

Source: Authors' calculations.

nowned Latino advocacy group to advocate for humane immigrant policies: "Undocumented immigrants contribute about $850 billion more per year than they cost—a huge net gain for the United States," said Brent Wilkes, national executive director of the League of United Latin American Citzens. "It's about time that we provide a legal avenue for them to come here in recognition of their tremendous contributions to our country" (Curry 2006). The article not only emphasized the positive economic contributions of immigrants, it also advocated for policies that would facilitate authorized immigration to the United States.

Although such arguments were common in African American papers, by far the most common defense of immigrants offered in the African American newspapers asserted that immigrants face discrimination or racism. Racism-discrimination claims constituted approximately 50 percent of all positive immigrant characterizations in the mainstream papers and higher than 70 percent in African American papers. An article from the *Jackson Advocate* illustrates these claims in its discussion of law enforcement and motorists. Quoting a local immigrant advocate, the article argued, "The past reports of 'driving while black' have been supplemented with accounts today of 'driving while brown'. . . with the new focus being on Latino immigrants" (Vern 2010). This quote illustrates not only the common trend in black papers to argue that immigrants face racism but also the parallel trend of equating black-targeted discrimination with discrimination targeting Latino immigrants. So common were references to racism and discrimination in this dataset that these claims dwarfed other two most commonly occurring positive characterizations: of immigrants as hard workers (22 percent) and of immigrants as contributing to the public good (17 percent). As in the mainstream press, racism and crime claims rise and fall in tandem over the study period, spiking concurrently in 2006, 2010, and 2013 (see figure 6).

Results from the African American newspapers also reveal distinct trends in the racial labels used in immigration-related news stories, particularly when compared to the mainstream press. Whereas 30 percent of mainstream newspaper articles used at least one racial descriptor in their coverage of immigration, 67 percent of articles from African American newspapers used at least one racial descriptor. The most commonly used racial category was African American–black (87 percent), followed by Latino-Hispanic (nearly 54 percent of all racial labels applied versus 80 percent in mainstream newspapers). These findings suggest that though immigration coverage focuses on Latinos in both venues, African American newspapers are far more likely than mainstream newspapers to also discuss immigration as it affects or connects to African American communities.

To assess African American press descriptions of Latino immigrants, we examined the application of negative and positive characterizations of Latino immigrants. Characterizations of immigrants as criminal were the majority (73 percent) of negative characterizations,

Figure 6. Racism and Crime Claims by Year in African American Newspapers

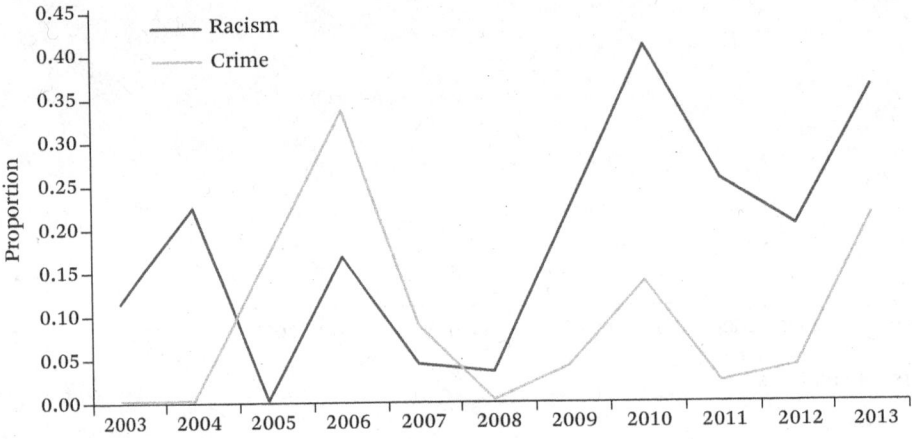

Source: Authors' calculations.

followed distantly by the claim that Latino immigrants drain collective resources (27 percent).

These patterns indicate that the dual racialization of Latinos as criminals and as victims of racism and discrimination appears in the African American as well as the mainstream press. The same time-series patterns from the mainstream press also arise in African American newspapers. Like in the mainstream press, the racialized arguments about Latino criminality and anti-Latino racism rise and fall in tandem, again suggesting a pattern in which immigration foes attack Latinos on the basis of perceived criminal tendencies and advocates respond with targeted claims of Latino immigrants facing racism and discrimination. The key difference between the mainstream and African American newspapers involves the prevalence of each argument and the timing of shifts in each argument. In the mainstream newspapers, criminality claims occur more frequently than racism claims in all but one year of the dataset (2012).[12] And, as noted, in the African American press, racism arguments surpass criminality arguments in 2008 and remain more frequent through the end of our analysis period. Coupled with the fact that the African American press offered more positive than negative characterizations of immigrants than did the mainstream press, these trends may evidence broader shifts in black-Latino relations in the South over the last decade and a half. As figure 7 makes clear, over the period of study, articles about Latinos became less likely to invoke negative characterizations of immigrants over time. The opposite pattern holds for positive portrayals, trending broadly upward after 2005. These patterns are specific to the African American newspapers. Mainstream newspaper articles about Latinos show slight declines in both positive and negative characterizations of immigrants during the study period. Time-series data indicates that characterizations of immigrants as criminal, followed by stealing jobs, diminish over time, and are less prominent than in the mainstream press, suggesting a shift in public discourse about black-Latino relations over the last decade and a half, characterized by increasingly positive characterizations of Latino immigrants as they increased in size and visibility across the region.[13]

12. This year marked widespread state and national-level attention to anti-immigration laws such as Alabama's HB56. Critics of these bills regularly cited them as evidence of racism and discrimination targeted at immigrants (Brown, Jones, and Dow 2016; Campbell 2016; Mohl 2016).

13. In the last years of our data, crime and racism claims also follow different patterns in the two data sets, both claims trending upward in the African American press and downward in the mainstream press. Our close read of the stories from these years does not suggest that these shifts were event driven.

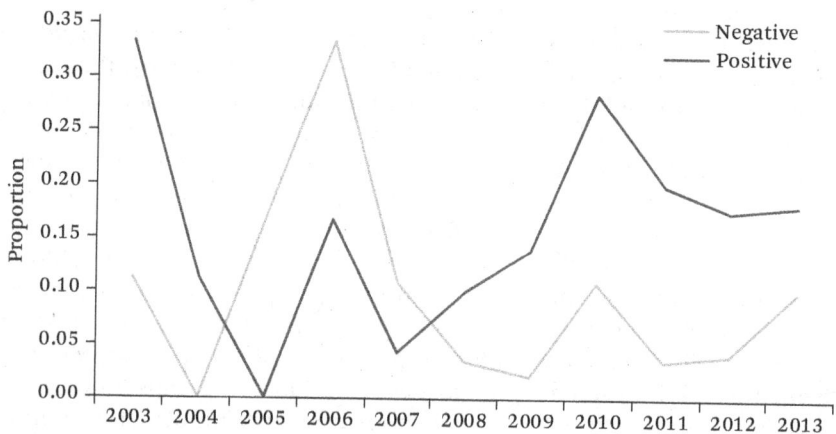

Figure 7. Co-occurrence of Positive and Negative Claims and Latino or Hispanic by Year in African American Newspapers

Source: Authors' calculations.

DISCUSSION AND CONCLUSION

In both the mainstream press and African American press, results indicate that since 2003 immigration discourse in Southern news media has crystallized around two themes: the criminality of Latino immigrants and the discriminatory treatment these immigrants face. Across both sets of newspapers, negative arguments about Latinos focus on their perceived criminal tendencies rather than characterizing immigrants as labor market competitors or economic threats. These claims arise in stories reporting disproportionately on Latinos under investigation for possible criminal offenses, suggesting the prominence of a racial threat narrative centered on public safety. These same characterizations also appear in news coverage about gang activity and in stories claiming that undocumented Latinos are criminals, by virtue of nothing more than their mere presence in the United States. Paralleling this criminality argument is the equally common claim that Latinos face mounting racism and discrimination akin to that African Americans face. That these trends are particularly pronounced for stories about Latinos and Hispanics (versus stories about Mexicans) further illustrates the racializing effects of these narratives. These trends appeared in both the mainstream and the African American press, with one important difference. Pieces in the African American press were far more positive toward immigrants relative to the mainstream press. These findings cast doubt on claims that Latinos in the region are assimilating into whiteness or occupying an elevated position in the racial hierarchy.

Our findings indicate key similarities between the racialization of Latinos and that of African Americans. The criminality claims that appear in our data are similar to patterns of media-driven racialization of African Americans in at least three respects: they emphasize Latinos as dangerous outsiders, assume inherent criminal tendencies among Latinos, and overrepresent the proportion of crimes committed by this demographic group (Alexander 2012; Mendelberg 2001; Dixon and Linz 2000a). The central difference between constructions of black criminality and of Latino criminality in our data is the emphasis on Latino illegality as evidence of criminality. There is, to our knowledge, no corresponding narrative about black illegality in the media; however, definitions of *criminal* and *illegal* are elastic (Gilroy 2008). Unauthorized presence in the United States is not a criminal violation but rather an administrative one. The assumption that unauthorized presence is somehow criminal is a social construction, and historical immigration debates in the United States have not always equated unauthorized presence with criminality (Ngai 2005). A key finding from our study is that the news media in our sample *choose* to portray illegality as reflective of criminality tendencies inherent to Latino immigrants rather opting to portray illegal presence as an administrative, human rights, or legal-bureaucratic issue. This choice is similar to constructions of black criminality that have long been used to demonize African Americans as unfit for legal, social, and other forms of citizenship (James 2010). In our data, the constructions of Latino illegality as criminality do the same work.

Our findings not only indicate similarities in the racialization of African Americans and Latinos, they also suggest that black political leaders and cultural elites perceive Latinos as sharing a common experience of racial discrimination at the hands of whites. The pronounced emphasis on anti-Latino discrimination in the African American press may be coincidental, but taken alongside new work on black-Latino alliances (Brown, Jones, and Dow 2016) and shifts in black elite public opinion (Williams and Hannon 2016) it may also reflect a strategic choice to shore up a sense of shared minority status between African Americans and Latinos. Although characterizations of Latinos as victims of discrimination and racism may spur alliances between minority groups, such claims may also feed a sense of racial threat among whites by emphasizing the challenges of Latino immigration to existing resource distributions. Regardless of the intent and consequences, these patterns indicate that media-driven racialization occurs through both negative characterizations of specific racial groups and through positive defensive pro-immigrant claims. As a counterpoint to the heightened racialization of Latinos as criminals, newspaper editors and journalists choose to publish stories that defend immigrants as the targets of racism and discrimination. In the latter instance, racialization may serve as a defensive resource, in which advocacy efforts draw on histories of civil rights activism to make their case. These results suggest that to make sense of the racially transformative effects of immigration requires a nuanced understanding of the racialization process. Existing research largely emphasizes explicit patterns of immigrant racial self-identification and state ascription. This focus neglects the effects that pro-immigration forces, meso-level organizations, and implicit racial appeals have on immigrants' place in and adjustment to U.S. racial hierarchies.

Although our use of the term *racialization* refers to discursive constructions, these discourses are meaningful in a racialized social system, characterized by systemic inequalities and the primacy of racial hierarchies and divisions (Bonilla-Silva 1997). As a result, these racialized appeals likely have important consequences for immigrant-native relations. Efforts to frame immigrants positively as racialized minorities and victims of discrimination serve different purposes and may even serve different purposes for different groups. In the case of nonwhites, the framing of Latino immigrants as racialized minorities and targets of discrimination may spur interminority sympathies and intergroup coalitions, particularly in the U.S. South, where civil rights organizations and language have unique political visibility. Collaborative efforts by civil rights organizations, immigrant rights organizations, and African American representatives to pass sanctuary city ordinances in Jackson, Mississippi, and Birmingham, Alabama, may be evidence of such effects. Such efforts may also stimulate a sense of threat among whites (see also Schildkraut and Marotta 2018; Craig and Richeson 2018) and may yield renewed local and state immigration enforcement.

Because these results are regional rather than constitutive of a single case, they have significant implications for the context of reception facing new immigrants. In using normative racial codes to situate Latino immigrants in relation to existing groups (Padín 2005), media not only discursively situate Latinos as most similar to blacks but also shape the patterns by which community and local level bureaucrats will extend access to services and social resources on the one hand, or engage in punitive behaviors on the other. In establishing the parameters by which Latinos are situated and understood in Southern communities, media discourses may play a significant role in shaping mobility opportunities for Latinos. A lingering question from this study involves the discursive tropes used by the Spanish-language press to characterize Latino immigrants in the region. Given our interest in ascriptive processes of racialization, this article focuses only on English-language sources. Further, at the time of our analysis and writing, Spanish-language media in the South was unavailable in digitized news databases. Future analyses of Spanish-language media in the region would provide a more detailed analysis of shifts in Latino racial identity, racialization, and incorporation during this period.

Media racialization of Latinos may affect Latino identities, producing new in-group meanings, boundaries, and political mobilization. A sense of proximity to blackness may play a significant role in shoring up a sense of Latino identity (Jones 2012; Sanchez 2008). This shared sense of group position can serve as a basis for political coalitions with long-term implications (Kaufmann 2003). Still, our results may reflect racialization processes particular to the South. Indeed, the often contradictory conclusions about the location of Latinos in the U.S. racial hierarchy may reflect regional differences in racialization and racial hierarchies. Greater attention to place-based variation in immigrant racialization will illuminate the mechanisms of Latino racialization across contexts.

REFERENCES

Alba, Richard. 2016. "The Likely Persistence of a White Majority." *The American Prospect*, January 11, 2016. Accessed January 19, 2018. http://prospect.org/article/likely-persistence-white-majority-0.

Alba, Richard, and Tariqul Islam. 2009. "The Case of the Disappearing Mexican Americans: An Ethnic-Identity Mystery." *Population Research and Policy Review* 28(2): 109–21.

Alexander, Michelle. 2012. *The New Jim Crow: Mass Incarceration in the Age of Colorblindness*. New York: New Press.

American Press Association. 2017. "Principles of Journalism." Los Angeles, Calif. Accessed January 19, 2018. http://americanpressassociation.com/principles-of-journalism/.

Apel, Therese. 2011. "Hit-and-Run Suspect Still at Large." *Clarion-Ledger*, November 30.

Augusta Chronicle. 2011. "Across the State." April 14, 2011.

Barrett, Barbara. 2011. "Illegal Immigrant Numbers Steady." *Raleigh News & Observer*, February 2, 2011.

Birmingham Times. 2010. "Undocumented Aliens Indicted for Transferring Counterfeit Documents." *Birmingham Times*. December 1.

Bloemraad, Irene, Fabiana Silva, and Kim Voss. 2016. "Rights, Economics, or Family? Frame Resonance, Political Ideology, and the Immigrant Rights Movement." *Social Forces* 94(4): 1647–74.

Bonilla-Silva, Eduardo. 1997. "Rethinking Racism: Toward a Structural Interpretation." *American Sociological Review* 62(3): 465–80.

———. 2004. "From Bi-Racial to Tri-Racial: Towards a New System of Racial Stratification in the USA." *Ethnic and Racial Studies* 27(6): 931–50.

Brodkin, Karen. 1998. *How Jews Became White Folks and What That Says About Race in America*. New Brunswick, N.J.: Rutgers University Press.

Brown, Hana E. 2013. "Race, Legality, and the Social Policy Consequences of Anti-Immigrant Mobilization." *American Sociological Review* 78(2): 290–314.

Brown, Hana, and Jennifer A. Jones. 2015. "Rethinking Panethnicity and the Race-Immigration Divide an Ethnoracialization Model of Group Formation." *Sociology of Race and Ethnicity* 1(1): 181–91.

Brown, Hana E., Jennifer A. Jones, and Taylor Dow. 2016. "Unity in the Struggle: Immigration and the South's Emerging Civil Rights Consensus." *Journal of Law and Contemporary Problems* 79(3): 5–27.

Browne, Irene, Natalie Delia Deckard, and Cassaundra Rodriguez. 2016. "Different Game, Different Frame?: Black Counterdiscourses and Depictions of Immigration in Atlanta's African-American and Mainstream Press." *Sociological Quarterly* 57(3): 520–43.

Browne, Irene, and Mary Odem. 2012. "'Juan Crow' in the Nuevo South: Racialization of Guatemalan and Dominican Immigrants in the Atlanta Metro Area." *Du Bois Review: Social Science Research on Race* 9(2): 321–37.

Calavita, Kitty. 2007. "Immigration Law, Race, and Identity." *Annual Review of Law and Social Science* 3(1): 1–20.

Campbell, Kristina. 2016. "The 'New Selma' and the Old Selma: Arizona, Alabama, and the Immigration Civil Rights Movement in the Twenty-First Century." *Journal of American Ethnic History* 35(3): 76–81.

Chavez, Leo R. 2008. *The Latino Threat: Construct-

ing Immigrants, Citizens, and the Nation. Palo Alto, Calif.: Stanford University Press.

Chavez, Nicole. 2012. "Asylum Requests on Rise Fourfold Jump in Wake of Georgia's Immigration Law, but Approval Is No Easy Feat." *Atlanta Journal-Constitution*, July 5.

Chiricos, Ted, and Sarah Eschholz. 2002. "The Racial and Ethnic Typification of Crime and the Criminal Typification of Race and Ethnicity in Local Television News." *Journal of Research in Crime and Delinquency* 39(4): 400–420.

Craig, Maureen, and Jennifer A. Richeson. 2018. "Majority No More? The Influence of Neighborhood Racial Diversity and Salient National Population Changes on Whites' Perceptions of Racial Discrimination." *RSF: The Russell Sage Foundation Journal of the Social Sciences* 4(5): 141–57. DOI: 10.7758/RSF.2018.4.5.07.

Crisp, Elizabeth. 2010. "Miss. Officials Eye Immigration Policy." *Clarion-Ledger*, July 12, 2010.

Curry, George. 2006. "Another Day of Absence." *Atlanta Daily Word*, May 4.

Dávila, Arlene M. 2012. *Latinos, Inc: The Marketing and Making of a People.* Berkeley: University of California Press.

De Genova, Nicholas, and Ana Yolanda Ramos-Zayas. 2003. *Latino Crossings: Mexicans, Puerto Ricans, and the Politics of Race and Citizenship.* New York: Routledge.

Deckard, Natalie Delia, and Irene Browne. 2016. "Constructing Citizenship: Framing Unauthorized Immigrants in Market Terms." *Citizenship Studies* 19(6-7): 664–81.

Dixon, Travis L., and Daniel Linz. 2000a. "Overrepresentation and Underrepresentation of African Americans and Latinos as Lawbreakers on Television News." *Journal of Communication* 50(2): 131–54.

———. 2000b. "Race and the Misrepresentation of Victimization on Local Television News." *Communication Research* 27(5): 547–73.

Domke, David. 2000. "Strategic Elites, the Press, and Race Relations." *Journal of Communication* 50(1): 115–40.

Dunaway, Johanna, Regina P. Branton, and Marisa A. Abrajano. 2010. "Agenda Setting, Public Opinion, and the Issue of Immigration Reform." *Social Science Quarterly* 91(2): 359–78.

Espiritu, Yen Le. 1993. *Asian American Panethnicity: Bridging Institutions and Identities.* Philadelphia, Pa.: Temple University Press.

Ewing, Walter, Daniel E. Martinez, and Rubén G. Rumbaut. 2016. "The Criminalization of Immigration in the United States." Washington, DC: American Immigration Council. https://www.americanimmigrationcouncil.org/research/criminalization-immigration-united-states.

Fanon, Frantz. 2004. "The Negro and Psycho-Pathology." In *Literary Theory: An Anthology*, 2nd ed., edited by Julie Rivkin and Michael Ryan. Oxford: Blackwell Publishing.

FitzGerald, David Scott, and David Cook-Martín. 2014. *Culling the Masses: The Democratic Origins of Racist Immigration Policy in the Americas.* Cambridge, Mass.: Harvard University Press.

Flores, Lisa A. 2003. "Constructing Rhetorical Borders: Peons, Illegal Aliens, and Competing Narratives of Immigration." *Critical Studies in Media Communication* 20(4): 362–87.

Fox, Cybelle, and Thomas A. Guglielmo. 2012. "Defining America's Racial Boundaries: Blacks, Mexicans, and European Immigrants, 1890–1945." *American Journal of Sociology* 118(2): 327–79.

Frank, Reanne, Ilana Redstone Akresh, and Bo Lu. 2010. "Latino Immigrants and the U.S. Racial Order How and Where Do They Fit In?" *American Sociological Review* 75(3): 378–401.

Frey, William H. 2015. "New Racial Segregation Measures for States and Large Metropolitan Areas: Analysis of the 2005–2009 American Community Survey." Ann Arbor: Michigan Population Studies Center. Accessed January 19, 2018. http://www.psc.isr.umich.edu/dis/census/segregation.html.

Fryberg, Stephanie A., Nicole M. Stephens, Rebecca Covarrubias, Hazel Rose Markus, Erin D. Carter, Giselle A. Laiduc, and Ana J. Salido. 2012. "How the Media Frames the Immigration Debate: The Critical Role of Location and Politics." *Analyses of Social Issues and Public Policy* 12(1): 96–112.

Fujiwara, Lynn. 2005. "Immigrant Rights Are Human Rights: The Reframing of Immigrant Entitlement and Welfare." *Social Problems* 52(1): 79–101.

Gans, Herbert J. 1999. "The Possibility of a New Racial Hierarchy in the Twenty-First Century United States." In *The Cultural Territories of Race: Black and White Boundaries*, edited by Michèle Lamont. Chicago / New York: University of Chicago Press / Russell Sage Foundation.

———. 2017. "The Census and Right-Wing Hysteria." *New York Times*, May 11. Accessed January 19, 2018. https://www.nytimes.com/2017/05/11

/opinion/sunday/the-census-and-right-wing-hysteria.html.

Gilens, Martin. 1999. *Why Americans Hate Welfare: Race, Media, and the Politics of Antipoverty Policy*. Chicago: University of Chicago Press.

Gilroy, Paul. 2008. "The Myth of Black Criminality." In *Ethnicity and Crime: A Reader*, edited by Basia Spalek. New York: McGraw-Hill.

Golash-Boza, Tanya. 2006. "Dropping the Hyphen? Becoming Latino (a)-American Through Racialized Assimilation." *Social Forces* 85(1): 27–55.

Gutiérrez, David G. 1995. *Walls and Mirrors: Mexican Americans, Mexican Immigrants, and the Politics of Ethnicity*. Berkeley: University of California Press.

Haney-Lopez, Ian. 1997. *White by Law: The Legal Construction of Race*. New York: New York University Press.

Hattam, Victoria. 2007. *In the Shadow of Race: Jews, Latinos, and Immigrant Politics in the United States*. Chicago: University of Chicago Press.

Hopkins, Daniel J. 2010. "Politicized Places: Explaining Where and When Immigrants Provoke Local Opposition." *American Political Science Review* 104(1): 40–60.

James, Joy. 2010. "'Campaigns Against "Blackness"': Criminality, Incivility, and Election to Executive Office." *Critical Sociology* 36(1): 25–44.

Janssen, Maria Carolina. 2010. "A Framing Analysis of Weblogs and Online Newspapers." Master's thesis, San Jose State University. Accessed January 19, 2018. https://www.scribd.com/document/192598515/A-Framing-Analysis-of-Weblogs-and-Online-Newspapers.

Jimenez, Tomas. 2009. *Replenished Ethnicity: Mexican Americans, Immigration, and Identity*. Berkeley: University of California Press.

Jones, Jennifer A. 2012. "Blacks May Be Second Class, but They Can't Make Them Leave: Mexican Racial Formation and Immigrant Status in Winston-Salem." *Latino Studies* 10(1): 60–80.

Kaufmann, Karen M. 2003. "Cracks in the Rainbow: Group Commonality as a Basis for Latino and African-American Political Coalitions." *Political Research Quarterly* 56(2): 199–210.

Kim, Claire Jean. 1999. "The Racial Triangulation of Asian Americans." *Politics & Society* 27(1): 105–38.

Kochhar, Rakesh, Roberto Suro, and Sonya Tafoya. 2005. "The New Latino South: The Context and Consequences of Rapid Population Growth." *Pew Research Center's Hispanic Trends Project* (blog), July 26, 2005. Accessed January 19, 2018. http://www.pewhispanic.org/2005/07/26/the-new-latino-south/.

Krogstad, Jens Manuel. 2015. "Hispanic Population Reaches Record 55 Million, but Growth Has Cooled." *Pew Research Center* (blog). June 25, 2015. Accessed January 19, 2018. http://www.pewresearch.org/fact-tank/2015/06/25/u-s-hispanic-population-growth-surge-cools/.

Lacayo, Celia Olivia. 2017. "Perpetual Inferiority: Whites' Racial Ideology Toward Latinos." *Sociology of Race and Ethnicity* 3(4): 566–79.

Lawlor, Andrea. 2015. "Local and National Accounts of Immigration Framing in a Cross-National Perspective." *Journal of Ethnic and Migration Studies* 41(6): 918–41.

LeDuff, Charlie. 2000. "At a Slaughterhouse, Some Things Never Die." *New York Times*, June 16.

Lee, Erika. 2002. "The Chinese Exclusion Example: Race, Immigration, and American Gatekeeping, 1882–1924." *Journal of American Ethnic History* 21(3): 36–62.

Lee, Jennifer, and Frank D. Bean. 2004. "America's Changing Color Lines: Immigration, Race/Ethnicity, and Multiracial Identification." *Annual Review of Sociology* 30(1): 221–42.

———. 2012. *The Diversity Paradox: Immigration and the Color Line in Twenty-First Century America*, reprint ed. New York: Russell Sage Foundation.

Lofquist, Daphne, Terry Lugaila, Martin O'Connell, and Sarah Feliz. 2012. "Households and Families: 2010." Washington: U.S. Census Bureau. Accessed January 19, 2018. https://www.census.gov/prod/cen2010/briefs/c2010br-14.pdf.

Marrow, Helen. 2011. *New Destination Dreaming: Immigration, Race, and Legal Status in the Rural American South*. Stanford, Calif.: Stanford University Press.

———. 2017. "The Difference a Decade of Enforcement Makes: Hispanic Racial Incorporation and Changing Intergroup Relations in the American South's Black Belt (2003–16)." In *The Politics of New Immigrant Destinations: Transatlantic Perspectives*, edited by Stefanie Chambers, Diana Evans, Anthony M. Messina, and Abigail Fisher Williamson. Philadelphia, Pa.: Temple University Press.

Massey, Douglas S. 2008. *New Faces in New Places: The Changing Geography of American Immigration*. New York: Russell Sage Foundation.

Massey, Douglas S., Jorge Durand, and Nolan J. Malone. 2003. *Beyond Smoke and Mirrors: Mexican Immigration in an Era of Economic Integration*. New York: Russell Sage Foundation.

McClain, Paula D., Niambi M. Carter, Victoria M. DeFrancesco Soto, Monique L. Lyle, Jeffrey D. Grynaviski, Shayla C. Nunnally, Thomas J. Scotto, J. Alan Kendrick, Gerald F. Lackey, and Kendra Davenport Cotton. 2006. "Racial Distancing in a Southern City: Latino Immigrants' Views of Black Americans." *The Journal of Politics* 68(3): 571–84.

McConnell, Eileen Diaz. 2011. "An 'Incredible Number of Latinos and Asians': Media Representations of Racial and Ethnic Population Change in Atlanta, Georgia." *Latino Studies* 9(2): 177–97.

Mendelberg, Tali. 2001. *The Race Card: Campaign Strategy, Implicit Messages, and the Norm of Equality*. Princeton, N.J.: Princeton University Press.

Menjívar, Cecilia. 2016. "Immigrant Criminalization in Law and the Media Effects on Latino Immigrant Workers' Identities in Arizona." *American Behavioral Scientist* 60(5–6): 597–616.

Migration Policy Institute. 2012. "2011 American Community Survey and Census Data on the Foreign Born by State." State Immigration Data Profiles. Washington, D.C.: MPI. Accessed January 19, 2018. http://www.migrationinformation.org/datahub/acscensus.cfm#rankings.

Mitchell, Amy, and Tom Rosenstiel. 2012. "The State of the News Media 2012." Washington, D.C.: Pew Research Center Project for Excellence in Journalism. Accessed January 19, 2018. http://www.stateofthemedia.org/2012/overview-4/major-trends/.

Mohl, Raymond A. 2016. "The Politics of Expulsion: A Short History of Alabama's Anti-Immigrant Law, HB 56." *Journal of American Ethnic History* 35(3): 42–67.

Molina, Natalia. 2013. *How Race Is Made in America: Immigration, Citizenship, and the Historical Power of Racial Scripts*. Berkeley: University of California Press.

Montejano, David. 1987. *Anglos and Mexicans in the Making of Texas, 1836–1986*. Austin: University of Texas Press.

Mora, G. Cristina. 2014. *Making Hispanics: How Activists, Bureaucrats, and Media Constructed a New American*. Chicago: University of Chicago Press.

Murji, Karim, and John Solomos, eds. 2005. *Racialization: Studies in Theory and Practice*. New York: Oxford University Press.

Newton, Lina Y. 2000. "Why Some Latinos Supported Proposition 187: Testing Economic Threat and Cultural Identity Hypotheses." *Social Science Quarterly* 81(1): 180–93.

Ngai, Mae M. 2005. *Impossible Subjects: Illegal Aliens and the Making of Modern America*. Princeton, N.J.: Princeton University Press.

Nobles, Melissa. 2000. *Shades of Citizenship: Race and the Census in Modern Politics*. Stanford, Calif.: Stanford University Press.

Nowrasteh, Alex. 2015. "Immigration and Crime—What the Research Says." Washington, D.C: CATO Institute. Accessed January 19, 2018. https://www.cato.org/blog/immigration-crime-what-research-says.

Oboler, Suzanne. 1995. *Ethnic Labels, Latino Lives: Identity and the Politics of (Re) Presentation in the United States*. Minneapolis: University of Minnesota Press.

Okamoto, Dina, and G. Cristina Mora. 2014. "Panethnicity." *Annual Review of Sociology* 40(1): 219–39.

Omi, Michael, and Howard Winant. 1994. *Racial Formation in the United States: From the 1960s to the 1990s*. New York: Routledge.

O'Neill, Saffron, Hywel T. P. Williams, Tim Kurz, Bouke Wiersma, and Maxwell Boykoff. 2015. "Dominant Frames in Legacy and Social Media Coverage of the IPCC Fifth Assessment Report." *Nature Climate Change* 5(4): 380–85.

Padín, José Antonio. 2005. "The Normative Mulattoes: The Press, Latinos, and the Racial Climate on the Moving Immigration Frontier." *Sociological Perspectives* 48(1): 49–75.

Passel, Jeffrey S., D'Vera Cohn, and Mark Hugo Lopez. 2011. "Hispanics Account for More than Half of Nation's Growth in Past Decade." Washington, D.C.: Pew Hispanic Center.

Portes, Alejandro, and Rubén G. Rumbaut. 2001. *Legacies: The Story of the Immigrant Second Generation*. Berkeley: University of California Press.

Ribas, Vanesa. 2015. *On the Line: Slaughterhouse Lives and the Making of the New South*. Oakland: University of California Press.

Rich, Brian L, and Marta Miranda. 2005. "The Sociopolitical Dynamics of Mexican Immigration in Lexington, Kentucky, 1997 to 2002: An Ambivalent Community Responds." In *New Destinations:*

Mexican Immigration in the United States, edited by Victor Zuniga and Rubén Hernandez Leon. New York: Russell Sage Foundation.

Rodriguez, Cassaundra. 2018. "Fueling White Injury Ideology: Public Officials' Racial Discourse in Support of Arizona Senate Bill 1070." *Sociology of Race and Ethnicity* 4(1): 83–97.

Rodriguez, Clara. 2000. *Changing Race: Latinos, the Census and the History of Ethnicity*. New York: New York University Press.

Roediger, David R. 2006. *Working Toward Whiteness: How America's Immigrants Became White: The Strange Journey from Ellis Island to the Suburbs*. New York: Basic Books.

Rumbaut, Rubén G. 2009. "Undocumented Immigration and Rates of Crime and Imprisonment: Popular Myths and Empirical Realities." New York: Russell Sage Foundation. Accessed January 19, 2018. https://www.russellsage.org/research/reports/undocumented-immigration-and-crime.

———. 2011. "Pigments of Our Imagination: The Racialization of the Hispanic-Latino Category." Washington, D.C.: Migration Information Source. Accessed January 19, 2018. https://www.migrationpolicy.org/article/pigments-our-imagination-racialization-hispanic-latino-category.

Russell-Brown, Katheryn. 2008. *The Color of Crime*, 2nd ed. New York: New York University Press.

Salter, Sid. 2003. "Opinion." *Clarion-Ledger*, August 20.

Sanchez, Gabriel R. 2008. "Latino Group Consciousness and Perceptions of Commonality with African Americans." *Social Science Quarterly* 89(2): 428–44.

Santa Ana, Otto. 2002. *Brown Tide Rising: Metaphors of Latinos in Contemporary American Public Discourse*. Austin: University of Texas Press.

Schildkraut, Deborah J., and Satia A. Marotta. 2018. "Assessing the Political Distinctiveness of White Millennials: How Race and Generation Shape Racial and Political Attitudes in a Changing America." *RSF: The Russell Sage Foundation Journal of the Social Sciences* 4(5): 158–87. DOI: 10.7758/RSF.2018.4.5.08.

Schneider, Craig. 2011. "In Georgia's Fields, a Growing Anxiety." *Atlanta Journal-Constitution*, June 4.

Schudson, Michael. 1981. *Discovering The News: A Social History of American Newspapers*. 2nd ed. New York: Basic Books.

Simon, Rita J., and Keri W. Sikich. 2007. "Public Attitudes Toward Immigrants and Immigration Policies Across Seven Nations." *International Migration Review* 41(4): 956–62.

Singer, Audrey. 2004. "The Rise of New Immigrant Gateways." Washington, D.C.: Brookings Institution. Accessed January 19, 2018. http://www.brookings.edu/research/reports/2004/02/demographics-singer.

Singer, Audrey, Susan W. Hardwick, and Caroline B. Brettell. 2008. *Twenty-First Century Gateways: Immigrant Incorporation in Suburban America*. Washington, D.C.: Brookings Institution Press.

Smiley, Calvin John, and David Fakunle. 2016. "From 'Brute' to 'Thug': The Demonization and Criminalization of Unarmed Black Male Victims in America." *Journal of Human Behavior in the Social Environment* 26(3–4): 350–66.

Smith, Jessica E. 2005. "Content Differences Between Print and Online Newspapers." M.A. thesis, University of South Florida. Accessed January 19, 2018. http://scholarcommons.usf.edu/etd/868/.

Smith, Robert Courtney. 2014. "Black Mexicans, Conjunctural Ethnicity, and Operating Identities Long-Term Ethnographic Analysis." *American Sociological Review* 79(3): 517–48.

Sohoni, Deenesh, and Jennifer Bickham Mendez. 2014. "Defining Immigrant Newcomers in New Destinations: Symbolic Boundaries in Williamsburg, Virginia." *Ethnic and Racial Studies* 37(3): 496–516.

Sommers, Laurie Kay. 1991. "Inventing Latinismo: The Creation of 'Hispanic' Panethnicity in the United States." *Journal of American Folklore* 104(411): 32–53.

Stuesse, Angela. 2009. "Race, Migration, and Labor Control: Neoliberal Challenges to Organizing Mississippi's Poultry Workers." In *Latino Immigrants and the Transformation of the US South*, edited by Mary Odem and Elaine Lacy. Athens: University of Georgia Press.

Vargas, Nicholas. 2015. "Latina/o Whitening?: Which Latina/os Self-Classify as White and Report Being Perceived as White by Other Americans?" *Du Bois Review: Social Science Research on Race* 12(1): 119–36.

Vern, Walker. 2010. "Jackson Ordinance Against Ethnic Profiling Draws Strong Support." *Jackson Advocate*, August 26.

Weigl, Andrea. 2005. "8 Plead Guilty in Formula Scheme." *Raleigh News & Observer*, January 19.

Williams, Kim M. 2016. "Black Political Interests on Immigrant Rights: Evidence from Black Newspapers, 2000-2013." *Journal of African American Studies* 20(3-4): 248-71.

Williams, Kim M., and Lonnie Hannon. 2016. "Immigrant Rights in a Deep South City: The Effects of Anti-Immigrant Legislation on Black Elite Opinion in Birmingham, Alabama." *Du Bois Review: Social Science Research on Race* 13(1): 139-57.

Wilson, Thomas C. 2001. "Americans' Views on Immigration Policy: Testing the Role of Threatened Group Interests." *Sociological Perspectives* 44(4): 485-501.

Wright, Matthew, Morris Levy, and Jack Citrin. 2015. "Public Attitudes Toward Immigration Policy Across the Legal/Illegal Divide: The Role of Categorical and Attribute-Based Decision-Making." *Political Behavior* 38(1): 229-53.

Yancy, George. 2016. *Black Bodies, White Gazes: The Continuing Significance of Race in America*. Lanham, Md.: Rowman & Littlefield.

Majority No More? The Influence of Neighborhood Racial Diversity and Salient National Population Changes on Whites' Perceptions of Racial Discrimination

MAUREEN A. CRAIG AND JENNIFER A. RICHESON

This article examines whether the size of racial minority populations is associated with whites' perceptions that different racial groups face discrimination. Correlational studies reveal that both the perceived size (studies 1 and 2) and actual size (study 2) of the racial minority population in their local environment predicts the extent to which whites report that they personally, and that whites as a group, face racial discrimination. Two experiments (studies 3 and 4) reveal that reading about growth in the racial minority share of the national population (versus control information) similarly increases whites' concerns about antiwhite discrimination. Overall, these findings suggest that increasing racial diversity, real or perceived, local or national, can elicit identity-relevant concerns among white Americans, including perceived vulnerability to racial discrimination.

Keywords: demographic changes, perceived discrimination, diversity, white identity

America's demographic makeup has changed radically in its racial and cultural diversity over the last five decades, a trend that is projected to continue for the foreseeable future (see Hing 2004). Whereas non-Hispanic whites made up 84 percent of the U.S. population in 1965, the number fell to 62 percent in 2015, and the prediction for 2065 is 46 percent (Pew Research Center 2015). This demographic trend toward increased diversity, in which the percentage of whites steadily decreases and the populations of various racial minority groups increase, is evident across most U.S. communities (Lee, Iceland, and Sharp 2012). In other words, the size of minority groups relative to whites is increasing nationwide.

Considerable social scientific research has examined majority group members' reactions to the perceived or actual size of minority groups in a relevant locale (neighborhood, town, county). For instance, psychologists Eric Knowles and Kaiping Peng find that whites

---

Maureen A. Craig is assistant professor of psychology at New York University. **Jennifer A. Richeson** is Philip R. Allen Professor of Psychology and faculty fellow at the Institution for Social and Policy Studies at Yale University.

© 2018 Russell Sage Foundation. Craig, Maureen A., and Jennifer A. Richeson. 2018. "Majority No More? The Influence of Neighborhood Racial Diversity and Salient National Population Changes on Whites' Perceptions of Racial Discrimination." *RSF: The Russell Sage Foundation Journal of the Social Sciences* 4(5): 141–57. DOI: 10.7758/RSF.2018.4.5.07. Direct correspondence to: Maureen A. Craig at maureen.craig@nyu.edu, Department of Psychology, New York University, 6 Washington Place, New York, NY 10003.

Open Access Policy: *RSF: The Russell Sage Foundation Journal of the Social Sciences* is an open access journal. This article is published under a Creative Commons Attribution-NonCommercial-NoDerivs 3.0 Unported License.

from largely nonwhite areas exhibited higher levels of implicit white identity centrality—the strength of the association between self-concept and race—than whites from predominantly white areas (2005). Minority group size has also been found to predict the extent to which racial majority group members feel threatened by racial minority groups and, in turn, express more negative racial attitudes (on threat, Fossett and Kiecolt 1989; Nadeau, Niemi, and Levine 1993; on attitudes, Blalock 1967; Quillian 1995). Perceived threat from minority neighbors may also shape whites' voting intentions and political behavior. For example, whites who live in areas with more black neighbors are more likely to both register as Republican and vote for a Republican candidate than whites who live in areas with fewer black neighbors (on registering, Giles and Hertz 1994; on voting, Enos 2016). Further, white Americans who estimate relatively larger proportions of blacks and Hispanics in the overall U.S. population are more likely to express antiblack and anti-Hispanic attitudes and to support restrictions on immigration (Alba, Rumbaut, and Marotz 2005). Taken together, this research suggests that larger minority groups—in terms of perceived or actual size—are often associated with greater perceptions of group threat among whites, which, in turn, predict the expression of negative social attitudes and conservative political attitudes and behavior.

Experimental work corroborates the results of this correlational research. For instance, white Americans considering a future in which the white population has declined to less than 50 percent of the national population (versus various control conditions) are more likely to perceive that the societal status of their racial group—in terms of resources or as the "prototypical" American—is under threat, which in turn leads to stronger identification as white (Outten et al. 2012), the expression of more negative racial attitudes and emotions (Craig and Richeson 2014a; Outten et al. 2012; Skinner and Cheadle 2016), greater opposition to diversity (Danbold and Huo 2015), and greater endorsement of conservative political ideology, political parties, and candidates (Craig and Richeson 2014b; Major, Blodorn, and Major-Blascovich 2016; Willer, Feinberg, and Wetts 2016; for a review, see also Craig, Rucker, and Richeson, forthcoming). Taken together, the social scientific literature to date reveals that larger minority populations can activate concerns in the white racial majority regarding their group's status that, in turn, yield a variety of seemingly in-group enhancing or out-group derogating responses. This article examines another potential consequence of increasing minority group size for white Americans; namely, greater perceptions that white Americans are likely to face racial discrimination.

PERCEIVED ANTIWHITE RACIAL DISCRIMINATION

Recent work finds that white Americans believe both that antiwhite discrimination is on the rise and that discrimination against racial minorities is decreasing (Norton and Sommers 2011). What might be the cause of these changing perceptions? Empirical research has identified a few factors that lead whites to perceive more discrimination against their racial group. For instance, the perception that minorities are making social progress (gaining societal power) has been found to increase perceptions of antiwhite discrimination, especially among whites who believe that the current societal status hierarchy is just (Wilkins and Kaiser 2014). Organizational messages that are favorable to racial diversity have also been found to enhance the sense among whites of personal and group discrimination against them compared with race-neutral messages (Dover, Major, and Kaiser 2016). This research suggests, in other words, that whites are likely to perceive more antiwhite discrimination under circumstances in which they perceive that their group's position in society is under threat. Given that larger or increasing racial minority populations have been found to induce perceived status threat among white Americans (Craig and Richeson 2014b; Fossett and Kiecolt 1989; Major, Blodorn, and Major-Blascovich 2016; Outten et al. 2012; Schildkraut and Marotta 2017), it may also be that perceiving or living in areas with larger racial minority populations may predict the extent to which whites are concerned about antiwhite discrimination. Across four studies, we investigated this possibility.

In studies 1 and 2, we examined the relationships between white Americans' estimates of the percentage of racial minorities in the total population with perceptions that different racial groups—whites, blacks, Hispanics, and Asian Americans—face discrimination and that they personally face race-based discrimination. Further, study 2 examined whether the percentage of racial minority group members living in the same communities as white respondents is related to perceived discrimination. To provide causal tests of whether perceived minority group size may heighten perceptions that whites face racial discrimination, studies 3 and 4 examined whites' reported expectations about the prevalence of antiwhite discrimination after the projected growth in the national racial minority population (and whites' relative decline) is made salient, compared with control information. Based on the literature reviewed, we predicted that larger racial minority group populations—be it perceived or actual size—will be associated with greater perceptions of and concerns about antiwhite discrimination.

STUDY 1

Study 1 provided an initial exploration of how whites' perceptions of the relative size of racial minority populations are associated with their perceptions of discrimination—especially that they personally and different racial groups face discrimination. Consistent with research finding a positive correlation between minority outgroup size and perceived threat among majority group members (Blalock 1967; Fossett and Kiecolt 1989), we predicted that the larger whites perceive racial minority groups to be in terms of their share of the population, the more they will report that whites as a group and they themselves experience discrimination.

Data and Methods

We used data from the National Politics Survey, a nationally representative telephone survey (N = 1,477) (Jackson et al. 2008). Analyses focused on the sample of self-identified white respondents who were U.S. citizens (n = 509; 62.48 percent women, and on average reported being between fifty-five and fifty-nine years old).

Perceived Discrimination

Respondents indicated their perceptions of racial discrimination faced by different groups (whites, blacks, Hispanics, Asians) as well as their perceptions that they personally faced racism. To assess perceived group-faced racial discrimination, respondents were asked how much different groups face discrimination in the United States (1 = a lot of discrimination, 4 = no discrimination at all). Respondents were also asked how often they personally felt discriminated against due to their race (1 = a lot of discrimination, 4 = no discrimination at all). All items were reverse coded such that higher numbers indicate greater perceived discrimination.

Perceived Racial Makeup

Respondents were also asked to estimate the racial makeup of the United States. Specifically, respondents were asked to give their best guess of the percentages of white, black, Hispanic, Asian American, and Native American in both the U.S. population and their city population. We created indices of the percentage of the total national population and city population that respondents perceived minority groups—blacks, Hispanics, Asian Americans, and Native Americans—to make up.[1]

Demographic Variables

The following indicators of respondents' demographic characteristics were also assessed: age (1 = eighteen to twenty-four, 13 = eighty and older), gender (0 = female, 1 = male), household income (1 = less than $25,000, 8 = more than $125,000),[2] and political ideology (1 = extremely liberal, 4 = extremely conservative).

---

1. See the appendix for supplementary tables listing the associations between the relative size of each racial group on white respondents' perceptions of discrimination for studies 1 and 2. In general, these analyses suggest that no single racial minority group's size was singularly responsible for the relationships reported across studies.

2. Supplementary analyses conducted to test whether respondents' household incomes moderated the relationships between perceived (and actual in study 2) racial makeup and perceived discrimination did not reveal reliable household income X minority group size interaction effects in either study 1 ($ps > .089$) or study 2 ($ps > .176$).

Table 1. Descriptive Statistics, Zero-Order Correlations, and Partial Correlations Between Percentage Racial Minority and Perceptions of Discrimination Among White Americans

	M	SD	Personal r	Personal $r_{partial}$	Antiwhite r	Antiwhite $r_{partial}$
Study 1						
Estimated percentage of racial minorities (United States)	55.97	13.88	.22***	.19***	.16**	.16**
Estimated percentage of racial minorities (city)	51.00	21.31	.28***	.26***	.13**	.08
Study 2						
Estimated percentage of racial minorities (county)	62.06	12.09	.19***	.20**	.20***	.23***
Actual percentages of minority groups						
Census block group	35.76	24.26	.12***	.13***	.06*	.08*
Census tract	37.75	23.36	.11***	.14***	.06*	.06*
Zip code	41.53	22.64	.12***	.15***	.04	.05†

Source: Authors' compilation.
Note. Partial correlations statistically control for age, gender, household income, and political ideology.
†$p < .10$; *$p < .05$; **$p < .01$; ***$p < .001$

Results

Subpopulation analyses focusing on the white respondents who were U.S. citizens were conducted in Stata (version 14.2). We report both zero-order correlations as well as partial correlations controlling for gender, age, household income, and political ideology.

As to perceptions of personally faced discrimination, as shown in table 1, consistent with predictions and robust to controlling for respondents' demographic characteristics, a positive relationship emerged between perceptions of personally faced discrimination and respondents' estimates of the percentage of racial minorities in the United States ($r = .22$, $p < .001$; $r_{partial} = .19$, $p < .001$) as well as their estimates of the percentage of racial minorities in their city ($r = .28$, $p < .001$; $r_{partial} = .26$, $p < .001$).

As to perceptions of antiwhite discrimination, a positive relationship also emerged between perceptions of group-level antiwhite discrimination and respondents' estimates of the national percentage of racial minorities ($r = .16$, $p = .001$; $r_{partial} = .16$, $p = .005$). A significant association emerged between perceived antiwhite discrimination and estimates of the local population of racial minorities (city estimates), $r = .13$, $p = .006$; however, this association was not robust to the inclusion of demographic controls ($r_{partial} = .08$, $p = .127$).

As to perceptions of discrimination faced by racial minorities, as shown in table 2, respondents' estimates of the national percentage of racial minorities were statistically unrelated to their perceptions of the extent of antiblack ($r = -.02$, $p = .645$; $r_{partial} = -.02$, $p = .605$), anti-Hispanic ($r = -.04$, $p = .331$; $r_{partial} = -.08$, $p = .092$), or anti-Asian ($r = .02$, $p = .647$; $r_{partial} = .00$, $p = .999$) racial discrimination. Respondents' estimates of the percentage of racial minorities in their city were similarly unrelated to their perceptions of antiblack ($r = -.04$, $p = .390$; $r_{partial} = -.08$, $p = .078$), anti-Hispanic ($r = -.03$, $p = .530$; $r_{partial} = -.09$, $p = .083$), or anti-Asian ($r = .00$, $p = .957$; $r_{partial} = -.05$, $p = .394$) discrimination.

Discussion

The results suggest that whites' estimates of the relative size of the racial minority population in both the nation and their local municipality are significantly related to the extent to which they perceived that whites as a group and they themselves face racial discrimination. Indeed, consistent with predictions, the more populous

Table 2. Zero-Order Correlations and Partial Correlations Between Percentage Racial Minority and Perceptions of Discrimination, Racial Minorities

	Antiblack		Anti-Hispanic		Anti-Asian	
	r	$r_{partial}$	r	$r_{partial}$	r	$r_{partial}$
Study 1						
Estimated percentage of racial minorities (United States)	−.02	−.02	−.04	−.08†	.02	.00
Estimated percentage of racial minorities (city)	−.04	−.08†	−.03	−.09†	.00	−.05
Study 2						
Actual percentages of minority groups						
Census block group	.06†	.07*	.01	.03	.01	.01
Census tract	.07*	.07*	.00	.01	.01	.02
Zip code	.02	.03	.02	.00	.01	.01

Source: Authors' compilation.
Note. Partial correlations statistically control for age, gender, household income, and political ideology.
†$p < .10$; *$p < .05$; **$p < .01$; ***$p < .001$

whites perceived racial minorities to be in the nation and their city, the more likely they were to perceive that whites as a group and that they personally face discrimination. Conversely, perceptions of discrimination faced by racial minority groups—blacks, Hispanics, and Asian Americans—were unrelated to whites' perceptions of racial minority group size. Taken together, these findings suggest that larger minority group size may be experienced as a threat to the in-group, reflected in increased concern about in-group vulnerability, such as group-based victimization (discrimination).

STUDY 2

Study 1 provided initial evidence that white Americans' perceptions of the size of racial minority groups are associated with their perceptions that both they and their racial group face discrimination. Study 2 sought to replicate this basic finding in another sample and explore whether the actual size of racial minorities in one's community may predict perceived antiwhite discrimination in a similar manner.

Data and Methods

We analyzed data from the Kinder Houston Area Survey, an annual telephone survey of the social and political attitudes of adults residing in Harris County, Texas (Klineberg 2010). Households are selected by randomly generated telephone numbers (to reach individuals who use cell phones as well as landlines) and an eligible respondent for each household was selected randomly from all household members age eighteen or older. Response rates in recent years have been around 40 percent (Klineberg 2010). Beginning in 2003, the survey authors matched individuals' responses to detailed demographic information about their neighborhoods from the 2000 U.S. Census at three levels (from largest to smallest): home zip code (the largest geographic area used to calculate demographic characteristics in these data), census tract (an area with roughly 1,200 to eight thousand residents), and census block group (an area with roughly six hundred to three thousand residents). In addition to exploring whether perceptions of minority group size are associated with perceived discrimination against oneself and one's group, then, in study 2 we can also examine whether whites who live in residential contexts that actually have larger racial minority populations (as estimated in the census) also perceive more discrimination against themselves and their racial group.

These data, moreover, are especially suited for exploring how changing demographics may relate to perceived antiwhite discrimination, because between 1990 and 2010, Harris County underwent a racial demographic shift, becoming majority-minority in 2000 (Emerson et al. 2012). We constrained the analyses to the sample of white respondents who completed the variables of interest for this study (perceived discrimination and perceived racial makeup) in the years in which their responses were matched to local demographics by U.S. Census data from 2003 to 2007. Thus, of the 7,940 respondents who participated in this time frame, 2,532 were self-identified white respondents who were U.S. citizens (51.37 percent women, M_{age} = 50.48, SD_{age} = 16.01) with complete data on the questions of interest.

Perceived Racial Makeup
Respondents were asked to provide their best guess of the white, Hispanic, Asian American, and black American percentages of the Harris County population. These estimates were only asked of respondents in one year of the survey (2007; n = 409 white respondents). As in study 1, we created an index of the perceived percentage of racial minorities in the total population.

Census-Matched Racial Makeup
As noted, the actual racial demographic characteristics of respondents' communities were gleaned from census data at three levels: home zip code, census tract, and census block group (U.S. Census Bureau 2013). Again, we were interested in the proportion of racial minorities—Hispanics, Asian Americans, black Americans, and individuals from racial minority groups that do not fall in any of the other groups—in the population at each level of respondents' local geographic area: the percentage of racial minorities in respondents' zip code, census tract, and census block group.

Perceived Discrimination
Respondents indicated their perceptions of the racial discrimination that different racial groups and they personally face. To assess perceptions of group discrimination, respondents were asked "How often, in general, are [Anglos/blacks/Hispanics/Asians] discriminated against in Houston?" (1 = never, 4 = very often). A second, similarly worded question that assessed perceived antiwhite discrimination ("How often are Anglos discriminated against in Houston?") was also asked in several years. Given that these questions were so similar and highly correlated with one another (r = .98), if both perceived antiwhite discrimination questions were asked in a given year, we computed the average of the two items to provide the measure of perceived antiwhite discrimination. If only one of the items was asked in a given year, as in 2006 and 2007, then responses to that item served as the index of perceived antiwhite discrimination. Respondents were also asked how often they personally felt discriminated against in Houston on the basis of their ethnicity (1 = never, 4 = very often). For both the group and personal discrimination measures, higher numbers indicate greater perceived discrimination.

Demographic Variables
The following indicators of respondents' demographic characteristics were assessed: age, gender (0 = female, 1 = male), household income (1 = less than $12,500, 8 = more than $100,000), and political ideology (1 = very conservative, 7 = very liberal).

Results
The descriptive statistics and correlations among the variables of interest are shown in tables 1 and 2. We report both zero-order correlations as well as partial correlations controlling for sex, age, household income, and political ideology.

On perceived racial makeup, consistent with the hypothesis and robust to controlling for respondents' demographic characteristics, a positive relationship emerged between perceived personally faced discrimination and respondents' estimates of the proportions of racial minorities in their county (r = .19, p < .001; $r_{partial}$ = .20, p = .001). A similar association emerged for perceptions of group-level (antiwhite) discrimination (r = .20, p < .001; $r_{partial}$ = .23, p < .001). That is, the more racial minorities that white respondents believed lived in their county, the more discrimination they reported facing personally and as a group.

As to census-matched racial makeup and personal discrimination, we also examined the associations between whites' perceptions that they personally face discrimination and the actual percentages of racial minorities in their communities at different geographic levels (census block group, census tract, zip code). Analyses revealed modest correlations in the direction consistent with predictions; the larger the percentage of racial minorities living in the geographic area, the more likely white respondents were to report that they personally face racial discrimination (census block group: $r = .12, p < .001; r_{partial} = .13, p < .001$; census tract: $r = .11, p < .001, r_{partial} = .14, p < .001$; zip code: $r = .12, p < .001; r_{partial} = .15, p < .001$).

On antiwhite discrimination, modest correlations in the expected direction emerged between respondents' perceptions of antiwhite discrimination and the percentage of racial minorities in their census block group ($r = .06, p = .010; r_{partial} = .08, p = .012$) and census tract ($r = .06, p = .019; r_{partial} = .06, p = .037$), but not their zip code ($r = .04, p = .130; r_{partial} = .05, p = .083$).

As to discrimination that racial minorities face, consistent with the results of study 1, the racial diversity of whites' residential areas was largely unrelated to their perceptions that different racial minority groups face discrimination (see table 2).[3] The only exception was for perceptions of antiblack discrimination, which was modestly (and positively) related to the number of racial minorities in respondents' census block group ($r = .06, p = .050; r_{partial} = .07, p = .045$) and census tract level ($r = .07, p = .028, r_{partial} = .07, p = .030$). Larger numbers of minority residents in one's census block group and tract, in other words, were associated with white respondents' greater endorsement that blacks face racial discrimination.

Discussion

The results of study 2 are largely consistent with the patterns observed in study 1: the larger white respondents perceived the local racial minority population to be, the more they tended to perceive that their group, and they themselves, face racial discrimination. Study 2 extended these findings by investigating whether actual rather than just perceived levels of local racial diversity are also related to perceived personal, antiwhite, and antiminority racial discrimination. Results revealed that white Americans who live in communities with larger percentages of racial minority groups tend to perceive more antiwhite discrimination toward the group and themselves personally. Although the effect sizes of these associations were modest, they are consistent with the idea that residing in areas with growing numbers of racial minority out-groups may evoke in-group threat and increase concern about the well-being of one's racial in-group.

The association between perceived antiwhite discrimination and the proportion of racial minorities in respondents' zip code was not reliable, however, perhaps because the area is too large for any effects of out-group presence to be realized. Future research should consider the ways in which individuals become aware of the actual racial composition of geographic regions and how that knowledge shapes perceptions of discrimination. An unexpected relationship also emerged between the percentage of racial minorities in one's community and perceived antiblack discrimination, a finding consistent with extant research noting potential benefits of racial diversity, such as increased perspective-taking and out-group empathy through contact (Pettigrew and Tropp 2008). Because this pattern was not observed for perceived discrimination against other racial minority groups, however, we do not discuss it further in this article.

INTERIM DISCUSSION

The data examined in studies 1 and 2 have several benefits, particularly in terms of ecological validity. These data include responses from adults in samples that are representative of the United States and of Harris County, respec-

---

3. Respondents were not asked about perceptions of antiminority discrimination in the same year that they were asked to give estimates of their county's racial demographics; thus, only associations between the actual percentage of racial minority populations in whites' surrounding area and perceived antiminority discrimination are reported.

tively, suggesting that the associations revealed and the phenomena under investigation in the present research are likely to be generalizable to the broader public. However, although these studies provide support for the hypothesis that larger racial minority populations—whether perceived or actual—may engender greater perceptions of antiwhite discrimination among white Americans, the cross-sectional, correlational nature of these survey designs limits the inferences that can be drawn regarding both causality and directionality of the effects. That is, it is possible that being sensitive to antiwhite discrimination leads individuals to perceive larger numbers of racial minorities, rather than the reverse. It is also possible that a third, unmeasured variable could be responsible for the observed associations between perceived discrimination and respondents' perceptions of the racial makeup of relevant residential regions (the county) or their actual racial makeup. Experimental research wherein the purported racial composition of a relevant residential region could be manipulated or, perhaps made salient, prior to assessing whites' perceptions of antiwhite discrimination would offer more clarity regarding the plausibility of the causal pathway underlying the associations found in studies 1 and 2. The goal of studies 3 and 4 was to provide such experimental tests.

STUDY 3

Studies 1 and 2 offer correlational evidence of the predicted positive relationship between minority population size and whites' perceptions of antiwhite discrimination. To examine this relationship from a different angle, study 3 considers how information about the increasing racial diversity of the nation (minority population growth and whites' relative decline) influences white Americans' perceptions of discrimination and, particularly, concerns about antiwhite discrimination. Building on past research, white participants read information about U.S. demographic trends (Craig and Richeson 2014a): either a racial demographic shift, often called a majority-minority shift, in which different racial minority populations are expected to increase in number and whites are expected to decrease as a percentage of the total population (racial shift condition) or the current racial demographics of the United States (control condition). Participants were subsequently asked about their expectations regarding the current and future prevalence of racial discrimination toward a variety of racial groups as well as their support for policies that would benefit workers from different racial groups. Consistent with the results of studies 1 and 2, we predicted that making the racial demographic changes toward a more racially diverse United States salient would elicit greater concern about growing antiwhite discrimination and more support for policies benefiting white workers than would exposure to the current (majority-white) racial demographics.

Methods

One hundred forty-six white participants (25 women, 120 men, and one individual who did not indicate gender, M_{age} = 31.21, SD_{age} = 11.98) were recruited from MTurk.com and participated for $0.30; all participants lived in the United States.[4] Data were collected in November and December 2012.

Materials and Measures

Participants were randomly assigned to read a newspaper article about either the projected future U.S. racial demographics (racial shift condition) or the current majority-white demographics of the United States (control condition). This manipulation is nearly identical to one used in prior research, but updated to reflect the 2012 rather than the 2010 demographics (control article) (Craig and Richeson 2014a). Each article included a graph of the current or projected racial demographics, broken down by racial category (white, black, Hispanic, Asian, Other). To ensure that participants understood the information presented in the articles, they responded to questions intended to assess their comprehension of the target article ("Which racial group is expected to be the largest contributor to the population growth in the

---

4. A gender imbalance is present because for most of data collection, female participants were filtered into a different study immediately following the initial demographic questions.

United States?"). Thus, both articles provided information about race in the United States, but the racial shift condition provided information about a future in which whites were a smaller percentage of population relative to the control article.

Perceived Discrimination

We assessed perceptions of current and future levels of discrimination faced by white Americans, Hispanics or Latinos, and black Americans. Participants were instructed to indicate the extent to which they thought that different racial groups currently face discrimination in the United States, and the extent to which they thought that different racial groups will face discrimination in the future. Participants responded on 1 (not at all) to 10 (very much) scales.

Workplace Policies to Benefit Different Racial Groups

We also assessed endorsement of policies that would benefit different racial groups (blacks, Latinos, whites) in the workforce. Specifically, participants indicated their agreement (1 = strongly disagree, 7 = strongly agree) that government policies should require employers to make special training programs for [black, Latino, white] workers and that government policies should require employers to make special efforts to recruit [black, Latino, white] workers. Similar to the perceived discrimination items, participants were asked to indicate their endorsement of implementing these policies now and in the future.

Procedure

Participants provided informed consent and completed initial demographic questions (race, gender). They were then randomly assigned to read the experimental (future demographics) or control (current demographics) article. Participants next completed the perceived discrimination items and then those related to support for targeted workplace policies. Half of the sample was randomly assigned to provide first their perceptions of currently faced discrimination and agreement with implementing policies now, followed by the future-focused questions; the other half completed the items in the reverse order. Last, participants completed additional demographic questions (for example, age) and were debriefed.

Results

No participants were excluded from the analyses. The final sample included seventy-five participants in the racial shift condition and seventy-one in the control condition. We conducted a series of 2 (timepoint: current perceptions, future perceptions) x 2 (experimental condition: racial shift, control) mixed-design ANOVAs (analyses of variance) on perceptions of discrimination and policy support.

Table 3 presents descriptive statistics for responses to the perceived discrimination items for the different racial groups by timepoint. Examining perceived antiwhite discrimination, main effects of timepoint [$F(1, 144) = 7.19$, $p = .008$, $\eta_p^2 = 0.05$] and experimental condition [$F(1, 144) = 4.57$, $p = .034$, $\eta_p^2 = 0.03$] emerged. Across experimental conditions, participants reported that whites would face more discrimination in the future than today. In addition, participants for whom the future, more racially diverse United States was salient reported that whites would and currently do face more racial discrimination than participants in the current majority-white control condition. Conversely, analyses of responses to the perceived discrimination against blacks and Latinos measures revealed only main effects of timepoint [blacks: $F(1, 143) = 33.25$, $p < .001$, $\eta_p^2 = 0.19$; Latinos: $F(1, 144) = 30.23$, $p < .001$, $\eta_p^2 = 0.17$]. Participants, regardless of condition, reported that blacks and Latinos would face less discrimination in the future than today.

On workplace policies to benefit different racial groups, in examining support for policies that would benefit white workers, a main effect of experimental condition emerged [$F(1, 144) = 5.42$, $p = .021$, $\eta_p^2 = 0.04$], such that participants for whom the future racially diverse United States was salient reported that white workers should benefit from special training programs and recruiting efforts, compared with participants in the (majority-white) control condition. Conversely, no reliable effects of timepoint, experimental condition or their interaction emerged for support for policies intended to benefit Latinos, $ps > .226$. Analyses of support

Table 3. Descriptive Statistics: Perceived Discrimination and Policy Support by Experimental Condition and Timepoint

	Current		Future	
	Control M (SD)	Racial Shift M (SD)	Control M (SD)	Racial Shift M (SD)
Perceived discrimination				
White Americans				
Study 3	2.21 (1.87)	3.19 (2.52)	2.83 (2.44)	3.39 (2.50)
Study 4	3.04 (2.19)	2.50 (1.93)	3.56 (2.82)	3.68 (2.76)
Black Americans				
Study 3	6.39 (2.27)	6.20 (2.50)	5.37 (2.58)	5.47 (2.45)
Study 4	6.20 (2.71)	6.15 (2.62)	4.99 (2.69)	4.94 (2.48)
Hispanics/Latinos				
Study 3	6.03 (2.25)	6.12 (2.04)	5.14 (2.43)	5.31 (2.21)
Study 4	5.96 (2.42)	5.73 (2.35)	4.67 (2.47)	4.39 (2.38)
Asian Americans				
Study 4	4.28 (2.16)	4.42 (2.09)	3.82 (2.22)	3.82 (2.03)
Native Americans				
Study 4	5.69 (2.57)	5.03 (2.27)	4.58 (2.51)	4.31 (2.17)
Support for policies benefiting the following groups (study 3 only)				
White Americans	2.05 (1.20)	2.57 (1.42)	2.15 (1.14)	2.63 (1.53)
Black Americans	2.73 (1.63)	2.94 (1.63)	2.49 (1.42)	2.94 (1.66)
Latinos	2.65 (1.54)	2.90 (1.51)	2.54 (1.45)	2.88 (1.55)

Source: Authors' compilation.

for policies that would benefit blacks revealed a main effect of timepoint [$F(1, 144) = 4.37, p = .038, \eta_p^2 = 0.03$] that was qualified by a timepoint × condition interaction [$F(1, 144) = 4.37, p = .038, \eta_p^2 = 0.03$]. Participants in the control condition supported policies that would benefit black workers more in the present than in the future, consistent with the expectation the racial discrimination against blacks is declining [$F(1, 144) = 8.50, p = .004, \eta_p^2 = 0.06$], whereas participants in the racial shift condition did not reveal this decline in support [$F(1, 144) < 1, p = .999$].

Discussion

Study 3 provided causal evidence that information about increasing minority populations (and a decreasing white population) influences white Americans' concerns about antiwhite discrimination and even support for employment policies benefiting whites (see also Craig and Richeson 2017). Concurrently, consistent with the results of studies 1 and 2, expectations regarding antiminority discrimination were not influenced by the experimental condition. Study 3 suggested not only that perceptions of discrimination are affected by shifting racial national demographics, but also that policies intended to benefit different racial groups may be influenced by these societal changes. Study 3, however, did not directly examine the putative psychological mechanism through which growing racial diversity is thought to increase concerns about antiwhite discrimination. Study 4 attempted to address this gap.

STUDY 4

In study 4, we again tested whether making the increasing racial diversity of the nation salient affects whites' perceptions of antiwhite discrimination. In addition, we explored whether increasing national diversity has these effects on perceived in-group vulnerability to discrimination because it also triggers concerns about in-group societal status. To this end, white participants read information about the growing racial-ethnic diversity of the nation (racial shift condition) or they read control information (increasing geographic mobility), prior to indicating their concerns about whites' status in society and their expectations regarding the current and future prevalence of racial discrimination toward a variety of racial groups, including white Americans (Craig and Richeson 2014a, 2014b). We predicted that making the U.S. racial population shift salient, relative to the control article, would elicit greater concern about whites' status in society, replicating our past work, as well as greater expectations regarding the prevalence of antiwhite discrimination, replicating study 3 and recent work (Craig and Richeson 2014b, 2017). We also tested (via mediational analyses) whether any observed effects of the racial shift information on perceptions of antiwhite discrimination might be due to heightened group status threat.

Methods

Two hundred and one white participants (113 women, 88 men, M_{age} = 38.14, SD_{age} = 12.45) were recruited from MTurk.com in exchange for $0.50.[5] Data were collected in March 2015.

Materials and Measures

As in study 3, we used a newspaper article paradigm to manipulate exposure to demographic change information suggesting larger minority populations. Depending on the experimental condition to which participants were randomly assigned, participants either read an article reporting on the growth of the rate of geographic mobility in the United States (control condition) or the article from study 3 that presents information on the projected future U.S. racial demographics in which whites are expected to make up less than 50 percent of the national population (racial shift condition).

Group Status Threat

One item assessed concerns about whites' societal status (group status threat; see Craig and Richeson 2014a, 2014b; Outten et al. 2012). Participants indicated their agreement (1 = strongly disagree, 7 = strongly agree) that if racial minorities gain status, white Americans' influence in society will likely decline.

Perceived Discrimination

As in study 3, participants indicated their perception that different racial groups—white Americans, Hispanics or Latinos, black Americans, Asian Americans, Native Americans—are currently facing discrimination and will face discrimination in the future (1 = not at all, 10 = very much).

Procedure

Participants provided informed consent and completed an initial set of demographic questions (for example, race, gender), followed by the article manipulation (racial shift or control). Participants then reported their level of group status threat and perceptions of discrimination faced by different racial groups, followed by additional demographic questions (for example, age), and were debriefed.

Results

No participants were excluded from analyses. The final sample included 101 participants in the racial shift condition and one hundred in the control condition.

We first tested whether the racial shift infor-

---

5. We explored moderation by participant gender. A statistically significant three-way (experimental condition x timepoint x participant gender) interaction emerged for perceived antiwhite discrimination [$F(1, 193)$ = 5.83, p = .017, η_p^2 = 0.03]. Probing this interaction revealed that women's responses were consistent with the effect reported in the main text: perceptions of rising antiwhite discrimination in the racial shift condition, but not the control condition [experimental condition x timepoint interaction: $F(1, 193)$ = 10.41, p = .001, η_p^2 = 0.05]. Conversely, men reported that antiwhite discrimination would be higher in the future, compared with current levels, regardless of experimental condition [experimental condition x timepoint interaction: $F(1, 193)$ < 1, p = .709]. We refrain from speculating further on this finding, given that study 3, which had a predominantly male sample, produced effects consistent with those found among women here. Future research that specifically examines how white men and white women may (or may not) differ in their reactions to the changing racial demographics of the nation is needed to fully explore this important issue.

mation influenced whites' perceived group status threat. Consistent with predictions and prior research, white participants in the racial demographic shift condition were more likely to report that whites' status in society is threatened by racial minorities ($M = 4.85$, 95% CI[4.55, 5.15], $SD = 1.42$), compared with participants in the control condition ($M = 4.19$, 95% CI[3.89, 4.49], $SD = 1.63$), $t(199) = 3.07$, $p = .002$, $d = 0.43$ (Craig and Richeson 2014b; Outten et al. 2012).

We next conducted a series of 2 (experimental condition: control, racial shift) x 2 (timepoint: current perceptions, future perceptions) mixed-design ANOVAs on the perceived discrimination measures. As shown in table 3, results revealed a main effect of timepoint [$F(1, 195) = 34.60$, $p < .001$, $\eta_p^2 = 0.15$], qualified by an experimental condition x timepoint interaction [$F(1, 195) = 5.18$, $p = .024$, $\eta_p^2 = 0.03$]. Consistent with study 3, participants in the control condition expected more antiwhite discrimination in the future, compared with current perceptions [$F(1, 195) = 6.34$, $p = .013$, $\eta_p^2 = 0.03$]. Reading about the increasing racial diversity of the United States, however, magnified this effect. Specifically, participants in the racial shift condition reported that antiwhite discrimination in the future would be strikingly more than in the present [$F(1, 195) = 34.14$, $p < .001$, $\eta_p^2 = 0.15$].

Consistent with study 3, further, analyses of perceived discrimination against different racial minority groups revealed only a main effect of timepoint [blacks: $F(1, 195) = 80.25$, $p < .001$, $\eta_p^2 = 0.29$; Latinos: $F(1, 195) = 74.85$, $p < .001$, $\eta_p^2 = 0.28$; Asian Americans: $F(1, 197) = 22.80$, $p < .001$, $\eta_p^2 = 0.10$; Native Americans: $F(1, 193) = 51.62$, $p < .001$, $\eta_p^2 = 0.21$]. Participants once again, regardless of experimental condition, expected that racial minority groups would face less discrimination in the future than they do currently (for descriptive statistics, see table 3).

Our mediation analysis is drawn on prior research revealing that concerns about whites' status in the societal hierarchy is one pathway through which exposure to information about the U.S. racial demographic shift affects whites' racial attitudes, intergroup emotions, and political ideology (Craig and Richeson 2014a, 2014b; Outten et al. 2012). We accordingly examined whether perceived group status threat may similarly mediate the observed effect of the racial shift information on perceptions that antiwhite discrimination in increasing (the difference between perceptions of future and current levels of antiwhite discrimination). We tested a simple mediation model to examine the indirect effect of the experimental manipulation on perceived antiwhite discrimination (future – current levels) via group status threat (Hayes 2013, model 4). No reliable indirect effect emerged, 95% CI[–0.09, 0.17], suggesting, somewhat surprisingly, that exposure to the racial shift information did not increase whites' tendency to anticipate growing antiwhite discrimination because it triggered concerns about group status.

Discussion

Overall, study 4 replicated past work finding that exposure to information about the rapidly diversifying racial composition of the nation increases whites' concerns about their racial group's status in society (Craig and Richeson 2014b; Major, Blodorn, and Major-Blascovich 2016; Outten et al. 2012). Study 4 also revealed, as predicted, that exposure to this racial demographic shift information heightens perceptions that whites will face discrimination. Perceptions of the discrimination faced by racial minority groups, however, were not affected by the experimental manipulation; instead, whites expected antiminority discrimination to decline in the future, regardless of their experimental condition. Further, a mediation analysis suggested that concerns about losing societal status in the future may not be the cause of the effect of exposure to the racial shift information on whites' perceptions of (and concerns about) future levels of antiwhite discrimination—a somewhat surprising finding given the documented role of group status threat in shaping whites' responses to other social and political outcomes upon exposure to increasing racial diversity (for a recent review, see Craig, Rucker, and Richeson 2017). Thus, the present data suggest that whites' concerns regarding their group's societal status and perceived antiwhite discrimination may be separable, co-occurring consequences of anticipating racial demographic change.

If concerns about white Americans losing influence or power in society do not account for the observed effects, what may? Recent social psychological research suggests that information about whites' relative population decline not only can be perceived as a threat to their in-group's material resources and sociopolitical standing (Craig and Richeson 2014a, 2014b; Major, Blodorn, and Major-Blascovich 2016; Outten et al. 2012), but also may threaten whites' understanding of their position as "prototypical Americans" (Danbold and Huo 2015)—that is, a more cultural threat (see also Zou and Cheryan 2017). Further, from the design of study 4, one cannot make strong causal attributions regarding the specific pathways through which information about racial minorities' population growth may influence perceived antiwhite discrimination and group status threat (group status threat could lead to perceived discrimination or vice versa). Thus, future research in which various potential threats (group status threat, prototypicality or cultural threats) of the rapidly changing demographics of the nation are manipulated, rather than measured, is necessary to investigate their potential causal role in shaping whites' reactions to increasing diversity and concerns about their racial in-group (see Craig and Richeson 2017).

GENERAL DISCUSSION

Together, the findings of the four studies reported here suggest that the size of relevant racial minority populations can increase whites' concerns about their racial identity and standing in society. Whites who live in areas with larger racial minority populations and those who perceive racial minority groups to be larger in size relative to the total population are also more likely to report that they personally, and whites as a group, face racial discrimination. Further, making the projected growth in the national population of racial minority groups salient (and thus the declining white population) similarly heightened white participants' concerns that their group may face discrimination, especially in this more racially diverse future. Perceptions of the discrimination faced by other racial groups (anti-Hispanic discrimination) were generally not associated with perceived or actual racial minority group size in white respondents' communities or nationally. Similarly, making the increasing national diversity salient did not affect whites' perceptions of the level of discrimination racial minorities currently face or are likely to face in the future. Indeed, consistent with classic research, these patterns of results suggest that larger racial minority groups activate whites' concerns that they or their in-group may lose ground in society and even face antiwhite discrimination (Blalock 1967; Blumer 1958). An initial test for a mechanism underlying this effect in study 4 suggested that though concerns regarding whites' relative material status in society are activated by information about increasing racial diversity, this type of group status threat is unlikely to account for the effects of this information on perceptions of discrimination.

Muted Effects of Actual Presence of Minorities

An important facet of the data examined in studies 1 and 2 is the general inaccuracy of respondents' estimates of racial diversity. On average, respondents estimated that racial minority groups constituted a larger percentage of the population than was accurate at the time of the surveys and that whites made up a lower percentage of the population than they did. On average, respondents in study 1 estimated that racial minorities already made up a majority of the national population, a milestone that is not expected to manifest for three decades (U.S. Census Bureau 2000, 2015). This kind of effect has been well documented in other, related research, but highlights a possible explanation for the relatively muted effects of actual levels of community racial diversity compared with perceived racial levels (Alba, Rumbaut, and Marotz 2005; Nadeau, Niemi, and Levine 1993). In study 2, for instance, perceptions of antiwhite (both group- and personal-level) discrimination tended to be more strongly associated with perceived racial minority group size (rs = .19 to .20), compared with actual racial minority group size (rs = .04 to .12). White respondents' overestimates of the size of racial minority groups relative to whites may be especially likely to both trigger and reflect concerns about their racial in-group.

Alternatively, the actual percentage of racial

minority group members in one's community may elicit opposing influences on racial threat, leading to smaller associations. That is, whereas larger percentages of racial minority groups can increase perceived group size and, subsequently, perceptions of threat to the in-group's interests, larger percentages of racial minority groups in one's community can also provide opportunities for positive intergroup contact, an important salve for strained intergroup relations (Allport 1954; Pettigrew 1998). Future work should examine the potentially separable mechanisms through which actual and perceived group size may influence racial threat and downstream effects for perceptions of discrimination (on threat, see Schlueter and Scheepers 2010). Regardless, these studies offer initial evidence that perceptions of and the actual size of racial minority out-groups are associated with white Americans' concerns about their racial in-group.

Personal Versus Group Discrimination

A well-established discrepancy exists between feelings of disadvantage for one's group and a sense of personal disadvantage: the personal-group discrimination discrepancy (Taylor et al. 1990; Taylor, Wright, and Porter 1994). That is, although most disadvantaged group members acknowledge that their group faces discrimination, far fewer report that they personally have (Crosby 1982; Kasschau 1977; Taylor et al. 1990). This pattern holds in these studies for white participants' perceptions that they and their group face racial prejudice (study 1: $M_{personal}$ = 1.73, 95% CI[1.65, 1.80], M_{group} = 2.15, 95% CI[2.07, 2.23]; study 2: $M_{personal}$ = 1.70, 95% CI[1.66, 1.73], M_{group} = 2.03, 95% CI[2.00, 2.07]). The results of studies 1 and 2, interestingly, suggest that racial makeup is more strongly associated with perceptions that one personally faces discrimination than that one's group does. This may suggest that larger minority populations in one's local environment activate concerns regarding potential unfair treatment to respondents themselves more so than concerns about the group as a whole. Future research, however, is needed to examine this possibility, as well as the processes involved in eliciting white Americans' concerns about group identity, material status, and cultural standing, processes that are likely to have considerable consequences for societal racial equality and cohesion.

Implications for White Americans' Identification

The present research has intriguing implications for how racial diversity, especially increasing racial diversity, may affect white Americans' racial identification and group consciousness. Although we did not specifically examine how increasing, actual, or perceived racial diversity affects whites' racial identification in these studies, research has found that exposure to information that whites are projected to become a minority in the United States or to information regarding the rapid increases in the Hispanic population can lead whites to express stronger racial identification (Abascal 2015; Outten et al. 2012; but see Major, Blodorn, and Major-Blascovich 2016). Of course, racial identification—even with a dominant group—is not necessarily negative, even for race relations, because racial identification can facilitate acknowledging white privilege (Croll 2007). Insofar as increasing racial diversity motivates in-group enhancing and out-group derogating reactions such as racial bias (Craig and Richeson 2014a), one possible downstream consequence of minority group growth is the emergence of more defensive forms of white identity (Goren and Plaut 2012; Knowles and Peng 2005). Future empirical research is needed to examine how and what forms of white racial identity may be shaped by racial diversity and, further, how these shifts in identification may subsequently affect societal intergroup relations.

It is entirely likely that the effects found here for perceived antiwhite discrimination reflect increased group consciousness. Further, according to the rejection-identification model, perceiving that one faces discrimination based on a group membership can itself increase identification with that group (Branscombe, Schmitt, and Harvey 1999). In other words, insofar as increasing racial diversity triggers greater concern about antiwhite discrimination among whites, it may also increase whites' racial identification (see Knowles and Peng 2005).

In Which Domains Might Whites Be Concerned About Discrimination?

One limitation of these studies is the use of general measures of perceived antiwhite discrimination. Preliminary research examining the domains (political influence, hiring decisions, dating) in which whites may expect to face discrimination suggests that information about increasing racial diversity can lead whites to express expectations that they will face discrimination across a variety of domains—particularly in employment and education, but also in interpersonal and more cultural areas (see Craig and Richeson 2017). That said, this question has only been explored in one study (of which we are aware) and, thus, it remains an open question for future inquiry.

Conclusions

The racial demographic trend toward a nation in which whites no longer number more than 50 percent and in which the combined total of all racial minority groups constitutes the majority of the population has received considerable media attention (Horowitz 2016; Wazwaz 2015). These studies offer an initial examination into how whites' racial concerns for their group and themselves personally are likely to be shaped by these changing racial demographics. This work suggests that as the U.S. populace becomes increasingly racially diverse, racial threat stemming from larger minority populations may have important consequences for whites' concerns about facing discrimination and racial group consciousness.

REFERENCES

Abascal, Maria. 2015. "Us and Them: Black-White Relations in the Wake of Hispanic Population Growth." *American Sociological Review* 80(4): 789–813.

Alba, Richard, Rubén G. Rumbaut, and Karen Marotz. 2005. "A Distorted Nation: Perceptions of Racial/Ethnic Group Sizes and Attitudes Toward Immigrants and Other Minorities." *Social Forces* 84(2): 901–19.

Allport, Gordon W. 1954. *The Nature of Prejudice.* Cambridge, Mass.: Perseus Books.

Blalock, Hubert M. 1967. *Toward a Theory of Minority-Group Relations.* New York: John Wiley & Sons.

Blumer, Herbert. 1958. "Race Prejudice as a Sense of Group Position." *Pacific Sociological Review* 1(1): 3–7.

Branscombe, Nyla R., Michael T. Schmitt, and Richard D. Harvey. 1999. "Perceiving Pervasive Discrimination Among African Americans: Implications for Group Identification and Well-Being." *Journal of Personality and Social Psychology* 77(1): 135–49.

Craig, Maureen A., and Jennifer A. Richeson. 2014a. "More Diverse Yet Less Tolerant? How the Increasingly-Diverse Racial Landscape Affects White Americans' Racial Attitudes." *Personality and Social Psychology Bulletin* 40(6): 750–61.

———. 2014b. "On the Precipice of a 'Majority-Minority' America: Perceived Status Threat from the Racial Demographic Shift Affects White Americans' Political Ideology." *Psychological Science* 25(6): 1189–97.

———. 2017. "Increasing Racial Diversity Triggers Concerns About Anti-White Discrimination Among the Prospective White 'Minority.'" *PLOS ONE* 12(9): e0185389.

Craig, Maureen A., Julian M. Rucker, and Jennifer A. Richeson. 2017. "The Pitfalls and Promise of Increasing Racial Diversity: Threat, Contact, and Race Relations in the 21st Century." *Current Directions in Psychological Science*, published online December 19, 2017. DOI: 10.1177/0963721417727860.

———. Forthcoming. "Racial and Political Dynamics of an Approaching 'Majority-Minority' United States." *Annals of the American Academy of Political and Social Science.*

Croll, Paul R. 2007. "Modeling Determinants of White Racial Identity: Results from a New National Survey." *Social Forces* 86(2): 613–42.

Crosby, Faye J. 1982. *Relative Deprivation and Working Women.* New York: Oxford University Press.

Danbold, Felix, and Yuen J. Huo. 2015. "No Longer 'All-American'?: Whites' Defensive Reactions to Their Numerical Decline." *Social Psychological and Personality Science* 6(2): 210–18.

Dover, Tessa L., Brenda Major, and Cheryl R. Kaiser. 2016. "Members of High-Status Groups Are Threatened by Pro-Diversity Organizational Messages." *Journal of Experimental Social Psychology* 62(1): 58–67.

Emerson, Michael O., Jenifer Bratter, Junia Howell, P. Wilner Jeanty, and Mike Cline. 2012. "Houston Region Grows More Racially/Ethnically Diverse, with Small Declines in Segregation." A Joint Report Analyzing Census Data from 1990, 2000, and 2010. Houston, Tex.: Kinder Institute of Urban Research and the Hobby Center for the Study of Texas.

Enos, Ryan D. 2016. "What the Demolition of Public Housing Teaches Us About the Impact of Racial Threat on Political Behavior." *American Journal of Political Science* 60(1): 123–42.

Fossett, Mark A., and K. Jill Kiecolt. 1989. "The Relative Size of Minority Populations and White Racial Attitudes." *Social Science Quarterly* 70(4): 820–35.

Giles, Michael W., and Kaenan Hertz. 1994. "Racial Threat and Partisan Identification." *American Political Science Review* 88(2): 317–26.

Goren, Matt J., and Victoria C. Plaut. 2012. "Identity Form Matters: White Racial Identity and Attitudes Toward Diversity." *Self and Identity* 11(2): 237–54.

Hayes, Andrew F. 2013. *Introduction to Mediation, Moderation, and Conditional Process Analysis: A Regression-Based Approach*. New York: Guilford Press.

Hing, Bill O. 2004. *Defining America Through Immigration Policy*. Philadelphia, Pa.: Temple University Press.

Horowitz, Evan. 2016. "When Will Minorities Be the Majority?" *Boston Globe*, February 26. Accessed May 28, 2017. https://www.bostonglobe.com/news/politics/2016/02/26/when-will-minorities-majority/9v5m1Jj8hdGcXvpXtbQT5I/story.html.

Jackson, James S., Vincent Hutchings, Cara Wong, and Ron Brown. 2008. National Politics Study, 2008. ICPSR36167. Ann Arbor, Mich.: Inter-University Consortium for Political and Social Research.

Kasschau, Patricia L. 1977. "Age and Race Discrimination Reported by Middle-Aged and Older Persons." *Social Forces* 55(3): 728–42.

Klineberg, Stephen L. 2010. "The Kinder Houston Area Survey." Houston, Tex.: Kinder Institute for Urban Research. Accessed January 29, 2018. http://has.rice.edu.

Knowles, Eric D., and Kaiping Peng. 2005. "White Selves: Conceptualizing and Measuring a Dominant-Group Identity." *Journal of Personality and Social Psychology* 89(2): 223–41.

Lee, Barrett A., John Iceland, and Gregory Sharp. 2012. "Racial and Ethnic Diversity Goes Local: Charting Change in American Communities Over Three Decades." New York: Russell Sage Foundation. Accessed May 28, 2017. https://www.russellsage.org/research/reports/racial-ethnic-diversity.

Major, Brenda, Alison Blodorn, and Gregory Major-Blascovich. 2016. "The Threat of Increasing Diversity: Why White Americans Support Trump in the 2016 Presidential Election." *Group Processes and Intergroup Relations*, published online October 20, 2016. DOI: 10.1177/1368430216677304.

Nadeau, Richard, Richard G. Niemi, and Jeffrey Levine. 1993. "Innumeracy About Minority Populations." *Public Opinion Quarterly* 57(3): 332–47.

Norton, Michael I., and Samuel R. Sommers. 2011. "Whites See Racism as a Zero-Sum Game That They Are Now Losing." *Perspectives on Psychological Science* 6(3): 215–18.

Outten, H. Robert, Michael T. Schmitt, Daniel A. Miller, and Amber L. Garcia. 2012. "Feeling Threatened About the Future: Whites' Emotional Reactions to Anticipated Ethnic Demographic Changes." *Personality and Social Psychology Bulletin* 38(1): 14–25.

Pettigrew, Thomas F. 1998. "Intergroup Contact Theory." *Annual Review of Psychology* 49(1): 65–85.

Pettigrew, Thomas F., and Linda R. Tropp. 2008. "How Does Intergroup Contact Reduce Prejudice? Meta-Analytic Tests of Three Mediators." *European Journal of Social Psychology* 38(6): 922–34.

Pew Research Center. 2015. *Modern Immigration Wave Brings 59 Million to U.S., Driving Population Growth and Change Through 2065: Views of Immigration's Impact on U.S. Society Mixed*. Washington, D.C.: Pew Research Center. Accessed January 29, 2018. http://www.pewhispanic.org/2015/09/28/modern-immigration-wave-brings-59-million-to-u-s-driving-population-growth-and-change-through-2065/.

Quillian, Lincoln. 1995. "Prejudice as a Response to Perceived Group Threat: Population Composition and Anti-Immigrant and Racial Prejudice in Europe." *American Sociological Review* 60(4): 586–611.

Schildkraut, Deborah S., and Satia A. Marotta. 2017. "Assessing the Political Distinctiveness of White Millennials: How Race and Generation Shape Racial and Political Attitudes in a Changing America." Paper presented to the Russell Sage Foundation, New York (September).

Schlueter, Elmar, and Peer Scheepers. 2010. "The

Relationship Between Outgroup Size and Anti-Outgroup Attitudes: A Theoretical Synthesis and Empirical Test of Group Threat- and Intergroup Contact Theory." *Social Science Research* 39(2): 285–95.

Skinner, Allison L., and Jacob E. Cheadle. 2016. "The 'Obama Effect'? Priming Contemporary Racial Milestones Increases Implicit Racial Bias Among Whites." *Social Cognition* 34(6): 544–58.

Taylor, Donald M., Stephen C. Wright, Fathali M. Moghaddam, and Richard N. Lalonde. 1990. "The Personal/Group Discrimination Discrepancy." *Personality and Social Psychology Bulletin* 16(2): 254–62.

Taylor, Donald M., Stephen C. Wright, and Lana E. Porter. 1994. "Dimensions of Perceived Discrimination: The Personal/Group Discrimination Discrepancy." In *The Psychology of Prejudice: The Ontario Symposium*, edited by Mark P. Zanna and James M. Olson. Hillsdale, N.J.: Lawrence Erlbaum.

U.S. Census Bureau. 2000. "Profile of General Demographic Characteristics: 2000." Accessed January 29, 2018. https://www.census.gov/prod/cen2000/dp1/2kh00.pdf.

———. 2013. "Geographic Areas Reference Manual." Accessed January 29, 2018. https://www.census.gov/geo/reference/garm.html.

———. 2015. "New Census Bureau Report Analyzes U.S. Population Projections." Press Release. Washington: Government Printing Office. Accessed January 29, 2018. https://www.census.gov/newsroom/press-releases/2015/cb15-tps16.html.

Wazwaz, Noor. 2015. "It's Official: The U.S. Is Becoming a Minority-Majority Nation." *U.S. News & World Report*, July 6. Accessed January 29, 2018. http://www.usnews.com/news/articles/2015/07/06/its-official-the-us-is-becoming-a-minority-majority-nation.

Wilkins, Clara L., and Cheryl R. Kaiser. 2014. "Racial Progress as Threat to the Status Hierarchy: Implications for Perceptions of Anti-White Bias." *Psychological Science* 25(2): 439–46.

Willer, Robb, Matthew Feinberg, and Rachel Wetts. 2016. "Threats to Racial Status Promote Tea Party Support Among White Americans." *SSRN* working paper. Stanford, Calif.: Stanford University Graduate School of Business. Accessed May 28, 2017. http://papers.ssrn.com/sol3/papers.cfm?abstract_id=2770186.

Zou, Linda X., and Sapna Cheryan. 2017. "Loathe Thy Neighbor: The Effects of Residential Diversity on Whites' Perceptions of Threat." *Social Psychological and Personality Science*, published online December 19, 2017.

Assessing the Political Distinctiveness of White Millennials: How Race and Generation Shape Racial and Political Attitudes in a Changing America

DEBORAH J. SCHILDKRAUT AND SATIA A. MAROTTA

White Americans will soon lose their majority status—news that provokes group threat and a conservative response. Yet an alternative outcome focused on white millennials is also possible. This study examines whether young whites are distinct in their racial attitudes and how they react to demographic change. Using two nationally representative surveys from 2012 and 2016 and a nationally representative experiment from 2016, we find that race affects attitudes more than generation, and in no case are white millennials as racially liberal as nonwhites. Exposure to information about changing demography makes white millennials more conservative on some questions, but what matters more is whether respondents are Republicans and identify as white. White millennials are hardly immune to the power of race to shape their attitudes.

Keywords: millennials, race, immigration, public opinion

Reading the news these days without seeing stories about race relations, immigration, or concerns about America's changing identity is difficult at best. The impending loss of majority status for whites in the United States often looms large in these stories, which feature headlines such as "It's Official: Minority Babies Are the Majority Among the Nation's Infants" (Cohn 2016) and "For First Time, Minority Students Expected to Be Majority in U.S. Public Schools this Fall" (Strauss 2014). In light of these changes, an unprecedented research question has emerged: how are white Americans reacting to the predicted loss of their majority status? Extant research concludes that this news drives a social and political wedge between whites and nonwhites. For example, exposure to information about these population changes can cause whites to become more conservative, less tolerant of diversity, and

Deborah J. Schildkraut is professor of political science at Tufts University. **Satia A. Marotta** earned her PhD in psychology at Tufts University in 2017.

© 2018 Russell Sage Foundation. Schildkraut, Deborah J., and Satia A. Marotta. 2018. "Assessing the Political Distinctiveness of White Millennials: How Race and Generation Shape Racial and Political Attitudes in a Changing America." *RSF: The Russell Sage Foundation Journal of the Social Sciences* 4(5): 158–87. DOI: 10.7758/RSF.2018.4.5.08. The authors wish to thank Kay Deaux, Katherine Donato, Nancy Foner, Suzanne Nichols, anonymous reviewers, and participants of the Immigration and Changing Identities conference at the Russell Sage Foundation. Direct correspondence to: Deborah Schildkraut at deborah.schildkraut@tufts.edu, Department of Political Science, Packard Hall, Tufts University, Medford, MA 02155.

Open Access Policy: *RSF: The Russell Sage Foundation Journal of the Social Sciences* is an open access journal. This article is published under a Creative Commons Attribution-NonCommercial-NoDerivs 3.0 Unported License.

more likely to think that being white is important to their sense of self (Outten et al. 2012; Hutchings et al. 2012; Danbold and Huo 2014; Jardina 2014; Craig and Richeson 2014b). These changing demographics and the threat they pose to the status of whites as the majority have been cited as key drivers of the success of Donald Trump's candidacy for president (Tesler and Sides 2016; Major, Blodorn, and Blascovich 2016; Sides, Tesler, and Vavreck 2018).

Over the past decade, however, a more optimistic story line about population change has also emerged, one focused on the so-called millennial generation, which consists of those Americans born after 1980 (Taylor 2014). The millennial narrative is more hopeful, portraying a group of young whites who are much more comfortable with diversity than their predecessors (Madland and Teixeira 2009; Teixeira 2011; Winograd and Hais 2011; Marcotte 2013; Feldmann 2014; Cillizza 2014; Tierney 2014; Simmons-Duffin 2014). Their alleged comfort with diversity is not due solely to millennials' being young; it is also a characteristic attributed to the diversity of the generation itself. As David Madland and Ruy Teixiera write, "Because of their diversity, Millennials' attitudes about and experiences with race are dramatically different from earlier generations . . . For millennials, race is "no big deal," an attitude that will increasingly characterize society as a whole as the millennials age and our march toward a majority-minority nation continues" (2009, 11). Although not stated directly, what underlies this expectation is the idea that increased diversity will promote increased contact with ethnic outgroups, which in turn will improve intergroup attitudes in the foreseeable future. This optimistic set of expectations has a long history in social science and is known as contact theory (Allport 1954). In the world of electoral politics, this portrait of a young generation comfortable with diversity fuels a narrative that the Republican Party has a "young person" problem, and comes with warnings that the Republican Party will age itself out of existence if it does not do more to appeal to the nation's young adults and their more racially liberal policy preferences (Rampell 2016; Cillizza 2014; Brownstein 2016).

If white millennials are as progressive as popular portrayals indicate, particularly with respect to racial issues, then white youth might be less susceptible to well-known psychological tendencies associated with racial group membership than whites in other generations, who have been shown to feel threatened by the nation's changing demography (see, for example, Craig and Richeson 2014a, also 2018). The goal of this study was therefore to assess claims made about white millennials. In particular, we examined whether white millennials are in fact more politically and racially liberal than older whites. We examine this question two ways. First, we used the 2012 and 2016 Cooperative Congressional Election Study (CCES) to compare the political views of white millennials to those of nonwhite millennials, older whites, and older nonwhites. In this portion of the study, we paid particular attention to questions about race, immigration, ideology, and partisanship. We then report the results of an experiment designed to examine whether white millennials and nonmillennials reacted similarly to information about demographic trends in the United States. This experiment built on important investigations conducted by Craig and Richeson (2014a, 2014b). Dependent variables in this portion of the analysis include attitudes about immigration policy, affirmative action, and evaluations of ethnic outgroups.

We find that white millennials are slightly more liberal than older whites, but that their views are closer to the views of older whites than they are to those of nonwhite millennials. We also find that white millennials are not more "immune" to the ways in which information about demographic change can promote more conservative attitudes. When such information moves attitudes in a more conservative direction, it does so for the young and old alike. We conclude that, on the issues examined here, race is a more powerful determinant of political preferences than generation. Moreover, the 2016 presidential election does not appear to have altered this pattern. Donald Trump's leadership of the Republican Party and his racially antagonistic campaign did not have a unique effect on young whites; Trump does not appear to have driven them toward or away from conservative policy stances, despite claims that his issue positions and rhetoric would drive them to the Democrats.[1]

WHO ARE MILLENNIALS?

According to Paul Taylor of the Pew Research Center, the millennial generation begins with those Americans born after 1980 (2014). Members of this group are called millennials because they came of age at the dawn of the new millennium (Pew Research Center 2015b).[2] This generation is notably large, and is now the largest generation in the American labor force (Fry 2015).

Taylor's analysis concludes that millennials are more liberal, Democratic, and racially diverse than other generations. Importantly, he notes that millennials are "at ease with racial, ethnic, and sexual diversity" (2014, 33). Taylor has a lot of company in depicting the millennial generation as unique in its comfort with diversity. Morley Winograd and Michael Hais, for instance, write that growing up in a more diverse society than its predecessors has led this generation to have "relatively colorblind attitudes on race relations" and "far more positive attitudes toward immigrants and their impact on society than older generations" (2008, 95, 96). Others echo this view (Madland and Teixeira 2009; Teixeira 2011; Winograd and Hais 2011; Marcotte 2013; Feldmann 2014; Cillizza 2014; Tierney 2014; Simmons-Duffin 2014). An important factor driving optimism about the racial harmony found among this generation is its own racial composition. According to recent estimates, this generation is only 57 percent white, non-Hispanic, relative to 72 percent of baby boomers, the next largest generation (Pew Research Center 2015a).[3]

What is missing from these optimistic characterizations of millennials, however, is an examination of their attitudes by race. Perhaps it is the relatively large proportion of nonwhites in this generation that makes the group seem so much more comfortable with diversity compared to older, but also whiter, generations. Whether millennial members of the country's racial majority share that comfort is an important question, particularly as whites edge ever closer to losing their majority status. The few extant examinations of the political attitudes of white millennials present a mixed picture. A 2014 report from the Pew Research Center uncovers gaps in attitudes among millennials by race, including presidential approval ratings and views on the scope of government, and a report by the Public Religion Research Institute describes a wide range of differences among millennials by race (Jones, Cox, and Banchoff 2012). A 2014 analysis by the Institute of Politics at Harvard also points to racial divisions among millennials on a range of issues (Harvard Public Opinion Project 2014). These reports, however, do not go beyond cross tabulations and do not include systematic comparisons of millennials to older Americans. They also fail to report the sample size for their nonwhite millennial respondents; given that most nationally representative surveys have few nonwhite respondents of any age, the subset of nonwhites who are born after 1980 in these surveys is likely to be quite small.

Scholarly analyses of the attitudes of millennials are also hard to find, though research on white attitudes by age exist. For example, Tatishe Nteta and Jill Greenlee find that white Americans who came of political age during Obama's first election are less likely to exhibit racial resentment than older white Americans (2013). Moreover, the ability of contact with

---

1. Whether the Trump presidency has affected partisanship and policy positions among white millennials remains to be seen. The most recent data included in our study were collected during the 2016 campaign.

2. Currently, neither name nor start date have been agreed upon for the generation following the millennials. This new generation, sometimes called Generation Z, is roughly defined as people born after 2000 (Sims 2015). Because they are still under eighteen and not yet included in national public opinion surveys, this group of Americans is not incorporated into the present analysis.

3. In the datasets analyzed here, 64 percent of millennial respondents are white in 2012 and 79 percent of boomers are; in 2016, the proportions are 63 percent for millennials and 79 percent for boomers. Millennials are also sometimes called *echo boomers* because they are primarily the offspring of baby boomers (born between 1947 and 1964), which, along with immigration, accounts for why their generation is so large.

blacks to mitigate racial resentment was enhanced for younger whites, whereas such contact exacerbated racial resentment among the oldest whites. Nteta and Greenlee conclude that coming of political age during Obama's presidency could diminish racial resentment among whites in the long term.

A study by Gary Jacobson suggests that this kind of "generational imprinting" is not confined to those young whites who might be predisposed to support Obama on account of their partisan identification (2016). Across many measures, he finds that young Republicans differ considerably from their older counterparts.[4] For example, young Republicans were much less likely to call themselves conservative and more progressive in their views on same sex marriage, immigration, and racial resentment. Notably, Democrats showed greater similarity in their views across age groups on these issues than Republicans did. Younger Republicans were also less likely to watch Fox News and to believe that Obama is foreign born or a Muslim than older Republicans. Jacobson concludes that younger Americans are less polarized along ideological lines than their older counterparts.

A contrasting perspective on racial attitudes among young adults comes from a study by Tyrone Forman and Amanda Lewis, who examined the attitudes of white high school seniors from 1976 to 2000 (2015). Their analysis finds that whites in the later period were more likely to agree that it is not their business if some minority groups get unfair treatment. Instead of finding an embrace of diversity, Forman and Lewis argue that their findings indicate "a growing sense of cognitive distance and disengagement from racial matters in general" (2015, 1418). In thinking that racial issues do not concern them, the so-called comfort with diversity that young whites seem to feel might actually be an indifference that ignores or denies ongoing racial injustice.

Overall, however, research suggests that younger whites today may in fact be more racially liberal than older whites. Additional research shows that people do not necessarily become more conservative with age, as previously thought, and that generational attitudes are formed by political events of the period in which people enter adulthood, as well as by the aggregate characteristics of the generation itself, such as whether the generation as a whole has more educational attainment than previous generations (Davis 2013; Schwadel and Garneau 2014; Danigelis, Culter, and Hardy 2007; Abrajano and Lundgren 2015; Cook 2014; Osborne, Sears, and Valentino 2011; Alwin and Krosnick 1991; Ghitza and Gelman 2014). Taken together, these studies suggest that the attitudes among the large millennial generation will be stable and will drive the socialization process among their children in the years to come. Put another way, there is reason to believe that the diversity of this generation, along with the political climate during its coming of political age (including the election of the first black president and the liberalization of several policies, such as gay rights and health care), will have a lasting cohort effect that will render this generation more politically and socially liberal than prior generations.

Although this study is framed as an examination of the millennial generation, people born in 1979 are likely to have similar experiences to those born in 1981. Yet a long line of research on political socialization focuses on younger members of the electorate, and in such studies it is routine to examine respondents by cohort. The "young adult" cohort varies in definition, but is often conceptualized as adults who are eighteen through twenty-nine, eighteen through thirty, or eighteen through twenty-five (Cook 2014; Nteta and Greenlee 2013; Alwin and Krosnick 1991; Dinas 2013; Abrajano and Lundgren 2015). This time frame is theoretically interesting and important because it is the time in which political attitudes appear most likely to be affected by contemporary political events and set the stage for a person's long-term political identity (Stoker 2014;

---

4. Jacobson's analysis does not break down Republicans by race, but given that self-identified Republicans are overwhelmingly white, it is reasonable to interpret his findings as descriptive of young white Republicans. In both surveys analyzed in this study, for example, 89 percent of self-identified Republicans are non-Hispanic whites.

Sears and Brown 2013; Ghitza and Gelman 2014; Kinder 2006; Hopkins 2014). Focusing on millennials, therefore, allows this analysis to engage with both conventional wisdom in popular culture, where the term *millennial* is used frequently, as well as with scholarly examinations of how political socialization affects cohorts, which focus on "young adults" more generally.[5]

EXPAND THE CIRCLE OF *WE* OR CIRCLE THE WAGONS?

Population change and perceived threats to the group's status can lead people to become more or less inclusive. Contact theory and generational imprinting would predict greater inclusivity, whereas social identity theory would predict greater defense of one's in-group and perhaps greater denigration of out-groups.

One theoretical process underlying the notion that today's young whites will be more comfortable with diversity than previous generations is contact theory. Contact theory, in its most basic form, posits that intergroup contact can enhance intergroup harmony and reduce prejudice (Allport 1954; Forbes 1997). Meta-analyses of contact theory studies conclude that the totality of evidence supports the theory's main tenets, particularly when the contact in question involves interpersonal friendships (Pettigrew and Tropp 2006; Pettigrew et al. 2011). For millennials, their diversity leads observers to believe that they will be more racially liberal and less threatened by demographic change than older Americans. Among a generation this diverse, increased interracial contact is an assumption. Recent polling supports this assumption, finding that Americans under thirty are much more likely to date and marry outside their race than older Americans (Dunsmuir 2013). Given the findings from research on contact theory, the diversity of this generation, and the rise of interracial and interethnic relationships, white millennials are therefore expected by many to react to demographic change more favorably than older whites.

White millennials may be more politically and racially liberal than older whites for other reasons as well. Chief among them is their pre-adult and early-adult socialization experiences across domains (home, school, politics, popular culture, and so on), that could reinforce racial liberalism. Growing up in a post–civil rights environment with new norms about acceptable racial discourse, witnessing the election of a black president during their politically formative years, seeing more diversity in entertainment, and more, could result in racially liberal generational imprinting, even for those young whites who maintain racially homogeneous interpersonal networks (Mutz and Goldman 2010; Dovidio et al. 2011; Mendelberg 2001; Nteta and Greenlee 2013; Goldman 2012).

Despite the potential power of interracial contact and the increased presence of more racially tolerant environments, there are reasons to believe that whites in the United States might not expand the circle of *we* so readily in the face of increasing ethnic diversity (Hollinger 1995). Studies show that nontrivial segments of the white population feel that whites are discriminated against, identify as white, and exhibit a sense of linked fate (Norton and Sommers 2011; Jardina 2014; Schildkraut 2017). Whites are more likely to think of themselves in terms of their racial identity when they are primed to consider threats to the group's status, and identification as white can promote group-interested preferences (Branscombe, Schmitt, and Schiffhauer 2007; Goren and Plaut 2012; Outten et al. 2012; Hutchings et al. 2012; Lowery et al. 2006). Maureen Craig and Jennifer Richeson find that informing white Americans of demographic projections leads them to adopt a more conservative political outlook on a range of issues and promotes greater levels of both implicit and explicit racial bias (on outlook, 2014b; on bias, 2014a). Felix Danbold and Yuen Huo find that such projections lead

---

5. We recognize that age and cohort are intertwined in this analysis. We do not have the over-time data needed for an analysis of how the two interact. Given the studies cited here, however, we have reason to believe that the patterns of preferences exhibited by Millennial respondents will be relatively stable as they age. We also ran all models presented in our cross-sectional analysis using age as a continuous variable instead of generation categories and found that our substantive conclusions remain the same.

whites to perceive that their status as the "prototypical" American is threatened which, in turn, decreases support for diversity (2014). Ashley Jardina finds that the impact of identifying as white on policy attitudes has increased over time. Together, this research suggests that as the nation's population is becoming ever more diverse, whites are reacting by closing ranks around the group, identifying more strongly as white, and having that identification become a more prominent influence over their political beliefs (2014).

These reactions are in line with the predictions of social identity theory, which maintains that salient group identities can be powerful forces shaping political attitudes and behaviors (Tajfel 1982; Tajfel and Turner 1986). Perceptions of threat to the group enhance the group's salience and lead group members to approach their environment in a group-interested manner (Schmitt and Branscombe 2002). Related to social identity theory is group position theory, the idea that perceived threats to the position of one's group in the social hierarchy, such as those whites feel in response to efforts to redress racial inequality, can generate group-interested attitudes and behaviors (Blumer 1958; Bobo and Hutchings 1996; Bobo 1999).

What we do not know, however, is whether white Americans of different generations respond similarly to information about the changing ethnic composition of the country. The studies described do not focus on age or generation. Several relied on small MTurk samples or college-age samples, which preclude meaningful analysis by generation. Of those that used larger nationally representative samples, analyses that control for age are rarely reported. In the exceptions where the results do control for age, it is used as a continuous variable: specific attention to millennials is lacking. Moreover, in studies that control for age, its effect is erratic: older Americans are more likely to identify as white than younger Americans in one study (Jardina 2014), but in another age is insignificant (Hutchings et al. 2012). In short, despite the value of the studies cited thus far, they do not address the specific question that motivates this analysis.

CROSS-SECTION ANALYSIS

Our first examination of whether white millennials are more racially and politically liberal than older whites relied on cross-sectional survey analysis, which allowed us to compare the attitudes of white millennials with those of other groups. The results show the relative effects of race and generation on attitudes about party, ideology, racial resentment, affirmative action, and immigration policy. This portion of the analysis does not include a measure of interracial contact, an important theoretical mechanism that might promote differences between white millennials and older whites; it is therefore not a direct test of contact theory. Nor do we have direct measures that capture the socialization experiences of our respondents. What we can do, however, is examine whether our results are more consistent with the expectations of social identity theory or more consistent with the expectations of theories that would predict greater racial and political liberalism. The goal here is to establish patterns of political preferences among whites of different generations and among millennials of different races. Establishing these patterns is an important step in assessing claims about the promise and expectations cast upon the nation's white young adults.

The data for this analysis come from the 2012 and 2016 Cooperative Congressional Election Studies. The CCES is a national survey conducted online by YouGov/Polimetrix that includes before and after election waves (Ansolabehere 2013). The 2012 survey included 54,535 respondents. Of those, 74 percent were white and 16.5 percent were millennials. Of the millennials, 5,121 were white and 3,881 were nonwhite. The 2016 CCES included 12,465 white millennials and 6,959 nonwhite millennials (Ansolabehere and Schaffner 2017). The large CCES sample sizes thus present a unique opportunity to examine the questions under investigation here.[6]

---

6. In the 2012 dataset, the millennial respondents were eighteen to thirty-two years old. In the 2016 dataset, they were eighteen to thirty-six years old. Although there are probably several compelling differences between older and younger millennials, examining that heterogeneity is beyond the scope of this study.

Despite the advantage of having a large number of nonwhite millennials, it is significant that the CCES is conducted only in English. Language use is an important marker of acculturation, and acculturation is a powerful predictor of political attitudes among Latinos and Asians in the United States.[7] Specifically, respondents with lower levels of acculturation tend to exhibit more liberal policy preferences and greater concern for racial issues, such as descriptive representation (Branton 2007; Barreto and Pedraza 2009; Manzano and Sanchez 2010; Sanchez and Masuoka 2010; Fraga et al. 2012; Schildkraut 2013). The lack of a non-English questionnaire makes it harder to detect differences between white and nonwhite millennials; any differences that do emerge are likely to be even stronger in the broader population.[8]

Across all dependent variables, we tested the extent to which race and generation shaped responses. In particular, we looked for whether the views of white millennials more closely resembled the views of nonwhite millennials or the views of older whites. If the former, then perhaps the optimistic portrait of how millennials feel about racial matters is true. If the latter, then we can conclude that being white still matters a great deal in shaping how white millennials form their political views. The 2012 analysis focused on five variables. First, we examined partisanship and ideology. These broad political outlooks are arguably more associated with race in our current era than in the past, and prior research argues that information about the nation's changing demographics leads whites to adopt more conservative preferences across a range of issues, even if those issues are not racial in nature (Abrajano and Hajnal 2015; Craig and Richeson 2014b; Pew Research Center 2012). Then we examined racial resentment, support for affirmative action, and attitudes about immigration policy. In 2016, a different set of questions was fielded to examine racial attitudes, and those variables were analyzed as well, in addition to partisanship, ideology, and attitudes about immigration policy.

For each dependent variable, we ran three statistical models. We first examined whether millennial respondents held more liberal preferences than older respondents. Then we controlled for race to determine whether being in the millennial generation still affects attitudes. The last model examined how being white and a millennial interact to shape attitudes. For models that include this interaction term, the coefficient on generation can be interpreted as the effect of being millennial on the political attitudes of nonwhites, and the coefficient on race can be interpreted as the effect of being white on the political attitudes of nonmillennials. The coefficient on the interaction term indicates whether being millennial has a unique effect on the attitudes of whites. Given the conventional wisdom about the political outlook of white millennials, the hypothesis examined was whether this coefficient is negative, which would indicate a more liberal attitude relative to older whites. All models also controlled for the respondent's level of education and whether the respondent resides in the South.[9] For ease of presentation, we display the results in terms of predicted outcomes derived from the full model.[10] Tables of results are included in the appendix (see tables A1 through A5).

Party and Ideology

Partisanship is measured on a 7-point scale that runs from strong Democrat to strong Re-

---

7. Throughout this study, *Hispanic* and *Latino* are used interchangeably.

8. Our aim is to compare the views of white millennials, nonwhite millennials, white nonmillennials, and nonwhite nonmillennials; differences among black, Latino, and Asian respondents are not explored here, nor are national-origin differences among Latino and Asian respondents, nor are differences between other generations, such as baby boomers or Gen Xers.

9. We define the South as the eleven states of the former Confederacy: Alabama, Arkansas, Florida, Georgia, Louisiana, Mississippi, North Carolina, South Carolina, Tennessee, Texas, and Virginia.

10. Predictions are calculated using the Margins command in STATA. South is set to 0 (not in south) and education is set to its weighted mean.

Figure 1. Predicted Partisan Identification, 2012

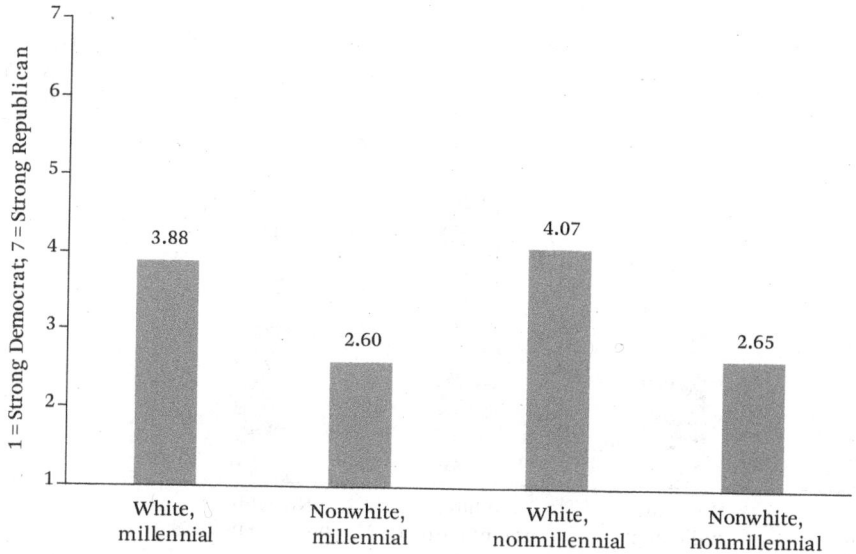

Source: Authors' calculations based on 2012 Cooperative Congressional Election Survey (Ansolabehere 2013).

Figure 2. Predicted Partisan Identification, 2016

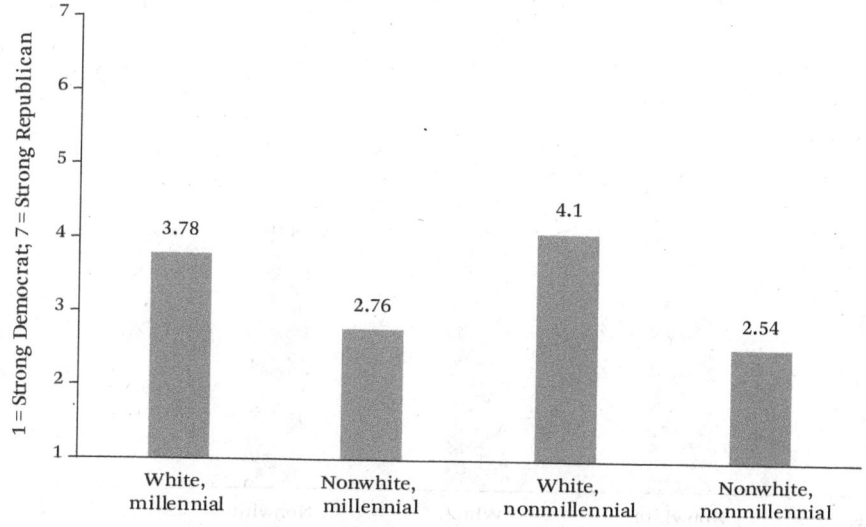

Source: Authors' calculations based on 2016 Cooperative Congressional Election Survey (Ansolabehere and Schaffner 2017).

publican, and ideology on a 7-point scale that runs from very liberal to very conservative. The results, which can be found in figures 1 and 2 (party) and 3 and 4 (ideology), indicate that being white is associated with greater identification as Republican and conservative. For partisanship, being in the millennial generation lessens one's attachment to the GOP, but only for whites (that is, the interaction was negative). It is clear from figures 1 and 2, however, that despite the statistical significance of being a white millennial, white millennials were actually closer to older whites in their partisan identification than to nonwhite millennials.

Figure 3. Predicted Ideology, 2012

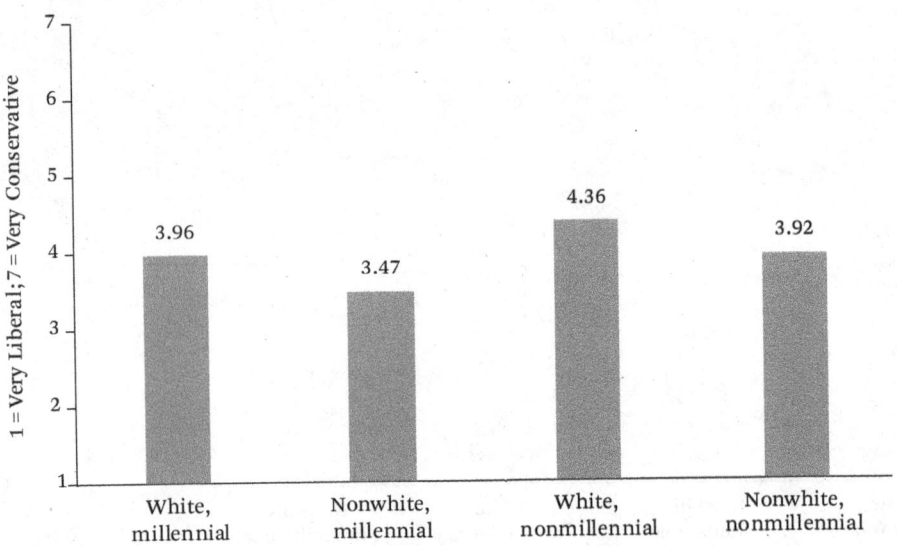

Source: Authors' calculations based on 2012 Cooperative Congressional Election Survey (Ansolabehere 2013).

Figure 4. Predicted Ideology, 2016

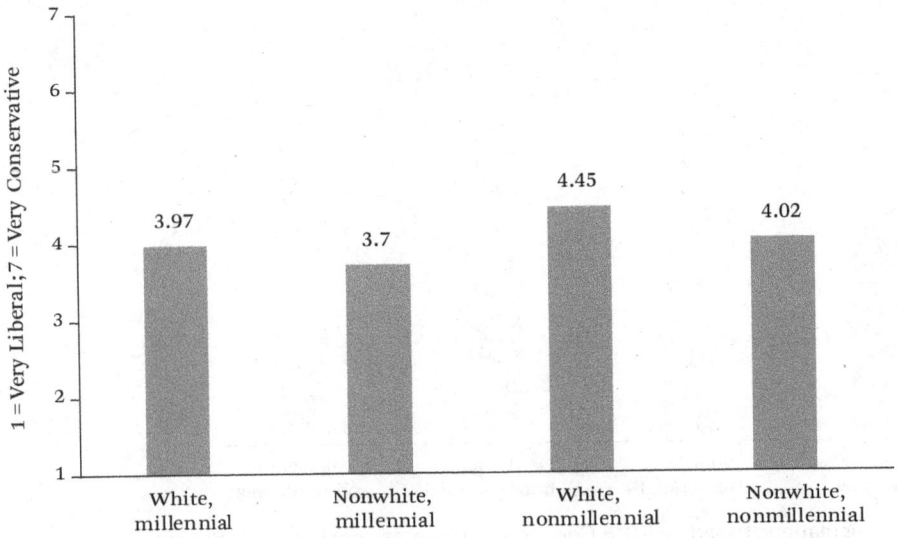

Source: Authors' calculations based on 2016 Cooperative Congressional Election Survey (Ansolabehere and Schaffner 2017).

For ideology, whites were more conservative than nonwhites, and millennials were more liberal than nonmillennials. The interaction between race and generation was significant in 2016 but not in 2012. The predicted outcomes displayed in figures 3 and 4 indicate that in 2012, the ideological self-categorization of white millennials was squarely in between that of older whites on the one hand and nonwhite millennials on the other. In 2016, white millen-

Figure 5. Predicted Level of Racial Resentment, 2012

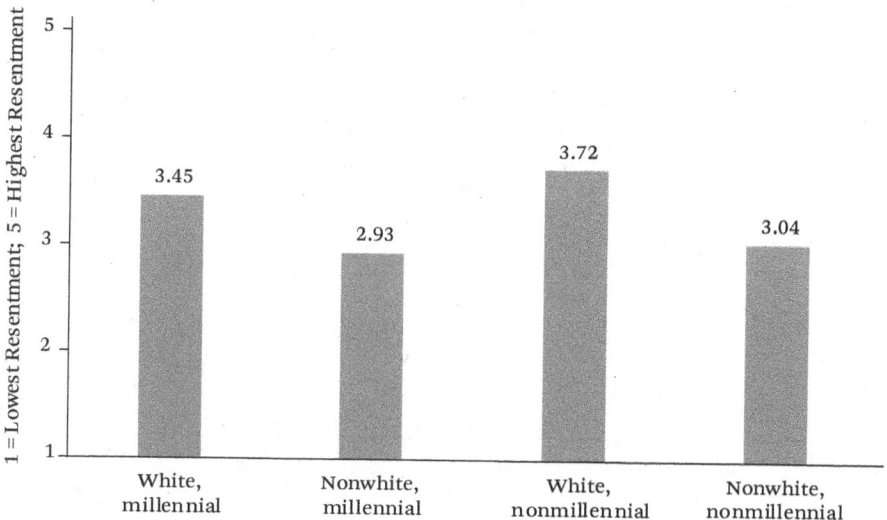

Source: Authors' calculations based on 2012 Cooperative Congressional Election Survey (Ansolabehere 2013).

nials were closer to their nonwhite counterparts than to older whites. Ideology in 2016 is the only analysis in this study where we find this to be true.

Little evidence indicates that the 2016 presidential campaign drove young people from the Republican Party. The mean predicted partisan affiliation and ideological categorization of white millennials is nearly identical in 2012 and 2016. In other words, the partisan and ideological makeup of white millennials was stable and—especially with respect to party—very close to the pattern exhibited among older whites.

Racial Resentment

No set of issues draws as much optimism among observers of millennials as racial issues. Observers claim that young people today are growing up amid so much diversity that we are witnessing a generation that is uniquely at ease with racial issues. As Winograd and Hais put it, "For Millennials of all backgrounds, racial and ethnic equality and inclusivity is a message they have been hearing all their lives and one in which they firmly believe" (2011, 32). To examine such optimism, we turn now to attitudes related to race, starting with racial resentment. The 2012 CCES measured racial resentment with two questions. Respondents were asked the extent to which they agreed with the following statements: "Generations of slavery and discrimination have created conditions that make it difficult for Blacks to work their way out of the lower class"; and "The Irish, Italians, Jews and many other minorities overcame prejudice and worked their way up. Blacks should do the same without any special favors" (for a discussion of these and other racial resentment measures, see Kinder and Sanders 1996; Tesler and Sears 2010). Both items were combined into a 5-point scale coded such that a higher score indicates more resentment ($\alpha=0.76$).

The results, presented in figure 5, are similar to the results for partisanship. For white millennials, being white led them to have more resentment than nonwhite millennials, and being a millennial led them have less resentment than older whites. Again, the interaction between race and generation is negative and significant, indicating that young whites are more racially liberal than older whites. Nonetheless, as is true of partisanship, the liberalizing effect of generation is modest; the predicted level of resentment for white millennials (3.45) is closer to that for older whites (3.72) than to the predicted level for nonwhite millennials (2.93).

Figure 6. Predicted Probability of Affirmative Action Preference, 2012

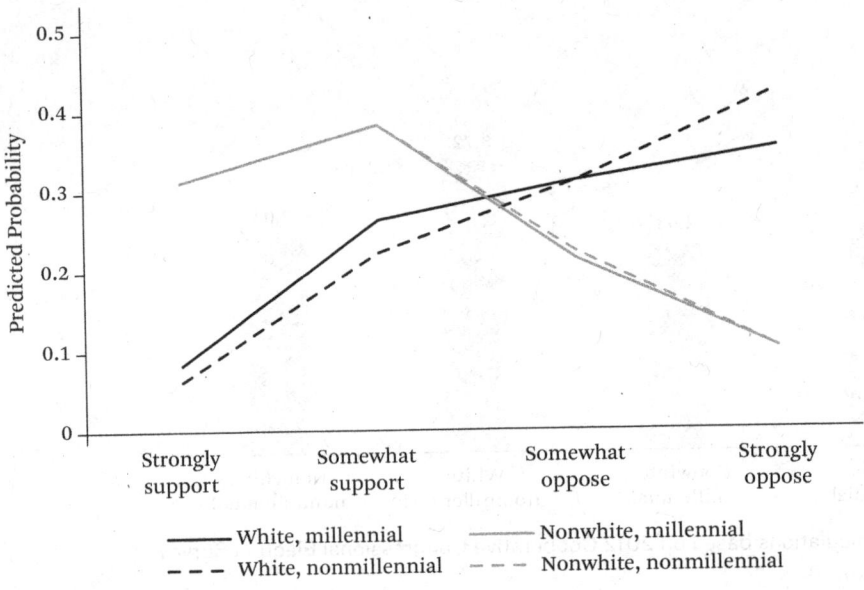

Source: Authors' calculations based on 2012 Cooperative Congressional Election Survey (Ansolabehere 2013).

Affirmative Action

Turning to affirmative action, respondents in 2012 were asked, "Affirmative action programs give preference to racial minorities in employment and college admissions in order to correct for past discrimination. Do you support or oppose affirmative action?" Four response options were given, ranging from strongly support to strongly oppose. Consistent with our other results, white millennials resembled older whites more than nonwhite millennials, despite a significant negative interaction between race and generation. White millennials were slightly less likely to strongly oppose affirmative action than older whites (35 percent versus 42 percent), but strong opposition is the plurality response for both groups, as illustrated in figure 6.

Attitudes About Discrimination

The 2016 CCES did not ask about racial resentment or affirmative action but instead about respondents' awareness of white privilege and racial discrimination. They were asked whether they agree or disagree with the following statements: "White people in the U.S. have certain advantages because of the color of their skin"; and "Racial problems in the U.S. are rare, isolated situations." The results for these questions, depicted in figures 7 and 8, conform to the pattern uncovered thus far. The interaction between being white and millennial was negative and significant in both cases. In one of them, whether having white skin confers advantages (figure 7), the liberalizing effect of being young was severely offset by being white. In sum, across 2012 and 2016, using a variety of measures about race, the general pattern remains: the racial attitudes of white millennials were remarkably similar to those of older whites.

Immigration Policy

Turning to immigration, the pattern is repeated yet again. Here, the dependent variable for 2012 was a 7-point scale, coded 0 to 1, on whether respondents support or oppose six immigration policies ($\alpha = 0.80$). The policies are to provide legal status for immigrants in the country illegally, increase border patrol, allow police to question anyone they think might be in the country illegally, fine U.S. businesses that hire immigrants who are in the country illegally, prohibit social services for people in the coun-

Figure 7. "White People in the U.S. Have Certain Advantages Because of the Color of Their Skin," 2016

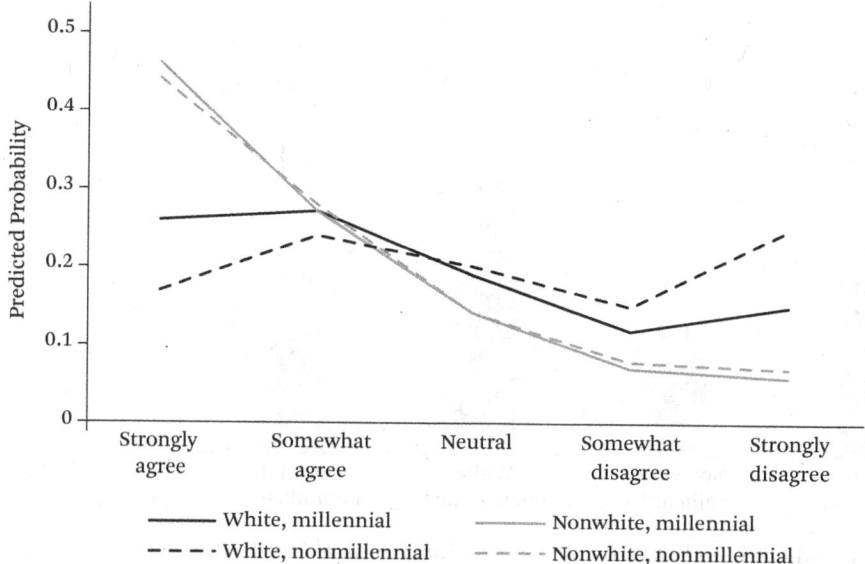

Source: Authors' calculations based on 2016 Cooperative Congressional Election Survey (Ansolabehere and Schaffner 2017).

Figure 8. "Racial Problems in the U.S. Are Rare, Isolated Situations," 2016

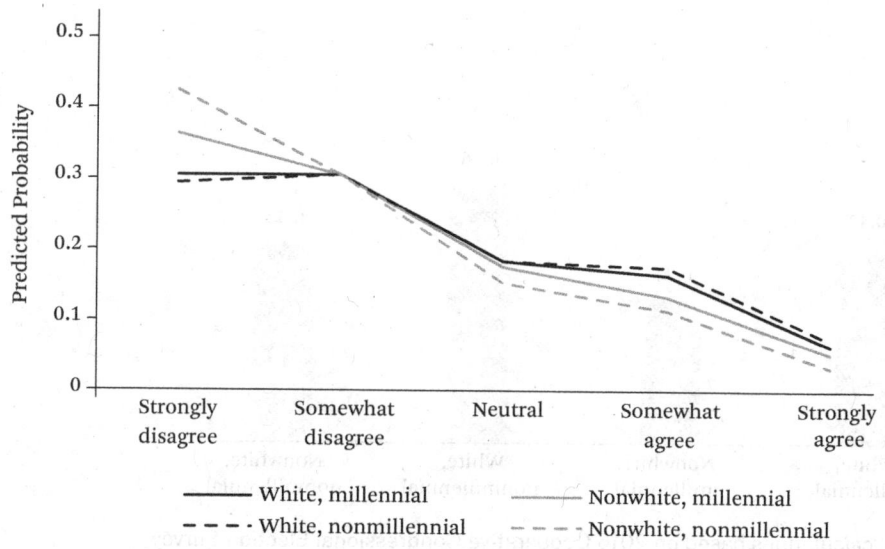

Source: Authors' calculations based on 2016 Cooperative Congressional Election Survey (Ansolabehere and Schaffner 2017).

try illegally, and deny birthright citizenship. In 2016, it was a 5-point scale made from four questions ($\alpha = 0.69$): to provide legal status for immigrants in the country illegally, increase border patrol, grant legal status to children who were brought to the United States illegally, and deport "illegal immigrants." In both years, a higher score indicates a greater preference for restrictive policies. Here again, the interaction between race and generation is negative and

Figure 9. Predicted Immigration Restriction Score, 2012

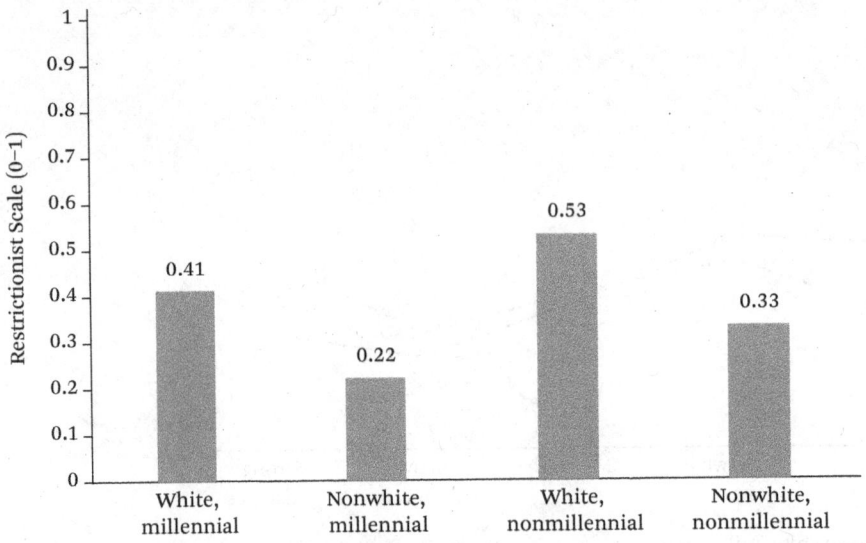

Source: Authors' calculations based on 2012 Cooperative Congressional Election Survey (Ansolabehere 2013).

Figure 10. Predicted Immigration Restriction Score, 2016

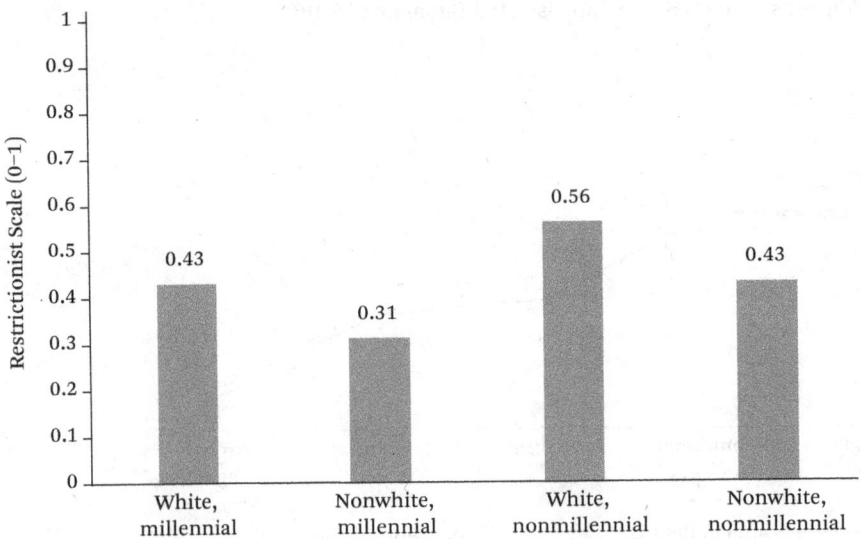

Source: Authors' calculations based on 2016 Cooperative Congressional Election Survey (Ansolabehere and Schaffner 2017).

significant, but the positive and significant effect for race, which promotes a more conservative stance, offsets the liberalizing push that being a millennial brings. As the predicted probabilities presented in figures 9 and 10 indicate, young whites had more restrictive immigration preferences than nonwhites, and their views more closely resembled those of older whites than of their nonwhite co-millennials.

In all models and with all dependent variables, residing in the South is associated with more conservative attitudes. Ideally, we would also have been able to control for whether respondents live in rural or urban settings. Unfortunately, such a measure was not available. Although white millennials appear in the aggregate to have views similar to those of older whites, heterogeneous preferences among whites need to be acknowledged and investigated. It is plausible that whites in urban settings are more racially liberal than whites in rural settings given the greater diversity found in urban areas. More relevant for our purposes, it is important to consider whether white millennials are *uniquely* affected by living in a rural or urban area relative to older whites. This question is one that future research should pursue.

To sum up, in four of the five tests in 2012 (all but ideology) and in all tests in 2016, the interaction between race and generation was negative and significant, indicating that white millennials showed a more liberal pattern of political preferences than their white elders did. Yet in all models, race maintains a significant and strong effect that offsets much of the racial and partisan liberalism promoted by being in the millennial generation. Across almost all tests, we see that white millennials tended to have views on party, ideology, race, and immigration closer to those of older whites than to those of nonwhite millennials.[11] In short, contrary to the claim Madland and Teixiera assert, race appears to remain a "big deal" for white millennials (2009).[12]

EXPERIMENTAL ANALYSIS

To probe this question further, we examined whether millennial whites and older whites responded similarly when presented with the specter of losing their status as the nation's racial majority. As noted earlier, social identity theory lays out reasons to expect whites to close ranks around their group in response to perceived threats to their status, and existing studies indicate that when shown information about population projections, whites do become more conservative on a wide range of issues. But are white millennials less prone to this tendency? Does the liberalizing effect of their generation offset their perception of threat? Exploring this question is the goal of the analysis presented in this section.

Here we show results of an experiment involving a nationally representative sample of white Americans (N = 955, 227 of whom are white millennials). The experiment was conducted online in 2016 by GfK Custom Research as part of a partnership with Time Sharing Experiments for the Social Sciences (Druckman and Freese 2016). It built on the important experiment conducted by Craig and Richeson, in which some respondents were shown a press release indicating that the nation will soon be majority-minority and a control group read about internal migration within the country. Their analysis reveals that whites in the treatment group were more likely than whites in the control group to have negative evaluations of ethnic groups (2014a) and to have more conservative preferences on a range of race-related and race-neutral public policies (2014b). Yet their study had only 415 white respondents, only eighty-five of whom were millennials. It also lacked measures of potential mechanisms that could drive the supposed differences be-

---

11. It is possible that despite having similar means across our dependent variables, one age group has more dispersion, which would indicate greater polarization. If the younger cohort is less polarized, as Gary Jacobson suggests, we would see smaller standard deviations for white millennials relative to older whites (2016). The CCES data, however, do not support this possibility. In 2012, white millennials had a slightly lower standard deviation on partisanship (2.06 versus 2.14), racial resentment (1.14 versus 1.15), and restrictionist immigration policy (0.32 versus 0.33) and a slightly higher standard deviation on ideology (1.79 versus 1.64) and affirmative action (0.93 versus 0.91); and in all cases the standard deviations are very close together. Nor do the 2016 data show any clear pattern in this regard.

12. All analyses in this section were rerun with age as a continuous variable. In almost all cases, the substantive conclusions presented here remain the same. With the immigration restriction scale, however, the interaction between age and race was not significant in 2012 or in 2016. Whites and older respondents were more likely than nonwhites and younger respondents to prefer stricter immigration policies; being younger did not have a unique effect on whites.

tween white millennials and older whites on matters of race.

Our experiment replicated features of the original Craig and Richeson study, using their press releases in our treatment and control conditions (see appendix). We included a larger sample of white millennials (N = 227), and to examine one potential mechanism, a measure of interracial contact. We asked respondents whether they personally knew anyone black, Hispanic, or Asian. If they said yes, we asked whether they had any close friends who are black, Hispanic, or Asian. Their answer to this question is our measure of interracial contact.[13] We concentrated on this form of close interpersonal contact because research indicates that contact through friendships is more likely to have a beneficial effect on intergroup attitudes than casual contact that results from diverse schools, workplaces, and neighborhoods (for a thorough example, see Ellison, Shin, and Leal 2011). We also asked respondents (before the manipulation) how important being white was to their identity.[14] The main hypothesis examined here is that white millennials are less likely than older whites to be affected by the treatment. In other words, white millennials are less likely than older whites to be moved in a conservative direction and are less likely to exhibit lower evaluations of ethnic outgroups after reading about demographic projections. After testing this hypothesis, we looked at interracial contact and examined whether millennial respondents were uniquely affected by having nonwhite friends.

Dependent Variables

In one paper, Craig and Richeson use their experiment to show that whites in the treatment group had more conservative preferences on several race-related and race-neutral policies than the control group (2014b). We used the same questions they did in their study. The first race-related policy item asked respondents whether they thought the time it takes for immigrants to become eligible for U.S. citizenship should be increased or decreased (5-point scale). The second asked whether the overall number of immigrants allowed into the United States should be increased or decreased (5-point scale). The third asked whether respondents agreed or disagreed with preferential hiring and promotion of racial minorities (7-point scale). In the interest of space, this analysis focuses on these three policy questions; analysis of race-neutral policies is not included.

In a second study, Craig and Richeson find that the treatment led whites to have more negative attitudes toward blacks, Latinos, and Asian Americans, but not toward whites (2014a). We assessed these group attitudes just as Craig and Richeson did, using traditional feeling thermometers in which respondents were asked to rate how warm (favorable) or cold (unfavorable) they felt toward particular groups in society, 100 being the warmest and 0 the coldest. In both of their papers, Craig and Richeson note that the treatment also promotes feelings of threat to group status. In keeping with their study, we asked participants the extent to which they agreed or disagreed with the following statement: "If they increase in status, racial minorities are likely to reduce the influence of white Americans in society" (7-point scale, higher feelings of threat coded as 7). In the Craig and Richeson study, whites in the treatment group were more likely to agree with this statement than whites in the control group.

Next, we tested whether exposure to information about population change affected white millennials and older whites similarly. We examined the three racial policy questions, the feeling thermometers, and the measure of status threat described here.

Are Millennials "Immune"?

To determine whether the treatment condition influenced the attitudes of millennials differently than older whites, we conducted two-way ANOVAs on all of the dependent variables described with the treatment condition (Racial Shift versus Control) and generation (Millen-

---

13. This measure is a modified version of the interracial friendship measure used in the General Social Survey.

14. The survey instrument also included a pre-manipulation set of policy questions as a distraction exercise, in response to reviewer suggestions (for the full questionnaire, see the appendix).

nial, Nonmillennial) as fixed factors. The findings regarding the main effects for being in the Racial Shift condition and for being a millennial appear in the first two blocks of results in table 1. The findings regarding the interaction of condition and generation are in the last block of results. Overall, the results are in line with the findings from the CCES analysis: white millennials were often more racially liberal than older whites, but their views were still powerfully shaped by their race.

Looking first at the direct effect of being in the Racial Shift condition as opposed to the control, we find a significant and direct effect moving people in a racially conservative direction on three of the eight measures (period of time to naturalize, feeling thermometer for blacks, and racial threat); a fourth measure is just shy of significance at the 95 percent confidence level (feeling thermometer for Asians).

Looking at the direct effect of being in the millennial generation, the results indicate more racially liberal views among millennials on the overall level of immigration and feelings of racial threat; the feeling thermometers for blacks and whites are just shy of significance. In sum, when looking at direct effects, the Racial Shift treatment results in more racially conservative views on four of the eight dependent variables and being in the millennial generation results in more racially liberal views on four of the eight dependent variables.

However, the last block of table 1 notably shows that for all eight dependent variables, the interaction between generation and condition was not statistically significant. In other words, in no case did we find that white millennials were less likely than older whites to be pushed in a conservative direction when they read about census population projections. When we saw significant results for the treatment, they applied to millennials and nonmillennials similarly.

What About Contact?

Despite finding that white millennials are not immune to the perceived threats that population changes promote relative to older whites, it is still possible that younger whites have more meaningful or significant interracial friendships than older whites, a possibility we began to explore in this final set of analyses. Using the same dependent variables analyzed in table 1, we ran a series of ordered probit and regression analyses that controlled for whether the respondent was in the treatment condition, whether the respondent was a millennial, how important the respondent said being white is to his or her identity, whether the respondent had any close friends who were black, Hispanic, or Asian, and his or her partisan identification. We also included a term to capture the interaction between one's generation and having any close nonwhite friends. The coefficient on this interaction term indicates whether having nonwhite friends affected millennials differently than older whites. In our sample, 67.7 percent of millennials reported having a close nonwhite friend, but so did 67.4 percent of older whites. In the aggregate, millennials were not more likely than older whites to report interracial friendships, a curious finding in and of itself that merits further scrutiny and additional data collection. But were those friendships a more powerful influence over racial attitudes?

The results for our analyses appear in table 2 (racial policy and racial threat) and table 3 (feeling thermometers). On racial policy and racial threat, we find that having nonwhite friends does not affect attitudes. If anything, white millennials with nonwhite friends were slightly more likely than others to say that immigration levels should be decreased. Rather, the most consistent factors leading to conservative racial policy views are whether respondents said that being white is important to them and whether they were Republican. Being in the Racial Shift condition also moved respondents in a conservative direction in two of the four measures (increase citizenship time and status threat).

Racial identity, partisanship, and being in the Racial Shift condition also mattered a great deal for the feeling thermometers (table 3). Here, however, we also find that nonwhite friendships led to higher thermometer scores for blacks, Hispanics, and Asians. Only on the feeling thermometers scores for blacks did we find that the millennials were affected more than older whites. In sum, interracial friendships mattered more for outgroup evaluations

Table 1. ANOVA Results for Condition and Generation

	Condition				Generation				Condition by Generation	
	Control M(SD)	Racial Shift M(SD)	F	p	Nonmillennials M(SD)	Millennials M(SD)	F	p	F	p
Period of time to naturalize	3.16 (0.84)	3.32 (0.89)	7.03	<0.01	3.28 (0.86)	3.14 (0.87)	3.7	0.55	0.36	0.55
Number of immigrants permitted	3.69 (1.14)	3.75 (1.16)	0.44	0.5	3.80 (1.13)	3.46 (1.18)	13.35	<0.01	0	0.98
Preferential hiring	5.42 (1.64)	5.53 (1.61)	0.85	0.36	5.52 (1.58)	5.35 (1.77)	1.68	0.2	0.02	0.88
Feelings of warmth toward blacks	63.67 (26.12)	59.55 (22.21)	5.16	0.02	60.81 (21.06)	64.14 (23.80)	3.56	0.06	0.04	0.83
Feelings of warmth toward Hispanics	63.67 (21.10)	61.41 (21.16)	1.56	0.21	62.04 (20.40)	64.15 (23.32)	1.56	0.21	0.03	0.86
Feelings of warmth toward Asians	68.38 (20.19)	65.47 (20.97)	3.68	0.06	66.36 (19.79)	68.70 (23.03)	1.94	0.16	0.08	0.77
Feelings of warmth toward whites	73.57 (19.38)	74.20 (19.00)	0.43	0.51	73.25 (18.92)	75.88 (19.91)	3.14	0.08	0.15	0.69
Feelings of threat toward in-group	4.42 (1.31)	5.26 (1.19)	62.41	<0.01	4.90 (1.34)	4.67 (1.25)	4.37	0.04	1.27	0.26

Source: Authors' compilation based on TESS_202 (Druckman and Freese 2016).
Note: The interaction between condition and generation was not significant for any dependent variable, thus only f-statistics and p-values are provided.

Table 2. Predicting Racial Policy Attitudes and Status Threat

	Decrease Immigration Level	Increase Citizenship Time	Oppose Affirmative Action	White Status Threat
Treatment	0.062	0.202***	0.103	0.824***
	(0.073)	(0.076)	(0.102)	(0.085)
Millennial	−0.541***	−0.101	−0.225	−0.281**
	(0.147)	(0.153)	(0.232)	(0.140)
White identity	0.165***	0.121***	0.091**	0.104***
	(0.029)	(0.031)	(0.036)	(0.033)
Nonwhite friend	−0.102	0.140	0.116	−0.136
	(0.090)	(0.093)	(0.120)	(0.103)
Party (Democrat coded higher)	−0.180***	−0.075***	−0.280***	0.009
	(0.018)	(0.018)	(0.025)	(0.021)
Millennial*nonwhite friend	0.339*	−0.114	0.115	0.190
	(0.182)	(0.190)	(0.279)	(0.186)
Constant			6.189	4.257
Cutpoint 1	−2.281	−1.894		
Cutpoint 2	−1.600	−1.097		
Cutpoint 3	−0.428	0.921		
Cutpoint 4	0.078	1.340		
N	899	901	900	897
R^2			0.141	0.115
χ^2	146.23	45.69		

Source: Authors' calculations based on TESS_202 (Druckman and Freese 2016).
Notes: Robust standard errors in parentheses. Immigration questions use ordered probit models. Affirmative action and status threat use OLS.
*$p \leq .1$; **$p \leq .05$; ***$p \leq .01$

than for policy preferences, though little evidence indicates that today's young whites are uniquely affected by such friendships. What mattered more was whether respondents were Republican and whether they said that being white was important to them. On this last measure, bivariate analysis shows that generation might matter: only 8.8 percent of millennials said that being white was extremely important, whereas 14.6 percent of nonmillennials did ($p = .01$). Exploring the relationship between age, race, and white racial identity—and how levels of white identity might change over time—is an important next step in this research agenda.

DISCUSSION AND CONCLUSION

The results of this analysis indicate that white millennials occupy a political space between their nonwhite counterparts and older whites. Notably, however, the findings fail to support the optimism about millennials commonly found in popular discourse with respect to racial attitudes. It is true that white millennials were somewhat more ideologically and racially liberal than older whites on some measures studied here, but far more often race was a stronger factor shaping their outlook. The first portion of our study showed that their partisan and racial policy views were closer to the views of older whites than to those of other millennials. The one exception was for ideological orientation in 2016, in which white millennials were closer to nonwhite millennials than they were to older whites. The second portion showed that they became more racially conservative on some measures after reading about population projections, just as older whites did.

Table 3. Predicting Feeling Thermometer Scores

	Blacks	Hispanics	Asians	Whites
Treatment	−4.611***	−2.799**	−3.365**	0.525
	(1.381)	(1.340)	(1.351)	(1.286)
Millennial	−3.223	−1.087	−0.985	2.311
	(3.054)	(2.978)	(3.127)	(2.757)
White identity	−3.660***	−2.929***	−2.130***	1.780***
	(0.551)	(0.551)	(0.530)	(0.489)
Nonwhite friend	5.823***	5.321***	5.390***	3.030*
	(1.631)	(1.579)	(1.578)	(1.594)
Party (Democrat coded higher)	1.749***	1.606***	1.318***	0.231
	(0.331)	(0.332)	(0.326)	(0.308)
Millennial*nonwhite friend	7.967**	3.482	1.067	1.493
	(3.674)	(3.647)	(3.747)	(3.327)
Constant	62.752	62.022	65.522	65.307
N	882	877	872	875
R^2	0.136	0.092	0.066	0.025

Source: Authors' calculations based on TESS_202 (Druckman and Freese 2016).
Notes: Robust standard errors in parentheses.
*$p ≤ .1$; **$p ≤ .05$; ***$p ≤ .01$

They did not become more conservative on every measure, but neither did nonmillennials. Together, these results offer a corrective to popular narratives that tell us that young Americans will usher in a more racially harmonious era and that the Republican Party needs to change if it hopes to count young Americans among its ranks. The Republican Party is mostly white (89 percent of GOP identifiers in our CCES samples were white), and white millennials are not very distinct from older whites on the issues examined here, including partisan identification.

Although our study focused on comparisons between older and younger whites on the one hand and white and nonwhite millennials on the other, our findings also reveal an intriguing pattern among older and younger nonwhite respondents in the CCES surveys. In nearly all cases, the predicted outcomes for nonwhite respondents differed very little by generation. Our study leads us to conclude that race affects attitudes more than generation among whites on many (but not all) of the issues under examination here, and this seems to be especially true for nonwhites. This degree of racial solidarity is perhaps not surprising, yet it is important that it provides an additional corrective to narratives claiming that millennials will be more comfortable with diversity than older Americans: among nonwhites, partisan and racial liberalism appears to be the norm among the young and old alike.

The analysis also raised many questions for future research to consider. First, if white millennials are only slightly more racially liberal than their predecessors and close ranks around the group in the face of group threat despite being a vastly more diverse generation, should we instead place our hopes for greater racial unity on the subsequent generation, which is going to be more diverse still? Or will white members of Generation Z also be significantly affected by being white? Similarly, to what degree is there heterogeneity on racial and ethnic matters within the millennial generation? Perhaps younger white millennials, having arguably come of political age in a more politically and racially polarized context than older white millennials, are more racially and ideologically conservative than older members of their generation. A related question is what happens to the views of millennials as they age. Will their slight racial liberalism (relative to older whites) remain, or will they become more conservative over time?

Second, what exactly is the nature of interracial contact among white millennials? We know that rates of interracial dating and marriage are rising, but to what extent do white millennials truly spend their time in racially diverse settings? Moreover, it is possible that their interracial relationships do matter, but in ways not captured by the blunt measure of interracial friendship used here. In our experiment, younger and older whites did not differ in their likelihood of reporting interracial friendships. That could be an anomaly, or it could be a product of the blunt measure we use. It could also mean that younger whites do not actually have more meaningful interethnic contact than older whites, despite conventional wisdom that says otherwise.

Third, the meaning and dynamics of white racial identity are poorly understood. We know that white millennials seem less likely to say that being white is important than older whites and that its importance moves whites in a racially conservative direction. But how will the presence and power of white racial identity change as whites lose their majority status, and how much will this dynamic vary across whites of different ages and contexts?

Fourth, the intersection of race, age, and partisanship needs to be analyzed further. Among whites, partisanship has become a major dividing line on matters pertaining to race, yet younger Republicans showed signs of having some policy preferences and ideological identities distinct from those of older Republicans (Jacobson 2016). How that divergence develops alongside demographic changes in the years to come will be important to observe.

Finally, the extent to which living in an urban or rural context shapes the dynamics under investigation here should be examined. One important narrative that emerged after the 2016 presidential election is that rural whites felt particularly ignored by political elites, which made them especially amenable to Donald Trump's campaign rhetoric (Cramer 2016; Hochschild 2016). The degree to which this sentiment exists and shapes how people respond to information about demographic change—and whether that effect varies across generations—is an important question for future research to address.

As the nation edges ever closer to having a majority-minority population, messages about racial divisions seem like they are becoming more, rather than less, common. These divisions are exacerbated by political parties that are becoming more racially distinct and as the standard bearer of the Republican Party takes positions that are explicitly racially antagonistic. It is increasingly important to examine how people feel about the implications of such divisions, whether preferences differ across generations, and the mechanisms that affect how people react to information about our changing nation. Uncovering practical ways to elicit racial harmony will be one of the most pressing questions of our time, our research suggesting that relying on the allegedly more tolerant attitudes of millennials may not be enough.

APPENDIX

Table A1. How Race and Generation Shape Party and Ideology, 2012 CCES

	Partisan Identification			Ideology		
	Model 1	Model 2	Model 3	Model 1	Model 2	Model 3
Millennial	-0.311***	-0.139***	-0.046	-0.474***	-0.420***	-0.458***
	(0.021)	(0.021)	(0.036)	(0.017)	(0.017)	(0.031)
White	—	1.373***	1.415***	—	0.457***	0.438***
		(0.020)	(0.024)		(0.017)	(0.020)
Millennial*white	—	—	-0.136***	—	—	0.055
			(0.044)			(0.037)
Education	0.006	-0.021***	-0.021***	-0.113***	-0.121***	-0.121***
	('(0.006)	(0.006)	(0.006)	(0.005)	(0.005)	(0.005)
South	0.110***	0.251***	0.251***	0.236***	0.282***	.0282***
	(0.020)	(0.019)	(0.019)	(0.016)	(0.016)	(0.016)
Constant	3.761***	2.748***	2.716***	4.638***	4.300***	4.313***
	(0.024)	(0.027)	(0.029)	(0.019)	(0.023)	(0.025)
N	53,398	53,398	53,398	51,391	51,391	51,391
R^2	0.005	0.083	0.083	0.028	0.041	0.041

Source: Authors' calculations based on 2012 Cooperative Congressional Election Survey (Ansolabehere 2013).
Notes: Robust standard errors in parentheses. Party: 1 = strong Democrat; 7 = strong Republican. Ideology: 1 = very liberal; 7 = very conservative.
*$p \leq .1$; **$p \leq .05$; ***$p \leq .01$

Table A2. How Race and Generation Shape Party and Ideology, 2016 CCES

	Partisan Identification			Ideology		
	Model 1	Model 2	Model 3	Model 1	Model 2	Model 3
Millennial	-0.331***	-0.151***	0.217***	-0.476***	-0.429***	-0.315***
	(0.018)	(0.018)	(0.032)	(0.015)	(0.015)	(0.028)
White	—	1.360***	1.561***	—	0.369***	0.430***
		(0.019)	(0.024)		(0.016)	(0.020)
Millennial*white	—	—	-0.537***	—	—	-0.165***
			(0.038)			(0.032)
Education	-0.052***	-0.076***	-0.073***	-0.129***	-0.135***	-0.134***
	(0.006)	(0.005)	(0.005)	(0.005)	(0.005)	(0.005)
South	0.166***	0.282***	0.283***	0.180***	0.210***	0.210***
	(0.019)	(0.018)	(0.018)	(0.015)	(0.015)	(0.015)
Constant	3.940***	2.940***	2.776***	4.768***	4.494***	4.445***
	(0.022)	(0.025)	(0.028)	(0.018)	(0.021)	(0.023)
N	62,008	62,008	62,008	60,513	60,513	60,513
R^2	0.008	0.086	0.089	0.032	0.041	0.041

Source: Authors' calculations based on 2016 Cooperative Congressional Election Survey (Ansolabehere and Schaffner 2017).
Notes: Robust standard errors in parentheses. Party: 1 = strong Democrat; 7 = strong Republican. Ideology: 1 = very liberal; 7 = very conservative.
*$p \leq .1$; **$p \leq .05$; ***$p \leq .01$

Table A3. How Race and Generation Shape Racial Resentment and Affirmative Action Attitudes

	Model 1	Model 2	Model 3	Model 1	Racial Resentment Model 2	Affirmative Action Model 3
Millennial	-0.292***	-0.229***	-0.110***	-0.239***	-0.128***	-0.011
	(0.013)	(0.013)	(0.024)	(0.010)	(0.011)	(0.019)
White	—	0.634***	0.679***	—	1.014***	1.068***
		(0.013)	(0.015)		(0.011)	(0.013)
Millennial*white	—	—	-0.164***	—	—	-0.174***
			(0.028)			(0.023)
Education	-0.131***	-0.138***	-0.138***	-0.020***	-0.042***	-0.042***
	(0.004)	(0.003)	(0.003)	(0.003)	(0.003)	(0.003)
South	0.106***	0.158***	0.158***	-0.062***	0.040***	0.040***
	(0.012)	(0.011)	(0.011)	(0.010)	(0.010)	(0.010)
Constant	4.020***	3.518***	3.481***			
	(0.014)	(0.017)	(0.018)			
N	47,084	47,084	47,084	54,297	54,297	54,297
R^2	0.040	0.088	0.089			
Chi-sq				571.47	9053.02	9109.89
Cutpoint 1				-1.292	-0.675	-0.634
Cutpoint 2				-0.427	0.304	0.345
Cutpoint 3				0.312	1.105	1.146

Source: Authors' calculations based on 2012 Cooperative Congressional Election Survey (Ansolabehere 2013).
Notes: Robust standard errors in parentheses. Racial resentment scale runs from 1 (lowest) to 5 (highest). Affirmative action: 1 = strongly support; 4 = strongly oppose.
*$p \leq .1$; **$p \leq .05$; ***$p \leq .01$

Table A4. How Race and Generation Shape Attitudes About Discrimination

	"Whites Have Advantages"			"Racial Problems Are Rare"		
	Model 1	Model 2	Model 3	Model 1	Model 2	Model 3
Millennial	-0.331***	-0.255***	-0.048***	-0.012	0.223**	0.156***
	(0.010)	(0.010)	(0.018)	(0.010)	(0.010)	(0.018)
White	—	0.706***	0.818***	—	0.276***	0.349***
		(0.011)	(0.014)		(0.011)	(0.014)
Millennial*white	—	—	-0.296***	—	—	-0.191***
			(0.022)			(0.022)
Education	-0.100**	-0.114***	-0.112***	-0.029***	-0.033***	-0.032***
	(0.003)	(0.003)	(0.003)	(0.003)	(0.003)	(0.003)
South	0.044***	0.109***	0.109***	0.054***	0.078***	0.079***
	(0.010)	(0.010)	(0.010)	(0.010)	(0.010)	(0.010)
N	52,837	52,837	52,837	52,778	52,778	52,778
Chi-sq	2129.31	6380.31	6560.18	118.92	790.60	867.10
Cutpoint 1	-1.083	-0.605	-0.515	-0.573	-0.372	-0.312
Cutpoint 2	-0.399	0.116	0.208	0.189	0.397	0.458
Cutpoint 3	0.081	0.620	0.713	0.708	0.919	0.980
Cutpoint 4	0.495	1.051	1.145	1.471	1.684	1.746

Source: Authors' calculations based on 2016 Cooperative Congressional Election Survey (Ansolabehere and Schaffner 2017).
Notes: Robust standard errors in parentheses. Ordered probit. For "whites have advantages," *strongly disagree* was coded higher. For "racial problems are rare," *strongly agree* was coded higher.
*$p \leq .1$; **$p \leq .05$; ***$p \leq .01$

Table A5. How Race and Generation Shape Restrictionist Immigration Sentiment

	2012			2016		
	Model 1	Model 2	Model 3	Model 1	Model 2	Model 3
Millennial	-0.141***	-0.116***	-0.105***	-0.149***	-0.132***	-0.121***
	(0.003)	(0.003)	(0.006)	(0.003)	(0.003)	(0.005)
White	—	0.196***	0.201***	—	0.129***	0.136***
		(0.003)	(0.004)		(0.003)	(0.004)
Millennial*white	—	—	-0.017**	—	—	-0.017***
			(0.007)			(0.006)
Education	-0.017***	-0.021***	-0.021***	-0.023***	-0.023***	-0.025***
	(0.001)	(0.001)	(0.001)	(0.001)	(0.001)	(0.001)
South	0.002	0.023***	0.023***	0.012***	0.023***	0.023***
	(0.003)	(0.003)	(0.003)	(0.003)	(0.003)	(0.003)
Constant	0.541***	0.397***	0.397***	0.609***	0.514***	0.509***
	(0.004)	(0.004)	(0.004)	(0.003)	(0.004)	(0.005)
N	54,535	54,535	54,535	64,600	64,600	64,600
R^2	0.038	0.103	0.103	0.049	0.075	0.075

Source: Authors' calculations based on 2012 Cooperative Congressional Election Survey (Ansolabehere 2013); 2016 Cooperative Congressional Election Survey (Ansolabehere and Schaffner 2017).
Notes: Robust standard errors in parentheses. Restrictionist sentiment is a 7-point scale (2012) or 5-point scale (2016). Both scales run from 0 to 1, where 1 = highest level of restriction.
*$p \leq .1$; **$p \leq .05$; ***$p \leq .01$

Experiment Questionnaire

We are conducting a study about how people feel about current issues in the United States. This survey is completely voluntary and has been approved by Tufts University. All of the information you provide will be kept strictly anonymous and confidential. You may skip any question for any reason by clicking the Next button on your screen. Thank you for agreeing to participate.

1. Please rate your feelings toward Barack Obama. Is your overall impression of him...

   Extremely favorable
   Favorable
   Somewhat favorable
   Neither favorable nor unfavorable
   Somewhat unfavorable
   Unfavorable
   Extremely unfavorable

2. How much do you think that what happens generally to white people in this country will affect what happens in your own life?

   A lot
   Some
   A little
   Not at all

3. How important is being white to your identity?

   Extremely important
   Very important
   Moderately important
   A little important
   Not at all important

4. Was the high school you attended...

   All white
   Mostly white
   About half white and half other races
   Mostly other races, or
   All other races?

5. Do you personally know anyone who is black, Hispanic, or Asian?

Yes

No

6. If yes to q5: Do you have any close friends who are black, Hispanic, or Asian?

Yes

No

7. Please read the following statements. Then indicate whether you strongly agree, agree, disagree or strongly disagree:

a. The use of marijuana should be legal.

b. If people work hard, they can still achieve the American Dream.

c. We would be safer if more Americans carried concealed weapons.

d. Banning large servings of soda would help to fight obesity.

e. Certain vaccines can cause autism in children.

We will now show you the text from a recent press release. After the text, please give your opinions about the topic. Please pay close attention while reading, as you will be asked questions about the content of the press release after you've read it.

[DISPLAY if in treatment group]

In a Generation, Racial Minorities May Be the U.S. Majority

New U.S. Census Bureau data suggest that America will become a "majority-minority" nation much faster than once predicted. The nation's racial minority population is steadily rising, advancing an unmistakable trend that could make minorities the new American majority by midcentury. The data show a declining number of white adults and growing under-18 populations of Hispanics, Asians, and other minorities. Demographers calculate that by 2042, Americans who identify themselves as Hispanic, black, Asian, American Indian, Native Hawaiian, or Pacific Islander will together outnumber non-Hispanic whites. The main reasons for the accelerating change are rapid immigration growth and significantly higher birthrates among racial and ethnic minorities. As white baby boomers age past their childbearing years, younger Hispanic parents are having children—and driving U.S. population growth. For example, there are now roughly 9 births for every 1 death among Hispanics, compared to a roughly one-to-one ratio for whites. The latest figures are predicated on current and historical trends, which can be thrown awry by several variables, including prospective overhauls of public policy.

[DISPLAY if in control group]

U.S. Census Bureau Reports Residents Now Move at a Higher Rate

New U.S. Census Bureau data suggest that the rate of geographical mobility, or the number of individuals who have moved within the past year, is increasing. The national mover rate increased from 11.9 percent in 2008 (the lowest rate since the U.S. Census Bureau began tracking the data) to 12.5 percent in 2014. According to the new data, 37.1 million people changed residences in the U.S. within the past year. 84.5 percent of all movers stayed within the same state. Renters were more than five times more likely to move than homeowners. The estimates also reveal that many of the nation's fastest-growing cities are suburbs. Specifically, principal cities within metropolitan areas experienced a net loss of 2.1 million movers, while the suburbs had a net gain of 2.4 million movers. For those who moved to a different county or state, the reasons for moving varied considerably by the length of their move. The latest figures are predicated on current and historical trends, which can be thrown awry by several variables, including prospective overhauls of public policy.

8. How interesting do you find the topic?

Extremely interesting

Somewhat interesting

Slightly interesting

Slightly uninteresting

Somewhat uninteresting

Extremely uninteresting

9a. [IF IN TREATMENT GROUP]
According to the press release, the minority population in the United States is . . .

Increasing

Staying the same

Decreasing

9b. [IF IN CONTROL GROUP]
According to the press release, the rate at which Americans move is . . .

Increasing

Staying the same

Decreasing

10. Please indicate how much you agree or disagree with the following statement:
If they increase in status, racial minorities are likely to reduce the influence of white Americans in society.

Strongly agree

Agree

Agree somewhat

Neither agree nor disagree

Disagree somewhat

Disagree

Strongly disagree

Now we're going to ask some questions about different policies in the United States. [Randomized]

11. Currently the United States requires immigrants to live in the U.S. for at least 5 years before being eligible to apply for citizenship. Do you think that the required amount of time should be increased a lot, increased a little, left the same as it is now, decreased a little, or decreased a lot?

Increased a lot

Increased a little

Left the same as it is now

Decreased a little

Decreased a lot

12. Do you think the number of immigrants from foreign countries who are allowed to come to the U.S. to live should be increased a lot, increased a little, left the same as it is now, decreased a little, or decreased a lot?

Increased a lot

Increased a little

Left the same as it is now

Decreased a little

Decreased a lot

13. Do you think the amount of federal funding dedicated to funding the U.S. military and defense departments should be increased a lot, increased a little, left the same as it is now, decreased a little, or decreased a lot?

Increased a lot

Increased a little

Left the same as it is now

Decreased a little

Decreased a lot

14. Some people say that because of past discrimination, racial minorities should be given preference in hiring and promotion. Others say that such preference in hiring and promotion of racial minorities is wrong because it discriminates against whites. What about your opinion—are you for or against preferential hiring and promotion of racial minorities?

Strongly support preferential hiring and promotion for racial minorities

Somewhat support preferential hiring and promotion for racial minorities

Slightly support preferential hiring and promotion for racial minorities

Neither support nor oppose preferential hiring and promotion for racial minorities

Slightly oppose preferential hiring and promotion for racial minorities

Somewhat oppose preferential hiring and promotion for racial minorities

Strongly oppose preferential hiring and promotion for racial minorities

15. Some people say that health care should be a right for all people and not a privilege only for those who are insured by their workplace or participate in some other private plan. Others say that the tax burden in this country is already high and it is unreasonable to expect people who are paying a part of their own private insurance plan to also pay for other people. How do you feel about universal, guaranteed health care?

- Strongly support universal, guaranteed health care
- Somewhat support universal, guaranteed health care
- Slightly support universal, guaranteed health care
- Neither support nor oppose universal, guaranteed health care
- Slightly oppose universal, guaranteed health care
- Somewhat oppose universal, guaranteed health care
- Strongly oppose universal, guaranteed health care

[DISPLAY]

We'd like to get your feelings toward groups that are in the news these days. We will use something called a feeling thermometer, and here is how it works:

You rate a group using a feeling thermometer that ranges between 0 degrees and 100 degrees. Ratings between 50 degrees and 100 degrees mean that you feel favorable and warm toward the group. Ratings between 0 degrees and 50 degrees mean that you don't feel favorable toward the group and that you don't care too much for that group. If you don't feel particularly warm or cold toward the group, you would rate the group at the 50 degree mark.

[RANDOMIZED ORDER of feeling thermometers]

[INSERT SLIDER SCALE 0 TO 100; LABEL 0 AS *COLD* AND 100 AS *WARM*]

16. Please rate your feelings toward blacks/African Americans.

17. Please rate your feelings toward Latinos/Hispanics.

18. Please rate your feelings toward Asian Americans.

19. Please rate your feelings toward whites/European Americans.

REFERENCES

Abrajano, Marisa, and Zoltan Hajnal. 2015. *White Backlash: Immigration, Race, and American Politics.* Princeton, N.J.: Princeton University Press.

Abrajano, Marisa, and Lydia Lundgren. 2015. "How Watershed Immigration Policies Affect American Public Opinion over a Lifetime." *International Migration Review* 49(1): 70–105. DOI: 10.1111/imre.12082.

Allport, Gordon. 1954. *The Nature of Prejudice.* Reading, Mass.: Addison-Wesley.

Alwin, Duane F., and Jon A. Krosnick. 1991. "Aging, Cohorts, and the Stability of Sociopolitical Orientations over the Life Span." *American Journal of Sociology* 97(1): 169–95. DOI: 10.1086/229744.

Ansolabehere, Stephen. 2013. Cooperative Congressional Election Study, 2012: Common Content [Computer File]. Accessed January 24, 2018. http://cces.gov.harvard.edu.

Ansolabehere, Stephen, and Brian F. Schaffner. 2017. Cooperative Congressional Election Study, 2016: Common Content [Computer File]. Accessed January 24, 2018. http://cces.gov.harvard.edu.

Barreto, Matt, and Francisco Pedraza. 2009. "The Renewal and Persistence of Group Identification in American Politics." *Electoral Studies* 28(4): 595–605.

Blumer, Herbert. 1958. "Race Prejudice as a Sense of Group Position." *Pacific Sociological Review* 1(1): 3–7.

Bobo, Lawrence. 1999. "Prejudice as Group Position: Microfoundations of a Sociological Approach to Racism and Race Relations." *Journal of Social Issues* 55(3): 445–72.

Bobo, Lawrence, and Vincent Hutchings. 1996. "Perceptions of Racial Group Competition: Extending Blumer's Theory of Group Position to a Multiracial Social Context." *American Sociological Review* 61(6): 951–72.

Branscombe, Nyla R., Michael T. Schmitt, and Kristin Schiffhauer. 2007. "Racial Attitudes in Response to Thoughts of White Privilege." *European Journal of Social Psychology* 37(2): 203–15.

Branton, Regina. 2007. "Latino Attitudes Toward Various Areas of Public Policy." *Political Research Quarterly* 60(2): 293–303.

Brownstein, Ronald. 2016. "How Trump Pushed Millennials Out of the Republican Party." *The Atlantic*, November 3, 2016. Accessed January 24, 2018. https://www.theatlantic.com/politics/archive/2016/11/trump-alienates-millennials/506345/.

Cillizza, Chris. 2014. "Republican's Young People Problem." *Washington Post*, March 9, 2014. Accessed January 24, 2018. http://www.washingtonpost.com/politics/republicans-have-another-major-demographic-issue-on-their-hands/2014/03/09/398deb46-a79d-11e3-8599-ce7295b6851c_story.html.

Cohn, D'Vera. 2016. "It's Official: Minority Babies Are the Majority Among the Nation's Infants, but Only Just." Pew Research Center. June 23, 2016. Accessed January 24, 2018. http://www.pewresearch.org/fact-tank/2016/06/23/its-official-minority-babies-are-the-majority-among-the-nations-infants-but-only-just/.

Cook, Zachary F. 2014. "How Impressionable Were the Younger Reagan Cohorts?" *The Forum* 12(3): 481–97. DOI: 10.1515/for-2014-5017.

Craig, Maureen A., and Jennifer A. Richeson. 2014a. "More Diverse Yet Less Tolerant? How the Increasingly Diverse Racial Landscape Affects White Americans' Racial Attitudes." *Personality and Social Psychology Bulletin* 40(6): 750–61.

———. 2014b. "On the Precipice of a 'Majority-Minority' America: Perceived Status Threat from the Racial Demographic Shift Affects White Americans' Political Ideology." *Psychological Science* 25(6): 1189–97.

———. 2018. "Majority No More? The Influence of Neighborhood Racial Diversity and Salient National Population Changes on Whites' Perceptions of Racial Discrimination." *RSF: The Russell Sage Foundation Journal of the Social Sciences* 4(5): 141–57. DOI: 10.7758/RSF.2018.4.5.07.

Cramer, Katherine J. 2016. *The Politics of Resentment: Rural Consciousness in Wisconsin and the Rise of Scott Walker*. Chicago: University of Chicago Press.

Danbold, Felix, and Yuen J. Huo. 2014. "No Longer 'All-American'? Whites' Defensive Reactions to Their Numerical Decline." *Social, Psychological, and Personality Science* 6(2): 210–18. DOI: 10.1177/1948550614546355.

Danigelis, Nicholas L., Stephen J. Culter, and Melissa Hardy. 2007. "Population Aging, Intracohort Aging, and Sociopolitical Attitudes." *American Sociological Review* 72(5): 812–30.

Davis, James A. 2013. "A Generation of Attitude Trends Among US Householders as Measured in the NORC General Social Survey 1972–2010." *Social Science Research* 42(3): 571–83. DOI: 10.1016/j.ssresearch.2012.11.002.

Dinas, Elias. 2013. "Opening 'Openness to Change': Political Events and the Increased Sensitivity of Young Adults." *Political Research Quarterly* 66(4): 868–82. DOI: 10.1177/1065912913475874.

Dovidio, John F., Samuel L. Gaertner, Tamar Saguy, and Eric Hehman. 2011. "Obama's Potential to Transform the Racial Attitudes of White Americans." In *The Obamas and a (Post) Racial America?*, edited by Gregory Parks and Matthew Hughey. New York: Oxford University Press.

Druckman, James N., and Jeremy Freese. 2016. "Time Sharing Experiments for the Social Sciences, TESS3_202." *TESS*. Accessed January 24, 2018. http://www.tessexperiments.org/.

Dunsmuir, Lindsay. 2013. "Many Americans Have No Friends of Another Race: Poll." Reuters, August 8. Accessed January 24, 2018. http://www.reuters.com/article/us-usa-poll-race-idUSBRE97704320130808.

Ellison, Christopher, Heeju Shin, and David L. Leal. 2011. "The Contact Hypothesis and Attitudes Toward Latinos in the United States." *Social Science Quarterly* 92(4): 938–58.

Feldmann, Linda. 2014. "Millennials See Themselves as 'Post-Racial.' What Does That Mean?" *Christian Science Monitor*, April 30, 2014. Accessed January 24, 2018. http://www.csmonitor.com/USA/2014/0430/Millennials-see-themselves-as-post-racial.-What-does-that-mean.

Forbes, Hugh Donald. 1997. *Ethnic Conflict: Commerce, Culture, and the Contact Hypothesis*. New Haven, Conn.: Yale University Press.

Forman, Tyrone A., and Amanda E. Lewis. 2015. "Beyond Prejudice? Young Whites' Racial Attitudes in Post-Civil Rights America, 1976–2000." *American Behavioral Scientist* 59(11): 1394–428.

Fraga, Luis, John Garcia, Rodney E. Hero, Michael Jones-Correa, Valerie Martinez-Ebers, and Gary M. Segura. 2012. *Latinos in the New Millennium: An Almanac of Opinion, Behavior, and Policy Preferences*. New York: Cambridge University Press.

Fry, Richard. 2015. "Millennials Surpass Gen Xers as the Largest Generation in U.S. Labor Force." Washington, D.C.: Pew Research Center. Accessed January 24, 2018. http://www.pewresearch.org/fact-tank/2015/05/11/millennials-surpass-gen-xers-as-the-largest-generation-in-u-s-labor-force/.

Ghitza, Yair, and Andrew Gelman. 2014. "The Great Society, Reagan's Revolution, and Generations of Presidential Voting." Department of Statistics and Political Science working paper. New York: Columbia University. http://www.stat.columbia.edu/~gelman/research/unpublished/cohort_voting_20140605.pdf.

Goldman, Seth K. 2012. "Effects of the 2008 Obama Presidential Campaign on White Racial Prejudice." Public Opinion Quarterly 76(4): 663–87. DOI: 10.1093/poq/nfs056.

Goren, Matt, and Victoria Plaut. 2012. "Identity Form Matters: White Racial Identity and Attitudes Toward Diversity." Self and Identity 11(2): 237–54.

Harvard Public Opinion Project. 2014. "Survey of Young Americans' Attitudes Toward Politics and Public Service, 26th edition." Cambridge, Mass.: Institute of Politics, Harvard University.

Hochschild, Arlie Russell. 2016. Strangers in Their Own Land: Anger and Mourning on the American Right. New York: The New Press.

Hollinger, David A. 1995. Postethnic America: Beyond Multiculturalism. New York: Basic Books.

Hopkins, Daniel J. 2014. "Partisan Loyalty Begins at Age 18." Fivethirtyeight, April 22. Accessed January 24, 2018. http://fivethirtyeight.com/features/partisan-loyalty-begins-at-age-18/.

Hutchings, Vincent, Ashley Jardina, Robert Mickey, and Haynes Walton. 2012. "The Politics of Race: How Threat Cues and Group Position Can Activate White Identity." Presented at the Annual Meeting of the Midwest Political Science Association. Chicago (April 12–15).

Jacobson, Gary C. 2016. "The Obama Legacy and the Future of Partisan Conflict Demographic Change and Generational Imprinting." Annals of the American Academy of Political and Social Science 667(1): 72–91. DOI: 10.1177/0002716216658425.

Jardina, Ashley. 2014. "Demise of Dominance: Group Threat and the New Relevance of White Identity for American Politics." Ph.D. diss., University of Michigan.

Jones, Robert, Daniel Cox, and Thomas Banchoff. 2012. "A Generation in Transition: Religion, Values, and Politics Among College-Age Millennials." Washington, D.C.: Public Religion Research Institute. Accessed January 24, 2018. http://publicreligion.org/research/2012/04/millennial-values-survey-2012/.

Kinder, Donald R. 2006. "Politics and the Life Cycle." Science 312(5782): 1905–08.

Kinder, Donald R., and Lynn M. Sanders. 1996. Divided by Color: Racial Politics and Democratic Ideals. Chicago: University of Chicago Press.

Lowery, Brian, Miguel Unzueta, Eric Knowles, and Phillip Atiba Goff. 2006. "Concern for the In-Group and Opposition to Affirmative Action." Journal of Personality and Social Psychology 90(6): 961–74.

Madland, David, and Ruy Teixeira. 2009. "The New Progressive America: The Millennial Generation." Washington, D.C.: Center for American Progress. Accessed January 24, 2018. https://www.americanprogress.org/issues/progressive-movement/report/2009/05/13/6133/new-progressive-america-the-millennial-generation/.

Major, Brenda, Alison Blodorn, and Gregory Blascovich. 2016. "The Threat of Increasing Diversity: Why Many White Americans Support Trump in the 2016 Presidential Election." Group Processes & Intergroup Relations, published online October 20, 2016. DOI: 10.1177/1368430216677304.

Manzano, Sylvia, and Gabriel Sanchez. 2010. "Take One for the Team? The Limits of Shared Ethnicity and Candidate Preferences." Political Research Quarterly 63(3): 568–80.

Marcotte, Amanda. 2013. "Are Millennials Killing Off the Religious Right?" XX Factor (blog), July 22. Accessed January 24, 2018. http://www.slate.com/blogs/xx_factor/2013/07/22/religious_progressives_outnumber_religious_conservatives_ages_18_33_does.html.

Mendelberg, Tali. 2001. The Race Card: Campaign Strategy, Implicit Message, and the Norm of Equality. Princeton, N.J.: Princeton University Press.

Mutz, Diana C., and Seth K. Goldman. 2010. "The Sage Handbook of Prejudice, Stereotyping and Discrimination." Sage chapter Mass Media. London: Sage Publications. Accessed January 24, 2018. http://iscap.upenn.edu/sites/default/files/GoldmanMutzchapter.pdf.

Norton, Michael I., and Samuel R. Sommers. 2011. "Whites See Racism as a Zero-Sum Game That They Are Now Losing." Perspectives on Psychological Science 6(3): 215–18.

Nteta, Tatishe, and Jill Greenlee. 2013. "A Change Is Gonna Come: Generational Membership and White Racial Attitudes in the 21st Century." *Political Psychology* 34(6): 877–97.

Osborne, Danny, David O. Sears, and Nicholas A. Valentino. 2011. "The End of the Solidly Democratic South: The Impressionable-Years Hypothesis." *Political Psychology* 32(1): 81–108. DOI: 10.1111/j.1467-9221.2010.00796.x.

Outten, H. Robert, Michael T. Schmitt, Daniel A. Miller, and Amber L. Garcia. 2012. "Feeling Threatened About the Future: Whites' Emotional Reactions to Anticipated Ethnic Demographic Changes." *Personality and Social Psychology Bulletin* 38(1): 14–25.

Pettigrew, Thomas F., and Linda R. Tropp. 2006. "A Meta-Analytic Test of Intergroup Contact Theory." *Journal of Personality and Social Psychology* 90(5): 751–83.

Pettigrew, Thomas F., Linda R. Tropp, Ulrich Wagner, and Oliver Christ. 2011. "Recent Advances in Intergroup Contact Theory." *International Journal of Intercultural Relations* 35(3): 271–80.

Pew Research Center. 2012. "Changing Face of America Helps Assure Obama Victory." Washington, D.C.: Pew Research Center, U.S. Politics and Policy. Accessed January 24, 2018. http://www.people-press.org/2012/11/07/changing-face-of-america-helps-assure-obama-victory/.

———. 2014. "Millennials in Adulthood." Washington, D.C.: Pew Research Center. Accessed January 24, 2018. http://www.pewsocialtrends.org/2014/03/07/millennials-in-adulthood/.

———. 2015a. "Comparing Millennials to Other Generations." Washington, D.C.: Pew Research Center's Social & Demographic Trends Project. Accessed January 24, 2018. http://www.pewsocialtrends.org/2015/03/19/comparing-millennials-to-other-generations/.

———. 2015b. "The Whys and Hows of Generations Research." Accessed January 24, 2018. http://www.people-press.org/2015/09/03/the-whys-and-hows-of-generations-research/.

Rampell, Catherine. 2016. "The GOP's Lost Generation of Millennial Voters." *Washington Post*. April 28, 2016. https://www.washingtonpost.com/opinions/the-gops-lost-generation-of-voters/2016/04/28/06f8efe4-0d7d-11e6-8ab8-9ad050f76d7d_story.html.

Sanchez, Gabriel, and Natalie Masuoka. 2010. "Brown-Utility Heuristic? The Presence and Contributing Factors of Latino Linked Fate." *Hispanic Journal of Behavioral Sciences* 32(4): 519–31.

Schildkraut, Deborah J. 2013. "Which Birds of a Feather Flock Together? Assessing Attitudes About Descriptive Representation Among Latinos and Asian Americans." *American Politics Research* 41(4): 699–729.

———. 2017. "White Attitudes about Descriptive Representation in the US: The Roles of Identity, Discrimination, and Linked Fate." *Politics, Groups, and Identities* 5(1): 84–106.

Schmitt, Michael T., and Nyla R. Branscombe. 2002. "The Meaning and Consequences of Perceived Discrimination in Disadvantaged and Privileged Social Groups." In *European Review of Social Psychology*, edited by Wolfgang Stroebe and Miles Hewstone. Essex: Psychology Press.

Schwadel, Philip, and Christopher R. H. Garneau. 2014. "An Age-Period-Cohort Analysis of Political Tolerance in the United States." *Sociological Quarterly* 55(2): 421–52. DOI: 10.1111/tsq.12058.

Sears, David O., and Christia Brown. 2013. "Childhood and Adult Political Development." In *The Oxford Handbook of Political Psychology*, 2nd ed. New York: Oxford University Press.

Sides, John, Michael Tesler, and Lynn Vavreck. 2018. *Identity Crisis: The 2016 Presidential Campaign and the Battle for the Meaning of America*. Princeton, N.J.: Princeton University Press.

Simmons-Duffin, Selena. 2014. "Why You Should Start Taking Millennials Seriously: NPR." *NPR Morning Edition*, October 6. Accessed January 24, 2018. http://www.npr.org/2014/10/06/352613333/why-you-should-start-taking-millennials-seriously.

Sims, David. 2015. "All Hail 'The Founders.'" *The Atlantic*, December 2, 2015. Accessed January 24, 2018. http://www.theatlantic.com/entertainment/archive/2015/12/all-hail-the-founders/418458/.

Stoker, Laura. 2014. "Reflections on the Study of Generations in Politics." *The Forum* 12(3). DOI: 10.1515/for-2014-5012.

Strauss, Valerie. 2014. "For First Time, Minority Students Expected to Be Majority in U.S. Public Schools This Fall." *Answer Sheet* (blog), August 21. Accessed January 24, 2018. http://www.washingtonpost.com/blogs/answer-sheet/wp/2014/08/21/for-first-time-minority-students-expected-to-be-majority-in-u-s-public-schools-this-fall/.

Tajfel, Henri, ed. 1982. *Social Identity and Intergroup Relations*. New York: Cambridge University Press.

Tajfel, Henri, and John Turner. 1986. "The Social Identity Theory of Intergroup Behavior." In *Psychology of Intergroup Relations*, edited by William Austin and Stephen Worchel. Chicago: Nelson-Hall.

Taylor, Paul. 2014. *The Next America: Boomers, Millennials, and the Looming Generational Showdown*. New York: PublicAffairs.

Teixeira, Ruy. 2011. "Millennials: Still Progressive After All These Years." Washington, D.C.: Center for American Progress.

Tesler, Michael, and David Sears. 2010. *Obama's Race: The 2008 Election and the Dream of a Post-Racial America*. Chicago: University of Chicago Press.

Tesler, Michael, and John Sides. 2016. "How Political Science Helps Explain the Rise of Trump: The Role of White Identity and Grievances." *Washington Post*, March 3. Accessed June 30, 2016. https://www.washingtonpost.com/news/monkey-cage/wp/2016/03/03/how-political-science-helps-explain-the-rise-of-trump-the-role-of-white-identity-and-grievances/.

Tierney, John. 2014. "How to Win Millennials: Equality, Climate Change, and Gay Marriage." *The Atlantic*, May 17. Accessed January 24, 2018. http://www.theatlantic.com/politics/archive/2014/05/everything-you-need-to-know-about-millennials-political-views/371053/.

Winograd, Morley, and Michael Hais. 2008. *Millennial Makeover: MySpace, YouTube, and the Future of American Politics*. New Brunswick, N.J.: Rutgers University Press.

———. 2011. *Millennial Momentum: How a New Generation Is Remaking America*. New Brunswick, N.J.: Rutgers University Press.

Hyper-selectivity, Racial Mobility, and the Remaking of Race

VAN C. TRAN, JENNIFER LEE, OSHIN KHACHIKIAN, AND JESS LEE

Recent immigrants to the United States are diverse with regard to selectivity. Hyper-selectivity refers to a dual positive selectivity in which immigrants are more likely to have graduated from college than nonmigrants in sending countries and the host population in the United States. This article addresses two questions. First, how does hyper-selectivity affect second-generation educational outcomes? Second, how does second-generation mobility change the cognitive construction of racial categories? It shows how hyper-selectivity among Chinese immigrants results in positive second-generation educational outcomes and racial mobility for Asian Americans. It also raises the question of whether hyper-selectivity operates similarly for non-Asian groups. While there is a second-generation advantage among hyper-selected groups, hyper-selectivity has not changed the cognitive construction of race for blacks and Latinos as it has for Asians.

Keywords: hyper-selectivity, racial mobility, assimilation, second generation, racial categories, identity

Today's immigrants have more diverse national origins than ever before in U.S. history. As a result, race and immigration have become inextricably linked in the United States; one can no longer understand the complexities of race without considering immigration; correlatively, one cannot fully grasp the debates in immigration without considering the role of race in U.S. society. Immigrants are diverse with respect not only to national origin, but also to selectivity. At one end of the extreme are Asian Indians, Chinese, Nigerians, Cubans, and Armenians who are, on average, hyper-selected; not only are they more likely to have graduated from college than their nonmigrant counterparts, but also more likely to have a college degree relative to the U.S. mean. At the other end of the extreme are groups such as Mexicans who are hypo-selected, that is, less likely to have graduated from college than their nonmigrant counterparts and the U.S. mean.

At 28 percent of the foreign-born population,

Van C. Tran is assistant professor of sociology in the Department of Sociology at Columbia University. **Jennifer Lee** is professor of sociology in the Department of Sociology at Columbia University. **Oshin Khachikian** is a PhD candidate in sociology at the University of California, Irvine. **Jess Lee** is a PhD candidate in sociology at the University of California, Irvine.

© 2018 Russell Sage Foundation. Tran, Van C., Jennifer Lee, Oshin Khachikian, and Jess Lee. 2018. "Hyper-selectivity, Racial Mobility, and the Remaking of Race." *RSF: The Russell Sage Foundation Journal of the Social Sciences* 4(5): 188–209. DOI: 10.7758/RSF.2018.4.5.09. Direct correspondence to: Van C. Tran at vantran @columbia.edu, Department of Sociology, Columbia University, 607 Knox Hall, 606 W. 122nd St., New York, NY 10027.

Open Access Policy: *RSF: The Russell Sage Foundation Journal of the Social Sciences* is an open access journal. This article is published under a Creative Commons Attribution-NonCommercial-NoDerivs 3.0 Unported License.

Mexicans are by far the largest immigrant group in the country—and one of the most socioeconomically disadvantaged. Their sheer size, coupled with their hypo-selectivity and disadvantaged socioeconomic and political status, have placed them at the center of research, debates, and policy prescriptions about immigrant assimilation and comprehensive immigration reform. By comparison, relatively little attention has focused on the assimilation patterns of hyper-selected immigrant groups such as the Chinese and Asian Indians, even though China and India have passed Mexico as the top sending countries for immigrants to the United States since 2013.

In this article, we shift the focus to hyper-selected immigrant groups, and ask how they may be changing our cognitive construction of U.S. racial categories in the twenty-first century. First, how does hyper-selectivity affect the educational outcomes of the second generation? Second, how have the achievements of hyper-selected immigrant groups and their second-generation children changed the cognitive construction of race? We tackle these questions by focusing on patterns of educational attainment among four hyper-selected groups—Chinese, Cubans, Nigerians, and Armenians who are racialized as Asian, Hispanic, black, and white, respectively, in the U.S. context. We adopt a cognitive approach and propose that a change in the selectivity of an immigrant group can change the host society's perceptions of the immigrant group and may also affect the perceptions of the racial group to which they are assigned (Brubaker, Loveman, and Stamatov 2004; Wimmer 2008).

IMMIGRATION, DIVERSITY, AND HYPER-SELECTIVITY

The influx of new immigrants to the United States became possible with the passage of the Hart-Celler Act in 1965, which eliminated quotas based on national origin and opened the door to newcomers from non-European countries. This change brought such a dramatic shift in national origins of immigrants that today more than four in five hail from Latin America, Asia, Africa, or the Caribbean, and only one in seven from Europe or Canada (Lee and Bean 2010). The shift is the single most distinctive feature of the country's "new immigration."

The change in the national origins of today's newcomers has made an indelible imprint on the nation's ethnoracial landscape, transforming it from a largely black-white society at the end of World War II to a kaleidoscope of ethnoracial groups (Alba and Nee 2003; Alba and Foner 2015; Foner and Fredrickson 2004; Waters, Ueda, and Marrow 2007). Since 1965, Latinos and Asians have more than quadrupled in size from 4 and 1 percent of the population to 18 and 6 percent, respectively. Latinos are now the largest minority group, and Asians the fastest growing group (Lee and Zhou 2015; Wong et al. 2011). Driving the growth of the Asian population is immigration; 65 percent of U.S. Asians are foreign born, a figure that increases to 80 percent among Asian adults. Among Latinos, 35 percent are foreign born. Although the total black population increased by only 1 percent (from 11 to 12 percent) since 1965, the foreign-born proportion grew to 10 percent of the total U.S. black population, up from 1 percent. The group that has decreased in size since 1965 is non-Hispanic whites. Although they remain by far the largest group in the country, accounting for some 65 percent of the population, their proportion has steadily declined since 1970, when the figure was 80 percent.

National origin and ethnoracial diversity are only two dimensions of contemporary immigrant diversity. Today's newcomers are also diverse with respect to socioeconomic status, legal status, selectivity, and phenotype—all of which affect patterns of immigrant and second-generation integration. For example, Asian Indians, Chinese, Koreans, Cubans, Nigerians, and Armenians are hyper-selected. Their positive selectivity places them and their U.S.-born children at a more favorable starting point in their quest for socioeconomic attainment compared to other second-generation groups, and even compared to third- and higher-generation whites and blacks.

At the other extreme are Mexicans, who are hypo-selected. Their negative selectivity, coupled with the lack of legal status, places Mexican immigrants and their second-generation children at a disadvantaged starting point

(Bean, Brown, and Bachmeier 2015). Although their second-generation children make enormous intergenerational strides, they remain below the U.S. mean with respect to educational attainment (Lee and Zhou 2015; Telles and Ortiz 2008; Tran and Valdez 2017).

Hyper- and hypo-selectivity have cultural, institutional, and social psychological consequences for the educational attainment of the second generation (Lee and Zhou 2017, 2015). The hyper-selectivity of Chinese immigrants can enhance the educational outcomes of the second generation, even among those from working-class families in ways that defy the classic status attainment model. For example, Chinese immigrants who arrive with more education and socioeconomic resources create ethnic capital in the form of supplemental education programs, SAT prep courses, and tutoring services that are accessible to working-class coethnics (see also Kasinitz et al. 2008; Tran 2016). Moreover, the high achievers become the role models and mobility prototypes to which group members aspire, and the reference group against whom they measure their success. These coethnic resources and cross-class social ties give second-generation Chinese—including those from working-class backgrounds—a leg up over other groups.

In addition, hyper-selectivity has social psychological consequences, which affect in-group and out-group perceptions. For example, the hyper-selectivity of Chinese immigrants drives the perception that all Chinese are highly educated, smart, hardworking, and deserving (Lee and Zhou 2015). And, critically, because of the racialization process that occurs in the United States, perceptions of Chinese extend to other Asian immigrant groups such as Vietnamese, even though the latter are not hyper-selected. These are the spillover effects of hyper-selectivity (Hsin 2016), which have resulted in the racial mobility of Asian Americans—the change in status or position of a racial group (Lee 2015). Here, we draw from Aliya Saperstein's racial mobility perspective, which accounts for the shift in an individual's racial status based on changes to their social status (2015). We build on this perspective by noting that racial mobility can also occur at the group level as a result of changes in an ethnoracial group's immigrant selectivity or socioeconomic status. These changes can affect out-group perceptions, alter the group's position in the U.S. hierarchy, and lead to racial mobility for both the ethnic group as well as their proximal host racial group.

This is precisely what happened in the case of U.S. Chinese and Asians. Less than a century ago, Chinese immigrants were described as illiterate, undesirable, and unassimilable foreigners, full of "filth and disease," and unfit for U.S. citizenship. In 1882 Senator John F. Miller, Republican of California, told the Senate on February 28, "It is a fact of history that wherever the Chinese have gone they have always taken their habits, methods, and civilization with them; and history fails to record a single example in which they have ever lost them. They remain Chinese always and everywhere; changeless, fixed and unalterable." Senator Miller added, "If the Chinese could be lifted up to the level of the free American, to the adoption and enjoyment of American civilization, the case would be better; but this cannot be done," he concluded. "Forty centuries of Chinese life has made the Chinaman what he is. An eternity of years cannot make him such a man as the Anglo-Saxon" (see Dunlap 2017, A2).

As "marginal members of the human race," they were denied the right to naturalize, denied the right to intermarry, residentially segregated in crowded ethnic enclaves, and legally barred from entering the United States for ten years beginning in 1882 with the passage of the Chinese Exclusion Act (Okihiro 1994; Takaki 1979). Despite decades of institutional discrimination, racial prejudice, and legal exclusion, Chinese have become one of the most highly educated U.S. groups and are now hailed as a successful group to be emulated. The change in their immigrant selectivity—and more specifically their hyper-selectivity—has led to the racial mobility of not only Chinese but also Asian Americans. Facilitating the group mobility of Asian Americans is that the Chinese are the largest Asian ethnic group in the United States.

Although Jennifer Lee and Min Zhou illustrate how hyper-selectivity affects second-generation Asian-origin immigrant groups (Chinese and Vietnamese), they do not consider how it may operate for non-Asian immigrant groups (2015). We expand the theoretical discussion of hyper-selectivity, and consider how it affects immigrant groups such as Cubans, Nigerians, and Armenians, and their U.S. proximal hosts—Latinos, blacks, and whites, respectively.[1] We posit that though the hyper-selectivity of Cubans, Nigerians, and Armenians positively affects the socioeconomic outcomes of immigrants and their second-generation children, it does not change group-based perceptions of their proximal hosts as it does for Asians. In other words, although hyper-selectivity has changed the cognitive construction of Chinese, and has led to the racial mobility of Asian Americans, it has not done the same for other U.S. racial groups. Instead, Cubans and Nigerians are perceived as the exceptions to Latinos and blacks—a perception that these ethnic groups actively strive to maintain as they distance and identify themselves in opposition to their proximal hosts. By contrast, Armenians—like European immigrant groups of the past—are becoming absorbed as whites.

FOUR HYPER-SELECTED IMMIGRANT GROUPS AT A GLANCE

We provide brief immigration histories of four hyper-selected groups: Chinese, Cubans, Nigerians, and Armenians that are racialized as Asian, Latino, black, and white, respectively, in the U.S. context.

Chinese

Since 1965, Chinese immigrants have become the most populous Asian-origin group, from 235,000 in 1960 to more than four million in 2010 (U.S. Census Bureau 2017). Although they constitute only 1.2 percent of the total U.S. population, more than half have graduated from college, making them one of largest, most visible, most educated, and upwardly mobile groups in the country. Their ascendance has captured the attention of the media, pundits, and researchers who have provided a bevy of explanations for their educational attainment—the most popular of which was the essentialist cultural argument in which pundits point to unique Chinese and Asian cultural traits and values to explain their high achievement (Chua and Rubenfeld 2014).

Social scientists, on the other hand, relied on the status attainment model to explain variance in socioeconomic attainment, parental education being the strongest predictor of children's educational attainment. This model explained differences between and within native-born whites and blacks, but it failed to account for a vexing achievement paradox. Left unanswered is how the children of Chinese immigrants whose parents have less than a high school education, and work in ethnic restaurants and factories, attain the same education (if not more) as their counterparts whose parents are college-educated professionals.

Immigration researchers tackle this paradox head on. Not only do they expose the fallacy of the culturally reductionist approach, they also explain how race and ethnicity serve as resources for immigrant and second-generation groups like the Chinese (Kasinitz et al. 2008; Hsin and Xie 2014; Portes and Zhou 1993; Zhou and Kim 2006). They point to both structural advantages such as contexts of exit and reception, ethnic capital, racial phenotype, favorable out-group perceptions, and cultural repertoires of achievement that affect second-generation success.

Lee and Zhou extend this literature by adding that hyper-selected immigrants import class-specific cultural institutions and practices from their countries of origin, and recreate those that have the most utility in their new host country (2015). Hence, what may be perceived and defined as the transmission of cultural traits and values is in fact class-specific in origin. In addition, they show that the chil-

---

1. *Proximal host* refers to "the racial category to which the immigrants would be assigned following immigration" (Mittelberg and Waters 1992, 412). Specifically, it refers to the native-born racial group in the host society that is closest to a given immigrant group. Although we use third-plus-generation whites and third-plus-generation blacks as the proximal hosts for Armenians and Nigerians, respectively, we depart from Philip Kasinitz and his colleagues and use third-plus-generation Latinos, rather than Puerto Ricans, as the proximal host for Cubans (2008). Finally, we add third-plus-generation Asians as the proximal host for Chinese.

dren of hyper-selected groups benefit from social psychological processes. For example, because Chinese immigrants are hyper-selected, teachers perceive all Chinese students as smart, hardworking, disciplined, and deserving. This can lead to *stereotype promise*—being viewed through the lens of a positive stereotype that can boost performance. Because of the racialization process in the United States, the hyper-selectivity of the Chinese extends to other East Asian groups, such as the Vietnamese. Hence, even mediocre second-generation Chinese and Vietnamese students gain advantages and second chances in the domain of education that are denied to other groups, including native-born whites. In turn, these cumulative advantages can result in a self-fulfilling prophecy of high achievement among Asian Americans.

Van Tran adds to this body of research by clarifying that not only does hyper-selectivity matter, but so does the socioeconomic diversity of the coethnic community (2016). Although Chinese immigrants are hyper-selected, the range of human capital attributes within the ethnic group is unusually wide. Thus, Chinese social networks serve to link poor and working-class people to upper-middle-class professionals more often than in other ethnic groups, providing working-class and working-poor Chinese immigrant parents with access to cultural knowledge often reserved for upper-middle-class professionals. These direct and indirect connections through ethnic social networks facilitate the transfer of practical knowledge of the strategies necessary for educational mobility—from magnet public high schools entrance exams to prerequisites for successful applications to the most selective universities. Furthermore, Tran finds that second-generation Chinese from working-class backgrounds strive to excel in school in order to obviate the prejudice experienced by their immigrant parents, and to repay them for the hardship that they have had to endure in their new host society.

Thus, the superior academic credentials and socioeconomic characteristics of the second-generation Chinese result from the hyper-selectivity of their immigrant parents, its spillover effects, and the socioeconomic diversity of Chinese Americans. These structural and social psychological advantages create ethnic-specific cross-class opportunities beyond the parental home for both middle- and working-class coethnics as the second generation come of age.

Cubans

More than 2.1 million Americans identify as Cuban and, like the Chinese, are hyper-selected (U.S. Census Bureau 2017). Among initial waves of the post-1965 migrants from Cuba, 33 percent had earned a college degree, relative to only 1 percent of the Cuban national population (Pedraza-Bailey 1985). This early form of hyper-selectivity was driven by the Cuban revolution, which dislodged the dominant social classes from their homeland and resettled them in Miami (Pérez 1986), leading researchers to call the first mass migration of Cuban elite to United States the Golden Exile (Portes 1969). As push factors in Cuba intensified and incentivized emigration, successive waves of coethnics—characterized by lower levels of education and professional qualifications—arrived and populated the Cuban enclave in Miami (Portes, Clark, and Bach 1977; Portes and Böröcz 1989).

Upon their arrival, the later waves were welcomed by a resource-rich ethnic enclave that facilitated their socioeconomic incorporation. The top-heavy class structure of the initial wave of Cuban migrants concentrated social and economic capital that would later cascade throughout the enclave and provide less-skilled coethnics with employment in the enclave (Portes and Bach 1985; Portes and Puhrmann 2015). Although the ethnic capital among Cubans in Miami has aided the socioeconomic incorporation among the first generation, the effects—beyond educational aspirations—are less clear among the second generation.

Hyper-selectivity and socioeconomic diversity among first-generation Cubans has led to graduate degree aspirations among the second, even among the children of later wave Cuban migrants whose parents are far less likely to have graduated from college (Feliciano 2006; Rumbaut and Portes 2001). However, evidence of cross-class learning that would bolster second-generation educational attainment—which is present among the Chinese—has yet to be empirically documented (Haller, Portes, and Lynch 2011).

Rather recent studies demonstrate that, unlike low-SES (socioeconomic status) second-generation Chinese who converge with high-SES coethnics in educational achievement, second-generation Cubans follow the pattern predicted by the status attainment model. Parental class predicts children's outcomes among second-generation Cubans, as reflected in the high college rates among the middle class at one extreme and high school dropout rates among the working class on the other (Portes and Puhrmann 2015). The favorable mode of incorporation and especially their context of reception has aided first-generation Cubans and has prevented downward assimilation among the second generation (Fernández-Kelly and Konczal 2005; Portes and Fernández-Kelly 2008; Portes and MacLeod 1996).

Nigerians

Numbering some 367,000, Nigerians make up less than 1 percent of the U.S. population, yet nearly two-thirds (62 percent) of Nigerian immigrants are college educated—far exceeding the U.S. mean at 28 percent. Nigerian migration to the United States began en masse following the political upheaval in Nigeria in the 1960s, increasing rapidly through the 1990s (Ogbaa 2003; Imoagene 2012). In this decade, larger proportions of graduate degree holders and highly skilled professionals continued to flee the economic and political uncertainty in Nigeria by resettling in the United States. This more recent, hyper-selected migration converged in three U.S. cities—New York, Houston, and Washington, D.C.—and contributed to the growing black middle class (Logan and Deane 2003).

Many of the most popular and active organizations among Nigerian Americans are not free-standing community associations created in the U.S. context, but rather American branches of hometown associations and community-based organizations with a long service history in Nigeria. Like the members of the Golden Exile who recreated Cuban private schools in Miami to ensure that Cuban parents would retain sustained authority over American-born children, Nigerians have founded mutual-aid associations across the United States that organize chain migration, assist with job placement, and direct remittances to the homeland (Konadu-Agyemang, Takyi, and Arthur 2006; Arthur 2000).

The tight ethnic networks that emerge from mutual-aid associations have consequences for nonmigrants, as well as for both first- and second-generation Nigerians. For example, Onoso Imoagene reveals how these networks sustain cultural norms of advanced educational attainment among U.S. Nigerians such that they believe that it is "un-Nigerian not to go to college" (2017). In fact, the educational expectations among the second generation is a graduate degree, similar to that of second-generation Chinese (Imoagene 2017; Lee and Zhou 2017, 2016, 2015). Although Nigerian immigrants and their children may reduce achievement to their ethnicity, Imoagene shows how the hyper-selectivity of the first generation affects the educational aspirations and attainment of the second generation (2017).

Armenians

Numbering approximately 460,000, Armenian Americans make up less than 1 percent of the total U.S. population, yet 44 percent of them have a bachelor's degree or higher (U.S. Census Bureau 2017). The earliest migrants fled in response to political violence and genocide, settled on the Eastern seaboard in the late 1800s (Bakalian 1992), and later moved to California to work in agriculture (Sabagh, Bozorgmehr, and Der-Martirosian 1990). Following the change in U.S. immigration law in 1965, Armenian immigrants were hyper-selected and racially classified as white, thanks to pre-1965 Armenian immigrants who successfully petitioned federal immigration officials in the U.S. Supreme Court to be classified as white. Their petition for racial classification earned them eligibility for U.S. citizenship in the 1920s (Craver 2009).

Like American Jews, who are diverse in national origin yet converge in the collective memory of the Holocaust, Armenian Americans emigrate to the United States from diverse sending countries, such as Syria, Iran, Armenia, Lebanon, Iraq, Turkey and Russia, but organize collectively for federal recognition of the

Armenian genocide (Waldinger and Bozorgmehr 1996). Iranian immigrants have the highest level of college completion among these groups, and Turkish immigrants, the highest level of self-employment (Sabagh, Bozorgmehr, and Der-Martirosian 1990).

Coordinated by a vocal and organized political lobby, Armenian Americans benefit from a host of professional societies, youth enrichment organizations, and nonprofit hometown associations that provide social services for both the local community as well as humanitarian relief in the Republic of Armenia (Waldinger 2015; Khachikian 2016). To our knowledge, no research has been published on the educational attainment of second-generation Armenians, making our analysis one of the first mobility snapshots for this immigrant group. Given the hyper-selectivity of the first generation, their favorable context of reception, and their white racial status in the United States, it is likely that the second generation will reproduce their parents' socioeconomic advantage. The ethnic capital that highly skilled professional immigrants create and sustain in a community with a high level of ethnic concentration like Los Angeles places second-generation Armenians at a favorable starting point in their quest for attainment (Der-Martirosian 2008; Phinney, Ong, and Madden 2000; Phinney, Baumann, and Blanton 2001).

PATTERNS OF IMMIGRANT AND SECOND-GENERATION EDUCATIONAL ATTAINMENT

We provide details of our data, methods, and analyses of patterns of immigrant and second-generation educational attainment.

Data and Methods

To examine the patterns of second-generation educational attainment among Chinese, Cubans, Nigerians, and Armenians, we used pooled data from the Annual Social and Economic Supplement of the Community Population Survey (CPS ASEC) from 2008, 2010, and 2012 (Bureau of Labor Statistics 2012). The CPS ASEC is the only data source that provides nationally representative samples of second-generation adults in the United States. The CPS ASEC is administered by the Census Bureau through both in-person and telephone interviews every month to monitor basic trends in the population. It uses a probability sample of about sixty thousand occupied households from all fifty states and the District of Columbia. The survey design features a 4-8-4 sampling scheme under which households are included in the survey for the first four consecutive months and excluded for the next eight, before returning again for the last four. Given this sampling design, the pooling of data from the 2008, 2010, and 2012 samples ensures the presence of non-overlapping individuals in the pooled dataset, because each of these surveys was collected two years apart. The pooled sample also ensures an adequate sample size for smaller groups such as Nigerians and Armenians.

The main outcome of interest is educational attainment by ethnoracial origin and immigrant generation. Our focus is on the second generation in each of the four ethnic groups. We compared their outcomes with those of the immigrant first generation from the same ethnic groups, with the proximal host from the same racial groups, and with their second-generation nonethnics from the same racial group. The four proximal host racial groups include third-plus-generation individuals from the same race (that is, native-born non-Hispanic whites, non-Hispanic blacks, non-Hispanic Asians and Hispanics). These three sets of comparisons were selected to reveal the complex linkages between hyper-selectivity and intergenerational mobility that underlie the cognitive construction of racial groups in the U.S. context.

The analysis is restricted to respondents age twenty-five or older, given our main outcome of interest in educational achievement. This age range also allowed us to effectively compare the first and second generation in the United States with nonmigrants in their home countries for whom data on educational attainment are available only for those older than twenty-five. Our key independent variables are ethnoracial origin and immigrant generation, operationalized based on the birthplace of the respondent and those of their parents. Those with one foreign-born parent and one native-born parent we classified based on the ethnic-

Table 1. Educational Attainment by Ethnoracial Origin and Immigrant Generation

Ethnic Group	% College Graduate	% Total Sample	N Sample Size
First generation			
Chinese	52.7	1.0	3,196
Cuban	23.5	0.6	1,868
Armenian	34.5	0.0	120
Nigerian	63.8	0.1	320
Second generation			
Chinese	61.2	0.2	611
Cuban	40.6	0.1	343
Armenian	57.6	0.0	31
Nigerian	73.5	0.0	44
Second generation			
Non-Chinese Asian	54.7	0.6	1,902
Non-Cuban Hispanic	19.5	2.3	7,003
Non-Armenian white	36.6	3.0	9,426
Non-Nigerian black	37.7	0.2	587
Third-plus generation			
Non-Hispanic Asian	52.0	0.8	2,338
Hispanic-Latino	16.9	4.8	14,730
Non-Hispanic white	32.9	74.1	229,480
Non-Hispanic black	18.9	12.2	37,661
Total	31.3	100.0	309,660

Source: Authors' compilation based on the 2008–2012 CPS ASEC (Bureau of Labor Statistics 2012).
Note: Combined sample is limited to population age twenty-five and older.

ity of the foreign-born parent to ensure the largest samples of the second generation.

The analyses proceeded in two stages. First, bivariate analyses provided statistical profiles for each ethnic group by ethnoracial origin. Second, multivariate logistic regression analyses examined the socioeconomic attainment of Latino ethnic groups, relative to third-plus-generation proximal hosts or to second-generation nonethnic individuals from the same racial group. Because the dependent variable is dichotomous, we used logistic regressions with robust standard errors and report the odds ratios. The control variables include age, the quadratic term of age, region of the country and survey year. Because CPS ASEC 2008–2012 pools data across three survey years, we controlled for changes over time. Region is a variable with four census categories: Northeast, Midwest, West, and South. Our analyses adjusted for the stratified survey design using appropriate final weights provided by CPS ASEC. We also present some of our findings using predicted probabilities based on the multivariate analyses in which values for control variables are held constant at the mean level.

Descriptive Analyses

Table 1 provides an overview of our CPS ASEC pooled sample by ethnoracial origin and immigrant generation, along with the proportion with a bachelor's degree or more. Chinese were the largest among the four groups, having the highest number of both immigrant and second-generation respondents, followed by Cubans. In contrast, the samples of Armenians and Ni-

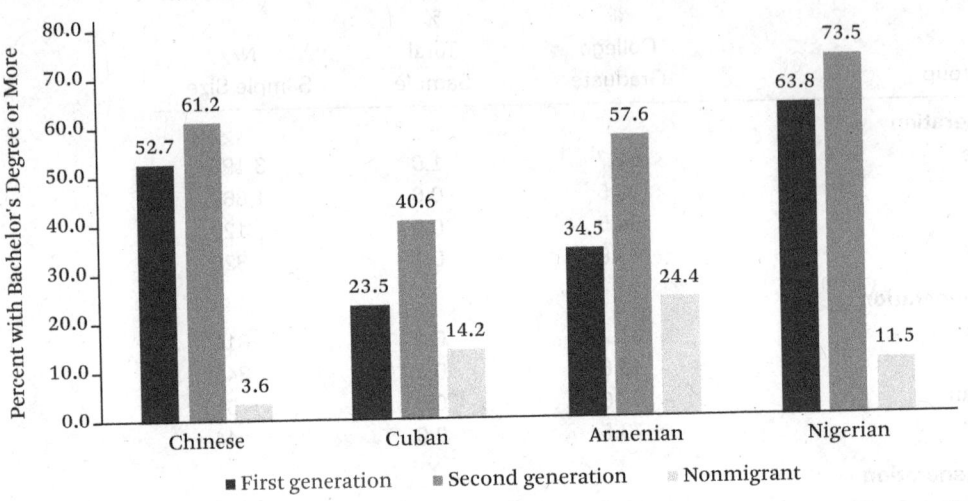

Figure 1. Educational Attainment by Ethnoracial Origin and Immigrant Generation

Source: Authors' compilation based on the 2008–2012 CPS ASEC (Bureau of Labor Statistics 2012), UNESCO Institute for Statistics 2012, and Education Policy and Data Center 2013.
Notes: Combined sample is limited to population age twenty-five and older. Nonmigrant data for Chinese, Cubans, and Armenians are extracted from United Nations Educational, Scientific and Cultural Organization's (UNESCO) Institute for Statistics. Nonmigrant data for Nigerians are extracted from Education Policy and Data Center.

gerians were rather small, reflecting both their relative group size and recency of immigration. We also specified the second-generation nonethnics from the same racial group and their third- and higher-generation proximal host groups. These two sets of comparisons provide benchmarks for second-generation progress against the U.S. mainstream and how well the four ethnic groups performed relative to other second-generation individuals of the same racial but not the same ethnic background. These two benchmarks capture the increasing diversity of the U.S. mainstream into which the second generation assimilate because recent research has shown how the choice of reference groups to compare second-generation attainment affects the conclusion of second-generation progress, mobility, stagnation, or decline (Jiménez and Horowitz 2013; Kasinitz et al. 2008; Portes, Aparicio Gomez, and Haller 2016; Tran and Valdez 2017).

Examining educational attainment among the four ethnic groups revealed two distinctive characteristics—hyper-selectivity and intergenerational mobility. Figure 1 presents descriptive results on the proportion with a bachelor's degree or higher within each ethnic group in the United States, contrasting these proportions with the educational attainment among nonmigrants in the sending countries. Among the population age twenty-five and older, first-generation immigrants reported significantly higher percentages of having a bachelor's degree or higher than their nonmigrant counterparts in respective home countries. This achievement gap is most striking between Chinese nonmigrants and Chinese immigrants in the United States, but also substantial for the other three groups. Only 3.6 percent of nonmigrant Chinese reported having a college education, but 52.7 percent of immigrant Chinese held a bachelor's degree. This hyper-selectivity ratio of 17:1 between immigrant and nonmigrant means that Chinese immigrants were disproportionately well educated relative to nonmigrants. This ratio is about 8:1 for Asian Indians. This gap is also quite stark among Nigerians. Immigrant Nigerians (63.8 percent) were six times more likely than their nonmigrant counterparts to report having a bachelor's degree or more (11.5 percent). Their hyper-selectivity ratio is about 6:1. Similarly, 23.5

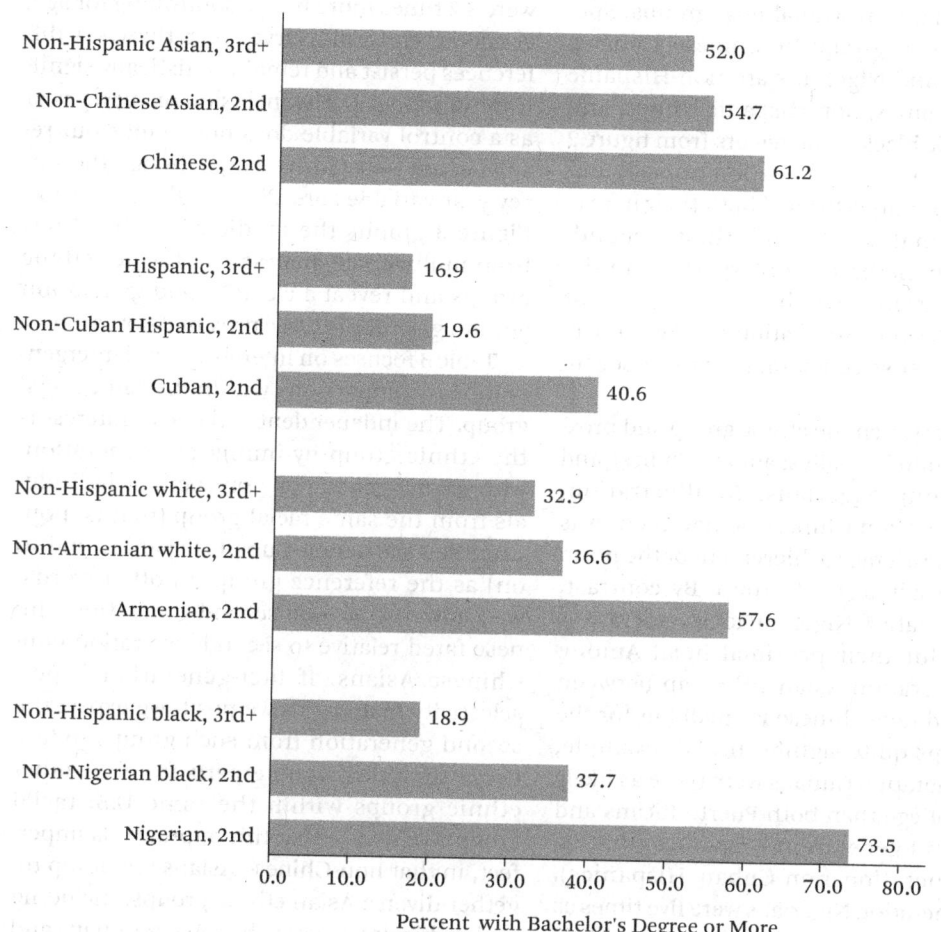

Figure 2. Educational Attainment by Ethnoracial Origin and Proximate Host

Source: Authors' compilation based on the 2008–2012 CPS ASEC (Bureau of Labor Statistics 2012).
Note: Combined sample is limited to population age twenty-five and older.

percent of immigrant Cubans reported having a college degree relative to only 14.2 percent of nonmigrant Cubans, a gap of 9 percent. Among Armenians, the corresponding gap is about 10 percent.

Between the first and second generation, intergenerational mobility is clear. A significantly higher proportion of the second generation from four ethnic groups reported having a bachelor's degree or higher than their immigrant first generation. Among Chinese, this number increased from 52.7 percent to 61.2 percent. Among Cubans, 23.5 percent among first-generation immigrants and 40.6 among the second generation reported having a college education. Among Armenians, the increase was from 34.5 percent to 57.6 percent. Among Nigerians, patterns of mobility were similarly robust, up approximately 10 percentage points to 73.5 percent in the second generation. The overall pattern is clear: the first generation was significantly more selective than the nonmigrants in the country of origin, and the second generation reported even higher education than the first.

Figure 2 presents descriptive results on the proportion with a bachelor's degree or higher for the second generation from the same four groups, contrasting these proportions with second-generation nonethnic counterparts from the same race and the third-plus-generation native proximal host groups. Specifically, the host groups for Chinese, Cubans, Armenians, and Nigerians are non-Hispanic Asians, Hispanics, non-Hispanic whites, and non-Hispanic blacks. The results from figure 2 show that the second generation from all four ethnic groups outperformed both their native-born proximal hosts and their second-generation nonethnic counterparts from the same racial group. The higher achievement among the second generation is a key consequence of hyper-selectivity among the first generation.

The gap between the ethnic group and proximal host group is smallest among Chinese and largest among Nigerians. By illustration, second-generation Chinese achievement was similar to the average achievement or the norm for their proximal host group. By contrast, second-generation Nigerian achievement was an outlier for their proximal host. Among second-generation Asians, the gap between Chinese and non-Chinese is small but for the other groups quite significant. For example, second-generation Cubans were twice as likely to finish college than both Puerto Ricans and other second-generation Hispanics (that is, second-generation non-Cuban Hispanics). Second-generation Nigerians were five times as likely as African Americans and twice as likely as other second-generation blacks (that is, second-generation non-Nigerian blacks) to have a college degree.

Multivariate Analyses
Further results from our multivariate analyses confirm the patterns documented in our descriptive analyses. Table 2 presents multivariate results from logistic regressions predicting college attainment for the four second-generation groups in comparison with the three native proximal host groups. Model 1 shows that blacks and Puerto Ricans were about half as likely as whites to have a bachelor's degree and that the second generation from all four ethnic groups were significantly more likely have graduated from college than the first generation. The largest differences are among Nigerians, who were 5.7 times more likely than whites to have a college degree, and among Chinese, who were 3.2 times more likely. Controlling for age, gender, region, and survey year, these key differences persist and remain statistically significant in model 2. The inclusion of survey year as a control variable does not change our results in any substantive way, although the survey year variables are statistically significant. Figure 3 graphs the predicted probabilities from multivariate analyses for the key ethnic groups and reveal a clear second-generation advantage over the three proximal host groups.

Table 3 focuses on interethnic and intergenerational comparisons within the same racial group. The independent variable of interest is the ethnic group by immigrant generation, with second-generation non-coethnic individuals from the same racial group (that is, non-Chinese Asians, non-Cuban Hispanics, and so on) as the reference group. In other words, we examine how well second-generation Chinese fared relative to second-generation non-Chinese Asians. If first-generation hyper-selectivity matters, as we posit, we expect the second generation from such groups to fare better than their counterparts from the other ethnic groups within the same U.S. racial group. We realize that this approach is imperfect, in that non-Chinese Asians still lump together diverse Asian ethnic groups, including high-achieving ones such as Asian Indians and Koreans as well as low-achieving ones such as Cambodians and Laotians.

Compared with other second-generation Asians, the second-generation Chinese reported significantly higher odds of having a bachelor's degree or more. They were also significantly more likely than first-generation Chinese to achieve more education. Among Hispanics, both first- and second-generation Cubans were significantly more likely to complete a college education or more than other second-generation Hispanics. Nigerians were in fact the most highly educated group. First-generation Nigerians were 2.5 times more likely and second-generation Nigerians 4.2 times more likely to have a bachelor's degree or higher than other second-generation blacks. Finally, first-generation Armenians were the only group that reported lower odds of having

Table 2. Logistic Regression for Second-Generation Educational Attainment, College Graduates

Variables	Model 1	Model 2
Ethnoracial origin and immigrant generation		
Non-Hispanic black, third-plus generation	0.475***	0.465***
	(0.007)	(0.007)
Hispanic/Latino, third-plus generation	0.419***	0.355***
	(0.011)	(0.009)
Non-Hispanic Asian, third-plus generation	2.216***	1.860***
	(0.124)	(0.105)
Chinese, second generation	3.235***	2.654***
	(0.296)	(0.235)
Cuban, second generation	1.403**	1.197
	(0.166)	(0.143)
Armenian, second generation	2.787*	3.111**
	(1.195)	(1.247)
Nigerian, second generation	5.692***	4.752***
	(2.360)	(1.988)
Control variables		
Age		1.018***
		(0.002)
Age-square		1.000***
		(0.000)
Male		1.008
		(0.010)
Midwest		0.720***
		(0.011)
South		0.802***
		(0.011)
West		1.048**
		(0.016)
CPS 2010 vs. CPS 2008		1.033**
		(0.012)
CPS 2012 vs. CPS 2008		1.106***
		(0.013)
Constant	0.488***	0.520***
	(0.003)	(0.028)
N	285,238	285,238

Source: Authors' compilation based on the 2008–2012 CPS ASEC (Bureau of Labor Statistics 2012).

Note: Odds ratios reported. Robust standard errors in parentheses. The reference group for ethnoracial origin is non-Hispanic white, third-plus generation. The reference category for region is northeast.

*$p < .05$; **$p < .01$; ***$p < .001$

Figure 3. Predicted Probabilities of Educational Attainment by Ethnoracial Origin

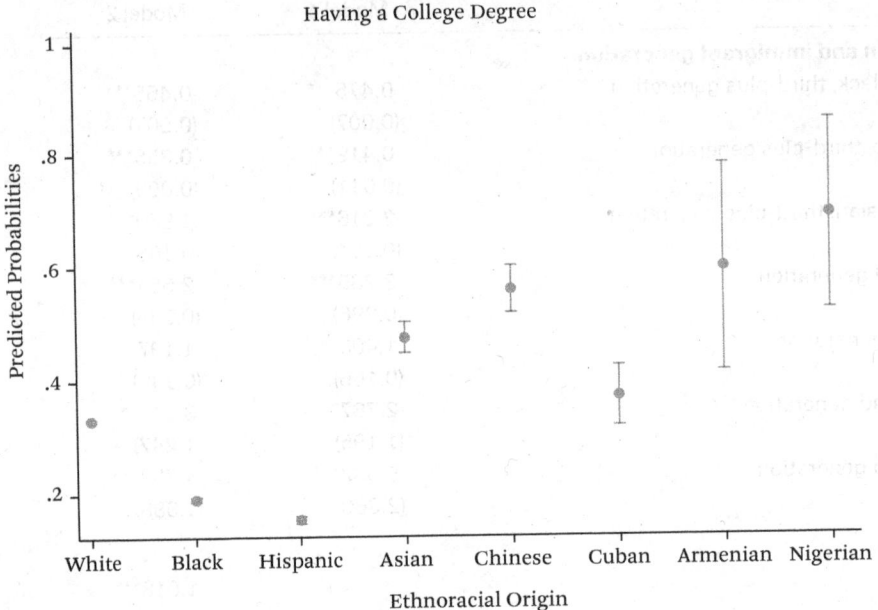

Source: Authors' compilation based on the 2008–2012 CPS ASEC (Bureau of Labor Statistics 2012).
Note: Combined sample is limited to population age twenty-five and older. The four native (third-and-higher-generation) groups are non-Hispanic white, non-Hispanic black, Hispanic and non-Hispanic Asian. The four second-generation groups are Chinese, Cuban, Armenian, and Nigerian. Predicted probabilities are based on multivariate models, which also controlled for gender, age, quadratic tem of age, region, and survey year, holding these control variables at mean value.

a bachelor's degree or more than other second-generation whites, whereas second-generation Armenians were 2.5 times more likely to have completed a college education.

Figure 4 graphs the race-specific predicted probabilities from the multivariate analyses in table 3, holding all the control variables at their mean value. Except for Asians, the other three racial groups show three clear patterns. First, there is upward mobility in educational attainment when comparing first- and second-generation respondents within each ethnic group. Second, second-generation respondents from the hyper-selected groups also reported significantly higher achievements than their second-generation nonethnic counterparts from the same racial group. Third, among Asian respondents, second-generation Chinese respondents slightly outperformed first-generation Chinese and other second-generation Asians.

HYPER-SELECTIVITY AND THE COGNITIVE CONSTRUCTION OF RACE

Our analyses point to the positive association between hyper-selectivity and second-generation educational attainment. The hyper-selectivity of first-generation Chinese, Cubans, Nigerians, and Armenians has led to even higher college completion rates among the second.

Although hyper-selectivity positively affects college graduation rates for the second generation, what remains to be seen is whether this advantage will last beyond the second generation. Drawing from research on immigration and race-ethnicity, we considered how hyper-selectivity might affect third- and later-generation Chinese, Cubans, Nigerians, and Armenians, and theorize what this suggests about the effects of hyper-selectivity on the cognitive construction of race and patterns of eth-

Table 3. Race-Specific Logistic Regression for Second-Generation Educational Attainment

Variables	Chinese Model 1	Cuban Model 2	Armenian Model 3	Nigerian Model 4
Immigrant generation				
First generation	1.215*	1.412***	0.592*	2.489***
	(0.096)	(0.112)	(0.129)	(0.436)
Second generation	1.441***	2.668***	2.462*	4.210***
	(0.158)	(0.335)	(1.064)	(1.773)
Control variables				
Age	1.012	1.076***	1.064***	1.094*
	(0.013)	(0.013)	(0.011)	(0.039)
Age-square	1.000***	0.999***	0.999***	0.999**
	(0.000)	(0.000)	(0.000)	(0.000)
Male	1.141*	0.738***	1.258***	1.017
	(0.071)	(0.042)	(0.066)	(0.158)
Midwest	1.978***	0.934	0.839*	1.286
	(0.236)	(0.115)	(0.062)	(0.350)
South	1.557***	0.843*	1.141	1.157
	(0.153)	(0.072)	(0.084)	(0.206)
West	1.356***	0.768**	1.049	0.921
	(0.103)	(0.066)	(0.072)	(0.248)
CPS 2010 vs. CPS 2008	1.034	1.036	1.038	0.822
	(0.082)	(0.071)	(0.065)	(0.162)
CPS 2012 vs. CPS 2008	0.996	1.019	1.209**	1.206
	(0.076)	(0.071)	(0.078)	(0.228)
Constant	1.152	0.080***	0.248***	0.092**
	(0.361)	(0.024)	(0.069)	(0.075)
N	5,709	9,214	9,577	951

Source: Authors' compilation based on the 2008–2012 CPS ASEC (Bureau of Labor Statistics 2012).
Note: Odds ratios reported. Robust standard errors in parentheses. The reference group for each race-specific regression is second-generation individuals in same racial group, excluding the ethnic group. For Chinese, it is second-generation non-Chinese Asian. For Cubans, it is second-generation non-Cuban Hispanic. For Armenians, it is second-generation non-Armenian white. For Nigerians, it is second-generation non-Nigerian black. The reference category for region is northeast.
*$p < .05$; **$p < .01$; ***$p < .001$

noracial identification. We contend that the effects of hyper-selectivity differ for groups depending on how they are racialized in the U.S. context, as well as the status of the proximal host group in relation to the hyper-selected immigrant group.

Members of the second-generation may identify by national origin or ethnicity, and enter U.S. institutions (such as schools) with entrenched racial categories and highly stratified racial hierarchies. These, in turn, affect how teachers, guidance counselors, and peers perceive, treat, and identify students of diverse immigrant and ethnoracial backgrounds (Calarco 2014; Drake 2017; Ferguson 2003; Lee and Zhou 2015; Lewis-McCoy 2014; Valenzuela 1999). For example, although second-generation Nigerian students may strongly identify with their ethnicity and immigrant origin, school officials may recognize neither; rather, they may identify the students as black and treat them accordingly.

Figure 4. Race-Specific Predicted Probabilities of Educational Attainment by Generation

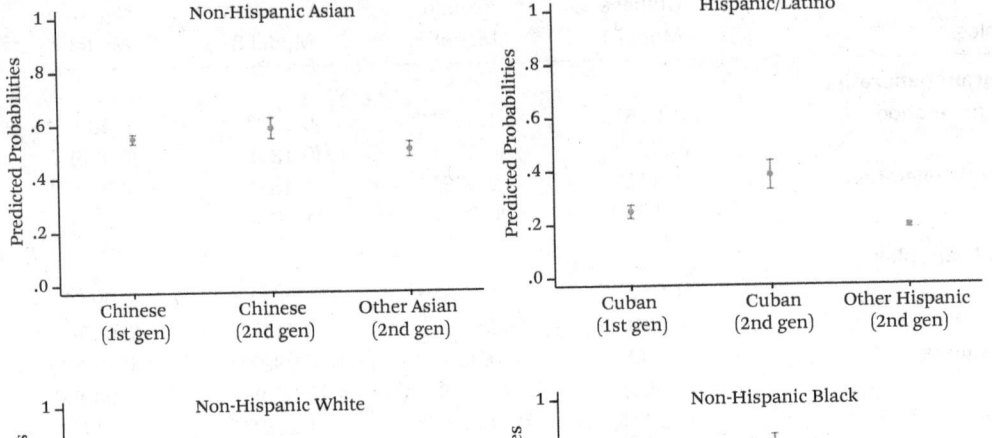

Source: Authors' compilation based on the 2008–2012 CPS ASEC (Bureau of Labor Statistics 2012).
Note: Combined sample is limited to population age twenty-five and older. Other Asian includes non-Chinese Asians; Other Hispanic includes non-Cuban Hispanics; Other White includes non-Armenian whites; Other Nigerian includes non-Nigerian blacks. Predicted probabilities are based on multivariate models, which also controlled for gender, age, quadratic term of age, region, and survey year, holding these control variables at mean value.

Research shows that internal ethnic identification among the second generation can be at odds with external racial ascription, and studies of the children of black immigrants underscore the relevant difference between the two (Imoagene 2017; Tran 2015; Waters 1999). In her study of second-generation Nigerians, Imoagene shows that they succeeded in part by actively choosing their ethnicity while negotiating their race (2017). Despite their extraordinary academic achievement, however, she also finds that because of their racial status as black, they faced biases and barriers that impeded their full integration into U.S. institutions (see also Owens and Lynch 2012; Owens and Massey 2011; Patacchini and Zenou 2016). Like Van Tran and Mary Waters, in their studies of second-generation West Indians, Imoagene cautions that the class and ethnic advantages of the second-generation Nigerians may not extend to the third and later generations because of their racial status and the cognitive construction of blackness in U.S. society (Imoagene 2017; Tran 2015; Waters 1999).

Here, we note that the size of the hyper-selected immigrant group in relation to their proximal host matters for changing the cognitive construction of race, and has implications for ethnoracial identification among descendants of immigrants. For example, in spite of the hyper-selectivity of Nigerian immigrants and the extraordinarily high level of education attained by the second generation, Nigerians make up only 1 percent of the total U.S. black population (see table 4). This fraction is not enough to change the cognitive construction of blackness, which was born out of the legacy of slavery, entrenched by Jim Crow laws, and

Table 4. Relative Distribution by Ethnoracial Origin and Immigrant Status by Racial Groups

	% Ethnic Group	% Foreign Born	% Racial Group	N
Asian respondents				
Chinese, first generation	83.4	19.6	15.2	3,196
Chinese, second generation	16.6		2.9	611
Other Asian, first generation	·	80.4	62.5	13,132
Other Asian, second-plus generation			19.4	4,076
Total	100	100	100	21,015
Hispanic respondents				
Cuban, first generation	83.3	5.2	3.2	1,868
Cuban, second generation	16.7		0.6	343
Other Hispanic, first generation		94.8	58.6	33,946
Other Hispanic, second-plus generation			37.5	21,733
Total	100	100	100	57,890
White respondents				
Armenian, first generation	88.2	0.9	0.05	120
Armenian, second generation	11.8		0.01	31
Other white, first generation		99.1	5.2	13,078
Other white, second-plus generation			94.7	238,894
Total	100	100	100	252,123
Black respondents				
Nigerian, first generation	79.6	6.5	0.7	320
Nigerian, second generation	20.4		0.1	44
Other black, first generation		93.5	5	4,584
Other black, second-plus generation			95	38,239
Total	100	100	100	43,187

Source: Authors' compilation based on the 2008–2012 CPS ASEC (Bureau of Labor Statistics 2012).
Note: Samples are limited to population age twenty-five and older.

embedded through the de jure and now de facto practice of the one-drop rule of hypodescent. Because of the distance between Nigerian and black American identity, Nigerians in the United States sometimes work to distinguish themselves from black Americans, and strategically emphasize their ethnic and immigrant identities over their racial identities (see Imoagene 2017).

Hyper-selectivity operates differently for Chinese immigrants than it does for Nigerians. Chinese immigrants are the largest Asian immigrant group, and Chinese Americans are the largest Asian ethnic group, which affects the cognitive construction of both the ethnic category Chinese as well as the racial category Asian. Foreign-born Chinese make up 20 percent of all foreign-born Asians, and first- and second-generation Chinese account for 18 percent of the total Asian American population. Because Chinese are a larger share of the U.S. Asian population than Nigerians are of the U.S. black population, the former will more strongly affect the cognitive construction of race than the latter. In short, the hyper-selectivity of Chinese immigrants and the high educational attainment among the second generation affect Americans' perceptions of not only U.S. Chinese but also Asian Americans. Furthermore, the perceived similar status of Chinese and Asian identity in the United States explains why Chinese do not strongly reject the racial label of Asian American (as Nigerians reject the black American one), but instead use ethnic and racial identifiers interchangeably (Lee and Zhou 2015).

Today, Asian Americans are the most highly educated racial group in the country and academic achievement has become racialized as the province of Asians (Drake 2017; Jiménez and Horowitz 2013; Lee and Zhou 2017, 2015). This racialization of achievement signals that the effects of hyper-selectivity may extend well beyond the second generation for Chinese and other Asian ethnic groups. This possibility is even more likely considering that Chinese and Indian immigration to the United States—two extremely hyper-selected immigrant streams—drives Asian immigrant replenishment. Finally, that 59 percent of the Asian American population are foreign born (73 percent of Asian adults) means that immigrant hyper-selectivity will influence the cognitive construction of race for Asian Americans. We contend that it has already led to the racial mobility of Asian Americans.

We hypothesize that the case of Cubans will more closely mirror that of Nigerians than Chinese with respect to both the cognitive construction of race and patterns of identification. Cuban immigrants make up only 5 percent of all Latino immigrants, and 97 percent of the U.S. Latino population is non-Cuban. Although they may be racialized as Latino in the U.S. context, first- and second-generation Cubans perceive themselves as distinct from other Latinos and Hispanics, and distance themselves from panethnic labels (Owens and Massey 2011; Portes and Fernández-Kelly 2008; Portes and MacLeod 1996; Tran and Valdez 2017). Although the second generation may benefit from this distinction and from immigrant optimism, this advantage does not extend to the third and later generations (Fernández-Kelly and Konczal 2005).

Given the racialization of Cubans as Latino coupled with the fact that Mexicans (a hypo-selected group)—rather than Cubans—are the largest immigrant group in the country, we posit that the hyper-selectivity of Cubans will not change the cognitive construction of the racial category Latino. Even in Miami, where the majority of Latinos are of Cuban descent, the cognitive construction of Latino has not changed because Cubans are more likely to identify ethnically rather than as Latino, have historically identified racially as white, and continue to reject the panethnic Latino label (Oboler 1995; Torres 1999). In other words, not only are Cubans more likely to identify with their ethnonym, but also, given their large group size in Miami, non-Cubans in Florida recognize them as Cubans rather than as Latino, thereby leaving the status of the Latino racial category intact (Mora 2014). In addition, in the popular imagination of most Americans, Latino is synonymous with Mexican, and invokes stereotypes of illegality and disadvantage (Donato and Massey 2016). Consequently, Cuban immigrants will continue to be perceived, perceive themselves, and identify themselves as the exceptions to and distinct from Latino immigrants, and Cuban Americans, the exceptions to and distinct from U.S. Latinos. We hypothesize that Cuban Americans will be hailed as exemplars of Latino exceptionalism, rather than alter the cognitive construction of Latino.

The hyper-selectivity of Armenian immigrants and the educational attainment of the second generation will be least consequential in changing the cognitive construction of white. Armenians are not only a small proportion—1 percent—of white immigrants, but also a tiny proportion—0.1 percent—of the total U.S. white population. Their negligible size in relation to both white immigrants and U.S. whites portends that they will be absorbed into the white racial category, which has historically stretched to include new European immigrant groups, and adopt a white racial identity. Moreover, other patterns point to the likelihood of further absorption: whiteness is expanding even further to include Asian-white and Latino-white multiracials, even as it continues to exclude black-white multiracials into the fold (Alba 2016; Lee and Bean 2010).

In table 5, we summarize the two factors at the core of our argument on racial mobility: an ethnic group educational attainment and its group size, both relative to its proximal host. We also compare the four ethnic groups with their proximal host racial groups. As we show, individuals of Chinese descent not only report educational attainment high in respect to their proximal host group, but also make up more than 16 percent (one-sixth) of the total popula-

Table 5. How Proximal Host, Educational Achievement, and Group Size Shape Racial Mobility

Ethnic Group	Proximal Host Group	Ethnic Group's Educational Attainment Relative to Proximal Host	Ethnic Group's Population Size as a Share of the Overall Racial Group	Perception of Ethnic Group's Achievement Relative to Proximal Host	Racial Mobility
Chinese	Asian	Same	Large	Norm	Yes
Cuban	Latino	Higher	Small	Exception	No
Armenian	White	Same	Small	Norm	No
Nigerian	Black	Higher	Small	Exception	No

Source: Authors' compilation.

tion of their racial group (Asians). As a result, Chinese ethnic group achievement is perceived as the norm for the proximal host racial group. For those of Nigerian descent, however, their educational achievement far exceeds the level for their proximal host (black). Moreover, Nigerians make up only a small share of the total black population in the United States, which renders the Nigerian achievement pattern the exception, not the norm, for the U.S. black population. A similar pattern is found among Cubans and their proximal host, Latinos. These differences in perceptions of each ethnic group's relative achievement compared with that of the proximal host, in turn, contribute to the shifting cognitive perceptions of Asian as a racial category while leaving black and Latino categories relatively stable, despite the high attainment of Nigerians and Cubans. Finally, despite the high achievement of individuals of Armenian descent, their small size relative to the U.S. white population does not change the perception and status of whiteness.

DISCUSSION AND CONCLUSIONS

Our comparative framework points to certain findings that dispel the popular myth of Asian Americans as the model for high academic achievement. The media and pundits racialize achievement as the province of Asians, yet Nigerians are the most highly educated. Nearly two-thirds (63 percent) of Nigerian immigrants have a bachelor's degree, versus just over half (53 percent) of foreign-born Chinese. Moreover, the most highly educated second-generation group is also Nigerian, 74 percent of whom have a bachelor's degree or higher, followed by second-generation Chinese at 61 percent. Although college graduation rates for second-generation Cubans and Armenians are evenly matched at 45 percent, the former have made the most intergenerational mobility; second-generation Cubans nearly double the college graduation rates of the first generation (41 percent to 24 percent). Critically, based on predicted probabilities, each group is more likely to have graduated from college than their U.S. proximal hosts.

To be sure, we have not considered other possible hyper-selected immigrant groups, such as Asian Indians, in this analysis. However, not all ethnic groups with high levels of human capital are hyper-selected. For example, British and Canadian immigrants, who are more highly educated than other immigrant groups, are not necessarily hyper-selected because they are not disproportionately more educated than their nonmigrant counterparts.

Our decision to focus here on Chinese, Cubans, Nigerians, and Armenians is analytical because we aim to highlight how hyper-selectivity facilitates racial mobility for ethnic groups that are differentially racialized in the U.S. context. Although Nigerians immigrants are the most highly educated, the Chinese are the most hyper-selected, revealing that educational outcomes alone do not change the cognitive construction of U.S. racial categories. By juxtaposing the largest and most hyper-selected Asian ethnic group—Chinese—with relatively smaller and more recently arrived groups such as Nigerians and Armenians, we underscore the significance of group size and how it affects perceptions of an ethnoracial group's relative standing and status. Consequently, these perceptions of racial mobility and immobility affect the cognitive construction and changing meaning of racial categories in the U.S. context, and affect patterns of ethnic and racial identification among hyper-selected immigrant groups and their second-generation children.

The choice of four ethnic groups from different U.S. racial categories also shows how assimilation of contemporary immigrant groups into American society is intricately linked to the outcomes and mobility of the proximal host groups. Because Chinese as an ethnic group do not have a proximal host, the racial mobility of Chinese and Asian immigrants and their children has fundamentally shifted the public perception of this group. In this sense, Chinese and Asians are not burdened by negative stereotypes often associated with native minority groups. At the same time, however, Chinese and Asians are often perceived as the "perpetual foreigners" because they are not immediately associated with or recognizable as a native ethnoracial group (Cheryan and Monin 2005; Tuan 1998). The public perception toward and perceived status of ethnoracial groups in turn profoundly affect how individuals from these ethnic groups might choose to identify themselves—as Chinese, Asian, Chinese American, or Asian American.

This essay broadens the concept of hyper-selectivity by applying it to four ethnic groups of diverse origins. By linking the achievements of immigrants and their children in the host society to the positive selection from the sending societies, it opens the black box of immigrant selectivity by showing how immigrants from these ethnic groups arrive with specific class-based resources that facilitate their assimilation into American society. Instead of treating immigrants as "blank slates" on arrival in the United States (Deaux 2006), hyper-selectivity as a concept provides both a theoretical and empirical link between home and host societies, while highlighting how it matters for second-generation achievement. More consequentially, it also reveals the global nature and origins of the cognitive construction of U.S. racial categories as well as patterns of ethnoracial identification.

If hyper-selectivity and racial mobility among Chinese have shifted public perceptions of Asian as a racial category, then hypo-selectivity and racial immobility among Mexicans have equated Hispanic and Latino with lingering disadvantages. The racial mobility among Asians has also provided an opportunity to potentially blur, and eventually reposition, the racial boundaries between U.S. Asians and whites (Wimmer 2008). What remains to be seen is how this process unfolds among hypo-selected groups. This contrasting exercise reveals the need for future studies that focus on how hypo-selectivity affects the achievement of the second generation, how it affects racial group formation and mobility (or immobility), and how it blurs or brightens group boundaries.

Finally, our analyses highlight the salience of a globally comparative context in the study of immigrant assimilation, educational achievement, and racial classifications. By adopting a comparative framework, our analyses show how hyper-selectivity and racial mobility interact to change the cognitive construction of U.S. racial categories and the choice of ethnoracial identities among the first and second generation. In doing so, we unveil the centrality of race in the U.S. context. Despite their exceptional achievement, first- and second-generation Nigerians remain the exception—rather than the norm—among U.S. blacks. Highly achieving and upwardly mobile Nigerians still find themselves on the other side of the rigid black-white divide. On the other hand, the racial mobility among Chinese and Asians have begun to blur the white-Asian boundary and the racial distinctions between these groups. Asian Americans are transforming the U.S. mainstream and remaking race in the process, whereas a similar process has yet to unfold for Cubans, Nigerians, and Armenians and their proximal hosts.

REFERENCES

Alba, Richard. 2016. "The Likely Persistence of a White Majority." *The American Prospect*. Winter. Published online January 11, 2016. Accessed May 1, 2018. http://prospect.org/article/likely-persistence-white-majority-0.

Alba, Richard, and Nancy Foner. 2015. *Strangers No More. Immigration and the Challenges of Integration in North America and Western Europe*. Princeton, N.J.: Princeton University Press.

Alba, Richard, and Victor Nee. 2003. *Remaking the American Mainstream*. Cambridge, Mass.: Harvard University Press.

Arthur, John A. 2000. *Invisible Sojourners: African Immigrant Diaspora in the United States*. Westport, Conn: Praeger.

Bakalian, Anny P. 1992. *Armenian-Americans: From Being to Feeling Armenian*. New Brunswick, N.J.: Transaction Publishers.

Bean, Frank D., Susan K. Brown, and James D. Bachmeier. 2015. *Parents Without Papers*. New York: Russell Sage Foundation.

Brubaker, Rogers, Mara Loveman, and Peter Stamatov. 2004. "Ethnicity as Cognition." *Theory and Society* 33(1): 31–64.

Bureau of Labor Statistics. 2012. *Current Population Survey: Annual Social and Economic Supplement (CPS ASEC), 2008–2012*. Washington: United States Department of Labor.

Calarco, Jessica McCrory. 2014. "Coached for the Classroom: Parents' Cultural Transmission and Children's Reproduction of Inequalities." *American Sociological Review* 79(5): 1015–37.

Cheryan, Sapna, and Benoît Monin. 2005. "Where are you really from? Asian Americans and Identity Denial." *Journal of Personality and Social Psychology* 89(5): 717–30.

Chua, Amy, and Jed Rubenfeld. 2014. *The Triple Package: How Three Unlikely Traits Explain the Rise and Fall of Cultural Groups in America*. New York: Penguin.

Craver, Earlene. 2009. "On the Boundary of White: The Cartozian Naturalization Case and the Armenians, 1923–1925." *Journal of American Ethnic History* 28(2): 30–56.

Deaux, Kay. 2006. *To Be an Immigrant*. New York: Russell Sage Foundation.

Der-Martirosian, Claudia. 2008. *Iranian Immigrants in Los Angeles: The Role of Networks and Economic Integration: The New Americans*. New York: LFB Scholarly Publishing.

Donato, Katharine M., and Douglas S. Massey. 2016. "Twenty-First-Century Globalization and Illegal Migration." *Annals of the American Academy of Political and Social Science* 666(1): 7–26.

Drake, Sean J. 2017. "Academic Segregation and the Institutional Success Frame: Separate and Unequal Schooling in an Integrated, Affluent Community." *Journal of Ethnic and Migration Studies* 43(14): 2423–39.

Dunlap, David W. 2017. "135 Years Ago, Another Travel Ban Was in the News." *New York Times*, March 17, 2017. Accessed March 19, 2017. https://www.nytimes.com/2017/03/17/insider/chinese-exclusion-act-travel-ban.html.

Education Policy and Data Center. 2013. National administrative data. Washington: Education Policy and Data Center. Accessed August 29, 2016. https://www.epdc.org/country.

Feliciano, Cynthia. 2006. "Beyond the Family: The Influence of Premigration Group Status on the Educational Expectations of Immigrants' Children." *Sociology of Education* 79(4): 281–303.

Ferguson, Ronald F. 2003. "Teachers' Perceptions and Expectations and the Black-White Test Score Gap." *Urban Education* 38(4): 460–507.

Fernández-Kelly, Patricia, and Lisa Konzcal. 2005. "'Murdering the Alphabet': Identity and Entrepreneurship Among Second-Generation Cubans, West Indians, and Central Americans." *Ethnic and Racial Studies* 28(6): 1153–81.

Foner, Nancy, and George M. Fredrickson. 2004. *Not Just Black and White: Historical and Contemporary Perspectives on Immigration, Race and Ethnicity in the United States*. New York: Russell Sage Foundation.

Haller, William, Alejandro Portes, and Scott M. Lynch. 2011. "Dreams Fulfilled, Dreams Shattered: Determinants of Segmented Assimilation in the Second Generation." *Social Forces* 89(3): 733–62.

Hsin, Amy. 2016. "How Selective Migration Enables Socioeconomic Mobility." *Ethnic and Racial Studies* 39(13): 2379–84.

Hsin, Amy, and Yu Xie. 2014. "Explaining Asian Americans' Academic Advantage over Whites." *Proceedings of the National Academy of Sciences* 111(23): 8416–21.

Imoagene, Onoso. 2012. "Being British vs Being American: Identification Among Second-Generation Adults of Nigerian Descent in the US and UK." *Ethnic and Racial Studies* 35(12): 2153–73.

———. 2017. *Beyond Expectations*. Oakland: University of California Press.

Jiménez, Tomás R. 2016. "Bringing Culture Back in: The Class Origins and Ethnoracial Destinations of Culture and Achievement." *Ethnic and Racial Studies* 39(13): 2385–90.

Jiménez, Tomás R., and Adam L. Horowitz. 2013. "When White Is Just Alright: How Immigrants Redefine Achievement and Reconfigure the Ethnoracial Hierarchy." *American Sociological Review* 78(5): 849–71.

Kasinitz, Philip, John H. Mollenkopf, Jennifer Holdaway, and Mary C. Waters. 2008. *Inheriting the City: The Children of Immigrants Come of Age.* New York: Russell Sage Foundation.

Khachikian, Oshin. 2016. "Ethnic Capital Revisited." Department of Sociology working paper. Irvine: University of California.

Konadu-Agyemang, Kwadwo, Baffour K. Takyi, and John A. Arthur, eds. 2006. *The New African Diaspora in North America: Trends, Community Building, and Adaptation.* Lanham, Md.: Lexington Books.

Lee, Jennifer. 2015. "From Undesirable to Marriageable: Hyper-selectivity and the Racial Mobility of Asian Americans." *Annals of the American Academy of Political and Social Science* 662(1): 79–93.

Lee, Jennifer, and Frank D. Bean. 2010. *The Diversity Paradox.* New York: Russell Sage Foundation.

Lee, Jennifer, and Min Zhou. 2015. *The Asian American Achievement Paradox.* New York: Russell Sage Foundation.

———. 2016. "Unraveling the Link Between Culture and Achievement." *Ethnic and Racial Studies* 39(13): 2404–11.

———. 2017. "Why Class Matters Less for Asian American Achievement." *Journal of Ethnic and Migration Studies* 43(14): 2316–30.

Lewis-McCoy, R. L'Heureux. 2014. *Inequality in the Promised Land: Race, Resources, and Suburban Schooling.* Stanford, Calif.: Stanford University Press.

Logan, John R., and Glenn Deane. 2003. "Black Diversity in Metropolitan America." Lewis Mumford Center for Comparative Urban and Regional Research, University at Albany.

Mittelberg, David, and Mary C. Waters. 1992. "The Process of Ethnogenesis Among Haitian and Israeli Immigrants in the United States." *Ethnic and Racial Studies* 15(3): 412–35.

Mora, G. Cristina. 2014. "Cross-Field Effects and Ethnic Classification: The Institutionalization of Hispanic Panethnicity, 1965 to 1990." *American Sociological Review* 79(2): 183–210.

Oboler, Suzanne. 1995. *Ethnic Labels, Latino Lives: Identity and the Politics of (Re) Presentation in the United States.* Minneapolis: University of Minnesota Press.

Ogbaa, Kalu. 2003. *The Nigerian Americans: The New Americans.* Westport, Conn.: Greenwood Press.

Okihiro, Gary. 1994. *Margins and Mainstreams: Asians in American History and Culture.* Seattle: University of Washington Press.

Owens, Jayanti, and Scott M. Lynch. 2012. "Black and Hispanic Immigrants' Resilience Against Negative-Ability Racial Stereotypes at Selective Colleges and Universities in the United States." *Sociology of Education* 85(4): 303–25.

Owens, Jayanti, and Douglas S. Massey. 2011. "Stereotype Threat and College Academic Performance: A Latent Variables Approach." *Social Science Research* 40(1): 150–66.

Patacchini, Eleonora, and Yves Zenou. 2016. "Racial Identity and Education in Social Networks." *Social Networks* 44(January): 85–94.

Pedraza-Bailey, Silvia. 1985. "Cuba's Exiles: Portrait of a Refugee Migration." *The International Migration Review* 19(1): 4–34.

Pérez, Lisandro. 1986. "Cubans in the United States." *Annals of the American Academy of Political and Social Science* 487(1): 126–37.

Phinney, Jean S., Kathleen Baumann, and Shanika Blanton. 2001. "Life Goals and Attributions for Expected Outcomes among Adolescents from Five Ethnic Groups." *Hispanic Journal of Behavioral Sciences* 23(4): 363–77.

Phinney, Jean S., Anthony Ong, and Tanya Madden. 2000. "Cultural Values and Intergenerational Value Discrepancies in Immigrant and Non-Immigrant Families." *Child Development* 71(2): 528–39.

Portes, Alejandro. 1969. "Dilemmas of a Golden Exile: Integration of Cuban Refugee Families in Milwaukee." *American Sociological Review* 34(4): 505–18.

Portes, Alejandro, Rosa Aparicio Gomez, and William Haller. 2016. *Spanish Legacies: The Coming of Age of the Second Generation.* Berkeley: University of California Press.

Portes, Alejandro, and Robert L. Bach. 1985. *Latin Journey, Cuban and Mexican Immigrants in the United States.* Berkeley: University of California Press.

Portes, Alejandro, and József Böröcz. 1989. "Contemporary Immigration: Theoretical Perspectives on Its Determinants and Modes of Incorporation." *International Migration Review* 23(3): 606–30.

Portes, Alejandro, Juan M. Clark, and Robert L. Bach. 1977. "The New Wave: A Statistical Profile of Recent Cuban Exiles to the U.S." *Cuban Studies* 7(1): 1–32.

Portes, Alejandro, and Patricia Fernández-Kelly. 2008. "No Margin for Error: Educational and Occupational Achievement Among Disadvantaged Children of Immigrants." *Annals of the American Academy of Political and Social Science* 620(1): 12–36.

Portes, Alejandro, and Dag MacLeod. 1996. "Educational Progress of Children of Immigrants: The Roles of Class, Ethnicity, and School Context." *Sociology of Education* 69(4): 255–75.

Portes, Alejandro, and Aaron Puhrmann. 2015. "A Bifurcated Enclave: The Economic Evolution of the Cuban and Cuban American Population of Metropolitan Miami." *Cuban Studies* 43: 40–63.

Portes, Alejandro, and Min Zhou. 1993. "The New Second Generation: Segmented Assimilation and Its Variants." *Annals of the American Academy of Political and Social Science* 530(1): 74–96.

Rumbaut, Rubén G., and Alejandro Portes. 2001. *Ethnicities: Children of Immigrants in America*. Berkeley: University of California Press.

Sabagh, Georges, Mehdi Bozorgmehr, and Claudia Der-Martirosian. 1990. "Subethnicity: Armenians in Los Angeles." *Institute for Social Science Research* working paper. Los Angeles: University of California. Accessed January 28, 2018. http://escholarship.org/uc/item/7jp6m12s .

Saperstein, Aliya. 2015. "Developing a Racial Mobility Perspective for the Social Sciences." *Work in Progress* (blog), March 3, 2015. Accessed January 28, 2018. https://www.russellsage.org/news/developing-racial-mobility-perspective-social-sciences.

Takaki, Ronald. 1979. *Iron Cages: Race and Culture in 19th-Century America*. New York: Oxford University Press.

Telles, Edward E., and Vilma Ortiz. 2008. *Generations of Exclusion: Mexican-Americans, Assimilation, and Race*. New York: Russell Sage Foundation.

Torres, María de los Angeles. 1999. *In the Land of Mirrors: Cuban Exile Politics in the United States*. Ann Arbor: University of Michigan Press.

Tran, Van C. 2015. "More Than Just Black: Cultural Perils and Opportunities in Inner-City Neighborhoods." In *Bringing Culture Back In: New Approaches to the Problems of Black Youth*, edited by Orlando Patterson. Cambridge, Mass.: Harvard University Press.

———. 2016. "Ethnic Culture and Social Mobility Among Second-Generation Asian Americans." *Ethnic and Racial Studies* 39(13): 2398–403.

Tran, Van C., and Nicol M. Valdez. 2017. "Second-Generation Decline or Advantage? Latino Assimilation in the Aftermath of the Great Recession." *International Migration Review* 55(1): 155–90.

Tuan, Mia. 1998. *Forever Foreigners or Honorary Whites? The Contemporary Asian Ethnic Experience*. New Brunswick, N.J.: Rutgers University Press.

UNESCO Institute for Statistics. 2012. "UIS Statistics Database, 2010–2012." Accessed August 29, 2016. http://data.uis.unesco.org/.

U.S. Census Bureau. 2017. "American FactFinder—Results." Accessed January 28, 2018. https://factfinder.census.gov/faces/tableservices/jsf/pages/productview.xhtml?pid=ACS_15_1YR_S0201&prodType=table.

Valenzuela, Angela. 1999. *Subtractive Schooling: U.S.-Mexican Youth and the Politics of Caring*. New York: State University of New York Press.

Waldinger, Roger D. 2015. *The Cross-Border Connection: Immigrants, Emigrants, and Their Homelands*. Cambridge, Mass.: Harvard University.

Waldinger, Roger D., and Mehdi Bozorgmehr, eds. 1996. *Ethnic Los Angeles*. New York: Russell Sage Foundation.

Waters, Mary C. 1999. *Black Identities: West Indian Immigrant Dreams and American Realities*. Cambridge, Mass.: Harvard University Press.

Waters, Mary C., Reed Ueda, and Helen B. Marrow, eds. 2007. *The New Americans: A Guide to Immigration since 1965*. Cambridge, Mass.: Harvard University Press.

Wimmer, Andreas. 2008. "The Making and Unmaking of Ethnic Boundaries: A Multilevel Process Theory." *American Journal of Sociology* 113(4): 970–1022.

Wong, Janelle, S. Karthick Ramakrishnan, Taeku Lee, and Jane Junn. 2011. *Asian American Political Participation: Emerging Constituents and Their Political Identities*. New York: Russell Sage Foundation.

Zhou, Min, and Susan Kim. 2006. "Community Forces, Social Capital, and Educational Achievement: The Case of Supplementary Education in the Chinese and Korean Immigrant Communities." *Harvard Educational Review* 76(1): 1–29.